THE
TOOL BOOK

THE
TOOL BOOK

Edited by Mike Lawrence

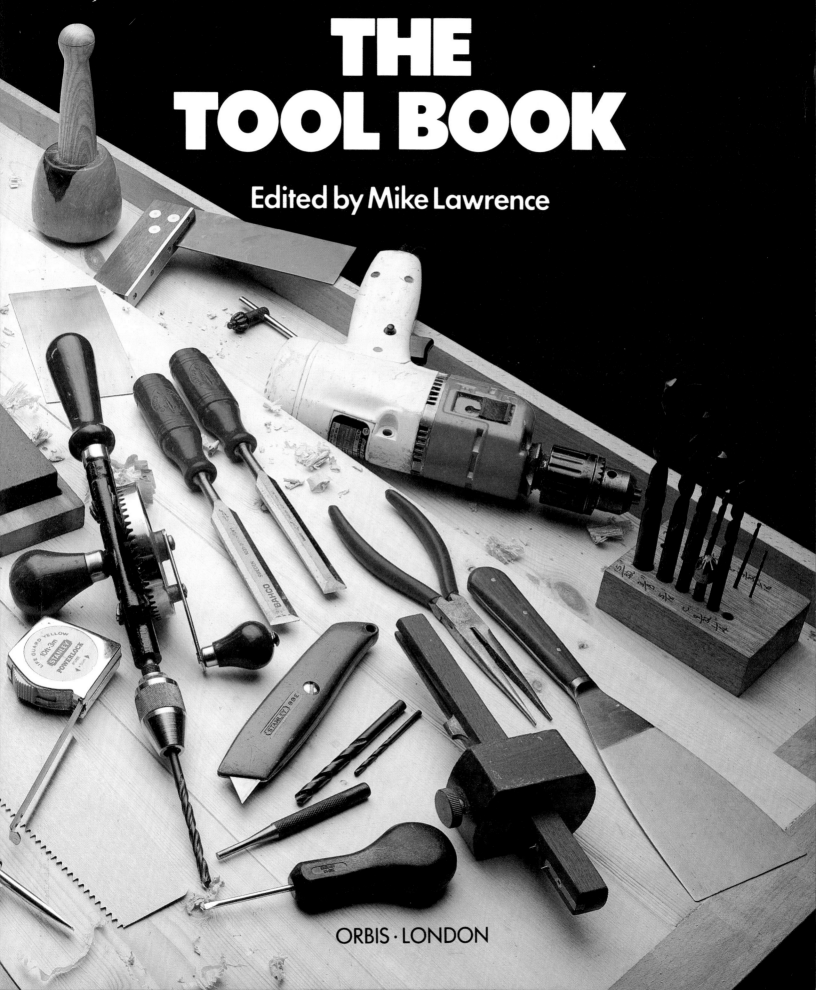

ORBIS · LONDON

Acknowledgements
Photographers: Barnaby's, Jon Bouchier, Simon Butcher, Jem Grischotti,
Karen Norquay, Ian O'Leary, Roger Tuff.

Artists: Nick Farmer, Val Hill, Linden Artists, Peter Robinson,
Mike Saunders, Ian Stephen, Ralph Stobart, Universal Studios,
Brian Watson, David Weeks.

This edition published 1985 by
Orbis Publishing Limited, London
under licence from
Whinfrey Strachan Limited
315 Oxford Street
London W1R 1AJ

Printed in Yugoslavia
ISBN: 0-85613-831-2

CONTENTS

1 Handtools for woodwork

Measuring and marking tools	8
Handsaws	10
Hammers	12
Screwdrivers	14
Bench planes	16
Specialist planes	18
Shaping tools	20
Chisels	22
Hand drills	24
Vices and cramps	27
Abrasives	30
Nails	32
Screws	34
Self-assembly fittings	36

2 Power tools

Power drill attachments	39
Power saws	42
Specialist power tools	45

3 Using hand tools

Making simple butt joints	49
Making halving and mitre joints	54
Making joints with dowels	58
Making housing joints	62
Mortise and tenon joints	66
Making dovetail joints	71
Shaping wood and boards	76
Gluing and cramping wood	80

4 Using power tools

Using drill stands and jigs	85
Using shaping cutters	89
Using circular saws	94
Using a saw table	99
Tools for woodturning	104
Basic woodturning techniques	107

5 Using a router

Setting up and cutting grooves	114
Profiling and box jointing	119
Using jigs, templates and spindles	124

6 Woodworking equipment

Making aids for woodwork	130
Building a workbench	135

7 Choosing and using other tools

Masonry tools	141
Paint brushes, rollers and pads	144
Tools for electrical jobs	147
Tools for plumbing jobs	150
Blowlamps	152
Spanners, bolts and machine screws	154

8 Working with metal

Tools for simple metalworking	158
Soldering irons	161
Drilling, cutting and bending metal	163
Making joints in metal	168

9 Access equipment

Ladders and steps	174
Ladder accessories	177

10 Looking after your tools

Simple tool maintenance	180
Sharpening tools by machine	185
Tool storage	188
Index	191

CHAPTER 1

HAND TOOLS FOR WOODWORK

When you're working with wood, you need tools to measure up and
mark out your workpiece, tools to cut it to length and give it
the shape you want, and tools to help you join everything together.
You'll also need a range of fixings – nails, screws
and self-assembly fittings – to reinforce the joints.

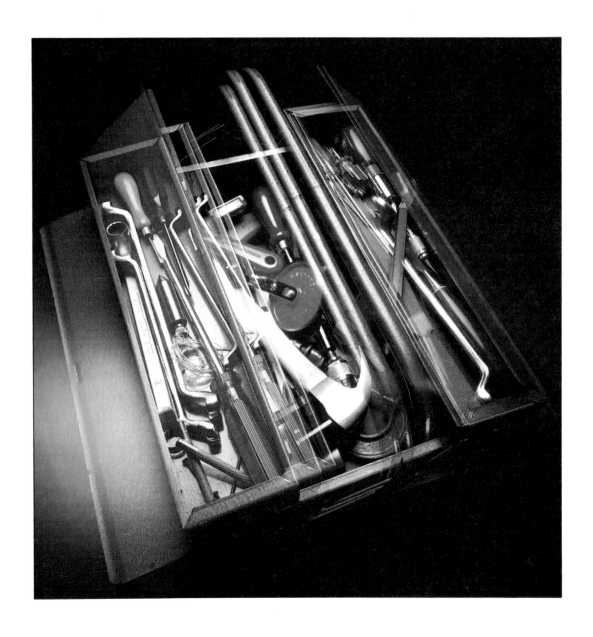

MEASURING & MARKING TOOLS

You may be proficient at using saws, planes and other tools for cutting and shaping wood, but for a perfect result you must be able to mark up with precision. And for that you will need a number of special tools.

Carpenter's tools are all designed for specific purposes and to use marking and measuring ones successfully the wood must be square. If not, this could be the reason why, for example, lines around timber don't meet where where they should. Never make the mistake of thinking that timber bought ready-planed is necessarily perfectly square. Always check for yourself.

The timber could also be warped, or its actual size may be different from the nominal size you ordered, and this could result in badly fitting joints.

Marking up square or rectangular-sectioned timber is relatively straightforward when the right tools are used. Marking up mouldings full of lumps and bumps is a different matter. All you can do here is draw a line on whatever raised and flat surfaces are available.

There are some mistakes or imperfections you can easily correct. A common cause of error, for instance, is to switch between imperial and metric measurements. Don't. Decide on one system and stick to it. For while some conversions are accurate, others may have been rounded up or down.

If a marking knife or the spur of a marking gauge leaves a ragged score mark, check to see if the knife or spur is sharp. If it is, you are probably digging too deeply into the wood. The best way to make a deep line is to build it up by going over it two or three times rather than trying to do it in one go. For marking across the grain, a cutting gauge is purpose-built and will avoid the problem.

Steel tapes
Flexible tapes are frequently marked off in both metric and imperial gradations. The tape – up to 5m (16ft 3in) long – is pulled from a spring-loaded holder and retracts automatically when released; some tapes can also be locked in any position. At the end of the tape is a tab which you hook over or butt up against whatever you are measuring.

Carpenter's rules
These are more accurate than tapes because they are not flexible and can be laid flat on a surface. They normally give both metric and imperial measurements up to 1m (3ft 3in). They are made from boxwood, steel or plastic and many are hinged so they can be folded up.

Straight-edges
These are precision-made plain metal bars up to 2m (6ft 6in) long, with one bevelled edge, which is used (bevel up) for drawing straight lines. Straight-edges can also be used to check the flatness of a surface.

Try-squares, combination squares and sliding bevels
A try-square is used for drawing and checking right angles by placing the wooden or plastic stock against the timber. The metal blade is usually between 150mm and 300mm (6in and 12in) long. Metal-stocked engineer's squares are also available – they are more accurate and more expensive.

A combination square is a versatile measuring tool for both 90° and 45° angles, and also incorporates a spirit level for checking the true vertical.

A sliding bevel is designed to measure awkward angles. The stock can be moved along the blade, then locked in position so that the angle can be transferred to the timber.

Carpenter's pencil and marking knife
A pencil is useful for shading waste areas (a sensible precaution against mistakes) and for making marks that must be

hints

- If you want to cut pieces to the same size, mark only one, and transfer the measurement to the others by cramping them together and striking across them in one go using a knife and try-square.

- A combination square, like a try-square, gives both internal and external right angles – but it can also be used to check 45° angles and to mark off measurements; it even has a built-in spirit level.

- When using tapes and rules, make sure your eye is immediately over the measuring mark.

- Measure along the edge, rather than down the middle: that way you'll keep the tape or rule parallel to the length of the timber.

- A sliding bevel is the handiest tool for transferring angles other than 90° or 45° from one place to another.

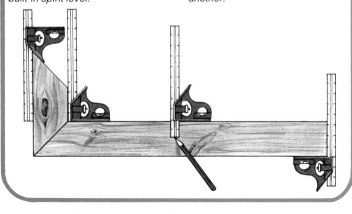

Craig Warwick

Jem Grischotti

cleaned off so they don't show on the finished job. The traditional carpenter's pencil is rectangular in section, but you can use an ordinary HB pencil sharpened to a chisel point.

Before sawing, chiselling or planing, it's best to use a knife to draw the guide-lines. This makes a thinner, more accurate line than a pencil, and also, by cutting through the surface fibres of the wood, helps to give the cut a neater finish. Knives with a specially angled cutting edge are manufactured specifically for marking, but any sharp craft knife or replaceable-blade knife is suitable.

Marking and mortise gauges
You can use a marking gauge to mark a line parallel with and close to the edge of the wood you're working on. It has a wooden block, called a stock, which you can fix with a thumbscrew at any point along the wooden shaft so it is a given distance from a sharp metal spur. You steady one end of the wood against a bench-hook or the edge of the bench, and press the other end into your stomach; then, holding the gauge's stock against the edge of the wood, with the spur angled so it points away from the direction of travel, slide the stock along so that the spur is dragged lightly at an angle along the surface.

A cutting gauge, with a blade instead of a spur, is ideally to be preferred for marking across the grain.

The mortise gauge is like a marking gauge but has two spurs, one fixed and one movable, allowing you to score a pair of parallel lines. It is mainly used for marking mortise-and-tenon joints, but by retracting the movable spur into the stock it can be used as an ordinary marking gauge instead. It is set in much the same way as a marking gauge, but before you fix the stock in relation to the movable spur you should set the latter at the correct distance from the fixed spur.

Combined marking and mortise gauges are also available. These have two spurs – one fixed, the other movable – on one edge, and a fixed spur on the opposite edge.

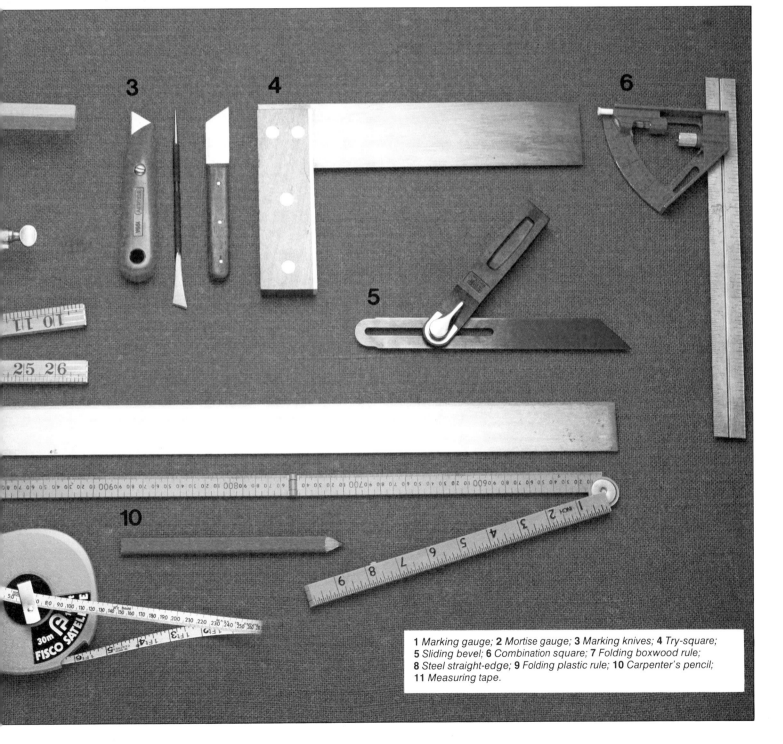

1 *Marking gauge;* 2 *Mortise gauge;* 3 *Marking knives;* 4 *Try-square;*
5 *Sliding bevel;* 6 *Combination square;* 7 *Folding boxwood rule;*
8 *Steel straight-edge;* 9 *Folding plastic rule;* 10 *Carpenter's pencil;*
11 *Measuring tape.*

HANDSAWS

Although you can make do with a limited range in your toolbox, it's useful to know what the different types of handsaw can do. These are eight of the most common.

All saws have certain things in common. Firstly the teeth are angled outwards alternately (called the 'set') and you can see this by looking directly down on any saw with the points of the teeth uppermost. The angled formation does two things – it makes the cut a little wider than the blade of the saw so the blade doesn't get stuck, and it allows saw dust to fall away without the teeth becoming clogged.

Saws are graded according to the number of teeth they have to the inch – measured in 'points' to the inch (p.p.i.). The main thing to remember is that the greater the number of teeth, the finer and slower the cut will be.

But the number of teeth a saw has isn't the only important characteristic. The *kind* of teeth it has also makes a difference – for instance, a saw specifically designed to cut *along* the grain of wood has teeth filed to form a chisel edge, while those of a saw designed to cut *across* the grain are filed to form a sharper point (see diagrams).

Blades themselves vary in thickness from about 1mm for a large panel saw, to about 0.5mm for a small tenon saw, and even less for a coping saw. And to help the blade clear the cut as you saw, the blade's width is itself tapered so it's thinner on top than at the cutting edge.

hints

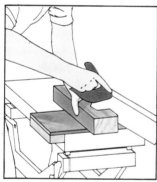

1 Saw with your shoulder, hand and eye in line with your saw. Drawing it backwards, use short strokes with the saw to start a cut.

2 To help saw a straight line, cramp a batten along the marking line and saw against it. Always make the cut on the waste side.

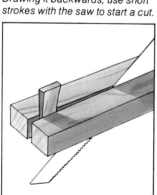

3 On a long cut the saw may be inclined to jam, so try wedging the cut open with a scrap of wood as you saw.

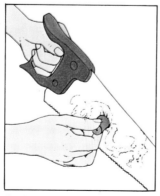

4 Clean a rusty saw blade with steel wool and turps/white spirit. Lubricate a blade by rubbing it with candle wax or soap.

Rip Saw Specifically designed for cutting large pieces of wood *along* the grain (for example, cutting down a length of timber to reduce its width). The tip of each tooth is filed to a flat chisel edge and cuts with a planing action. With only 4-6 points per inch, the teeth are large and slice through thick wood easily. (Limited use).

Cross-cut Saw Designed to cut *across* the grain, (that is, cutting a piece of wood to the correct length), the teeth are bevelled to a knife point, as well as being set, so the sharp points of alternate teeth point outwards. As you saw, the teeth cut two parallel grooves, and the wood in between crumbles away as sawdust. With 7-8 points per inch, the saw can also be used for cutting *along* the grain, but it's slower than with a rip saw.

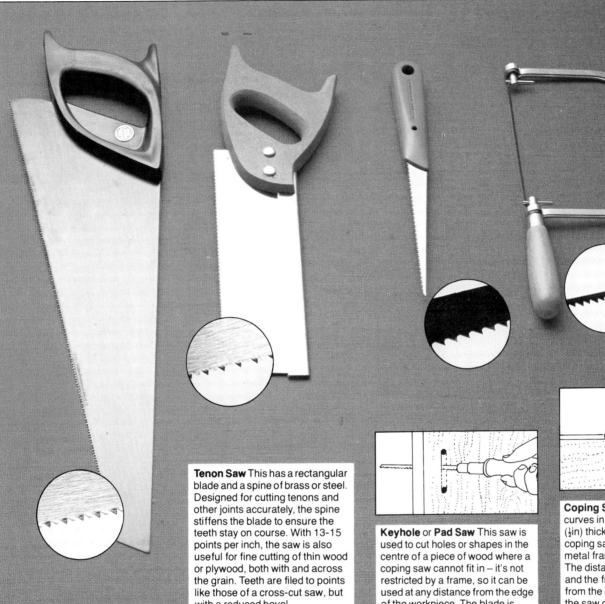

Tenon Saw This has a rectangular blade and a spine of brass or steel. Designed for cutting tenons and other joints accurately, the spine stiffens the blade to ensure the teeth stay on course. With 13-15 points per inch, the saw is also useful for fine cutting of thin wood or plywood, both with and across the grain. Teeth are filed to points like those of a cross-cut saw, but with a reduced bevel.

A Dovetail Saw is simply a smaller version of the tenon saw, designed for rather finer work and – as the name implies – for cutting dovetail joints. It has a thinner blade with 20 points to the inch, so it's particularly useful for cutting timber less than 12.5mm (½in) thick.

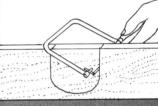

Keyhole or **Pad Saw** This saw is used to cut holes or shapes in the centre of a piece of wood where a coping saw cannot fit in – it's not restricted by a frame, so it can be used at any distance from the edge of the workpiece. The blade is fairly thick to keep it rigid, and means that the saw makes a coarse cut. It's used for cutting out keyholes (hence the name) and letter-boxes in doors. It's easiest to drill a hole at each corner of the shape to be cut, so allowing the blade of the saw to change direction.

Coping Saw Designed for cutting curves in wood less than 12.5 mm (½in) thick, the thin blade of a coping saw is held in tension in a metal frame and makes a fine cut. The distance between the blade and the frame determines how far from the edge of a piece of wood the saw can be used. The angle of the blade can be adjusted so you can saw in different directions.

Fret Saw Similar to the coping saw, but has a much deeper frame or 'throat'. It allows more freedom in cutting shapes and patterns in wood.

Panel Saw This is basically a smaller version of the cross-cut saw, with smaller teeth and more of them (10 points per inch). Makes a finer cut and is adequate for cutting large joints and mitres. Again, it will cut both across and along the grain, so it's probably the most versatile of the large handsaws. Also available with 'hardened' teeth designed to resist the blunting effect of sawing manmade boards like plywood and chipboard. Many also now come with a teflon-coated finish which is designed to reduce friction when sawing and to prevent rust.

Saw teeth

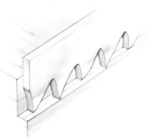

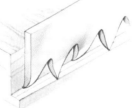

The teeth of a rip saw are filed to a chisel-like edge. The teeth cut along the grain with a planing action.

The teeth of a cross-cut saw and smaller saws are bevelled to fine points. Alternate teeth are angled outwards so that the cut is wider than the blade. The teeth cut with a slicing action.

HAMMERS

Sooner or later, just about all do-it-yourself activities require a hammer. But there are more types of hammer than you may think – some suitable for general-purpose work and others intended to cope with specific tasks.

It's most important that, when buying a hammer, you select the right one for the job. There are nine main types of hammer you're likely to come across in the ordinary course of events.

Cross-pein hammer

Also called the Warrington pattern or joiner's hammer, this is primarily for use in joinery. However, so long as it's not employed for very heavy work, it also makes a good general-purpose hammer for the handyman. It has a flat face for normal striking, and a wedge-shaped 'cross pein' ('cross' because it's at right angles to the line of the handle) for starting small pins held between the fingers and for driving nails into awkward corners. Its handle is either of ash or hickory. Head weights range between 170 and 450g (6 to 16oz).

Ball-pein hammer

Often called an engineer's hammer, this is a general-purpose tool for the metalworker and mechanic rather than the woodworker. It has a flat face for normal striking operations such as driving cold chisels and punches, and a rounded pein for riveting, bending and shaping metal, and so on. Its head comes in a range of weights between 113 and 1360g (4oz and 3lb), with those between 113 and 680g (4oz and 1½lb) the most generally useful and therefore the most widely available. The handle is usually ash, but hickory and glass fibre are also sometimes used.

Pin hammer

Occasionally known as a 'telephone hammer', this is used to drive very small tacks and pins. It has a long ash handle, and a head weight of either 100g (3½oz) or, more usually, 113g (4oz). While usually of the cross-pein design, it's also found with a ball pein.

Claw hammer

This is the heavy-duty, general-purpose hammer for all structural carpentry and building work. With a head weight of 450, 570 or 680g (16, 20 or 24oz), it drives the largest nails with ease and, thanks to its specially shaped claw, it can grip them and pull them out too.

The shaft will be of wood (ash on cheap models, otherwise hickory), steel or glass fibre. Steel and glass fibre handles are permanently bonded to the head, eliminating the risk that it will come loose (a common problem with all timber-shafted hammers). They're also fitted with shock-absorbing rubber grips – though these can make your hands rather sweaty, which in turn makes the grip slippery.

Carpenter's mallet

A wooden mallet is very useful in woodwork. It's used where a hammer might cause damage (for example, when tapping together joints, and when driving wooden-handled chisels). It's usually made entirely of beech, with a rectangular-sectioned head which is specially shaped to compensate for your swing; this is to ensure it strikes squarely. Head weights vary between 400 and 1000g (14 and 35oz), but it's more usual to buy a wooden mallet according to the size of its striking face. This will be between 100 and 150mm (4 and 6in) long.

Club hammer

This is used mainly in building work, where you need a very heavy hammer for such jobs as driving a cold chisel into masonry. It has a square-sectioned head weighing 1135, 1360 or 1820g (2½, 3 or 4lb), either end of which can be used for striking.

Sledge hammer

Basically a larger version of the club hammer, the sledge hammer

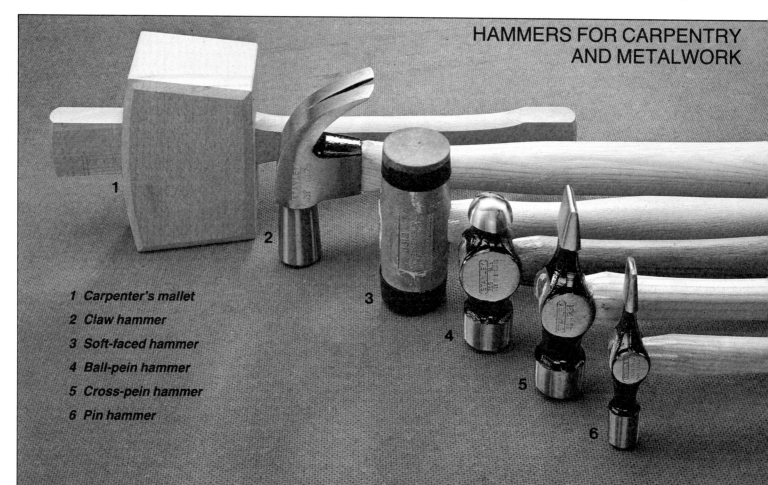

HAMMERS FOR CARPENTRY AND METALWORK

1 *Carpenter's mallet*
2 *Claw hammer*
3 *Soft-faced hammer*
4 *Ball-pein hammer*
5 *Cross-pein hammer*
6 *Pin hammer*

is used for breaking up concrete and stone, driving stakes into the ground, and so on. It has a head weight of 1820, 3180, 4540 or 6360g (4, 7, 10 or 14lb), and a shaft between 610 and 915mm (2 and 3ft) long. Usually, the heavier the head, the longer the shaft.

Brick hammer
A brick hammer has a long, tapering head, ending in a sharp, chisel-pointed edge which is used for cutting and shaping bricks. However, it takes practice to use a brick hammer well. The shaft is normally of hickory, and the hammer is sold either by the length of its head, or by head weight. Generally this is between 680 and 1820g (1½ and 4lb).

Soft-faced hammer
Like a wooden mallet, a soft-faced hammer is used where you want to apply force without damaging the surface you're working on. Many types are available, with head weights of between 230 and 1360g (8oz and 3lb), but all adopt the same basic format. Replaceable faces of plastic, nylon, copper, rawhide or rubber (rubber faces may be shaped or flat) are fixed to both ends of a cylindrical plastic or metal head.

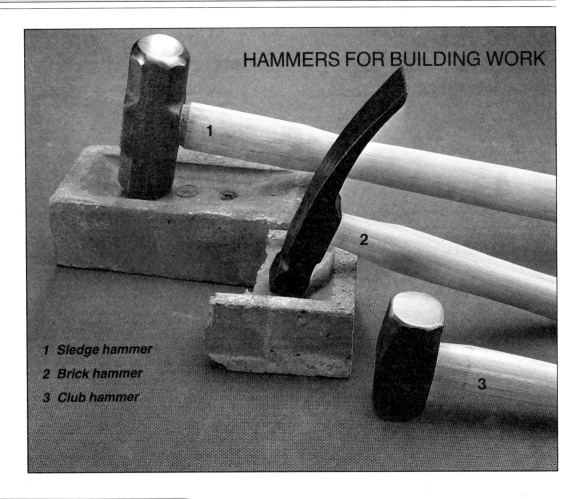

HAMMERS FOR BUILDING WORK

1 Sledge hammer
2 Brick hammer
3 Club hammer

hints

● To gain most benefit from the weight of the head, hold a hammer near the end of its shaft. The club hammer is an exception; holding the shaft about halfway along gives you better control.

● Except when using a sledge hammer (where you have no choice) don't swing the tool from your shoulder. Once the nail is established in the timber, you'll get better control swinging it from the elbow. For light use, swing from your wrist only. But always be firm, keep your eye on the nail, and try to bring the head down vertically onto it.

● If you find the hammer skipping off nail heads as it makes contact, clean its striking face by rubbing it across a sheet of abrasive paper or emery cloth laid flat.

● If a hammer handle works loose or breaks, don't throw the tool away. You can easily buy and fit a new handle yourself. Leave it somewhere hot first to dry it out thoroughly and thus shrink it.

Then saw a slot across (1), in the same direction as on the old shaft, to take the wedge (two in the case of large hammers). Plane or

pare the shaft down to fit, and drive it into the head. Saw the

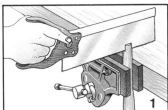

handle off flush if necessary (2), and (3) drive in the wedge or

wedges (available in various sizes from any tool shop).

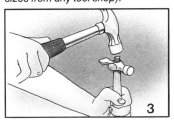

Choosing a hammer
Whatever type of hammer you're looking for, you need to ask yourself a number of questions before actually buying.

First of all, is it the right size? 'Size', here, refers to the weight of the head. It's the head's weight that does most of the work. If it's too light, your blows will lack force. If, on the other hand, it's too heavy, the tool will be difficult to control and tiring to use; moreover, there's a good chance that it will bend nails, damage the work piece, or – if you're talking about sledge hammers – damage you. Aim for a compromise between the two extremes.

Is the hammer well made? Poorly-made hammers break easily, which makes them rather hazardous and a waste of money. The head should be forged, not cast. Cast heads tend to chip on impact, sending bits of metal flying off in all directions. In any case, to reduce this risk still further, the edge of the striking face should be neatly chamfered.

Check the shaft too. It should be both strong and resilient. In this respect, ash is suitable only for fairly light hammers. Heavy hammers need a shaft of hickory or, if the hammer is likely to come in for rough treatment, of steel or glass fibre.

Make sure the shaft and head are securely joined, so that there's no chance of the head flying off. With steel and glass fibre shafts, you must take this on trust, because you can't see the fixing – which makes it a good idea to buy a well-known brand. With wooden shafts, examine the hammer end-on to see that the joint between shaft and head is tight and free from gaps. As insurance, iron wedges (only one if the hammer is light) are normally driven into the end of the shaft. Shoddy workmanship here is sometimes covered up with paint, so beware.

Finally, remember that even a first-rate hammer can be dangerous if misused. Never use a hammer to do a job it's not designed for. Never use it on metal harder than itself. Avoid glancing blows. And never hit one hammer with another.

Check, too, that the hammer is in good condition before you use it. If the shaft is at all loose, fit another. If the striking face is badly worn, replace it.

Lastly, wear safety goggles if there are likely to be chips and splinters flying about, as when breaking concrete, chiselling into masonry and driving masonry nails (which are notorious for shattering).

SCREWDRIVERS

You're sure to need more than one screwdriver if you're to tackle every job properly: in fact you need a selection. But how will you choose the right ones? Here's the full range available to help you.

There's more to screwdrivers than meets the eye. Firstly, there are several tip shapes, which must be matched to the screws you're using (see pages 34-35). The two commonest are the familiar flat tip, for driving slotted screws, and the cross-shaped tip, which comes in several varieties (see Hints).

Secondly, screwdrivers vary widely in their dimensions. These include the tip width or diameter. If the tip is too big, it won't fit the screw head – or, if it will, and it's the flat type, it will damage the surrounding material. If it's too small, you'll damage the screw or the tool.

A thick bar (blade shank) means more strength than a thin one; and increased turning power comes from a thicker handle and greater overall length. However, a short screwdriver can be fat, a long one can be thin (useful for awkward corners), and vice versa.

A third point is that there are many other variations on the basic principle – some gimmicky, and some extremely useful. All the better ones are shown and described here, so you can make your choice. The only point to watch is the one that applies to all tools: buying cheap brands is a false economy. A screwdriver blade of inferior steel will soon twist or break; and poor design will mean that the blade and handle may come apart.

Engineer's screwdrivers (10) are general-purpose tools, primarily for mechanical and engineering work. The idea is that the fluted plastic handle can be gripped firmly by greasy hands. Unfortunately, it can also be uncomfortable to use for long periods, especially on stubborn screws.

The bar may be cylindrical, square or even hexagonal in cross-section. Square- and hexagonal-section shanks can be gripped with a spanner to increase turning power. Lengths range between 75 and 450mm (3 to 18in), but the great majority are between 100 and 250mm (4 to 10in) long. Tips are normally between 5 and 12mm (³⁄₁₆

to ⁷⁄₁₆in) wide, though larger and smaller versions can be found.

Very small engineer's screwdrivers (like electrician's screwdrivers and mains testers – see below) are often fitted with a fountain-pen-style clip for your pocket. In fact, they're sometimes called 'pocket screwdrivers'.

Stubby screwdrivers (11) are very short engineer's screwdrivers (about 38mm/1¹⁄₂in long, and with a 6mm/¹⁄₄in wide tip), for awkward corners and confined spaces. The handle may be fitted with a tommy bar (a transverse piece of metal) for extra leverage.

Cabinet screwdrivers (8) are general-purpose tools for the carpenter. They are distinguished by their comfortable, smoothly-contoured handles, made of hardwood or plastic in roughly the shape of a lightbulb. Most have a cylindrical bar which is flattened just before it enters the handle. A similar type (12), with a plain bar, is widely used as a universal screwdriver. Blade lengths range from 75 to 250mm (3 to 10in), with those above 100mm (4in) rising in 50mm (2in) steps. Tip widths range between 5 and 13mm (³⁄₁₆ to ¹⁄₂in).

The **London pattern screwdriver** (7), the forerunner of the modern cabinet screwdriver, is becoming rarer. However, it's a sturdy tool, and many would say it has more turning power than the screwdrivers that have superseded it. This is due mainly to the shape of the blade – flat along its whole length, so there's less risk of twisting in use.

Its wooden handle, though superficially like that of a cabinet screwdriver, is larger and rounder, offering a better grip. It also has two flat faces, which are there partly to give a better fit in the hand, and partly to stop the tool rolling off the bench. Blade lengths range between 100 and 300mm (4 to 12in); tip widths from 8 to well over 13mm (⁵⁄₁₆ to over ¹⁄₂in).

A stubbier version of the London pattern screwdriver is the **crutch screwdriver.**

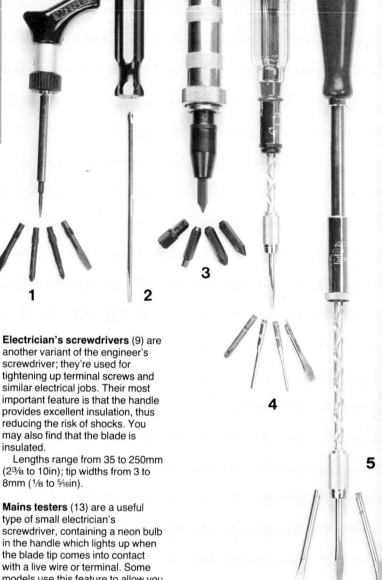

1   **2**

3

4

5

Electrician's screwdrivers (9) are another variant of the engineer's screwdriver; they're used for tightening up terminal screws and similar electrical jobs. Their most important feature is that the handle provides excellent insulation, thus reducing the risk of shocks. You may also find that the blade is insulated.

Lengths range from 35 to 250mm (2³⁄₈ to 10in); tip widths from 3 to 8mm (¹⁄₈ to ⁵⁄₁₆in).

Mains testers (13) are a useful type of small electrician's screwdriver, containing a neon bulb in the handle which lights up when the blade tip comes into contact with a live wire or terminal. Some models use this feature to allow you to test cartridge fuses. There's just one point to watch: if you drop the tool, ensure – before using it again – that the bulb hasn't been damaged. If a broken bulb misleads you into thinking that a live wire is safe, the result could be fatal so always check the bulb functions.

Instrument screwdrivers are also known as instrument maker's screwdrivers. But there's little agreement on what their impressive-sounding name properly denotes. Some manufacturers apply it to engineer's or other screwdrivers (eg, 17) with tip widths of less than 5mm (³⁄₁₆in); others to engineer's screwdrivers with unusually long blades (between 75 and 250mm/3 and 10in) for their narrow tips (which are between 3 and 8mm/¹⁄₈ and ⁵⁄₁₆ wide); and still others reserve the title for other specialised tools. The real point,

however, is that instrument screwdrivers are used on the smallest screws.

The **ratchet screwdriver** (1 and 6) is a cabinet screwdriver whose blade is connected to its handle via a ratchet. This enables you to twist the handle back between turns – as you have to anyway – yet still grip it, while the blade remains in the same position. It does make screwdriving easier.

Most ratchet screwdrivers offer three settings: one for driving, one for withdrawing, and a third that locks the blade so you can use the tool as an ordinary screwdriver. Lengths range between 75 and 200mm (3 to 8in); tip widths between 5 and 8mm (³⁄₁₆ and ⁵⁄₁₆in).

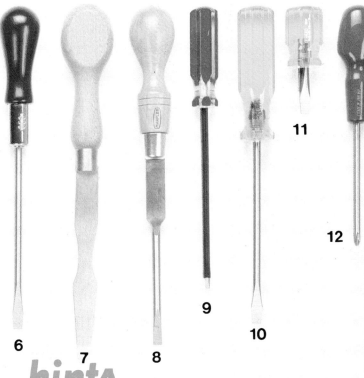

18

11

14

12

13 **15** **17**

9

10

6

7

8

16

hints

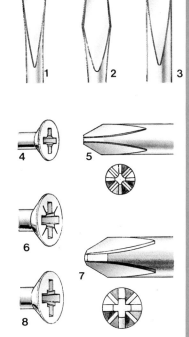

● Ordinary flat screwdriver tips come in two varieties: flared (1 and 2) and parallel (3). Flared tips are stronger, but a parallel tip will reach into tight corners and counterbored holes, which a flared tip cannot. For most jobs, either will do.

● Recessed screws are easier to drive and unscrew, because they give the screwdriver a more positive location in the head, and it's less likely to slip out. Their only disadvantage is that they're harder to remove if the recess is damaged or clogged.

They come in three main types, for which there are two special screwdrivers. Phillips screws (4) aren't widely available for home use, but you'll often encounter them on industrial products, domestic appliances, etc. Only a Phillips screwdriver (5) will fit them properly.

Pozidriv (6) and Supadriv (8) screws are more sophisticated. The latter have now superseded the former, but the Pozidriv screwdriver (7) is used for both. ('Supadriva' is simply another name for it.) It comes in five sizes, numbered from 0 to 4. The commonest are size 2, which fits screw gauges 5 to 10, and size 3, for larger gauges. However, both these types of screw also accept Phillips screwdrivers.

1 **2** **3**

4 **5**

6

7

8

● For real screwdriving power (eg, on screws which are stuck fast) you can't beat a screwdriver bit in a brace (see page 679). Such bits come in widths of 6 and 10mm (¼ and ⅜in).

An alternative is a screwdriver bit in a power drill – but the drill must have variable speed control.

Spiral ratchet screwdrivers (4 and 5) are also known as pump-action screwdrivers. To operate them you pump the handle up and down; this action turns the screw by means of a ratchet and a long shaft with spirals cut into it. At the tip of the shaft is a chuck which accepts separate, interchangeable screwdriver bits (including drill points – see page 25). What's more, the spiral shaft can be retracted for storage, which is just as well, since its fully extended length can run from 240 to as much as 700mm (9½ to 28in), depending on the model. You can also use the tool as an ordinary ratchet screwdriver.

The pump action obviously makes this a useful tool where large numbers of screws have to be driven. However, the bit does slip very easily, so it's best not to use it for fine cabinet work and the like, where scarring would be a disaster.

The **combination screwdriver** (1 and 2) is the fruit of an attempt to create a single tool that will cope with a variety of sizes and types of screw. Several kinds are available, the simplest consisting of a collection of mini-screwdrivers which can be mounted in a full-sized handle. Alternatively, as on spiral ratchet screwdrivers, the handle may have a chuck that accepts various bits; the spares may be stored inside the handle (4). You can also find handles which take double ended blades (2) with one tip for slotted and one for recessed screws. At the top end of the market are models comprising a handle and a tipless blade, into which you push one of a range of tips; the tip may clip in, or even be held by a small magnet.

Like most compromises, combination screwdrivers are only partly satisfactory. They're useful as standbys (eg, kept in the car), because they can handle a variety of situations. But they tend not to be rugged enough for everyday use.

Impact drivers (3) are for shifting really stubborn screws and bolts. Not normally used in woodwork because they exert such force, they are struck with a hammer: gearing converts the downward thrust into turning power. Impact drivers come with interchangeable bits suitable for the various screw and bolt heads.

Offset screwdrivers are designed for work in corners which can't be reached at all with an ordinary straight screwdriver. The basic version (16) is no more than a double-ended screwdriver blade with a double bend in it. Each tip may simply be a different size, or their shapes may differ. The H-shaped type (15) offers four tips instead of just two.

More sophisticated versions (14) are available, which are single-ended but take interchangeable bits. Some have a longer lever arm, to give more turning power, and many have a ratchet.

Allen keys (18) are for hex screws, which have heads with internal hexagonal recesses; these are now widely used in domestic appliances, power tools and the like. The Allen key is a bit like an offset screwdriver, but L-shaped, and with the hexagonal section running throughout its length. It's normally sold in sets to suit most sizes of hex screw, either metric or imperial – though the latter are becoming rare.

A less common alternative is the Allen key screwdriver – an engineer's screwdriver with a hexagonal blade and tip.

The **screw-holding** or **self-grip screwdriver** holds the screw onto its tip so it can be driven with one hand. It's handy when using machine screws (a metalworking type) in confined spaces; it doesn't work that well with wood screws.

It holds screws in one of three ways. The tip may be magnetic; it may have a pair of sprung jaws (models with this feature are sometimes called gasfitter's screwdrivers); or it may be split in such a way that it wedges itself into the screw slot.

BENCH PLANES

The plane has evolved over centuries into a precision tool for squaring and smoothing wood. Whatever sort of carpentry you're doing, at least one plane is an essential part of your kit.

A plane may look complicated, but in fact it's no more than a wide chisel blade mounted in a holder to control the thickness of shaving it removes. This gives it a consistency of performance which is essential for reducing the width or thickness of a piece of wood, smoothing its surface, and, perhaps most importantly, ensuring that its sides and edges are truly at right angles to each other.

There are five types to choose from: the smoothing plane, jack plane, fore plane, jointer plane, and block plane. All are known as 'bench planes'. Each is designed to do a different job, but (with the exception of the block plane) all are made in exactly the same way. The only obvious difference between them is their size.

Although a few traditional wooden models are still in use, all modern bench planes are made from metal. They are not only more accurate and durable, but also much easier to adjust to give exactly the thickness of shaving required.

The bulk of the plane consists of an iron body with a flat bottom (the sole), a slot through which the blade protrudes (the mouth), and handles at the front and back. The blade itself (often called the iron) is mounted, with the bevels forming the cutting edge facing downwards, on a wedge-shaped component known as the frog.

The frog contains most of the plane's mechanism. At its rear is a wheel-nut which raises and lowers the blade, thus altering the amount protruding through the mouth, and controlling the thickness of shaving produced. A lever at the top of the frog angles the blade from side to side so you can make sure the cutting edge is parallel with the sole.

In addition, by loosening the screws holding the frog onto the body, and usually by adjusting another below the wheel-nut, you can move the frog backwards and forwards, increasing or decreasing the size of the mouth. A smaller mouth helps stop the wood from splitting and gives a finer finish, but making it too small will slow the work, as it will be harder for shavings to escape.

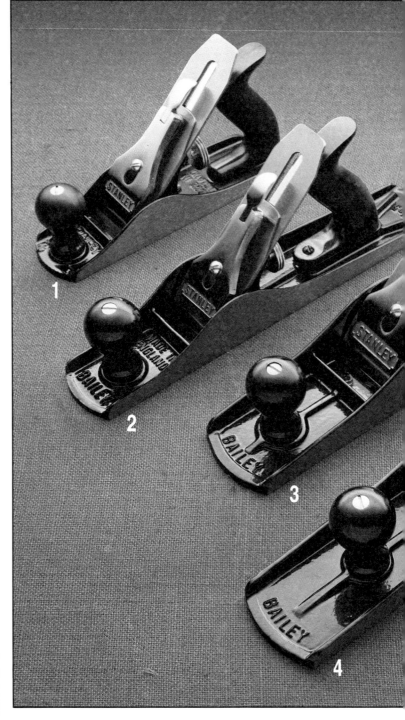

THE PARTS OF A PLANE

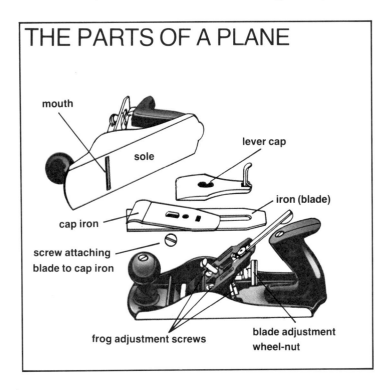

mouth
sole
lever cap
cap iron
iron (blade)
screw attaching blade to cap iron
frog adjustment screws
blade adjustment wheel-nut

1 *The smoothing plane,* at between 200 and 250mm (8 to 10in) long, is the smallest of the standard bench planes. It's really for giving a final smoothing (before sanding) to timber that has already once been roughly planed to size, but in practice is useful all round on smaller jobs.

2 *The jack plane* is a general-purpose tool (its name is short for 'Jack of all trades') for reducing timber to size, squaring up and

smoothing. About 380mm (15in) long, it doesn't give as good a finish as a smoothing plane, and on rough timber is not 100 per cent accurate. But it's the one to buy first.

3 *The fore plane* is a longer version of the jack, up to 450mm (18in) long. It does the same sort of job but does it more accurately, the reason being that the additional length enables it to ride over and thus to level off

5

hints

● Plane irons are honed like chisels, on an oilstone and to an angle of 30°. The blade will already have a bevel ground on it at a 25° angle (see Chisels, page 22). Smoothing and jack plane irons can also have the corners rounded over to stop them digging in.

● Set the blade for the right depth of cut by holding the plane bottom-up with light behind it and sighting down the sole while turning the wheel-nut. When the barest sliver of the cutting edge emerges from the mouth, use the lever to straighten the blade, then try the plane out and adjust until it cuts as you want.

● Thin shavings give the finest finish; thick ones make for speed when you're reducing wood to size, but may mean widening the mouth and raising the cap iron in relation to the blade.

● Press down on the plane's front end at the beginning of your stroke, then on both ends, and on the rear end as you finish; this avoids a tendency to give the surface a curve.

● While planing an edge, keep the plane square to the face by placing the last three fingers of your left hand under the sole as a guide.

● Alternatively you can make the simple wooden guide called a 'shooting-board' and place the work on that.

● Avoid splitting end grain by chamfering off the front edge first; by cramping waste wood to it; by using a shooting-board; or by working alternately from both ends.

● Constantly check the wood you're planing for 'flatness' (with a straight edge, a steel rule, a square or the sole of the plane), on diagonals as well as in length and width. Use a try-square to see whether the edge is square to the face.

● If the plane drags on the wood surface despite being correctly adjusted, rub a candle-end over the sole to reduce friction.

● Always plane with the grain if possible. If you can't identify which way it runs, set the plane for a very fine cut and work slowly and carefully.

slight undulations in the timber, instead of merely following them as a shorter plane would.

4 The jointer or trying-plane is the largest of all, and, with a sole between 510 and 610mm (20 and 24in) long, is even more accurate for sizing and squaring wood. If you have one, you should use it after removing initial roughness with the jack plane. Like the jack and fore planes, the jointer itself gives rather a rough finish.

5 The block plane, although it can be used like a tiny ordinary plane, is primarily designed to plane end grain efficiently. It is only 140 to 200mm (5½ to 8in) long, and is meant to be used with one hand. Moreover, the blade is set at a different angle. Its simpler construction limits the amount of adjustment you can make, though this varies from one model to another. The block plane iron, unlike all others, is mounted bevel-upwards.

SPECIALIST PLANES

Each of these strange and wonderful planes is ideal for certain types of job.

Left: The finger plane is used in certain delicate craft operations.

For most carpentry you can get by with basic tools. However, if you start to spend a lot of time working wood, you'll soon find jobs to which they're not really suited. In particular, you'll want to be aware of the startling range of specialist planes available.

Note that these tools are really for working solid timber, though some will tackle plywood or blockboard at a pinch.

Rebating planes
Rebating – cutting a 'step' along the edge of a piece – is the simplest variation on straightforward planing.

Rebate planes have their cutting irons at various angles, and bevel upwards. Generally, however, the iron's protrusion can be adjusted to take thick or thin shavings (according to the timber and grain) by means of a screw mechanism just like that on bench planes (see pages 16 -17).

In fact the **bench rebate plane** (2) is simply a bench plane whose iron runs the full width of the sole. It can be used for general work as well as very wide rebates. Another version has blades which you replace (rather than resharpen) when blunt – plus an adjustable 'fence' which guides the tool along the edge of the workpiece.

The **rebate plane** itself (1) – also called the **duplex rebate** or **filister plane** – looks a bit more unusual. It includes not only a guide fence, but also an adjustable depth gauge which you set so that it stops the tool against the top of the workpiece when you've planed deep enough. Another feature is a spur to score a line in advance of the iron – useful to prevent tearing when planing across the grain.

Moreover, the iron can be used in either of two positions. The front one is for 'bullnose' work: planing up into corners.

A **bullnose** or **bullnose rebate plane** (5) does a similar job, but has no fences or spur. It's best used for deepening and cleaning up rebates and suchlike, rather than making them in the first place.

There's also the **shoulder** or **shoulder rebate plane** (3 and 4) – so called because it's ideal for shaving the shoulders (inside faces) around a tenon so it fits properly into its mortise. This has absolutely flat sides as well as a flat sole, so it can be used both upright and horizontally.

The **bullnose shoulder rebate plane** (4) is similar, but has a short nose for bullnose work. On some models this can be removed completely, making a 'chisel plane' – which, unlike even a bullnose plane, cuts right up to a vertical surface.

The **side rebate plane** (6) is unique in being able to widen a rebate or groove by planing its sides, rather than its bottom. It has an adjustable depth stop, and two cutters so it can be used in either direction. Each end has a detachable nose for bullnose work.

Grooving planes and routers
Two sophisticated variants of the rebate plane will cut grooves.

The **plough plane** (14) is the simpler of the two. It makes grooves and rebates from 3 to 19mm (⅛ to ¾in) wide, depending on which cutter you use, and up to 15mm (⅝in) deep. Its adjustable guide fence can keep a groove parallel to a straight edge for a distance of up to 125mm (5in) inwards, and there's also a depth stop.

The **combination plane** (15) is very similar, except that its greater range of cutters (of which 16 shows some) give you the additional ability to channel out shaped 'beadings', plus tongues to match your grooves. Its plain grooving cutters usually come slightly wider, too, and it may cut deeper than the plough plane. Like the rebate plane, it's generally fitted with retractable spurs for cross-grain work.

The **hand router** or **router plane** (17) is another grooving tool. It will cut grooves which are curved in plan (see Shaping wood, pages 76 -79); it has an adjustable depth stop, and a small fence for following straight or even curved edges.

It's ideal for levelling and smoothing off the bottoms of grooves and wide recesses which have already been made (or at least begun), but not for starting grooves off, especially across the grain. A housing, for example, should have its sides sawn out before the router is used.

You can also get a miniature router for fine work such as inlaying.

Planes for curved surfaces
No ordinary bench plane, nor any of the special planes so far described, is built to tackle curved surfaces (with the exception shown on page 911). However, others can do so readily.

The **flat spokeshave** (11) deals with simple curves, or compound curves which are convex in both directions (see *Ready Reference*, page 79). The **radius spokeshave** (12) planes concave curves too. You can get a 'hollow' or 'half-round' spokeshave as well, whose body and blade have a concave curve; and there are other variations.

Though the knack of using a spokeshave takes time to acquire, it's a handy tool. However, it's really meant for narrow surfaces such as board edges. The **compass** or **circular plane** (13) will tackle curved surfaces of any size (though not those which are concave in both directions). The knob on top revolves a screw which flexes the springy steel blade to the desired radius – either convex or concave.

Scrapers
Scrapers belong with planes because, unlike abrasive paper, they remove very fine shavings.

The **cabinet scraper** can be straight-edged (7) or **goose neck** (8) – the latter, of course, being for curved surfaces. Its function is to provide an absolutely smooth finish. To sharpen it, you burr the edge over with, say, a screwdriver shank, after grinding it square on an oilstone. As it blunts with use, you can repeat this operation three times before re-grinding.

One problem with the scraper is that friction soon makes it painfully hot. An answer is to mount it in a holder, forming a **scraper plane** (9). The iron is gripped at an acute angle, as when hand-held. Some scraper planes have wing-type handles, like spokeshaves.

The **scratch stock** (10) is for cutting short runs of moulding, on their own or along the edges of boards. Once used whenever the workman had no wooden 'moulding plane' of the right shape (there was a separate one of these for each profile), it comes in handy nowadays if you have no power router, or lack the right cutter for one.

Its wooden 'stock' is L-shaped so you can run it along the edge of the work as a guide, like the fence of any other plane. In it there's a slot, into which you clamp the cutter with wood screws or bolts. The cutter itself is home-made from any handy piece of steel (eg, a hacksaw blade).

You sharpen the cutter like a cabinet scraper, and simply work the tool along the timber (tilting it away from you slightly) until the moulded shape appears.

The proprietary version shown (10) is especially long, and the guide part of its stock is movable for fine adjustment. Cutters (not yet shaped) have been fitted in two of the many alternative positions; in practice, you'd usually use one at a time.

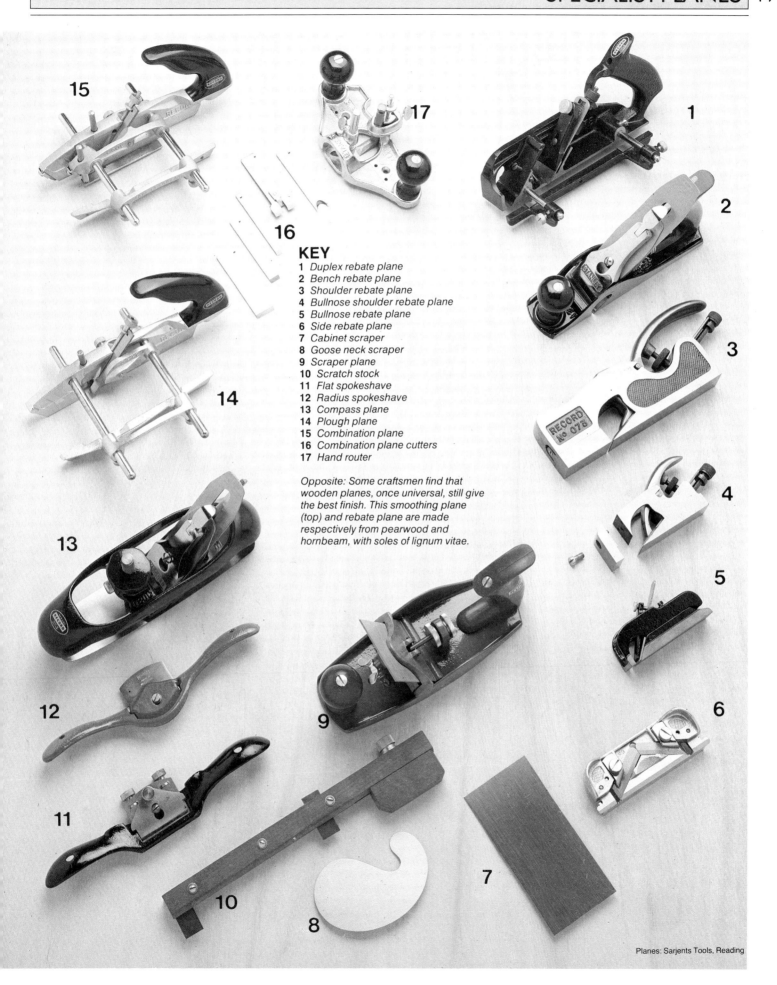

KEY

1 Duplex rebate plane
2 Bench rebate plane
3 Shoulder rebate plane
4 Bullnose shoulder rebate plane
5 Bullnose rebate plane
6 Side rebate plane
7 Cabinet scraper
8 Goose neck scraper
9 Scraper plane
10 Scratch stock
11 Flat spokeshave
12 Radius spokeshave
13 Compass plane
14 Plough plane
15 Combination plane
16 Combination plane cutters
17 Hand router

Opposite: Some craftsmen find that wooden planes, once universal, still give the best finish. This smoothing plane (top) and rebate plane are made respectively from pearwood and hornbeam, with soles of lignum vitae.

Planes: Sarjents Tools, Reading

SHAPING TOOLS

There's a whole group of tools designed to make wood-shaping easy – especially if you're dealing with awkward contours. When the need arises, it's invaluable to know which is which.

The tools shown here belong somewhere between abrasive papers and planes. They're all designed for removing waste from the surfaces of timber and other materials. But they do the job by means of sharp teeth which cover their cutting faces.

Surforms and rasps can be thought of as rough shaping tools, while files are for fine shaping and final smoothing.

Surforms
The Surform – sometimes known as the shaper or perforated rasp – is really a patented variation on the traditional rasp, described below. It removes material faster, for it actually shaves it off, rather than just wearing it away. This is because it has very sharp teeth which are 'open': gaps in the blade enable shavings to pass right through, so it doesn't clog. Its action is like that of a plane, with the difference that it takes numbers of small shavings instead of single large ones.

Surforms come in a range of shapes. Some (1 and 3) correspond to bench planes (including the block plane, 1); some have curved 'soles' (2); one is designed for use as a scraper; and one simply consists of a blade with handles at either end.

There's also a cylindrical pattern (6), which is the equivalent of a round rasp or file, and others (such as 4) like flat rasps or files. These last are the only two types which work in awkward corners.

All Surforms consist of a plastic holder and a steel blade (5), which is replaceable. Some blades have a standard cut, others are fine, and others are made to cut plastics, ceramics and even metal (as long as it's softer than steel).

Rasps
The Surform's chief disadvantage is its general unsuitability for tight corners and intricate shapes. The rasp doesn't share this problem.

Chiefly a woodworking tool (though usable on plastics and very soft metals such as lead), it has coarse, protruding teeth that look as if they've been individually clawed

out of the metal. It comes in several shapes, all suited to working unusual contours.

● The **cabinet rasp** (10) is usually half-round, like the one shown, and therefore suitable for flat, convex and concave surfaces. As for grades of coarseness (see the *Hints* panel), you may find a choice between 'second' (medium) and smooth cuts. Its length varies from 200 to 300mm (8 to 12in).

● The so-called **wood rasp** (11 and 12) can be half-round, in which case it's virtually the same as the half-round cabinet rasp – perhaps with a slightly more pronounced curve to the rounded face. But there are three other versions. The **flat wood rasp** is flat on both faces; the **hand** or **parallel wood rasp** (12) resembles it, but is unique in having parallel edges. You can also get a **round** (ie, cylindrical) pattern (11).

Wood rasps can be bastard (coarse), second or smooth cut, and they come in lengths from 150 to 400mm (6 to 16in).

● **Needle rasps** (9) are tiny, narrow rasps, made in various sections and used for fine detail work. You can get special handles for them.

● **Rifflers,** also known as woodcarver's rasps or riffler rasps (7 and 8), are similar, but double-ended. On all except the 'knife' type (7), both ends are curved for access to corners. The section of a curved riffler can be flat (tapered or parallel), square, 'three-square' (ie, triangular), round, half-round or oval.

Rifflers usually come with a bastard or smooth cut. You can also get rasp teeth at one end and file teeth at the other.

Files
Almost all files are primarily for metalwork (eg, tool sharpening) but also widely used on wood, where they give a finer finish than a rasp.

The exception is the **wood file**, usually a 'hand' (ie, flat-faced and parallel-edged) pattern with a coarse 'single' cut. This is specifically made for cleaning up timber surfaces after using a rasp.

● The **flat file** is a general-purpose type. Flat on both faces, it tapers in width and thickness. It's usually 'double' cut on the faces and single cut (ie, finer) on the edges. Lengths range from 100 to 500mm (4 to 20in).

Surforms

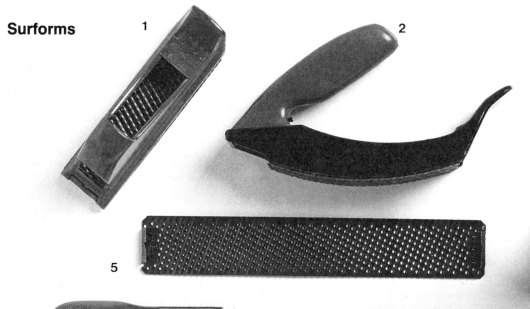

● **Hand files** (16) taper only in the thickness. They have one 'safe' (ie, un-toothed) edge, which is useful in situations where having both edges 'live' (toothed) would mean filing bits you didn't want filed. The range of lengths and cuts is similar to that for flat files.

● The **mill file** is a flat, usually parallel-edged type, always single cut, which is used not only for sharpening tools but also for general fine finishing. It has at least one rounded edge, and is between 200 and 250mm (8 to 10in) long.

● The **pillar file** is a narrow hand file with one safe edge.

● If you're only getting one file for your toolkit, the **half-round file** (18) is the one to choose. You can use its flat face for flat surfaces and convex curves, and its rounded face for concave curves. It tapers like a flat file, and comes in a similarly wide range of lengths, cuts and degrees of coarseness.

● **Round files** (17) are cylindrical and slightly tapered. They're essential for filing tight curves, such as the insides of pipes, where the curve on a half-round file is too gradual. Lengths are between 100 and 500mm (4 to 20in); the smaller versions are often called rat-tail files.

● The **three-square** or **triangular file** (14) is handy for cleaning out angles which are smaller than 90°.

● **Needle** or **jeweller's files** (13) are unbeatable for their own particular task – precision finishing of intricate, high-class work. They're usually sold in sets which include several different sections – flat (parallel), round, half-round, square, three-square and knife-shaped. Their coarseness, unlike that of other files, is indicated by a number.

● There are also **riffler files**, or **jeweller's rifflers** – just like riffler rasps except for having file teeth.

Rasps

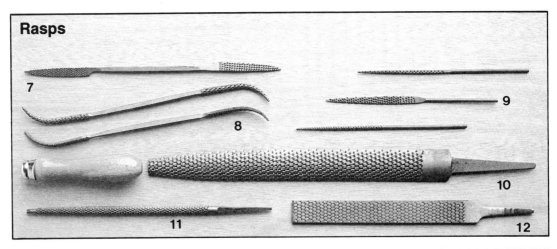

Which tool is which?

Shaping tools come in a great variety of patterns, sizes and shapes. Shown here are most of those readily available.

Left: Surforms
1 block plane
2 ripping plane
3 standard plane
4 flat file
5 blade
6 round file

Above: rasps
7 riffler (knife type)
8 rifflers (curved)
9 needle rasps
10 cabinet rasp
11 round rasp
12 hand rasp

Right: files
13 needle files
14 three-square file
15 square file
16 hand file
17 round file
18 half-round file
19 file card

Files
Mainly for working metal, files will also tackle fine wood-shaping. Like rasps, they come without handles. Use a file card (19) to unclog them.

hints

● *Choosing the right tool means identifying 'cut' and coarseness.*

*The **cut** is the shape of the teeth. Rasps, by definition, are rasp-cut (A). Files can be single-cut (in slanting parallel ridges – B), double-cut (in criss-cross ridges – C) or curved-tooth (D).*

Single-cut files give a finer finish, especially on soft metals. Double-cut files work faster, and are thus for more general use. A dreadnought file has very coarse curved teeth, and is especially suitable for aluminium.

*For each of these cuts there are up to six possible degrees of_ **coarseness**. (Confusingly, these are also sometimes known as the 'cut'.) They're determined by the number of teeth per 25mm (1in).*

The range is: rough or coarse; bastard, medium, medium coarse, middle, regular or common; second-cut; smooth; dead smooth; and double dead smooth.

● *What all this boils down to is that a double-cut second-cut file will do for most jobs.*

With rasps, the categories (if any) are usually less precise.

● *Almost all rasps and files are sold without handles. Don't use them that way – the pointed 'tang' can be dangerous. Instead, buy a metal or plastic file handle of a suitable*

size, insert the tang, and tap the handle gently on the workbench so it grips firmly. If it proves stubborn, use a wooden mallet.

Worn rasps and files can't be sharpened – they must be replaced. Handles, however, can be pulled or tapped off for re-use.

● *Keep files sharp and efficient for as long as possible by stroking them with a file card (in the photograph), parallel to the ridges, to remove clogging fragments.*

After cleaning, rub chalk well into all the teeth. This helps prevent them from clogging again.

● *Store files separately – not all jumbled up together, or they'll blunt one another.*

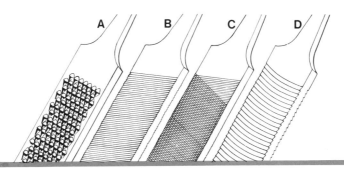

CHISELS

A set of chisels will help your carpentry progress beyond the most basic. But you need to know some facts about choosing and using them.

There are half a dozen common types of woodworking chisel and the main thing that affects your choice is the design of the chisel's blade. With all of them the actual cutting edge is at the end of the blade, but the blade profile varies. If strong and thick it will take a lot of bashing; if it is more delicate with sloping sides it is designed to reach into awkward corners. For some jobs you may find a chisel with an extra long blade handy and, for cutting curves, it's best to use one with a curved cross section (called a gouge).

The handle material is also important. Traditionally, handles are made from wood. But although comfortable to hold, wood is likely to split or mushroom out at the end if hit with a hammer, so a wooden mallet must be used instead. If the chisel is likely to be subjected to very heavy blows — when chopping out a housing or a mortise, for example — then a wooden handle must also be fairly chunky, or else have the end strengthened with a metal band. There are no such problems with plastic handles. You can hit these as hard as you like with a hammer or a mallet without fear of damaging them.

Having got the right chisel, look after it: don't use it for opening paint cans and so on, and take care when working on old, used timber not to run into any nails or screws and nick the cutting edge. You should also make sure you sharpen it correctly. If you don't, over the years the angle forming the cutting edge can become misshapen so that accurate work will almost be impossible to do — and a blunt chisel is useless.

CHISEL SAFETY

Chisels can be dangerous unless you follow a few safety rules. When working, never allow your hands or any other part of your body to get in front of the cutting edge, just in case you slip. When you have finished with the chisel, put it away. Don't leave it lying about where it might cause an accident. To be doubly safe, fit it with a plastic blade guard — often supplied with the chisel when you buy.

Sharpening chisels

A new chisel isn't ready for use. Although the end is angled at between 20° and 25° (called the grinding bevel) to give what seems to be a cutting edge, this won't cut for long — if at all. So, to provide a more durable edge, the very tip of the chisel has to be honed down to an angle between 30° and 35°.

To do this, you will need an oil stone — a rectangular block of abrasive material, normally carborundum. A combination oil stone is best. One face is a fine abrasive for normal sharpening; the other is coarser and is for drastically reshaping the grinding bevel if and when it gets damaged.

Before you begin sharpening, liberally cover the surface of the stone with oil which will carry away the metal removed from the chisel, preventing it from becoming embedded in the stone. A thin mineral oil is best.

You now simply hold the chisel bevel down, checking that it is at the correct angle, and work it back and forth over as much of the stone's surface as possible — merely running it up and down will wear a groove in the stone's surface. A useful additional tool is a honing guide – a sort of small trolley into which you lock the chisel to keep it at the correct angle on the stone.

After a while, run your finger down the chisel's flat side and over the edge. If you feel a slight burr or ridge of metal the chisel is ready for the next stage. Place it flat side down on the stone and gently stroke away the burr.

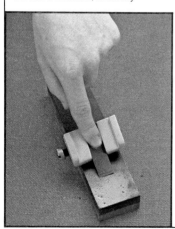

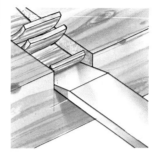

Don't try to chisel away too much timber in one go. To begin with, taking off about 3mm (¹/₈in) slivers is safe — reduce this to 1mm or less for a fine finish.

For most jobs, hold the chisel with the cutting bevel facing towards the wood which you are cutting away. However, for fine work, some carpenters hold it the other way round. They say it gives more control because the chisel is less likely to try to follow the grain of the wood and dig in too deep.

Unless you're using a mallet to knock the chisel through the wood, always keep both hands on the chisel. Use one hand to provide the driving force, and hold the handle with the other hand to guide it.

When making a mortise or a housing choose a chisel of the same width as the cut-out. With mortises you have more control if you hold the chisel by the blade rather than the handle, steadying your hand by resting it on the wood as you're cutting.

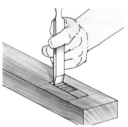

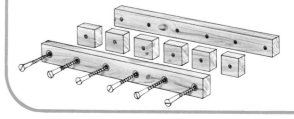

The best way to store chisels is in a rack which you can make for yourself. Use two thin battens of timber with 19mm (³/₄in) blocks spaced between them to slot the chisels into. Make up using screws long enough to go through the rack and into the wall.

Mortise chisels

Specially designed to take the battering they get when cutting a mortise, these have a thick, almost square-sectioned blade, and either a very chunky handle (the sash mortise chisel) or one bound with a metal ring (the 'registered' pattern). Traditionally, a leather 'shock absorber' is included between the handle and the blade.

Bevel-edged chisels

These get their name from the blade's sloping (bevelled) sides, and can cope with most jobs. They are particularly good at getting into corners and undercutting, but aren't strong enough for very heavy chopping or levering. The most commonly available sizes — chisels are sized by blade width — are between 6mm (¼in) and 38mm (1½in), in 3mm (⅛in) steps.

Firmer chisels

A rectangular-sectioned blade makes the firmer chisel stronger and capable of quite heavy chopping-out operations. Unfortunately, it also makes it too unmanageable for cutting fiddly joints. Sizes are as for bevel-edged chisels.

Firmer bevel chisels offer the best of both worlds — they look like bevel-edge chisels but have thicker blades and are as strong as firmer chisels.

Paring chisels

Available in both firmer and bevel-edged patterns, these have a very long blade for cutting long housings and slots.

Gouges

Gouges are really just specialist chisels — the blade has a C-shaped section. There are two types: scribing gouges have the bevel forming the cutting edge on the inside of the 'C' and are for cutting shallow grooves and the like; firmer gouges have the bevel on the outside and are for trimming curves.

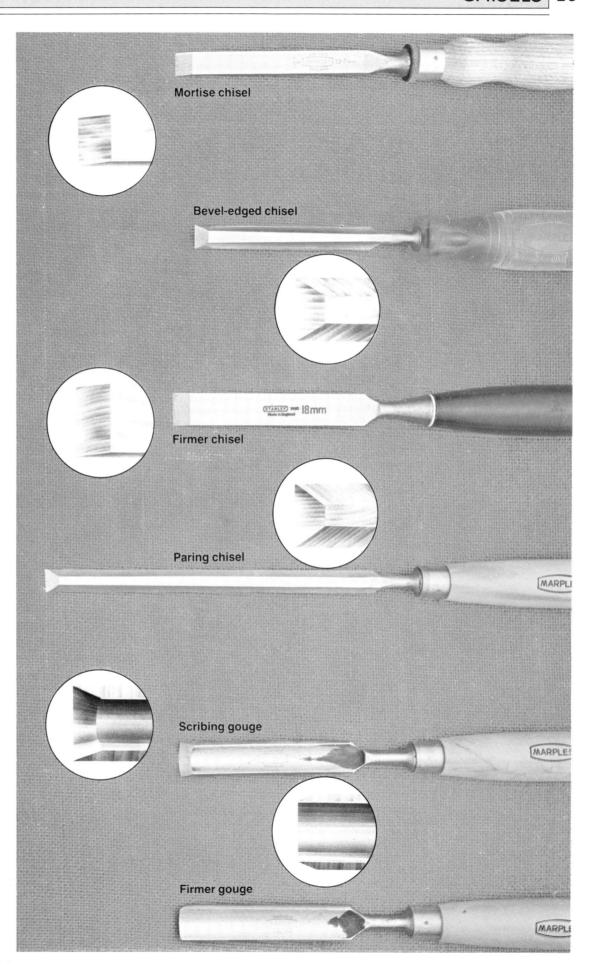

Mortise chisel

Bevel-edged chisel

Firmer chisel

Paring chisel

Scribing gouge

Firmer gouge

HAND DRILLS

Drilling holes by hand gives you more control than is possible with power tools. Here's the equipment you need for the job.

A hand drill, a carpenter's brace and a selection of bits for each – you can buy the bits in sets to start you off – are essential ingredients of any tool kit. The bit is the part that makes the hole; the drill or brace drives it round and round. Just avoid getting anything so large and clumsy that you'll be uncomfortable using it, or so insubstantial that it will only tackle the lightest work.

Hand drills

Also known as a **wheelbrace**, the **hand drill** (6) is used for fairly light drilling in a variety of materials. A detachable side knob is usually fitted for use when more pressure is required. On most hand drills, the *chuck* – the adjustable jaws – is designed to accept straight-shanked bits up to 6mm (¼in), or more commonly 8mm (⅜in), in diameter.

The chuck is turned via a small pinion gear when you rotate the main gear wheel. A second 'balancing' pinion may also be fitted to give a smoother action. In some modern designs the gears are enclosed for protection against sawdust and so on.

● The **breast drill** (7) is a heavy-duty version of the single-pinion hand drill. It has not only a side handle but also a breast plate against which you can lean to provide extra pressure. It's therefore well suited to making large holes and to drilling masonry. Most breast drills accept ordinary straight-shanked drill bits up to 12mm (½in) in diameter, and up to 25mm (1in) in diameter provided their shanks are reduced (see below). Gears may be exposed or enclosed – drills with the latter feature are sometimes called *Continental pattern* – and most breast drills offer a choice of two speeds. Speed selection is achieved on Continental types by moving the crank handle; on the rest, the main gear is moved to engage one or the other of two concentric sets of cogs.

Bits for hand drills

Twist drill bits (10), often called 'twist drills', are the ones most commonly used in hand drills. 'High-speed' versions cope with most jobs in most materials, including metal – for which, in fact, they are primarily designed.

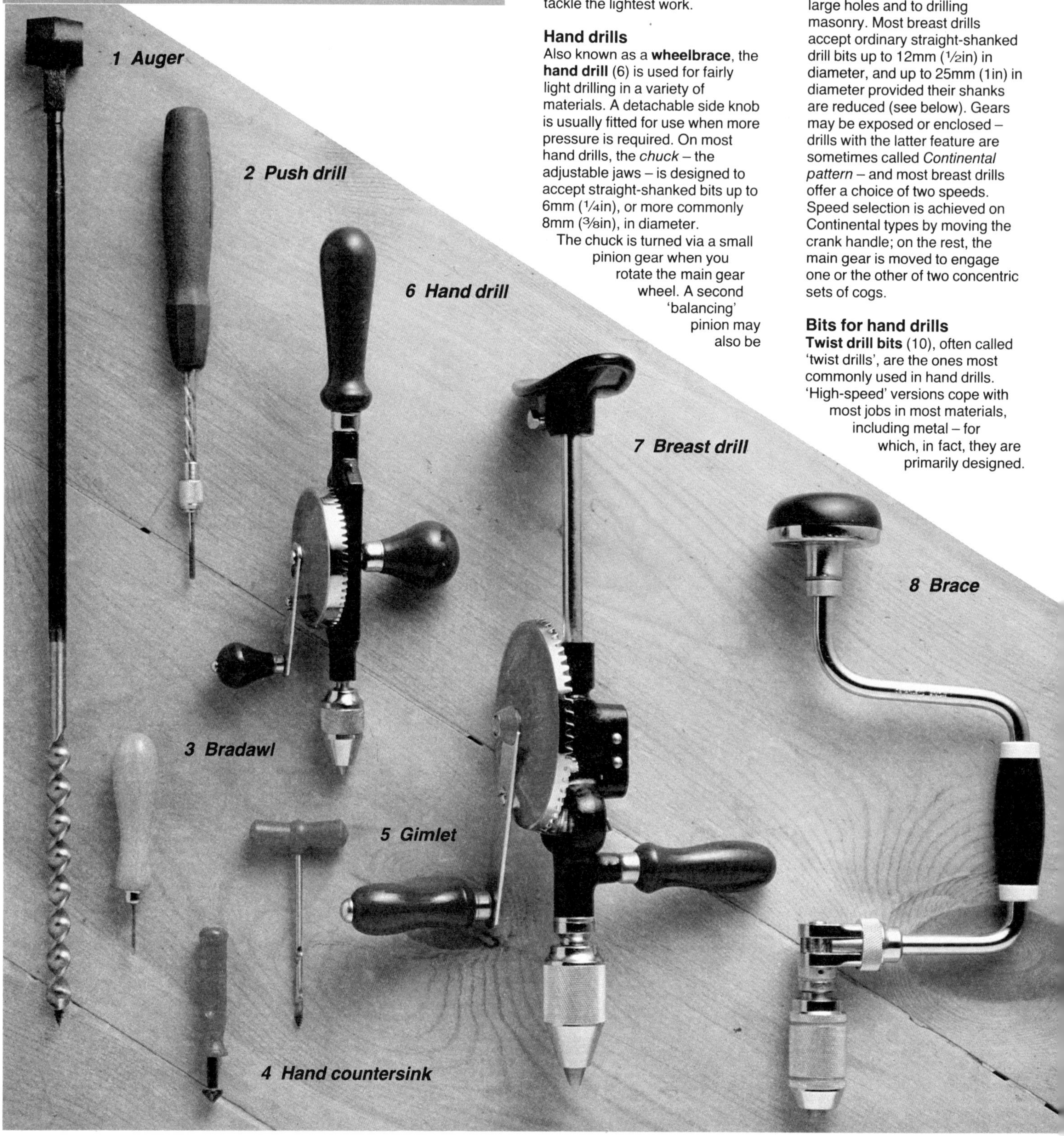

1 Auger

2 Push drill

6 Hand drill

7 Breast drill

8 Brace

3 Bradawl

5 Gimlet

4 Hand countersink

The cheaper carbon steel types are suitable only for drilling wood.

Most have a straight shank, and can be anything from 0.4 to 25mm (up to 1in) in diameter, though sizes between 1.5 and 12mm (¹⁄₁₆ and ½in) are the most common.

Bits up to 19mm (¾in) across are also widely available; they can be used in chucks that don't have such a large capacity, for some have reduced shanks – in other words, the upper end of the shank has a smaller diameter than the lower, as on the dowel bit illustrated (11).

Bit lengths vary according to the diameter, and type of steel.

● Although **masonry bits** are best used with power drills, small 'plugging drills' work well in hand drills if you have enough strength to drive them. They're basically twist drills with very hard tungsten carbide tips which have special cutting lugs, and are available in diameters between 4.5 and 10mm (³⁄₁₆ to ⅜in).

● Unlike twist drill bits, **dowel bits** (11) have a shape which is purpose-designed for clearing timber waste efficiently, and ideal for dowel joints. They also have a sharp point to centre the bit accurately where you want it, and two sharp spurs at the outside of the tip to help it cut a clean hole and stay on course – especially when drilling into end grain (which is where dowels are generally inserted). Dowel bits are available in diameters from 3 to 13mm (⅛ to ½in). On some, the top end forms a square-sectioned tapered *tang* to fit alligator-jawed braces (see below).

● The **drill and countersink bit** (12) is very useful: it drills pilot, clearance holes and countersinks.

Push drills

The **push drill** (2) is for making very small holes in timber more quickly and easily than a gimlet can. You pump the handle up and down, and the drill turns on each push stroke. It needs special bits called *drill points*. Sold with the drill and stored in its hollow handle, these are normally between 2 and 4.4mm in diameter, though other sizes are sometimes available.

Non-mechanical drills

Some drills are operated entirely by hand, without any gears.

● The **auger** or screw auger (1) is in effect a long bit, with a hole in the top end to take a removable dowel handle. It's for drilling large and very deep holes, having a diameter of 6-38mm (¼-1½in) and a length generally in the region of 600mm (2ft).

● The **bradawl** (3) will make complete holes for the smallest screws. It's also very useful for making starting holes for slightly bigger screws – and before using a twist bit or push drill, so that the bit doesn't wander off centre. Another pattern of bradawl has a square-sectioned shaft tapering to a point, which makes it stronger.

● The **hand countersink** (4) makes countersinks when turned by hand.

● The **gimlet** (5) is a small drill, complete with lead screw point and a twist to clear the waste.

Carpenter's braces

The **brace** (8) or **swingbrace** is traditionally the woodworker's chief tool for making large holes in wood. It consists of a crank with a toadstool-shaped head at one end (so you can steady it and apply pressure) and a chuck

Bits for hand drills

10 A range of twist bits
11 Dowel bit
12 Drill and countersink bit

Tools for making holes

*1 The **auger** drills very deep holes. 2 The **push drill** makes small holes quickly. 3 The **bradawl** makes starting holes for screws and drill bits. 4 The **hand countersink** makes recesses for screw heads. 5 The **gimlet** drills holes where hand pressure suffices. 6 The **hand drill** is ideal for all smallish holes. 7 The **breast drill** allows greater pressure. 8 You need the **brace** for large and deep holes. 9 The **joist brace** is for confined spaces.*

9 Joist brace

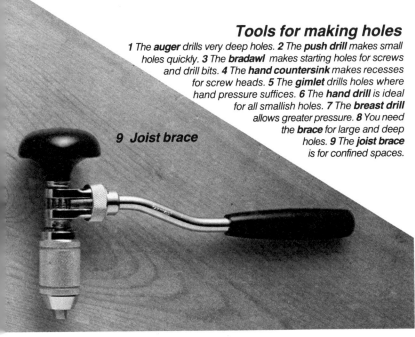

which is attached to the other end.

The chuck may be fixed, but is usually attached via a ratchet which allows drilling in awkward corners where you can't rotate the crank fully. It will have one of two types of jaws. Alligator jaws accept only bits with square tangs. Universal jaws also accept straight-shanked bits, such as twist drill bits, up to about 12mm (½in) in diameter.

Braces are sized according to the crank's turning circle or 'sweep'. This varies between 200 and 350mm (8 and 14in), with 250mm (10in) the best for general work. A version with a sweep as little as 150mm (6in), called an **electrician's brace,** is also available, and is used for making holes in confined spaces – through joists, floor boards and the like.

● The **joist brace** (9) is the modern alternative to the electrician's brace. It's simply a variation on the ratchet type of carpenter's brace in which the large crank handle is replaced by a lever, thus reducing the length of the tool. Fitted with universal jaws, it's for drilling in confined spaces – for example, sideways through floor joists.

Bits for braces

The traditional bits for making holes in timber are **auger bits,**

whose long twists mean efficient waste clearance, plus accuracy when boring deep holes. They also have a screw point, which centres the hole – and, once it takes hold, pulls the bit through the wood and so reduces the amount of pressure you will have to apply.

Two basic types of auger bit are available. Both come in diameters between 6 and 25mm (¼ and 1in), and are normally between 200 and 250mm (8 and 10in) long.

● The **Jennings pattern auger bit** (14) has a twist in the shape of a double helix. It clears the waste especially well and is marginally the more accurate of the two. It also comes in a 125mm (5in) length, suitable for dowelling, when it may be known (confusingly) as a dowel bit.

● The **solid centre** or **Irwin auger bit** (15) has a single helix around a central core, which makes it stronger and a little faster in use, and thus a good choice for drilling deep holes.

● Auger bits usually have two spurs at the tip, like those on a dowel bit (11) but sharper, to sever the wood fibres and so make a neater hole. But some solid centre bits have just one spur; and the **Scotch auger bit** or wagon bit (13) is a Jennings pattern bit without any spurs at all, for hard timber and rough work,

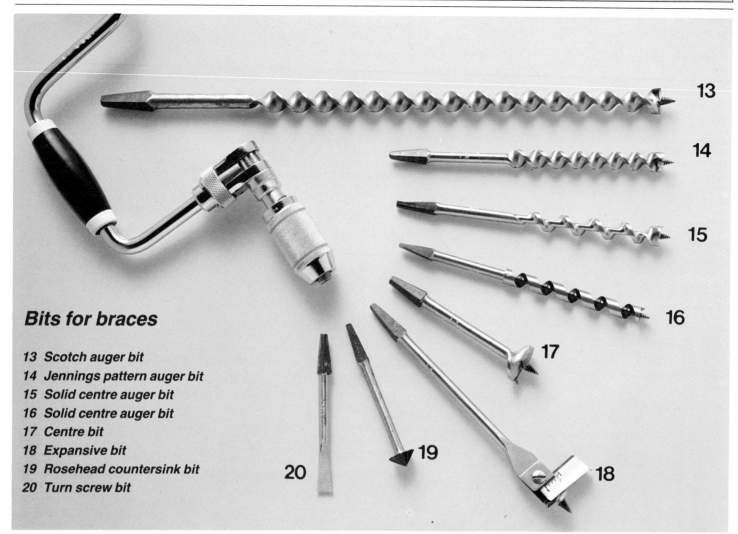

Bits for braces

13 Scotch auger bit
14 Jennings pattern auger bit
15 Solid centre auger bit
16 Solid centre auger bit
17 Centre bit
18 Expansive bit
19 Rosehead countersink bit
20 Turn screw bit

where plenty of pressure is more important than a clean cut.

● 16 is a type of solid-centre auger bit with a single spur and a twist shaped for an exceptionally accurate, straight-sided hole.

● **Centre bits** (17) are used to bore fairly shallow holes of large diameter – between 6 and 50mm (¼ and 2in). They have a short, helical cutting head whose twist doesn't continue up the shank. This bit is equipped with two cutters which remove the waste, plus a spur which paves the way for them. Centre bits are 100-150mm (4-6in) long, and not good at boring deep holes – they tend to wander.

● The **expansive bit** (18) is an ingenious device – essentially a centre bit with an extra spur/cutter that can be adjusted to alter the diameter of the hole. This can be extremely economical as you can get away with just one expansive bit instead of a whole range of different sizes. There are two common sizes. The smaller makes holes between 12 and 38mm (½ and 1½in) in diameter; the larger, holes between 22 and 75mm (⅞ and 3in) in diameter. Some manufacturers offer additional cutters which increase

the capacity of the larger size to as much as 150mm (6in).

● The **countersink bit** is for making a circular sloping-sided (countersunk) recess to take the head of a screw. Shown is the **rosehead** type (19), which is the commonest.

● The **turn screw bit** or screwdriver bit (20) is useful when you want to exert more force on the screw than is possible with a screwdriver on its own.

Looking after your tools
Once you've bought your equipment, look after it. Keep gears, ratchets etc free from dust and shavings, and lubricate them now and again with light machine oil. Keep your drill bits sharp, too, if you want good results without undue hard work. With auger bits, centre bits and the like, the cutting edges can easily be restored with a file. Sharpening twist drill bits is more difficult, and takes skill even if you use one of the do-it-yourself aids now available. So, unless you can afford to keep buying new twist drill bits all the time, it's worth finding out if a local tool shop can arrange to have them sharpened for you. Bits can be spoilt by incorrect sharpening.

hints

● When drilling right through a piece of wood, remember that as the drill bit breaks through the other side, the wood there will splinter out. Either stop drilling halfway (with auger, centre and expansive bits, wait till the screw point breaks through – A) and finish the hole by drilling from the other side – B; or else firmly clamp scrap wood to the workpiece and drill right through into that – C.

● Particularly when drilling deep holes, withdraw the bit from the hole now and then to clear out the waste. Keep turning it in the same direction as when drilling – unless the bit has a lead screw, when you must obviously turn it anti-clockwise first to disengage the screw.

● Where a hole's depth is critical, fit the drill with a depth stop – D. You can make one easily by drilling through a piece of scrap wood, fitting it around the bit like a collar, and adjusting the bit in the chuck till only the amount you need protrudes beyond the collar.

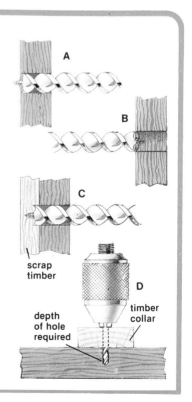

VICES & CRAMPS

While many tools are luxuries, rather than bare necessities, you'll soon find that a vice and some cramps are an absolute must for effective woodwork.

Before going into the details of the various appliances for gripping woodwork, it's worth thinking for a moment about your needs.

Even the most basic tool kit requires some sort of vice. Without one, you simply won't be able to hold the timber still while you work on it – and that's a certain recipe for inaccuracy, if not for accidents. In fact, it makes many cutting operations impossible.

The snag is, of course, that a vice must be mounted on a bench. You may consider a proper wooden bench too expensive for the amount of woodworking you do; besides, few homes have room for one. So what are the alternatives? If you have any sort of workshop or hobbies room, it's worth considering the type of vice that can be clamped to the edge of a table or firmly supported shelf. Otherwise a Workmate may be the most sensible investment.

And what about cramps? Without them you'll probably never make a decent glued joint, because all woodworking adhesives, except for the contact type, need pressure during setting in order to get the joint tight (see Chapter 3, pages 76 -79 for full information on gluing and cramping techniques). Cramps are also indispensable for securing wide and flat workpieces to a table or bench. However, you often need to use them in pairs (or even fours), and buying a full set can be expensive.

For the average handyman, perhaps the best plan is just to buy a couple of medium-sized G-cramps (or at least one of the other types that do a similar job) and leave it at that. If you do find yourself tackling the occasional job that requires sash cramps, you can hire them for a usually negligible fee. The only specialist cramp it may be worth getting is a mitre cramp.

When shopping, remember that cramps and clamps are just different names for the same thing.

G-cramps

These are extremely useful for general work. They consist simply of a C-shaped metal frame (usually steel, but occasionally aluminium in the smallest sizes) with a pivoting shoe attached to one end of a threaded shaft which passes through one arm of the C. The shaft moves the shoe towards the other arm in order to grip the work. The main variations in design lie in the means by which the shaft is turned – usually either a tommy bar (1, 2, 3 and 10), often sliding for even greater leverage, or by a thumbscrew rather like a wing nut (5). The **spin grip** type (2) uses a knurled wheel – generally in conjunction with a tommy bar, and often in small sizes intended for modelling and other delicate work.

Other G-cramp variants are:
Deep-throat cramps (1) now perhaps more commonly known as **long-reach cramps**. These have especially long arms which allow them to grip some distance from an edge.
Edge cramps (10), for securing things against the edge of a workpiece. Sometimes known as 'edge-lipping cramps' because of their primary use, they usually have a second threaded shaft emerging from the back of the C.
Fret cramps (4), used for very light, delicate work such as modelmaking, where ordinary G-cramps would prove unmanageable. They are therefore constructed accordingly. The main frame is normally made from a strip of spring steel, bent to shape, and the clamping is generally done by means of a simple thumbscrew. Capacities range from 50 to 100mm (2 to 4in).

Quick-release cramps

These are G-cramps with a difference. Both jaws are fixed to a metal bar – plain (9) or serrated (12). At least one jaw is movable; it locks in any position along the bar's length when you tighten up its screw mechanism to clamp the work. This mechanism is operated by means of a wooden handle (9) or a tommy bar (12). Capacities range from 150 to 915mm (6 to 36in).

Rak cramps

These attempt to combine the virtues of the sash cramp – see below – and the G-cramp. There are two main patterns. The **fixed-jaw** type (6 and 7), which is closer to the G-cramp, consists of a long bar with deep serrations, which curves round at one end to form a jaw, plus a movable second jaw which slides along the bar and is itself fixed in place by means of a locking screw operated by a tommy bar.

The **beam** version, which is closer to the sash cramp, has a straight bar, and both jaws are movable. They're also reversible; they can be made to face outwards – allowing you, for example, to cramp something to the inside of a framework. Another model, the **Jet cramp**, has a plain rather than a serrated bar.

For both types, sizes vary widely.

Web cramps

A unique solution to the problem of holding together awkwardly-shaped structures while the adhesive sets, the **web cramp** (8) is little more than a strong belt made from 25mm (1in) wide nylon webbing, fitted with a specially designed locking 'buckle'. You simply wrap it around whatever you want to cramp, and tighten it up.

Cam clamps

Made in timber (with cork-faced jaws) or in metal, these are types of quick-release clamp which have no screw mechanism. Instead you move a lever to exert pressure.

Mitre cramps

Used almost solely for cramping up mitred corner joints during glueing (eg, for picture frames), the **mitre** or **corner cramp** (11) consists of a right-angled cast metal frame fitted with two screw assemblies which simply squeeze the mitre together. They come in a variety of sizes, so you can choose the one best suited to the scale of the work.

Woodworking bench vices

The bench vice holds workpieces conveniently and firmly in place. The basic version (13) consists simply of two cast metal jaws; these are linked by means of two guide rods, plus a screw mechanism (operated with a tommy bar from the front of the vice) which moves the outer jaw. More sophisticated versions include features such as quick-release mechanisms and easily interchangeable linings.

There are two vital points to bear in mind. Firstly, before using a vice you must fit wooden jaw linings – screwing them in place through holes supplied for the purpose in each jaw. If you don't, workpieces will be badly bruised. Secondly, you must secure the vice to a substantial, heavy workbench. There's little sense in fixing something immovably in a vice if the vice itself can move. However, if you have no bench, there is a way out. Some vices are fitted with what amounts to a small G-cramp, so that you can secure them to the edge of any heavy table.

Remember, too, that even the biggest bench vice is limited in use by its size. It won't grip large boards, or even sizeable widths or lengths of timber. On the whole, vices have more application in furniture-making and other relatively small-scale work than in general carpentry.

Sash cramps

Sash cramps (16) are absolutely invaluable for keeping carcases and frameworks tight and square during glueing. The clamp consists of a long, flat steel bar with two jaws. One jaw is fixed to one end of the bar, but adjusted with a screw mechanism and tommy bar; the second jaw (the 'tail slide') slides freely along the bar, but is locked in position where required – usually by inserting a metal peg into one of the regularly spaced holes in the bar. Alternatively, the bar may have notches on the underside to receive a pin built into the tail slide. Here the second jaw locks automatically in position when pressure is applied to it – ie, when the main jaw is tightened.

Sizes vary considerably, but even the smallest sash cramps generally have a capacity of about 600mm (2ft), while the largest can run to as much as 1525mm (5ft). It's worth remembering, though, that some suppliers size sash cramps according to the length of bar, which is always 150mm (6in) or so greater than the capacity.

T-bar cramps

These are just heavy-duty versions of the sash cramp – the only difference being that the bar is T-shaped in section (14), rather than rectangular. This strengthens its ability to resist bending, so you can exert more cramping force.

Cramp heads

These provide what amounts to a do-it-yourself sash-cramp kit (15) – they're simply a sash cramp without the bar. You mount them on a long timber batten in which you've drilled peg holes to suit your needs.

KEY (OVERLEAF)

Cramps for light work and everyday jobs
1 *Deep-throat G-cramp*
2 *Spin grip cramp*
3 *Lightweight G-cramp*
4 *Fret cramp*
5 *General-purpose G-cramp*
6 *Fixed-jaw Rak cramp*
7 *Fixed-jaw Rak cramp*
8 *Web cramp*
9 *Quick-release cramp (note the plastic jaw covers, which help to protect the workpiece from damage when tightening)*
10 *Edge cramp*
11 *Mitre cramp*
12 *Quick-release cramp*

Woodworking bench vice (13)

Cramps for large structures
14 *T-bar cramp*
15 *Cramp heads*
16 *Sash cramp*

CRAMPS FOR LIGHT WORK AND EVERYDAY JOBS

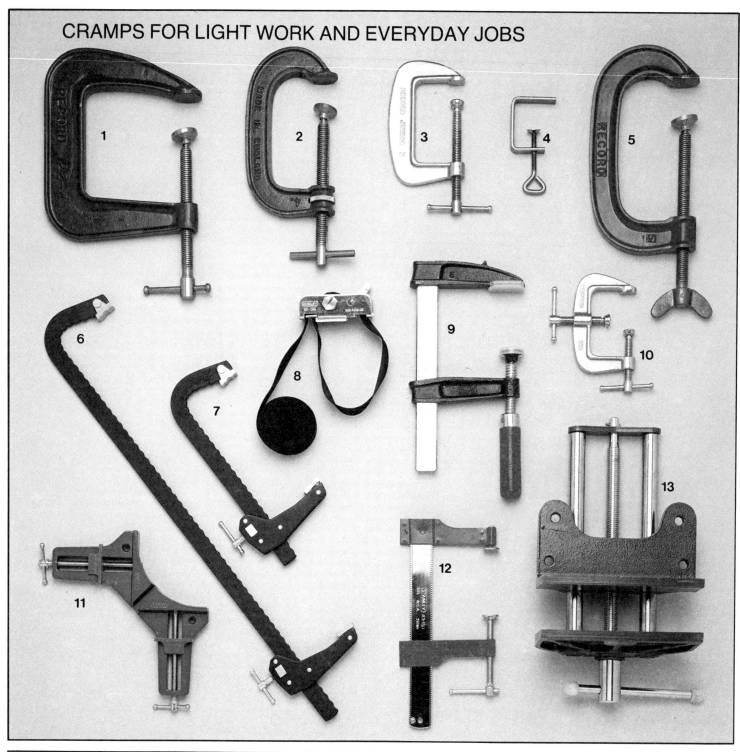

CRAMPS FOR LARGE STRUCTURES

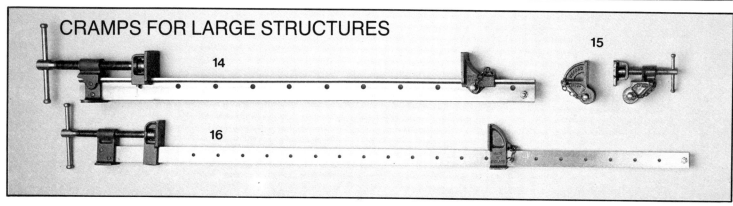

The Workmate

The Workmate is a unique product which solves many of the problems associated with traditional vices.

It is, in essence, a huge vice on legs. That means, for a start, that you don't need a separate mounting. In fact, the Workmate does duty as a workbench too – but it folds up so you can carry it about. That removes the need for the permanent location required by more massive benches, and of course it enables you to take the bench to the job where necessary.

The Workmate's weight is a compromise; it's light enough to carry without much strain, but still heavy and stable enough.

On standard models at least, the actual working surface is small; for any job that's at all complex, you'll certainly need additional space – if only to stow your tools. Objects left on a Workmate tend to fall off, especially since its top actually moves whenever you clamp something. That's because the jaws have their edges parallel, rather than their faces, so the bench is formed by their upper surfaces.

They're opened and closed by a pair of screw mechanisms, each with its own handle. This means that (within limits) you can align the jaws out of parallel, thereby gripping tapered workpieces. V-shaped grooves are milled horizontally and vertically in their edges, which is handy for holding cylindrical things like pipes.

Holes through the jaws take plastic pegs, which can be used as bench stops (ie, to prevent work slipping) or in any number of arrangements to cramp workpieces which are too large for the vice.

Moreover, the Workmate's small surface area can be increased with a set of 'extender arms'. These are strips of metal with holes in them. You peg them into the holes in the bench, so that they stick out beyond it to provide a firm support for large items. Plastic brackets or 'angle grips' can be fitted on top, to grip the workpiece by its edges or corners; the use of these can replace sash cramps, and they also enable corner cramping of frames both large and small.

There are several variants on the basic design. Retractable stub legs raise the Workmate from sawbench to workbench height. A wall-mounted version folds up flat against the wall. And there's also an extra-large model which opens very wide; one of its jaws swings up to a 45° or 90° angle if you want. These last two both incorporate an additional working surface.

ABRASIVES

In woodwork and decorating, a smooth surface is often vital for good results. Sanding is the way to achieve it. Here are the tools and techniques you need to know about.

Old-time woodworkers gave their jobs a final smooth finish by rubbing them with all sorts of materials — dogfish skin, for example. Now modern abrasives have taken over; sand isn't among them, but we still use 'sandpaper' and 'sanding' as general terms.

Of course, smoothing wood isn't the only job that calls for sanding. In decorating, it helps shift dust stuck in paintwork, remove excess filler from cracks in walls, and much more besides. Fine sandpaper can equally well be used to smooth a matt surface — such as that of natural timber — and to take the shine off a glossy one, such as varnish (often in order to help a subsequent coat to stick).

Sanding can also be used for minor wood-shaping operations, such as rounding off sharp corners; but the emphasis is on 'minor'. It's too slow for removing large amounts of material. If you don't believe this, try sanding out a scratch from a piece of wood. In any case, other tools are much better suited to the job — planes, rasps and so on.

But, of all the different abrasives on the market, which should you use? It depends on what you're sanding and the surface you want.

All abrasives — except for steel wool and various harsh metal and plastic discs — consist of a backing coated with grains of 'grit'. Grits can be crushed glass or garnet, or modern synthetic materials. The latter are more efficient, longer-lasting, less likely to become clogged, and able to cope with a wider range of materials. Unfortunately, they also make the abrasives more expensive.

But choosing the right kind of grit isn't everything. It's also essential to pick the right 'grade'. A large, coarse grit will cut faster than a small, fine one, but also leave a rougher finish. For this reason, most sanding operations need at least three different grades: a coarse one to remove most of the material, a medium one to remove any residual material, and a fine one for the final finish.

Sadly, however, abrasive manufacturers don't often use simple terms like 'fine' and 'coarse' to describe their products. They use a numbering system; and the snag is that it varies with the type of abrasive. With glasspaper you talk about 00 (the finest grade) and 3 (the coarsest). But with silicon carbide paper, for example, you deal in hundreds.

What's more, similar numbers may not mean the same thing. Silicon carbide 100 is a lot coarser than aluminium oxide 100 (another type). All you can do is look at the paper and decide for yourself. If in doubt, ask your supplier for advice.

The type of backing also matters. The commonest is paper, and it's usually more than adequate. But some power-tool abrasives use cloth; and tungsten carbide uses a steel backing.

Then you have to consider the way the grit is stuck on. Is, for example, the adhesive waterproof? The most common waterproof abrasive, 'wet-and-dry' silicon carbide paper, unlike glass- and garnet paper, can be lubricated with water without falling to pieces — a very useful property. And how much of the backing's surface is actually covered with grit? For abrasives described as 'close coat' it's between 70 and 100 per cent, so they're faster and more durable. 'Open coat' abrasives, on the other hand, are cheaper and less prone to clogging.

You can sand either by hand or by machine. Electric orbital, drum, disc, belt and floor sanders are all available, each for a different type of job. You fit them with replaceable sheets, belts or loops of abrasive, usually aluminium oxide. Belt and floor sanders are large and expensive, but can readily be hired (see overleaf).

Machines are faster than hand work, and a great help over large surfaces, but they must be used with care — and, above all, kept moving. It's all too easy to make unwanted hollows, and to rub away details such as sharp edges that you want to keep. Besides, machines won't go into awkward angles or over complex mouldings. In such situations the only answer is to work by hand.

SHEET ABRASIVES

1 to 5 Glasspaper

The traditional abrasive for hand sanding of wood; can also be used for keying paintwork, although other abrasives stay 'sharp' longer and are less likely to clog up. Sheet size usually 280 × 230mm (11 × 9in). The cheapest sheet abrasive. Nine grades available: 2/0 or 00 (the finest, also called flour paper), 0, 1, 1½, F2, M2, S2, 2½ and 3 (very coarse).

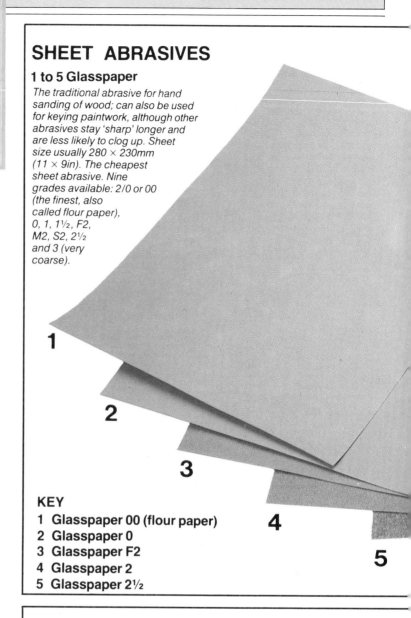

KEY
1 **Glasspaper 00 (flour paper)**
2 **Glasspaper 0**
3 **Glasspaper F2**
4 **Glasspaper 2**
5 **Glasspaper 2½**

SANDING BLOCKS

Sanding any but the smallest area is a tedious chore without a sanding block to give you easier handling and a more level surface. For smooth results a block needs resilience:
1 *is wood with a felt pad.*
2 *is cork. You wrap the paper round them.*

The re-usable flexible sanding block (3) is a fairly new product which consists of a piece of foam plastic with its faces and edges covered with abrasive paper. On some types the abrasive is aluminium oxide, for use on wood; on the one shown, it's silicon carbide — medium on two sides and coarse on the other two. The latter can be used on wood or metal, but it works well on paintwork if used wet.

1 wood bloc
with fe
pad

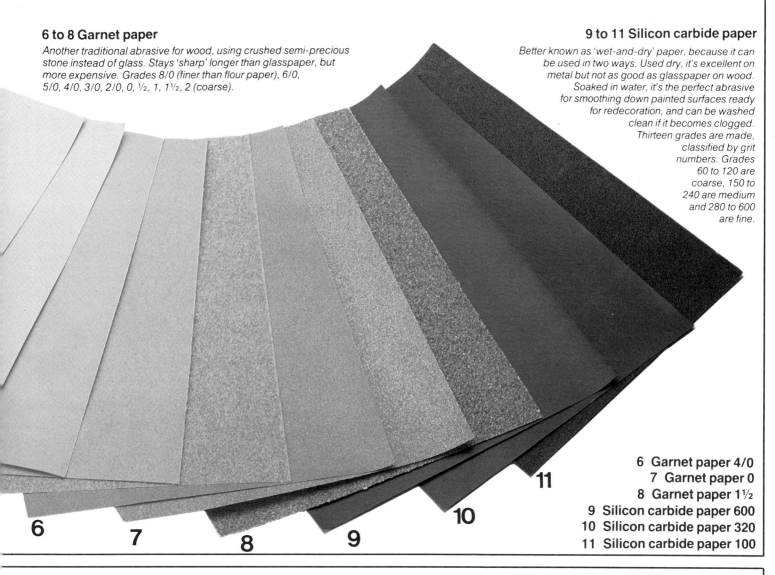

6 to 8 Garnet paper

Another traditional abrasive for wood, using crushed semi-precious stone instead of glass. Stays 'sharp' longer than glasspaper, but more expensive. Grades 8/0 (finer than flour paper), 6/0, 5/0, 4/0, 3/0, 2/0, 0, ½, 1, 1½, 2 (coarse).

9 to 11 Silicon carbide paper

Better known as 'wet-and-dry' paper, because it can be used in two ways. Used dry, it's excellent on metal but not as good as glasspaper on wood. Soaked in water, it's the perfect abrasive for smoothing down painted surfaces ready for redecoration, and can be washed clean if it becomes clogged. Thirteen grades are made, classified by grit numbers. Grades 60 to 120 are coarse, 150 to 240 are medium and 280 to 600 are fine.

6 Garnet paper 4/0
7 Garnet paper 0
8 Garnet paper 1½
9 Silicon carbide paper 600
10 Silicon carbide paper 320
11 Silicon carbide paper 100

2 cork block

3 flexible sanding block

NAILS

The nail is almost as old as carpentry itself, yet even today few fixing devices are so convenient. Moreover, woodworkers over the years have developed a host of tricks to make its use easier still.

Nails come in many guises for all sorts of different jobs, though some are easier to find than others. Before looking at them all, a few general points are worth considering.

The first is strength. Friction is what makes a nail grip. Therefore long, thick nails provide a better fixing than short thin ones. Another factor is the shape of the nail's shank. Nails which are drawn out from wire have round or oval shanks; those cut from sheets of metal have rough but vaguely rectangular shanks; and there are also nails whose shanks are either twisted or roughened in some way.

The holding power of any nail depends a lot on the material into which it's driven, and on the forces to which the nail and the joint are subjected. If possible, such forces should always be either in the same direction as the nail is driven, or 'in shear' (ie, at right angles to it). And in carpentry, wherever you need a tight joint or expect any appreciable stress at all, you should glue the timber first. But on the whole, nails with specially shaped shanks are strongest, and cut nails are stronger than wire nails.

The maxim 'the bigger the better' is not always true. For one thing, fat nails are more likely to split wood. But cut nails cause fewer splits than wire nails because, being blunt, they break the wood fibres and create their own holes, while wire nails merely force the fibres apart. It's a pity cut nails are becoming rarer.

Another point is that, with a few deliberately decorative exceptions, nails aren't very attractive. The standard method of hiding them is to punch their heads below the surface of the wood and to fill the resulting hollows with stopping (a type of wood filler). Large, flat nail heads are difficult to punch in even a little way. But if you're securing such things as carpet, fabric or sheet roofing, the large head found on most tacks and roofing nails is essential to hold the material in place without the risk of tearing.

Finally, think about rust. In most indoor work ordinary mild steel nails are fine. Outdoors – and indoors if there's likely to be a lot of moisture

about – you need a nail with more rust resistance. Normally this means a galvanised nail, but other rust-resisting finishes are available – and you can also get nails made entirely from metals that don't rust at all, such as brass, copper and even bronze. But few are as strong as mild steel; many are used solely for their decorative value.

Buying nails

When buying nails, there are three things to remember. Firstly, they're described by length rather than diameter. Secondly, names vary a lot, so you may have to describe what you want.

Thirdly, though it may be sensible (if more expensive) to buy small amounts in boxes or packets, loose nails are sold by weight, not quantity. But how many do you get in a kilogram or a pound? Either tell your supplier roughly how many you need and get him to do the conversion – or simply judge the amount by eye, bearing in mind that piles of small nails tend to contain far more than you think.

General-purpose nails

Round wire nails (12), sometimes called French nails, are used only for rough carpentry. While giving a strong fixing, they tend to split the wood, and their large heads can be hard to disguise. They're available plain (12) or galvanised (15), and they come in lengths from 20 to 150mm (¾ to 6in).

Oval wire nails (14) are used in all types of general woodwork, and as a substitute for cut floor brads. Their heads naturally lie flush with the surface of the wood, making them unobtrusive; and, if the long axis of the oval runs along the timber's grain, oval nails tend not to split the wood. They're sold in lengths from 20 to 150mm (¾ to 6in), and galvanised versions can be found.

Lost-head nails (16) are often used instead of oval wire nails – they're stronger, because they're round, and easier to punch below the timber's

surface (hence their name). You'll find them in lengths of 12 to 150mm (½ to 6in) – either plain steel or galvanised.

Cut floor brads (11) are traditional nails for fixing floorboards to joists, though they're becoming harder to find. They grip strongly, and tend not to cause splits. They're available in lengths from 20 to 150mm (¾ to 6in), with the 50 to 75mm (2 to 3in) range the most common, and have a plain steel finish.

Cut clasp nails (17) are very like cut floor brads, and share their advantages. Used for rough fixings in wood, and in masonry if it's not too hard, they grip so strongly they can be very difficult to remove. Their lengths range from 25 to about 100mm (1 to 4in). Like cut floor brads, they're growing scarcer.

Masonry nails (4) are specially designed to make a reasonably strong general-purpose fixing in brickwork and the like. Those with twisted shanks should grip better than those with plain shanks. Both types have the drawback that, because they're hardened to penetrate masonry, they're rather brittle: they may snap if not hit cleanly, or if the masonry proves extra hard, so goggles are a wise precaution. Masonry nails come in various gauges (thicknesses) and in lengths from about 12 to 100mm (½ to 4in). They should be galvanised or blued.

Annular nails (10), also called ringed-shank nails, have ribs along the shank to prevent them pulling out. This makes them particularly useful for fixing sheet materials, for example

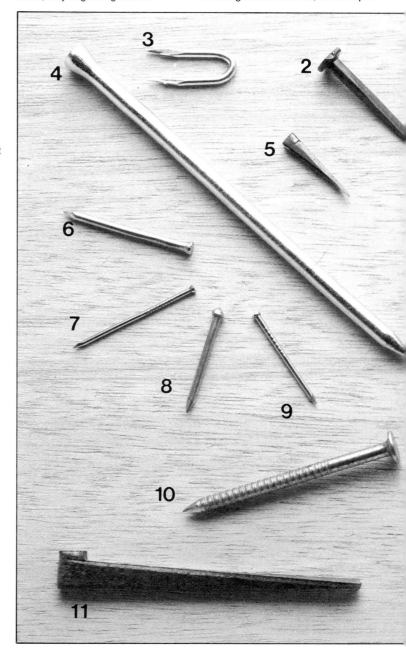

when levelling a floor with hardboard. Their lengths range between 25 and 75mm (1 and 3in), and they're normally either plain steel or coppered.

Clout nails (13) have extra-large heads which make them ideal for fixing roofing felt, slates, sash window cords and so on. Their lengths range between 12 and 50mm (½ to 2in), and most are galvanised, given some other rustproof finish or made from a rustless metal.

You can also get a **plasterboard nail,** used for fixing plasterboard to timber frameworks (eg, on ceilings and in stud partitions); this is similar except for its jagged shank, which provides extra grip.

Panel pins (6) are slim versions of the lost-head nail, used in fine work for fixing sheet materials, mouldings and so on. Normally of bright steel, they come in lengths between 12 and 50mm (½ to 2in).

Moulding pins (9) and **veneer pins** (7) are still thinner lost-head nails, extremely useful for almost invisible fixing of thin, narrow mouldings and lippings, where the main problem is to avoid splitting, and where the pin's weakness is unimportant. Veneer pins have even smaller heads than moulding pins. You'll find both in lengths from 12 to 25mm (½ to 1in), with a plain steel finish.

Specialised nails
Hardboard pins (8) are for fixing hardboard. Their grip is weak, but their diamond-shaped heads burrow into the surface as the pin is driven home, making punching and filling almost unnecessary. Most have a coppered finish, and they usually vary in length from 10 to 38mm (⅜ to 1½in).

Sprigs (5), also called cut brads, are mainly used for holding glass in window frames, though they can also be used to secure heavy linoleum (be careful here: because they have no heads, they won't grip if driven in too far). Normally plain, the range from 12 to 19mm (½ to ¾in) long. They are usually plain steel, but other finishes are sometimes available.

Cut tacks (2) are like sprigs, but with large flat heads for holding fabric in place; they're used for carpet laying and upholstery. They come with a blued, coppered or galvanised finish, and are from 6 to 30mm (¼ to 1¼in) long.

Twisted-shank roofing nails are used to fix corrugated sheet roofing. There are two main types. One (1) must be used in conjunction with curved washers; the other has a built-in sprung head. Both are usually galvanised. The first type ranges from 63 to 112mm (2½ to 4½in) long, and the second is usually 63mm (2½in) long.

Staples, in this context, mean heavy-duty versions (3) of the familiar gun-dispensed staple. They're used to fix wire fencing or upholstery springs, and are galvanised or left plain accordingly. Sizes vary from 12 to 40mm (½ to 1½in).

Though not suitable for such demanding tasks, the staple gun itself (which has no baseplate, unlike the office stapler) is also useful for a wide range of fixing jobs.

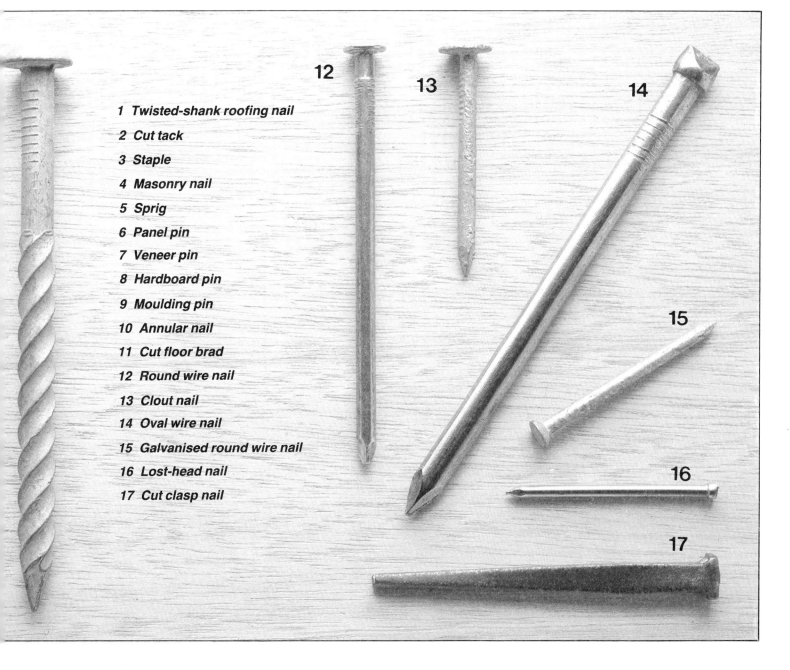

1 Twisted-shank roofing nail
2 Cut tack
3 Staple
4 Masonry nail
5 Sprig
6 Panel pin
7 Veneer pin
8 Hardboard pin
9 Moulding pin
10 Annular nail
11 Cut floor brad
12 Round wire nail
13 Clout nail
14 Oval wire nail
15 Galvanised round wire nail
16 Lost-head nail
17 Cut clasp nail

SCREWS

Wood screws are the usual way of making a secure fixing in carpentry. But they come in a very wide variety of shapes, sizes and finishes. Here's how to choose the right screw for the job.

To be able to pick exactly the screw you need for a particular purpose, it helps to know what each part of the screw does.

The thread is the spiral which actually pulls the screw into the wood and holds it there. Most have the same profile, but chipboard screws combat the material's crumbly quality with their shallower spiral; and some have a double thread, which means the screw won't wander off-centre, and can be driven into the wood twice as fast. Most wood screws have about two-fifths of the length unthreaded, forming a shank, but chipboard screws are threaded all the way up to the head for better grip.

Screw heads come in at least nine shapes, but wood screws use only three. Countersunk is the commonest. This name describes how the screw head fits into the surface of what you're fixing: that is, in a hole with sloping sides. Such 'countersunk holes' are common in hinges and other fittings. In timber they have to be made with a special drill bit or hand tool (a countersink) – except where the screw cuts its own way in, as may

happen in softwood.

You often need an ordinary countersunk head, because it lies flush with the surface. But the raised countersunk head looks more handsome, and is frequently used with metal fittings. The round head is useful when fixing a metal fitting without countersunk screw holes to wood, perhaps with a washer underneath it to spread the pressure.

On all screws either a slot or a recess is cut into the head so that the screwdriver tip can engage in it. Recessed heads need special screwdrivers, but they offer a more positive grip for the tip, so that it won't slip out in use and perhaps scar the work. On the other hand, they make it harder to get screws out if they're damaged or clogged with paint.

On wood screws the Pozidriv recess has now given way to the similar-looking Supadriv type. Each has its own screwdriver tip shape, but you can get away with using a Pozidriv screwdriver for both, or even a Phillips screwdriver (made for another recess type, found on screws for metalwork

rather than on wood screws). Recessed heads need fewer sizes of screwdriver to fit the range of screw gauges.

Accessories and unusual screws

Screws for special purposes include the clutch-head screw, which can't be undone by a thief, or by you (so make sure you know what you're doing when you drive it in). The coach screw, for heavy work, has a square head and is tightened with a spanner. The mirror screw is inserted in the usual way: then a shiny chrome-plated dome is screwed into the head in turn, covering it and making a decorative feature. You can also get several types of snap-on cover for similar effects.

A screw cup or collar fits under a countersunk or raised head, enhancing the appearance and spreading the load; it also enables screws to be easily withdrawn, and (like a round head) to hold thin materials such as hardboard and plastic laminate.

A screw socket is similar but flush with the surface.

Sizes and materials
How big is a screw? Its length – the amount hidden beneath the timber surface – ranges from 5mm ($^3/_{16}$in) to 150mm (6in). The gauge – the diameter of the shank – has a number from 0 (the smallest) to 32; 4, 6, 8, 10 and 12 are the commonest. A No 14 screw, for example, is 6.3mm ($^1/_4$in) in

diameter. With practice you'll soon be able to tell the gauge of a screw without having to measure it against others (all screws of the same gauge have the same head diameter). Remember that you can have the same length in different gauges and the same gauge in different lengths.

And what are screws made of? Steel is the commonest and cheapest metal, but it has disadvantages — it's not pretty, it rusts at the slightest sign of water (including that in water-based filler and emulsion paint), and it stains certain hardwoods such as oak, sycamore and afrormosia.

Luckily there are quite a few alternatives. Steel itself comes with several different coatings, from nickel plate to black japanning (paint). However, most are purely decorative; the exception is bright zinc plate, which is corrosion-resistant as well as attractive. When painted, it survives well outdoors.

Of other metals, brass (available plain or chrome-plated) is fairly corrosion-proof, but weak. Aluminium (also weak), stainless steel and silicon bronze are virtually corrosion-free. Stainless steel is the strongest of these, but is expensive.

So even the smallest screw has a long title, which you have to spell out fully when buying. Remember to give all the following details, preferably in this order: length, gauge number, head type, material, recess type (if applicable), and finish (if applicable).

HEADS AND THREADS
1 *The commonest head profile is countersunk, with a flat top and sloping sides.*
2 *Raised countersunk heads have a slightly domed top, and are used with metal fittings.*
3 *Round-head screws are used to fix metal fittings without countersunk screw holes.*
4 *The screw thread usually extends to about three-fifths of the screw length, but chipboard screws are threaded all the way up.*
5 *Most screws have a slot in the head.*
6 *Supadriv recesses need a special screwdriver.*

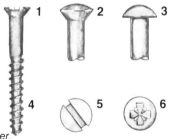

HIDING SCREW HEADS
*Often you may want to hide the heads of fixing screws, and there is a variety of plastic screw head covers available which do this neatly and effectively. The cover may snap onto a collar fitted beneath the screw head (**7** and **8**), or may fit into a counterbore (see Hints, right) to conceal the hole (**9**). The mirror screw (**10**) hides the screw head beneath a plated screw-on dome.*

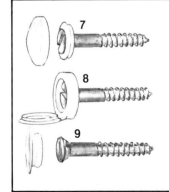

THE FINISHES YOU CAN CHOOSE
Screws are commonly made from steel, but other materials and finishes are also available. Here are some of them.

bright zinc plated

brass

chrome plated

brass chrome plated

light bronze metal antique

aluminium

dark bronze metal antique

black japanned

stainless steel

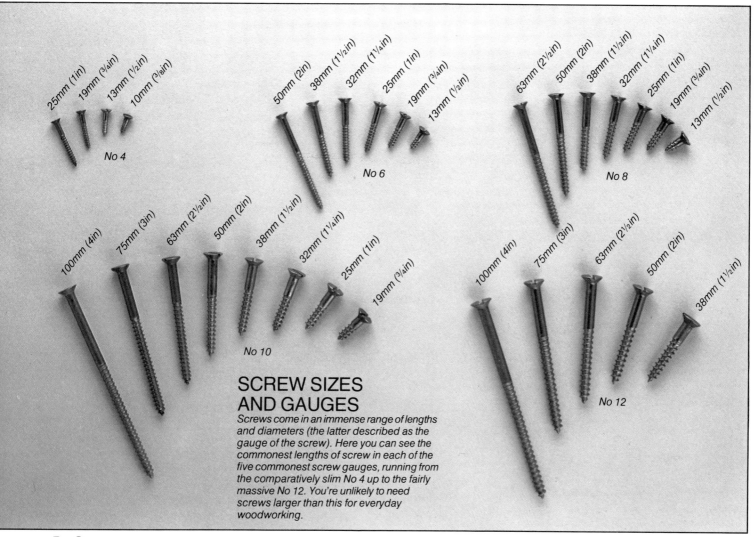

25mm (1in) 19mm (³/₄in) 13mm (½in) 10mm (³/₈in)

No 4

50mm (2in) 38mm (1½in) 32mm (1¼in) 25mm (1in) 19mm (³/₄in) 13mm (½in)

No 6

63mm (2½in) 50mm (2in) 38mm (1½in) 32mm (1¼in) 25mm (1in) 19mm (³/₄in) 13mm (½in)

No 8

100mm (4in) 75mm (3in) 63mm (2½in) 50mm (2in) 38mm (1½in) 32mm (1¼in) 25mm (1in) 19mm (³/₄in)

No 10

100mm (4in) 75mm (3in) 63mm (2½in) 50mm (2in) 38mm (1½in)

No 12

SCREW SIZES AND GAUGES

Screws come in an immense range of lengths and diameters (the latter described as the gauge of the screw). Here you can see the commonest lengths of screw in each of the five commonest screw gauges, running from the comparatively slim No 4 up to the fairly massive No 12. You're unlikely to need screws larger than this for everyday woodworking.

hints

● When screwing wood to wood, always drill clearance and pilot holes first. The clearance hole accepts the screw shank; it should be about the same length and diameter. The pilot hole eases insertion; it should be about two-thirds of the thread diameter, and penetrate 5mm (³/₁₆in) or so less than the screw.

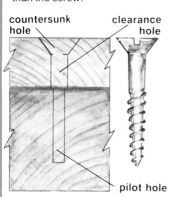

countersunk hole

clearance hole

pilot hole

● The cheapest way to buy screws is in bulk, not in little plastic packets (unless you want only a few screws of an unusual size or type). Some sizes ('preferred sizes') are cheaper even than smaller ones, because they're more common. For example, a 50mm (2in) No 6 screw costs less than a 44mm (1³/₄in) screw of the same gauge.

● You need a bigger pilot hole in hardwood than in softwood, but in softwood you don't need one at all if the screw is smaller than a No 7. Use a bradawl to make pilot holes for the smallest screws.

● If you're screwing two pieces of wood together, always screw the thinner one to the thicker. Use a screw whose length is three times the thickness of the thinner piece, and drill the clearance hole through the thinner piece only.

● To screw on a very thick piece, you may do better to drill counterbores than use extra-long screws.

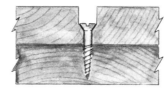

● End grain won't grip screws well. One answer is to insert dowels first, in such a way that the screws bite into them sideways.

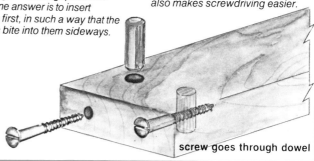

screw goes through dowel

● For general use, select a screw long enough to bury at least four twists of thread in the wood, and not so thick as to cause splitting.

● Always use the right size of screwdriver; it makes life a lot easier. And when using brass or aluminium screws, it's a good idea to drive steel ones into the holes first to prevent the softer metals breaking, especially in hardwood. Wax, grease or soap on the thread also makes screwdriving easier.

SELF-ASSEMBLY FITTINGS

The simplest fitting for assembling woodwork is the humble screw. But nowadays there are many others, made for a vast range of problems.

Traditionally all furniture was jointed. Pieces which fitted together provided its strength.

Today, however, many people make their own furniture who have had no opportunity to acquire the skill of cutting accurate joints. Moreover, a lot of modern furniture is made from chipboard, a crumbly material which is impossible to join by conventional means.

Add to that the needs of industry, which demand speed and simplicity (in particular for 'self-assembly' or 'flat-pack' furniture, sold as a set of components and put together by the customer), and you have the reasons for self-assembly fittings.

These often very ingenious pieces of hardware are made of metal, plastic or both. All but the simplest are unobtrusive, and yet they make strong, rigid joints. Many are commonly known as KD (knock-down) fittings, because all enable the joint to be dismantled easily – usually by unscrewing.

One problem with these fittings is availability. The less sophisticated ones are sold widely in hardware and DIY stores. For others, you may have to buy from specialist suppliers, or by mail order.

One-piece fittings
The simplest self-assembly fittings of all are stamped from sheet metal. Those with countersunk (sloping-sided) holes are fitted using countersunk or raised-head screws; others need round-head screws.
● Straight and T-shaped plates (1), plus L-shaped ones, are used primarily for repairing frames.
● Corner plates (2) are useful for stiffening box corners; they're fitted to the outside at the rear. A central

hole lets you screw the plate into the wall as well (provided the cabinet has no back panel) – giving

a handy means of hanging a wall unit simply and securely.
● **Shrinkage plates** (3) allow for the natural shrinkage and swelling of timber. Their round holes are used to attach the fitting to one component with countersunk screws. You then screw into the other component through the elongated hole, which is aligned in the direction of maximum timber movement (ie, across the grain). That way, when the timber moves, it moves the screw along the slot, instead of distorting. A round-headed screw with a small washer gives least friction.

● **Table shrinkage plates** (4) are similar, but right-angled for fixing solid timber table-tops to the side or end rails of their supporting frames. The choice of two elongated holes, one in each direction, enables you to use them on all four sides of a table.
● **Angle brackets** (also called corner brackets and angle repair brackets – 5) form a simple way of holding components together at right angles.
● However, for the rigidity which a joint usually needs, you really require a purpose-designed fitting. Invisible from outside the cabinet, these are made wholly or partly of plastic, and you can generally choose from white, brown and sometimes beige. You'll need at least two per joint.
Simplest of all is the **modesty**

block (6), so called because it was originally used for fixing front panels to typing desks to hide their occupants' knees. It fits inside the angle made by two boards. Two screws go in one direction (usually horizontal), and one in the other (ie, vertically).

● Other types of block joint (7 and 8) have holes for two screws in each direction, plus a cover to conceal their heads. With 8 you can also screw into the wall or attach a back panel.
● The **mini block joint** (9) has only a single screw – a coarse machine screw (see pages 154 -155), which is supplied with the fitting. You drill a pilot hole for that in one component, and in the other a larger hole, into which you tap the barbed protruding part.
This is really only a high-quality shelf support; it's unsuitable for joints subject to appreciable stress.

Two-piece fittings
With many self-assembly fittings you fix half to one component and half to the other, then fit the two together. These are true KD fittings, because dismantling them involves just undoing a single screw – in the case of 10, not even that. This type of design also makes assembly easy. However, careful marking-up is needed so that both parts are perfectly aligned.
● The steel fitting (10) makes a very strong joint, especially in heavy frames such as bed frames. For rigidity it relies largely on the weight of the component being supported.

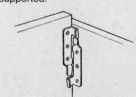

● The **KD block joint** (11 and 12) is a development of the ordinary block joint, made in two parts. In 11

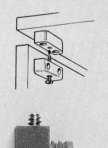

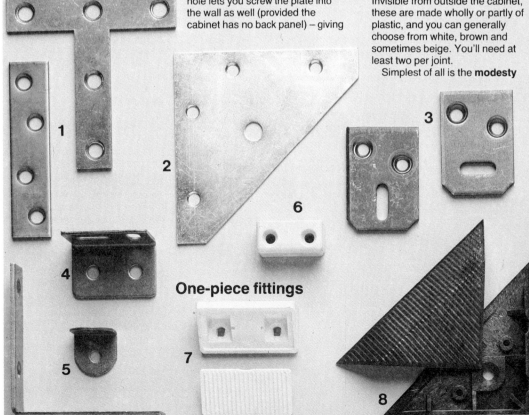

One-piece fittings

1 2 3 4 5 6 7 8 9

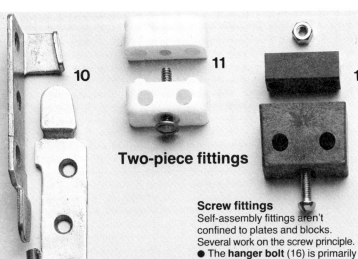

10

11

12

Two-piece fittings

13

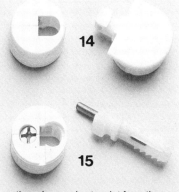

14

15

one part is prevented from twisting in relation to the other by projecting knobs which fit into sockets. The fixing is a machine screw, passing through one part into a nut retained in the other.

● 13 is a **cam joint**; one half is held inside the other by a revolving cam, turned by a screwdriver. This makes it compact and therefore inconspicuous.

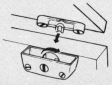

● 14 and 15 are variants common in industry. Both require a special drill bit (an end mill, or a centre bit in a brace) to make a flat-bottomed hole for one or both parts to sit in. This is trickier than using the screw-on types of fitting described above, but the result is almost invisible.

With 14, you just insert the projecting peg in one half into the hole in the other, and revolve the cam which locks it in place by turning the screw in one side.

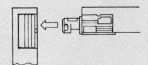

In 15, the projecting half is tapped into a hole bored in the edge of the panel, rather than the face. You then insert a steel pin to wedge it there, before assembling the two halves and locking them via the screw (visible in the photograph).

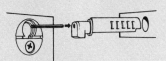

Screw fittings

Self-assembly fittings aren't confined to plates and blocks. Several work on the screw principle.

● The **hanger bolt** (16) is primarily for fixing table legs to their connecting rails. Its pointed end has a wood-screw thread, driven into the leg, and its blunt end a machine thread which takes a wing-nut, used to fasten a metal plate.

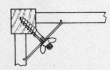

● The **chipboard connector screw** (17), unlike ordinary chipboard screws, is designed to go into panel edges. Its special thread resists pulling out. It needs a clearance hole through the face of the outer panel, and a pilot hole into the edge of the inner one; you can get a jig to make these accurately. Its head can be covered with a push-in plastic cap.

● An alternative is the **chipboard plug** (18), which acts like a wall plug. It's tapped into a pre-drilled hole in the board edge, and expands parallel to the board surface when you drive a screw into it. It grips more firmly than a screw alone.

● Other types of plug (or '**bush**' – 19) are threaded on the inside to receive a machine screw. This gives more security on re-assembly, and so makes them useful in plywood, blockboard and solid timber too.

● The familiar nut and bolt themselves form a more conspicuous type of KD assembly fitting. Both ends, of course, are visible. But a neat alternative to the conventional nut is the **T-nut** (20).

Its body fits into a drilled hole, and the prongs on its rim are drawn firmly into the timber as you tighten the bolt or machine screw – so that vibration can't loosen it.

● **Scan fittings** (21) are so called because of their frequent use on Scandinavian furniture. On the whole their shape suits them best to frame construction (eg, on tables and chairs), where they often provide an exceptionally neat solution, rather than to box construction. A brass-finished screw with a countersunk head passes through a drilled hole in one component and into a threaded hole in a steel 'cross dowel', which fits at right angles into a hole in the second component. This has a slot at one end so you can turn it to align the threaded hole with the screw.

The screw head, which sits in a matching metal socket, isn't unattractive; it has an hexagonal recess which enables it to be tightened with an Allen key (see pages 14 -15).

Where there's any risk of the components' rotating in relation to each other, use a **guide dowel** (22). One half of this has a projecting knob, which fits into a socket in the other. Each is pushed into a drilled hole in one of the two components.

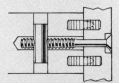

● The **cabinet connecting screw** (23) is a simple two-part device for fastening cabinets together through the faces of adjacent panels. You need to drill holes for both parts of the fitting first. It's made for combined panel thicknesses of between 30 and 39mm ($1^3/_{16}$ to $1^1/_2$in), but you can easily make it shorter by cutting it down.

● **Panel butting connectors** (24) are mainly for joining panels end to end – two lengths of a worktop, for example. You drill a large-diameter hole in the underside of each, near

the edge, and cut a slot from the edge of each hole to the edge of the board. Then you insert the connector and use a spanner to tighten the elongated nut on the end, thus drawing the two panels together.

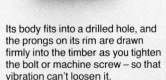

Screw fittings

17

16

18

19

20

21

22

23

24

CHAPTER 2

POWER TOOLS

The heart of the do-it-yourself workshop these days is
the power drill, which does a great deal more than simply drill holes.
You can choose relatively small — and inexpensive — single-speed models, or
more powerful (and more costly) multi-speed versions with extra features
like hammer action (for drilling masonry) and reversible gearing.
Then you can add various attachments for extra versatility,
or buy other integral tools for jobs like sawing and sanding.

POWER DRILL ATTACHMENTS

A tremendous number of accessories are available for your power drill. They can come in all shapes and sizes, and you'll find that they greatly increase its usefulness – often in unexpected ways. All sorts of jobs can now be done quite easily.

Perhaps the most basic power-drill accessory is the drill stand, which allows accurate vertical drilling of smallish pieces. Shaping attachments and the special cutters that go with them, plus dovetailing and dowelling attachments, can also come in very handy. The sections on using power drills provide full information about these items – and in addition, there are drill mountings for horizontal boring.

However, that's not the full range by any means. You can also get accessories for sawing, stripping, sanding, grinding and sharpening, planing, woodturning and screwdriving, plus a host of more general (and more specialised) jobs.

Some attachments are just gripped in the drill chuck in the normal way. To fit others, you have to remove the chuck first. This is a simple matter of inserting the chuck key and tapping it with a hammer – in an anticlockwise direction when looking at the drill head-on; see page 95.

But, before you buy any attachment at all, you ought to check whether it's compatible with your drill. Several factors, including the chuck capacity, the size of the drill's nose (its 'collar'), and the positions of any fixing lugs, may affect this.

General accessories

If you have no drill stand, or your workpiece is too big to fit below one, a **drill guide** (1) is invaluable for accurate drilling. It's simply a portable frame, sometimes spring-loaded, in which you mount the drill before positioning it to do the job. Both of its slide bars can be extended to tilt it for drilling at an angle; one will act as a 'fence' so holes can be kept at a fixed distance from an edge. Being movable, it can be used for drilling into walls.

An **angle drive** (2) is used where you otherwise couldn't drill square to the workpiece – for example, when drilling through the side of a joist in order to run pipes. Types vary; some reduce the drill speed to about half the normal rate. Another increases or reduces the speed according to which way round it's fitted.

A **flexible drive** (3) consists of a drive cable encased in another cable of spiral steel, perhaps with a plastic sleeve. At one end is a handle and chuck, into which you fit the accessory which does the actual work – eg, a disc sander. The other end usually fits into the drill chuck; but some types require the chuck to be removed, so that the threaded shank of the flexible drive can be screwed straight into the drill.

The flexible drive has two uses. First, it enables small accessories

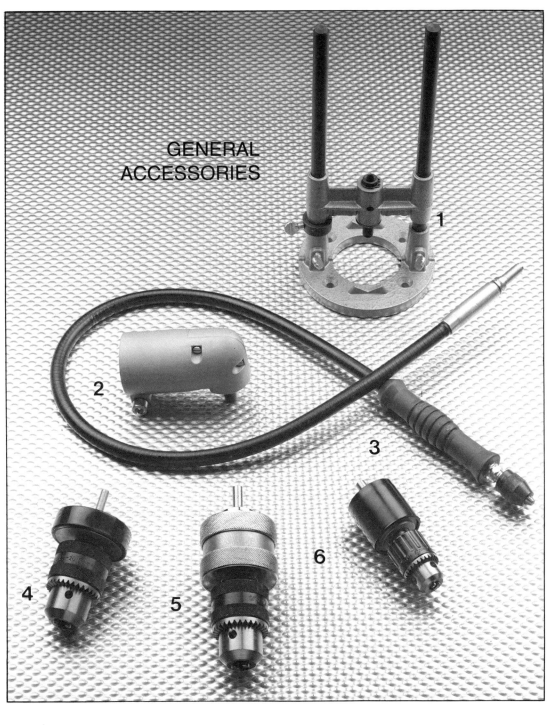

GENERAL ACCESSORIES

1

2

3

4

5

6

such as wire brushes to be manipulated more comfortably; second, it lets you get into awkward corners. The length of the cable ranges from under 1000mm up to 1200mm (3 to 4ft).

Reduction gears (4 and 5) increase turning power by reducing the drill's speed. They fit into the chuck, and enable you to drill large holes in concrete, hard brick or steel. Depending on the make of gear, the speed can be reduced up to twelve times. One type (5) incorporates a reverse speed as well.

There are also **electronic speed reducers**, which you connect into the drill power cable. You vary the speed by turning a knob. However, this doesn't give you any more turning power at slow speeds – and it's really only a substitute for buying a drill with variable-speed control in the first place.

Anyone with an ordinary rotary electric/drill can quite simply fit a **hammer adaptor** or percussion attachment (6) to give the hammering action which is needed to drill holes in hard building materials.

Saw attachments

You can get fitments which convert your drill into a **circular saw** (7) or **jigsaw** (9). These have the advantage of cheapness compared with power saws which have their own integral motors; on the other hand, they tend to be awkward in use – and a drill doesn't always have enough power for heavy sawing jobs. See page 95 for details of how to fit a circular saw attachment.

A **cutting wheel** (10) can be fitted directly into a drill chuck if you use a spindle or **arbor** (11) – unlike circular-saw blades, which must only be used in an integral saw or a saw attachment. Cutting wheels are for use on masonry, ceramics (eg, tiles) and metal; they come in a number of different materials and grades.

Stripping and finishing

There's also a whole range of drill accessories for removing rust, old paintwork and other deposits, plus others whose purpose is to smooth woodwork as part of your final finishing procedure.

In the first group come the **metal sanding disc** (12) coated in tungsten-carbide grit, and the **open-meshed sanding disc** (13), which sometimes doubles as a cutting wheel. Both of these are used with an arbor. The **flap wheel** (14) has leaves of abrasive paper.

While all these sanding devices are available in a number of grades, the fearsome **heavy-duty deposit destroyer**, with its toothed wheels, is for heavy stripping jobs only.

General accessories

1 *Drill guide*
2 *Angle drive*
3 *Flexible drive*
4 *Reduction gear*
5 *Reduction gear incorporating reverse drive*
6 *Hammer adaptor (percussion attachment)*

Saw attachments

7 *Circular saw*
8 *Circular saw blade and blade guard*
9 *Jigsaw and blade*
10 *Cutting wheel*
11 *Arbor (for cutting wheels and the like)*

Stripping and finishing

12 *Metal sanding disc (tungsten-carbide coated)*
13 *Open-meshed sanding discs*
14 *Flap wheel*
15 *Wire cup brush*
16 *Wire end brush*
17 *Wire wheel brush*
18 *General-purpose abrasive wheel*
19 *Backing pad*
20 *Sanding discs*
21 *Abrasive foam pad*
22 *Drum sander with abrasive loop fitted*
23 *Polishing bonnet*
24 *Orbital sander and abrasive sheets*

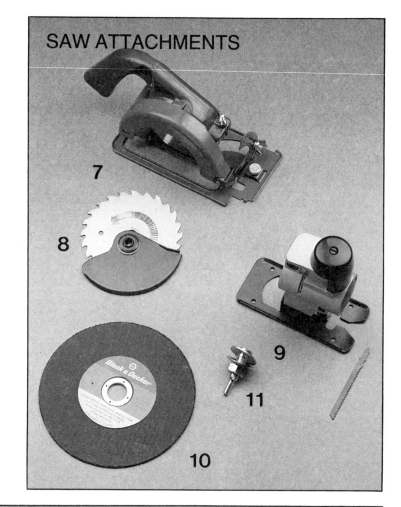

SAW ATTACHMENTS

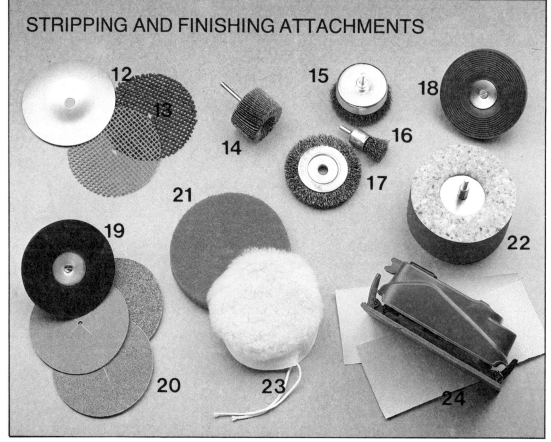

STRIPPING AND FINISHING ATTACHMENTS

There are also **wire brushes** (15, 16 and 17) of various shapes and sizes – the circular **wheel brush** (17) being intended for use in a fixed drill, rather like a grinding wheel (see below). The arbor-mounted **general-purpose abrasive wheel** (18) is capable of quite a smooth finish.

The flexible circular rubber **backing pad** (19) accepts paper **sanding discs** (20) – coarse for stripping, or fine for finishing – or an **abrasive foam pad** (21), which can be used either dry, or wet with a detergent: the higher the speed, the finer the finish. All these are held on by a simple screw and washer.

The **drum sander** (22), which takes special abrasive loops, is mainly a finishing tool, and is especially handy for curved surfaces. However, like all the accessories just mentioned, it needs care in use if you're not to remove more material than you intend, causing ugly scratches or hollows.

The **orbital sander** attachment (24) is easier to control, but only really suitable for flat surfaces. It accepts rectangular sheets of abrasive paper or metal.

See pages 30 -31 for fuller information on sanding materials and attachments.

If you want a really fine, glossy finish – perhaps waxed – after varnishing or lacquering, you can get soft felt pads or even a lambswool **polishing bonnet** (23), which fit over the rubber backing pad. These are used for 'burnishing'. You can even buy special burnishing cream, which you apply at the same time in order to obtain a real mirror finish.

Specialist attachments
The other drill accessories on the market just don't fit neatly under a single heading. They do all sorts of jobs.

One of the most useful is a **grinder** (1). Fitted with a **grinding wheel** (2) of the appropriate material and grade for the job, its main use lies in restoring worn cutting edges – such as those on chisels, plane irons and knives – without having to send the tools away.

Make sure you work at the correct angle, and don't weaken the metal by overheating it with the friction. This is all too easily done, so it's wise to keep a container of water nearby and keep plunging the work into it.

If you acquire further know-how and the right grinding wheels, you can even tackle more difficult tasks such as sharpening router bits.

When using a grinder, it's imperative to wear goggles because of sparks and flying fragments of abrasive and metal.

The **knife and scissor sharpener** (3) is basically a small grindstone with a shank which fits in the chuck; plus a device or devices to hold blades at the right angle against the revolving wheel.

Drill bits are among the trickiest items to sharpen correctly, even with a grinder. But you can buy a small **drill sharpener** (4) for sharpening twist bits. You have only to switch on, press the blunt bit into the appropriate hole, and rotate it. The beauty of this attachment is that it will pay for itself via the savings you make.

A **screwdriving attachment** (5)

is a step up from the basic screwdriving bit. It fits into the chuck, and the head of the screw is enclosed in a sprung sleeve. This sleeve acts as a depth gauge, and ensures that the bit doesn't slip out of the screw slot or recess. It also relieves the pressure on the screw after it's been driven home (some models do this via a clutch). If you have a reversible drill, you can use this attachment to withdraw screws as well.

Most screwdriving attachments can be fitted with interchangeable bits to accommodate a range of screw sizes.

A **pump** attachment (6) has two hose connection points (inlet and outlet). They may be push-on or threaded (you may need connecting nuts), and the required hose diameter is 12 or 18mm (1/2 or 3/4in). A drive spindle fits into the drill chuck.

This can be most useful for emptying garden ponds, washing machines, blocked sinks, flooded cellars and the like. Water will be displaced at a rate of 900 litres (200 gallons) per hour.

The **paint mixer** (7) is a simple device which is mounted in the chuck and revolves to do its work. Extension pieces are available in some cases.

The **hedge trimmer** (8) is another popular accessory. Its side handle allows you full control.

The lathe
A particularly large and versatile accessory is the **lathe** (9). This isn't something to buy unless you intend to use it seriously, because it will take a fair bit of practice and

even study to get the hang of how it works and what you can do with it.

'Woodturning', as using a lathe is called, is a complex craft in its own right and its possibilities are enormous. The lathe will enable you to produce anything which is wholly or partly cylindrical in section – from elegantly-shaped table legs to bowls and candlesticks. The basic technique is to clamp the workpiece between the jaws or 'centres' at either end of the machine, and shape the revolving timber with chisel-like 'turning tools' of various shapes which you steady on a 'rest' at one side. However, the refinements go far beyond what can be described in a small space – so we deal with them more fully on pages 104 -112.

Specialist attachments

For sharpening tools:
1 *Grinder*
2 *Grinding wheel*
3 *Knife and scissor sharpener*
4 *Twist bit sharpener*

For other jobs:
5 *Screwdriving attachment (available with a range of screwdriving bits to suite both slotted and recessed screws)*
6 *Pump*
7 *Paint mixer*
8 *Hedge trimmer*
9 *Lathe. You clamp your power drill in position at the left-hand side, and the 'stock' on the right can be moved backwards or forwards according to the length of your workpiece. The tool rest, also adjustable, is in the middle.*

SPECIALIST ATTACHMENTS

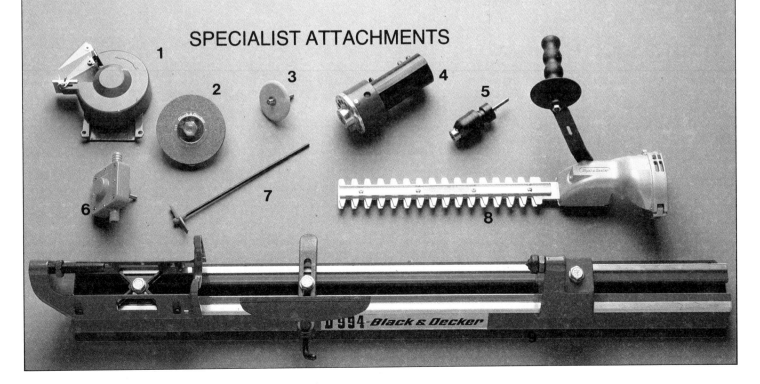

POWER SAWS

Power saws take the hard work out of sawing, and do a lot of things that hand saws can't cope with. Their general uses, and the particular tasks to which they're suited, are set out below.

If you start to do a lot of wood-work, you'll soon find that at least one power saw is an essential piece of equipment, especially when you're working with man-made boards.

Portable saws

Circular saws are for fast straight cutting of timber, man-made boards, plastic laminates, sheet plastics, thin sheet steel, thicker soft (non-ferrous) metals, bricks, building blocks, soft stone and ceramic tiles.

They come in several sizes, usually identified by the diameter of the rotating blade each will accept. The commonest size is 125mm (5in), but larger models that will take 150mm (6in) and 184mm (7¼in) diameter blades are also available. The latter naturally make deeper cuts (ie they'll cut through thicker material), and have more power for faster cutting. A 125mm blade cuts up to a maximum depth of 35mm (1⅜in); a 150mm saw cuts up to 47mm (1⅞in) deep, and a 184mm saw up to 62mm (2½in).

A spring-loaded safety guard protects your hands from the exposed part of the blade. The edge of the piece you're cutting automatically pushes the guard out of the way as you work, but there should be a lever which allows you to retract it for 'pocket cutting': that is, starting a cut in the middle of a piece.

It's vital to fit circular saw blades the right way round. The direction of rotation printed on the blade should tally with that on the guard. Also, ensure that the blade retaining nut is tight!

Jig saws will cut a similar range of materials to circular saws – and their great attraction is that they'll make curved cuts as well as straight ones. The jig saw has a straight, narrow blade, 75 to 100mm (3 to 4in) long, which moves up and down at up to 3000 strokes per minute.

Some types have an alternative lower speed of 2400 strokes per minute – useful for plastics, nonferrous metals and thin sheet steel.

Integral jig saw

Integral circular saw

Circular saw attachment for power drill

Circular saw blades

Blade guard

saws from Black & Decker and Bosch

With **variable-speed** models, cutting at anything between 500 and 3000 strokes per minute, you can exactly tailor the speed to suit the material, and also make more accurate starts by beginning the cut slowly and then speeding up. Variable speed control may be combined with electronic feedback, which maintains the speed when you meet resistance.

Most domestic jig saws have

enough power to cut softwoods up to 70mm (2¾in) thick, hardwoods 25mm (1in) thick and steel 2.4mm (³⁄₃₂in) thick. A newer type has 'orbital' action, in which the blade swings forward slightly on the upward stroke. This increases its speed and cutting capacity, so that you can tackle steel up to 10mm (⅜in) and aluminium up to 20mm (¾in) thick. Of course, the thickness of

wood you can cut is always limited by the blade length.

Because jig saws cut much more slowly than circular saws, they're much safer to use. But they're also less powerful, and harder to control when cutting in a straight line. In fact, curves are what they're best at. They're ideal for cutting out square, circular or irregular pieces from panels. Drill a starting hole so you can insert

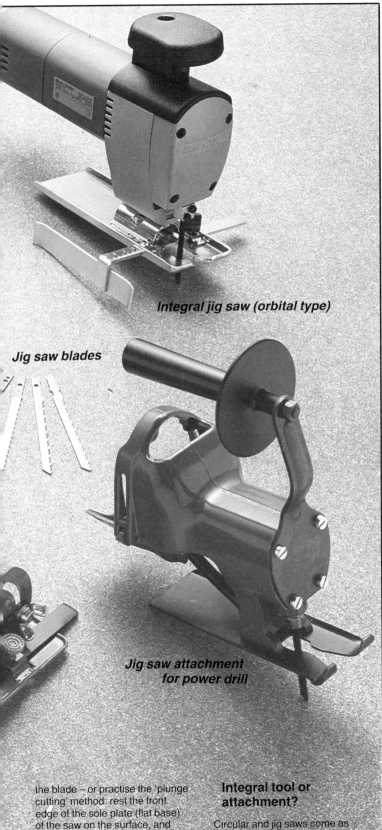

Integral jig saw (orbital type)

Jig saw blades

**Jig saw attachment
for power drill**

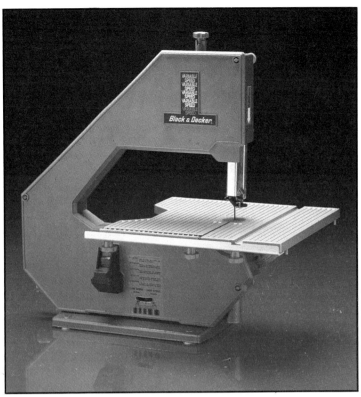

Lightweight band saw

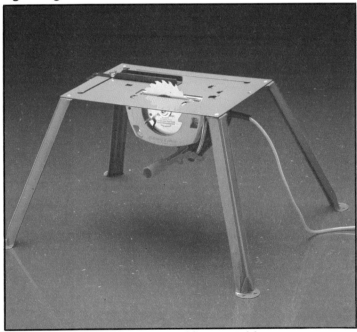

Portable circular saw mounted in saw table

the blade – or practise the 'plunge cutting' method: rest the front edge of the sole plate (flat base) of the saw on the surface, and gradually ease the blade into the workpiece.

A very useful feature on a jig saw is a blower to keep the cutting line free from sawdust, so you can see it. This is because you rely entirely on hand and eye to give you an accurate cut.

Integral tool or attachment?

Circular and jig saws come as tools on their own (integral tools) but also as attachments for an electric drill. Integral tools, though dearer, are better because they're always ready for use, they're properly balanced, they have enough power for the job, and they run at the right speed. These

Warning.
* Wear sensible close-fitting clothes and tough shoes. Never wear a tie.
* Keep both hands clear of the blade. Keep them firmly on the hand grips of a portable saw.
* Unplug the saw to adjust it or change blades, and whenever it is not in use.
* Switch off at the plug after each cut.

* Lock it away from children after use.
* Never use a power saw with children nearby – they could run into it.

When power sawing, a moment's thoughtlessness can mean serious injury – so think what you're doing at all times.

things are not often true of saw attachments, for they take time to set up, and they tend not to be all that well matched to the all-purpose drills they're fitted to. But their cheapness certainly makes them worth considering if you have to do a lot of sawing in one go, yet are not likely to need a power saw again in the near future. They'll serve the purpose without incurring the investment needed to buy an integral tool.

Fixed saws
Bench-mounted saws are more convenient than hand-held models in many instances, because they leave both hands free to guide the work. This makes it easier to achieve accurate results and to cut small pieces.

You can convert a portable circular saw (whether an integral tool or a drill attachment) into a bench saw by mounting it in a saw table, through which the blade protrudes upwards. This should have a 'rip fence' so you can cut pieces of timber accurately to width, and a 'mitre fence' for cutting ends square or at a particular angle.

But for the keen woodworker there are more solidly-built circular bench saws which come already fixed to the table.

There's one other type of fixed saw which has recently been produced in a lightweight, fairly

inexpensive version: the band saw. This is especially useful for making intricate curved cuts. Its blade is a narrow, continuous loop of steel which travels around pulleys inside the casing. The maximum depth of cut (dictated by the amount of the blade exposed) is usually about 100mm (4in). The width of material you can cut is limited by the depth of the 'throat' – the area between the exposed blade and the casing at the back; it's usually about 330mm (13in). There should be a rip fence, a mitre fence, and provision for tilting the saw table when making angled cuts.

Jig saw blades
1 General purpose.
2 Coarse wood cutting.
3 Fine wood cutting.
4 Scroll – for tight curves.
5 Metal cutting – also right for plastic laminates.
6 Knife – for fabrics, rubber and foam plastics.
7 Flush cutting – for cutting right up to vertical surfaces.
8 Carbide chip – very tough and smooth cutting.

Circular saw blades
1 Combination – for general use in wood. May have a rust-resistant lacquer, a non-stick coating to reduce binding in the cut as well as corrosion, or

Jig saw blades
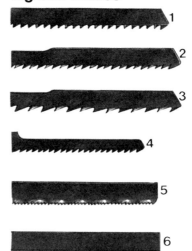

Circular blades
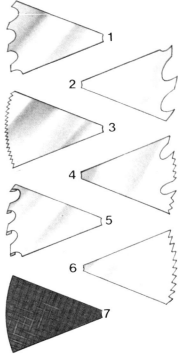

chrome-plating to make the blade stay sharper longer.
2 Ripping – for cutting wood lengthwise.
3 Crosscut – for cutting wood across the grain.
4 Planer – for extra-smooth cuts in wood.
5 Tungsten carbide tipped – for

fast, coarse cuts in wood and man-made boards. Chipboard quickly blunts ordinary blades, but tungsten has a very long life.
6 Metal cutting.
7 Abrasive discs – can be aluminium oxide, for metal cutting, or silicon carbide, for brick and stone.

hints

● *You can use portable power saws freehand, and for curved cuts with a jig saw. Watch the siting notch or mark on the sole plate of a circular saw, or the blade of a jig saw, and keep it just on the waste side of your cutting line.*
● *For precise straight cuts, you need a guide. Many power saws come with an adjustable fence – a metal T which fixes to the sole plate (A).That keeps the saw in line as long as you're cutting parallel with and close to a straight edge.*

If not, clamp a straight piece of timber or plywood parallel to the cutting line, and keep the sole plate against that as you cut.

● *On most power saws you can tilt the sole plate by up to 45° – useful for bevelled cuts (eg, when mitring panel edges for the corners of a box).*

● *Remember that a circular saw's depth of cut can be doubled by cutting from one side of the material, then turning it over*

and cutting from the other side (B).

In thick or hard materials, it's a good idea to make two cuts, even if working from one side only – the first with the blade set at half depth and the other to complete the job.

● *A jig saw blade must cut right through the material. But in use it's not as long as it looks, because much of it is hidden (C).*

● *As a saw blade emerges from the surface while cutting, it tends*

to splinter the material. With circular saws you can prevent this by setting the blade to the minimum possible depth, so it emerges at a flatter angle (D).

● *On plastic laminates, and veneered and laminated boards, avoid splintering by first scoring through the surface on each side of the cutting line, then laying clear adhesive tape over it. A jig saw, unlike a circular saw, cuts upwards, so saw with the decorative face down if possible.*

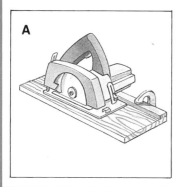

A

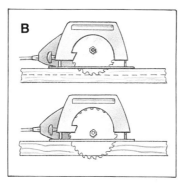

B

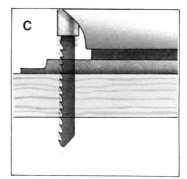

C

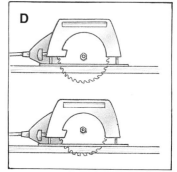

D

SPECIALIST POWER TOOLS

The basic power tools – a drill, a circular saw, a jigsaw – will serve most everyday purposes. But there's a range of more specialised machines which are well worth looking at if you want to invest in professional results.

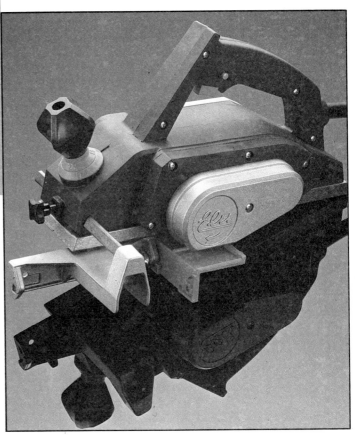

You've probably noticed that woodworking can be slow and hard. More than that, you may have wondered how professionals succeed in achieving such immaculate finishes.

Leaving aside practice and natural ability, the difference is that they have a far greater range of precision power tools at their disposal than the average do-it-yourselfer. Even where the tools look similar, you'll probably find they're more powerful and rugged, with refinements that improve accuracy.

So why not simply buy them? The main problem is cost. What's more, many perform only one type of task – probably one which you yourself undertake once or twice a year. However, there are exceptions. Here's a selection of advanced power tools that are both generally useful and not too dear.

You can still expect to pay more for most of these tools than for your basic electric drill. In many cases they're really only worth considering if you're becoming a keen woodworker. Even then, think carefully. Will you get enough use from the machine to justify the cost?

If it's a borderline decision, steer clear of versions aimed at the professional. In the main, you'll be paying for the ability to work hard day in, day out, year after year – something you're unlikely to need. The cheaper models are a better bet. They won't be as rugged, or have quite as many refinements, but they'll get the job done – and that's what matters.

Power planes
Even a modest portable power plane will make light work of smoothing and sizing sawn timber, and manufacturers claim that these machines will give acceptable results irrespective of the grain direction; that includes tackling endgrain.

They're ideal for almost all heavy jobs, especially where sawing is an awkward alternative to hand planing because the piece is too narrow to support properly.

They work by means of a rotating cutter (normally twin-bladed and between 75 and 83mm/3 and 3½in wide) turning at speeds from 14500 to 19000rpm. In general, the faster the speed the quicker the job, and the smoother the resulting finish. The plane's 'input power rating' (usually between 300 and 500 watts for do-it-yourself models) must also be taken into account, because it affects the thickness of wood that can be removed at a single pass (the maximum depth of cut). Low-powered models can normally manage only about 0.5mm, while the most powerful will cope with up to about 3.5mm (⅛in).

But power planes can do more than straightforward planing. Most will also tackle simple rebating, and some have specially grooved soles to allow accurate chamfering. If either task is important to you, see what maximum depths can be achieved. For chamfers, the depth will be between 3.5 and 4.5mm (about ⅛in). For rebates it can be as little as 8mm (⅜in) or as much as 20mm (¾in).

Check the other features too. Can the machine be cleaned easily after use? How simple is it to adjust the depth of cut? Can the cutters be retracted to protect them in storage? Is a front knob fitted so you can control the machine with two hands? Think, too, about whether you want a model with replaceable blades, or one with blades you can re-sharpen. If you decide on the latter, are the necessary bits and pieces – blade-sharpening holders, etc – included?

Finally, look out for accessories. Many models come with a guide fence as standard; on others it counts as an extra. Special guides may also be available to help with rebating and chamfering, and occasionally it may be possible to mount the tool in a special stand to convert it into a small-scale bench planer – handy for small workpieces. Perhaps the most useful accessory, though, is a waste collection tray. Without this, the shavings – actually chips – are normally just sprayed out across the room.

Routers
Using a power router is dealt with extensively in Chapter 5 pages 114 -128. However, it's worth noting that the ranges available include bigger and more sophisticated models than the one shown there.

In particular, check the power rating. Even in the do-it-yourself price range, you can get units rated at 750 watts (about 1 hp) and more. High power – especially when coupled with high rpm – means better control (with less tendency for the bit to 'chatter') and smoother, cleaner results.

Remember the distinction between fixed-base and plunging routers (page 114). The latter are safer and more versatile, because you can pre-set the depth of plunge before positioning the machine accurately. To start cutting, you just push down on the handles. This is invaluable for cuts which start in the middle of a piece.

For both types, you need an accurate and finely adjustable gauge for the depth of cut. Plunging routers should also have a precise indication of the plunge depth; top-quality models have special stops for quick adjustment, too.

Also very useful, although not always provided, is a clear view of the bit while you work. Comfortable handles are important – and it's worth finding out how easy it is to change bits. On some models this is an awkward two-spanner job; on others (page 115) the spindle can be locked, so you need to use only one spanner.

Lastly, routers often come with all manner of useful accessories – principally various types of fence and guide. It's well worth comparing what's available before you decide on your purchase.

Belt sanders
The belt sander works by means of a 75-100mm (3-4in) wide strip of abrasive paper looped round two rollers.

One, normally the front roller, merely holds the belt under slight tension, and enables you to adjust its tracking to stop it working its way off the ends of the rollers. The other, thanks to a motor rated at around 1000W, drives it round at considerable speed, moving the abrasive over the work at between 350 and 450m (1100 to 1600ft) per minute. To help keep the belt flat against the work, a rubber, steel or cork pad, sometimes called a 'platen', is fitted between the rollers. In the best models, platens of different materials are interchangeable, allowing you to choose the best backing for the job. To complete the set-up, it's usual these days for the sander to be fitted with a dust-collection bag.

Often considered the professional's choice, the belt sander has two main virtues. Firstly, unlike other powered sanders, it works the abrasive in just one direction, so you can keep it in line with the timber grain at all times.

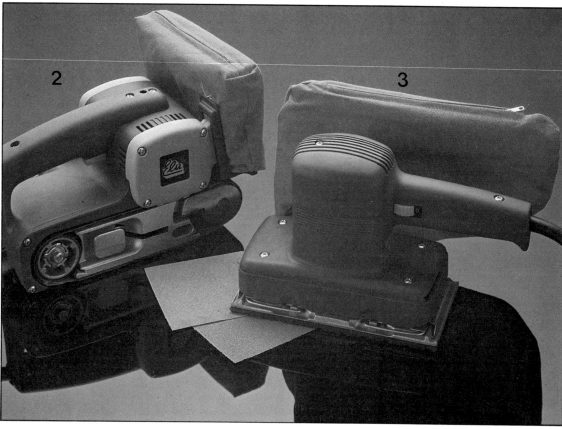

2

3

PLANES, SANDERS AND ROUTERS

1 *Off-the-shelf timber only comes in standard sizes. Unless you design around these, what you can get may not be what you want – and if the wood is rough-sawn it often needs smoothing too. The portable* **power plane**, *with its revolving cutter, solves these perennial problems once and for all. It removes material a lot more quickly than a hand plane, and in many situations where you can't use a saw.*

2 and 3 *Portable* **belt sanders** *(2) and* **orbital sanders** *(3) are the fast, efficient way to finish timber and most man-made boards – and they also cut out a lot of exhausting work when stripping paint and varnish.*

4 *The* **router** *will do all sorts of things that most other tools can't tackle easily or at all. These include grooving, rebating, and cutting profiles of many different types.*
   The more powerful and sophisticated models will give you greater accuracy, and enable you to make wider and deeper cuts in one go.

4

Secondly, it removes waste very efficiently, which makes it ideal if you need to strip off old paint or varnish, or get from a rough finish to a smooth one in a hurry.

However, it does have drawbacks. It needs rather more skill and effort to operate than other types. Like the orbital sander, it works well only on flat surfaces. And some models are very expensive.

At least one belt sander can also be mounted on the bench top in a special stand, so that you hold the workpiece against the abrasive rather than vice versa. The belt may run upright or sideways, in which case a table – perhaps combined with a fence – supports the piece and enables you to work at precise angles, and indeed to use the tool for fine shaping. On the better models the table also tilts at 45°.

If mounted upright or flat on its back, the belt is ideal for grinding tools: see Sharpening tools, pages 185 -187. Purpose-built bench belt sanders are also available – not as integral tools in their own right, but in the form of drill attachments, or mounted on one end of a bench grinder.

The bench disc sander (not to be confused with the humble rubber-backed disc sander drill attachment) works on a very similar principle. It possesses a hard rotating disc, 100 to 300mm (4 to 12in) in diameter, mounted upright Again a table, often adjustable, is standard, and a fence may also be provided.

Orbital sanders

These are also known as finishing sanders, because that's what they're designed for: producing a perfectly smooth finish.

They take their name from the way the abrasive sheet fixed to the rubber sole plate is worked over the surface with a rapid, near-scrubbing action – though in fact, on some models, this can be switched to merely work the paper back and forth for a really fine surface. The rapidity of the action varies. Some models achieve just 4000 orbits per minute; others manage as many as 25,000.

For most purposes, a higher speed means a better result. However, there are other factors to consider when choosing. As with belt sanders, a dust bag is always useful. On some models, the dust escapes directly into it through perforations in the abrasive sheet. You make these with a special jig.

You may also feel more comfortable using a machine designed for a two-handed grip. And do look at the ease with which the sheet can be replaced; the clipping arrangements on some models are extremely awkward. Finally, consider the overall size of the sanding surface. This will probably be given as a fraction of a standard sheet of abrasive – most being one-third sheet size, with a few taking half sheets. Precise measurements vary, though; there's no real agreement on what constitutes a standard sheet.

Glue guns

Really just a pistol-shaped hot glue pot, the glue gun melts sticks of solid adhesive and dispenses the resulting liquid through a nozzle at the squeeze of its trigger.

Why bother, when there are so many excellent cold woodworking adhesives on the market? The main reason is that this adhesive sets quickly under no more than hand pressure, eliminating the need for cramping. In addition, the gun does make it easy to glue small fiddly pieces and awkward corners without a lot of mess.

Glueing is an important area of woodwork which should be treated as more than an afterthought. You may well find the glue gun has a useful part to play here.

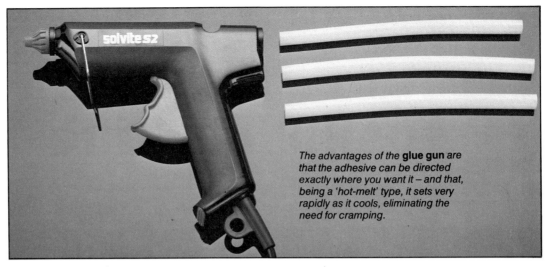

*The advantages of the **glue gun** are that the adhesive can be directed exactly where you want it – and that, being a 'hot-melt' type, it sets very rapidly as it cools, eliminating the need for cramping.*

*The **bench grinder/belt grinder** (above) makes sharpening almost effortless. You can fit a fairly coarse grinding wheel at the same time as a fine belt for honing.*

The grinder should be fitted with a clear plastic eyeshield for safety.

*The **grindstone** (right) or whetstone grinder is regarded by some craftsmen as the best sharpening device available, because it doesn't revolve fast enough to harm the steel in your tools.*

Bench grinders

Used mainly for the drastic re-sharpening of tools (see Sharpening tools, pages 185 -187 again), bench or 'high-speed' grinders come in all sorts of shapes and sizes. Just about the only thing they have in common is a bench-mounted electric motor with a spindle sticking out of each end. Usually one spindle, if not both, is fitted with a grinding wheel between 125 and 250mm (5 and 10in) in diameter, plus a guard and tool rest. The latter is most essential.

But it's quite possible for the motor to drive two different tools, and it's in the choice of the second tool that the differences become noticeable. Belt sanders, wire brushes, and slow grindstones are all available. See also page 186.

Grindstones

The traditional grindstone or whetstone (see page 186 for other patterns) basically consists of a motor and a horizontally-mounted, rotating ring of stone, onto which a lubricant (usually water) is dripped from an overhead reservoir to carry away waste metal. A guide rail for accurate positioning of blades will probably also be fitted. Accessories include replacement stones of various types. However, you'd need to do a fair bit of sharpening to make buying a grindstone worthwhile.

Further information

For more on power tools, consult the following sections: Abrasives – pages 30 -31; power saws – pages 42 -44; masonry tools – pages 141 -143; power tool attachments – pages 39 -41; using circular saws – pages 94 -103; using power drills – pages 85 -93; using a router – pages 114 -128; grinding – pages 185 -7.

Routers, circular saws and bandsaws are the most versatile do-it-yourself power tools. If you get one, do take the time to explore its possibilities.

CHAPTER 3

USING HAND TOOLS

Whatever you're making in wood, you have to join all the
bits together. There's a wide range of joints to choose from,
ranging from the simple butt joint to eye-catching dovetails.
The skill lies in choosing the right one for the job,
and cutting it carefully and accurately, ready for final assembly.

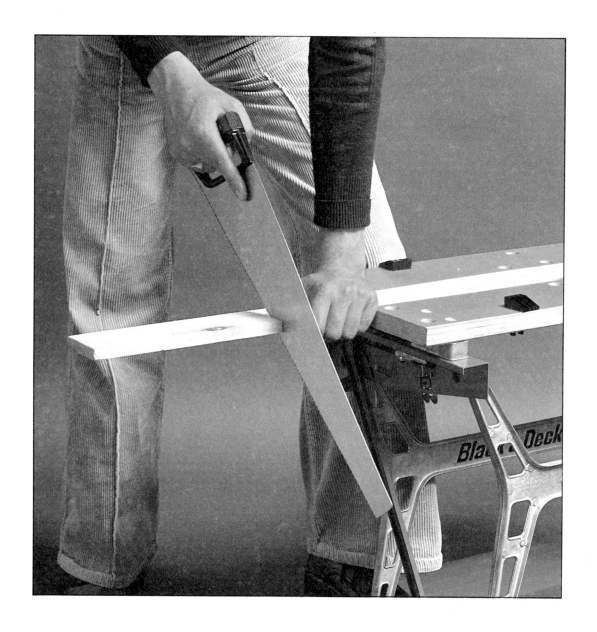

MAKING SIMPLE BUTT JOINTS

There are simple ways to join timber, and one of the simplest is the butt joint. It's easy to make, can be used on natural timber or man-made boards, and it's neat.

The great thing about butt joints is their simplicity. You can use them on any kind of timber or man-made board, provided it isn't too thin – not under 6mm (¼in). The only problem you will run into is where you are joining chipboard. A special technique is needed here to get the screws to grip, as is explained later.

Although it is possible to simply glue two pieces of wood together, unless you add some kind of reinforcement the result won't be very strong. So in most cases, the joint should be strengthened with either screws or nails. The question is which? As a rule of thumb, screws will give you a stronger joint than nails. The exception is where you are screwing into the endgrain of natural timber. Here, the screwthread chews up the timber to such an extent that it has almost no fixing value at all. Nails in this case are a much better bet.

Choosing the right adhesive
Even if you are screwing or nailing the joint together, it ought to be glued as well. A PVA woodworking adhesive will do the trick in most jobs, providing a strong and easily achieved fixing. This type of adhesive will not, however, stand up well to either extreme heat or to moisture; the sort of conditions you'll meet outdoors, or in a kitchen, for example. A urea formaldehyde is the glue to use in this sort of situation. It isn't as convenient – it comes as a powder that you have to mix with water – but your joints will hold.

Choosing the right joint
There are no hard and fast rules about choosing the best joint for a particular job. It's really just a case of finding a joint that is neat enough for what you're making, and strong enough not to fall apart the first time it is used. And as far as strength is concerned, the various kinds of butt joint work equally well.

Marking timber
Butt joints are the simplest of all joints – there's no complicated chiselling or marking out to worry about – but if the joint is to be both strong and neat you do need to be able to saw wood to length leaving the end perfectly square.

The first important thing here is the accuracy of your marking out. Examine the piece of wood you want to cut and choose a side and an edge that are particularly flat and smooth. They're called the face edge and face side.

Next, measure up and press the point of a sharp knife into the face side where you intend to make the cut. Slide a try-square up to the knife, making sure that its stock – the handle – is pressed firmly against the face edge. Then use the knife to score a line across the surface of the timber. Carry this line round all four sides of the wood, always making sure that the try-square's stock is held against either the face edge or the face side. If you wish, you can run over the knife line with a pencil to make it easier to see – it's best to sharpen the lead into a chisel shape.

Why not use a pencil for marking out in the first place? There are two reasons. The first is that a knife gives a thinner and therefore more accurate line than even the sharpest pencil. The second is that the knife will cut through the surface layer of the wood, helping the saw to leave a clean, sharp edge.

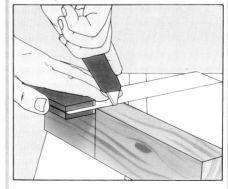

Sawing square

One of the most useful – and easiest to make – aids to sawing is a bench hook. It'll help you to grip the wood you want to cut, and to protect the surface on which you are working. You can make one up quite easily, by gluing and screwing together pieces of scrap timber (see *Ready Reference*).

You also need the ability to control the saw, and there are three tips that will help you here. Always point your index finger along the saw blade to stop it flapping from side to side as you work. And always stand in such a way that you are comfortable, well balanced, and can get your head directly above the saw so you can see what you are cutting. You should also turn slightly sideways on. This stops your elbow brushing against your body as you draw the saw back – a fault that is often the reason for sawing wavy lines.

Starting the cut

Position the piece of wood to be cut on the bench hook and hold it firmly against the block furthest from you. Start the cut by drawing the saw backwards two or three times over the far edge to create a notch, steadying the blade by 'cocking' the thumb of your left hand. Make sure that you position the saw so that the whole of this notch is on the waste side of the line. You can now begin to saw properly using your arm with sort of piston action, but keep your left (or right as the case may be) hand away from the saw.

As the cut deepens gradually reduce the angle of the saw until it is horizontal. At this point you can continue sawing through until you start cutting into the bench hook. Alternatively, you may find it easier to angle the saw towards you and make a sloping cut down the edge nearest to you. With that done, you can saw through the remaining waste holding the saw horizontally, using the two angled cuts to keep the saw on course.

Whichever method you choose, don't try to force the saw through the wood – if that seems necessary, then the saw is probably blunt. Save your muscle power for the forward stroke – but concentrate mainly on sawing accurately to your marked line.

Cleaning up cut ends

Once you have cut the wood to length, clean up the end with glasspaper. A good tip is to lay the abrasive flat on a table and work the end of the wood over it with a series of circular strokes, making sure that you keep the wood vertical so you don't sand the end out of square. If the piece of wood is too unmanageable, wrap the glasspaper round a square piece of scrap wood instead and sand the end of the wood by moving the block to and fro – it'll help in keeping the end square.

DOVETAIL NAILING

This is a simple way of strengthening any butt joint. All you do is grip the upright piece in a vice or the jaws of a portable work-bench, and glue the horizontal piece on top if it – supporting it with scrap wood to hold the joint square – and then drive in the nails dovetail fashion. If you were to drive the nails in square, there would be more risk that the joint would pull apart. Putting them in at an angle really does add strength.

The only difficulty is that the wood may split. To prevent this, use oval brads rather than round nails, making sure that their thickest part points along the grain. If that doesn't do the trick, try blunting the point of each nail by driving it into the side of an old hammer. This creates a burr of metal on the point which will cut through the wood fibres rather than parting them.

Once the nails are driven home, punch their heads below the surface using a nail punch, or a large blunt nail. Fill the resulting dents with wood stopping (better on wood than ordinary cellulose filler) and sand smooth.

1 *Drive nails at angle: first leans to left; next to right, and so on.*

3 *Fill resulting dents with stopping compound to cover up nail heads.*

THE OVERLAP

This is the simplest of all and is one you can use on relatively thin timber. The example shown is for a T-joint, but the method is the same if you want to make an X-joint.

Bring the two pieces of wood together as they will be when joined, and use a pencil to mark the position of the topmost piece on the one underneath. To reinforce the joint, countersunk screws are best, so mark their positions on the top piece of wood, and drill clearance holes the same diameter as the screw's shank – the unthreaded part – right the way through. The screws should be arranged like the spots on a dice (two screws are shown here, but on a larger joint where more strength is needed five would be better) to help stop the joint twisting out of square. Enlarge the mouths of these holes with a countersink bit to accommodate the screw heads, and clean up any splinters where the drill breaks through the underside of the wood.

Bring the two pieces of wood together again using a piece of scrap wood to keep the top piece level. Then make pilot holes in the lower piece using either a bradawl or a small drill, boring through the clearance holes to make sure they are correctly positioned. Make sure the pilot holes are drilled absolutely vertically, or the screws could pull the joint out of shape. Finally, apply a thin coating of adhesive to both the surfaces to be joined (follow the adhesive manufacturer's instructions), position the pieces of wood accurately and, without moving them again, drive home the screws.

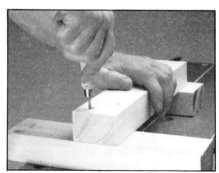

3 *Reassemble joint and bore pilot holes in bottom piece with bradawl.*

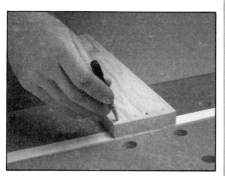

2 *With nail punch or large blunt nail, hammer nail heads below surface.*

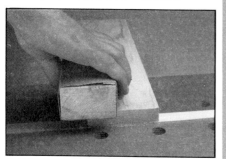

4 *When stopping is dry, sand flush with surface of surrounding timber.*

CORRUGATED TIMBER CONNECTORS

Another simple way of holding a butt joint together is to use ordinary corrugated timber connectors. Simply glue the two pieces of wood together, and hammer the connectors in across the joint. Note that they are driven in dovetail fashion – the fixing is stronger that way.

For strength, hammer in connectors diagonally rather than straight.

READY REFERENCE

MAKING YOUR OWN BENCH HOOK

This a very useful sawing aid to help grip the wood when cutting. Hook one end over the edge of the workbench and hold the wood against the other end. Make it up from off-cuts and replace when it becomes worn.

You need:
● a piece of 12mm (½in) plywood measuring about 250 x 225mm (10 x 9in)
● two pieces of 50 x 25mm (2 x 1in) planed softwood, each about 175mm (7in) long. Glue and screw them together as shown in the sketch. Use the bench hook the other way up if you're left-handed.

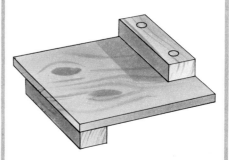

TIP: SAWING STRAIGHT

● hold wood firmly against bench hook and start cut on waste side of cutting line with two or three backward cuts
● decrease angle of the saw blade as cut progresses
● complete cut with saw horizontal, cutting into your bench hook slightly

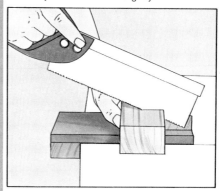

TIP: TO SMOOTH CUT END

● rub with a circular motion on glasspaper held flat on the workbench, so you don't round off the corners
● on large pieces of wood, wrap glasspaper round a block of wood and rub this across the cut end

1 *Bring pieces squarely together. Mark position of each on the other.*

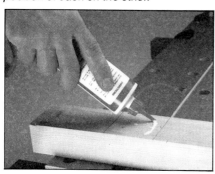

4 *Apply woodworking adhesive to both pieces and press them together*

2 *Drill and countersink (inset) clearance holes for screws in uppermost piece.*

5 *Carefully drive in screws. If they're tight, remove and lubricate with soap.*

FIXING INTO CHIPBOARD

Because neither nails nor screws hold well in chipboard, how do you hold a butt joint together? The answer is that you do use screws, but to help them grip, you drive them into a chipboard plug. Chipboard plugs are a bit like ordinary wall plugs. In fact, you can use ordinary plugs, but you have to be careful to position the plug so that any expanding jaws open across the board's width and not across the thickness where they could cause the board to break up.

The initial stages of the job are exactly the same as for the overlap joint – marking out, drilling the clearance holes, and so on. The difference is that instead of boring pilot holes in the second piece of wood, you drill holes large enough to take the chipboard plugs. Pop the plugs into the holes, glue the joint together and drive home the screws.

Incidentally, if you can't use any sort of plug at all – for example, when screwing into the face of the chipboard – the only way to get the screw to hold properly is to dip it in a little woodworking adhesive before you drive it home.

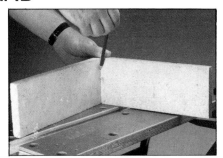

1 *Bring pieces together and mark position of overlap with a pencil.*

2 *Drill and countersink clearance holes in overlapping piece.*

3 *Mark screw positions through holes onto end of second piece.*

4 *Drill chipboard to take plugs, then glue and screw joint together.*

REINFORCING BLOCKS

The joints described so far are fairly robust, but if a lot of strength is needed it's worth reinforcing the joint with some sort of block. The simplest is a square piece of timber.

First drill and countersink clearance holes through the block and glue and screw it to one of the pieces you want to join so that it's flush with the end. To complete the joint, glue the second piece in position, and drive screws through into that. You can arrange for the block to end up inside the angle or outside it. Choose whichever looks best and is easiest to achieve.

With the block inside the angle, you'll have a neat joint and the screw heads won't be openly on display. However, in most cases it means screwing through a thick piece of wood (the block) into a thin piece (one of the bits you want to join), so it's not as strong as it might be. If greater strength is needed work the other way round, driving the screws through the pieces to be joined, into the block. You can neaten the result to a certain extent by using a triangular rather than a square block.

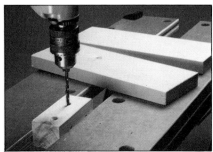

1 *Drill and countersink clearance holes through reinforcing block.*

2 *Glue and screw block in place level with end of one piece of wood.*

3 *Glue second piece in place and drive screws into it through block.*

4 *In some cases this joint looks better with block outside angle.*

JOINTING BLOCKS

Made from plastic, these are just sophisticated versions of the wooden blocks you can make yourself, and they're used in similar situations. Their only real advantage is that they tend to give a neater result when you're working with veneered or melamine covered chipboard, but only because they come in the right colours. There are basically two kinds to choose from.

The simplest is just a hollow triangular 'block' that comes with a snap-on cover to hide the screws. More complicated versions come in two parts. You screw one half of the block to each piece of wood, and then screw the two halves together using the machine screw provided. It's essential here that both halves of the block are positioned accurately, and since the blocks vary from brand to brand in the details of their design, you should follow the manufacturer's instructions on this point.

1 *Screw half of block to one piece of wood and mark position on other.*

2 *Next, screw second half of block in place on second piece of timber.*

3 *Finally, connect both halves of block using built-in machine screw.*

4 *Treat blocks that come in one piece as wooden reinforcing blocks.*

ANGLE IRONS

If still greater strength is needed, use either an angle iron or a corner repair bracket to reinforce the joint. These are really just pieces of metal pre-drilled to take screws and shaped to do the same job as a reinforcing block (the angle irons) or to be screwed to the face of the two pieces of timber across the joint (the flat T-shaped and L-shaped corner repair brackets).

In either case, bring together the pieces of wood to be joined, position the bracket, and mark the screw holes. Drill clearance and pilot holes for all the screws, then screw the bracket to one of the pieces before glueing the joint together and screwing the bracket to the second piece. They don't look very attractive, so use where appearance isn't important, ie, at the back of a joint, or where the joint is going to be concealed in some other way.

1 *Corner joints strengthened with plywood and an angle repair iron.*

2 *T-joints can be simply made with angle irons or repair brackets.*

SKEW NAILING

There'll be some situations where you cannot get at the end of the wood to use dovetail nailing. Here you must use skew nailing instead. This means gluing the two pieces securely together and then driving a nail into the upright piece of wood at an angle so it also penetrates the horizontal piece. Put a couple of nails into each side of the upright so that they cross. To stop the upright moving, clamp a block of wood behind it or wedge it against something solid.

Stop movement while driving nails with scrap wood block and G-cramp.

MAKING HALVING & MITRE JOINTS

Getting joints to fit snugly is one of the major objectives in carpentry, and nothing introduces the techniques so well as the halving joint. As for the perfect finish, that's the role of the mitre.

There are many situations in woodwork when you need a joint that's fast and simple, but also neat and strong. And this is where halving joints come into their own. Despite their simplicity, they're very effective joints because the two pieces of wood are cut so they interlock together, either face to face or edge to edge, making the joint as strong as — if not stronger than — the timber itself. They are used almost exclusively for building frameworks, joining the rails (side pieces) either at a corner or in a cross absolutely flush. You end up with a frame that's neat enough to be on show and sturdy enough to need no reinforcement.

Mitre joints, though not strictly speaking considered halving joints as there's no interlocking, are halved to make up a perfect 90° angle. In this section, only the simple mitre is dealt with — the more complicated forms (eg, mitred secret dovetails) are covered in another section.

Strength of joints

There are three things that affect the strength of a halving joint — the size of the timber, the quality of the timber, and any reinforcement you add.

The size of timber is important because it governs the amount of adhesive in the joint; the greater the areas glued together, the stronger the joint will be. Usually problems only arise when you are trying to join thin pieces of timber together — it's almost impossible to get the joint to stay rigid. Regarding timber quality, hardwoods rarely present a problem, but with softwoods, splitting can occur which will seriously weaken the joint. You should, therefore, reject timber containing knots, cracks and other potential weak spots.

In many cases, the correct adhesive is all the reinforcement you need — use a good quality PVA woodworking adhesive, or, if the joint will be subjected to heat or moisture, a urea formaldehyde woodworking adhesive. If still greater strength is required — this is more likely on corner halving joints than on cross halvings — you should drive screws through the overlaps, or, for a more natural look, drill a hole right through and glue in a

length of dowel. Both the dowels and screws are set like the spots on a dice to stop the joint twisting.

Butt joints (see pages 48 -52 for details) must be reinforced in some way to have strength, but with mitred butt joints this would defeat the decorative aim. Because of this, they are normally reserved for situations where strength is not required – picture frames and decorative edgings, such as door architraves for example.

Marking corner halving joints

Having sawn the ends of the two pieces of wood to be joined perfectly square (see pages 48 -52 again) place one on top of the other, and mark the width of the top piece on the one below. Carry this mark right round the timber using a knife and a try-square, then repeat the process, this time with the bottom piece of wood on top.

Next divide the thickness of the timber in two. You need a single-tooth marking gauge for this: it consists of a wooden shaft with a sharp metal pin called a spur near one end, and a block of wood (the stock) which can be moved along the shaft and be fixed at any point with the aid of a thumbscrew.

Position the stock so that the distance between it and the spur is roughly half the timber's thickness, and place it against one edge of the wood. Use the spur to dent the surface of the timber, then repeat with the stock against the other edge. If the dents co-

incide, the gauge is set correctly. If they don't, reset the gauge. Don't try to make small adjustments by undoing the thumbscrew and moving the stock — you'll go on for ever trying to make it accurate. Instead, with the screw reasonably tight, tap one end of the shaft sharply on a hard surface. Depending which end you tap and how hard you tap it, the setting will increase or decrease by the merest fraction.

With the setting right, wedge one end of the timber into the angle of a bench hook, place the stock of the gauge firmly against the timber's edge and holding it there, score the wood from the width line to the end. You'll find this easier if, rather than digging the spur right into the wood, you merely drag it across the surface. Score identical lines on the other side and the end.

Use a pencil to shade the areas on each piece of wood that will form the waste (the top of one, the bottom of the other), then grip the first piece upright in a vice. The lower down you can get it the better. If you can't get it low, back it with a piece of scrap wood to reduce vibration. Using a tenon saw, carefully saw down until you reach the width line — the first one you marked. The golden rule of sawing any kind of joint is to saw on the waste side of the marked line (it's *always* better to saw or chisel off too little rather than too much since you can always take off a little more but you can never put it back). And remember that the closer the fit, the

MAKING A CORNER HALVING JOINT

1 *First mark the width of each piece of wood on the other. Then, using a knife and square, continue these width lines round all four sides of each piece.*

2 *To mark the thickness line, set a marking gauge to half the thickness of the wood and, holding the stock firmly against one edge, scribe the line.*

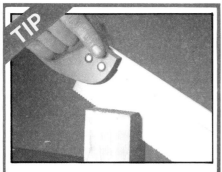

3 *It's easier to start sawing at an angle, then gradually bring the saw to the horizontal. Keep the wood gripped firmly in the vice until you're finished.*

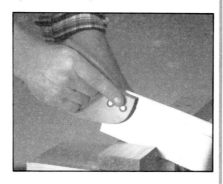

4 *Transfer the wood to a bench hook and cut down along the width line to remove the waste wood. Be sure to cut on the waste side of the guide line.*

5 *Smooth both parts to be joined with glasspaper and apply adhesive. Clamp together with a G-cramp until dry, protecting the wood with scrap timber.*

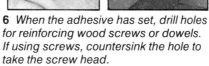

6 *When the adhesive has set, drill holes for reinforcing wood screws or dowels. If using screws, countersink the hole to take the screw head.*

stronger the joint will end up. Basically, it should fit like a hand in a glove.

Remove the wood from the vice, put it on a bench hook and cut down along the width line to release the waste wood. Again make sure you cut on the waste side of the line and be prepared to make final adjusments with a chisel. Treat the second piece of wood in exactly the same way, then bring the two together and check the fit.

You can use either a chisel or a piece of glasspaper to take off any unevenness in the timber, although it'll be quicker to use a chisel to clear out the edges so that the corners are absolutely square. When the pieces finally fit neatly, spread adhesive on both faces of the joint and hold them in place with a G-cramp (protecting the wood's surface with scrap timber) until the glue has set. Remove the cramp, and add any re-

READY REFERENCE

WHERE TO USE HALVING JOINTS

Halving joints are usually used for making frameworks. Here you can see which joint to use where, and how each one is assembled.

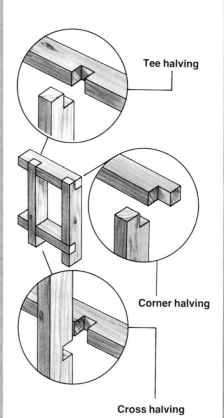

Tee halving

Corner halving

Cross halving

TOOLS FOR HALVING JOINTS

For measuring and marking: use a *handyman's knife* rather than a pencil for marking; use a *marking gauge* on each face of the joint – it'll be more accurate than using a tape measure; a *try-square* ensures accurate squaring off.
For cutting: use a *tenon saw* and a broad-blade *chisel* (25mm/1in) for cutting out cross halvings.

TIP: LABELLING JOINT PARTS

Avoid mixing up the pairs of joints by labelling the two parts with a letter and a number as soon as you cut them.

MAKING A CROSS HALVING JOINT

1 First mark out the waste area to be removed, then cut down the width lines with a tenon saw.

2 Hold the timber in a vice or against a bench hook and remove the waste by chiselling at a slight upward angle.

3 Do the same on the other side until there's a 'pyramid' of waste in the middle. Gradually flatten this.

4 When nearing the thickness line, hold the cutting edge at an angle to the wood grain. Trim fibres in the corners.

The next step is to turn the wood round and slope the other edge to leave a sort of pyramid of waste. With that done, pushing the chisel through the wood rather than hitting it, gradually flatten off the pyramid until you have brought it level with the halfway lines. You'll get a neater finish here if, in the final stages, you work with the chisel's blade flat but at an angle to the grain of the wood. Finally, again pushing the chisel, remove any ragged fibres lodged in the angles of the housing.

Once you've sawn and chiselled out the housing in the second piece of wood, the next step is to try fitting the two together. Don't try forcing them if they don't quite fit — you're in danger of splitting the wood. Instead, carefully chisel off a fraction more wood, bit by bit, until you can fit the pieces together without undue force. If, on the other hand, you've cut the housing too wide so the fit is very loose, you'll have to add some reinforcement like screws or dowels, and fill in the gaps with a wood filler, stopping or a mixture of fine sawdust and PVA adhesive. It's not worth trying to add a wedge unless the gap is very wide (over 6mm/¼in) because the result can be very messy.

Making a mitre joint
With wood that's square or rectangular in section, the first job is to make sure that both pieces are absolutely squarely cut. Use the try-square to check this — if they're not, it's better to cut another piece of wood than attempt to make adjustments. Next, place one piece on top of the other to form a right angle. Mark an internal and external corner on both, then take them apart and carry the marks across the edge with a knife and try square. Join up the marks on each piece of wood — this will give sawing lines at 45°. Mark the waste side of each with a pencil.

Wood that is raised on one side (eg, mouldings for picture frames) cannot be marked in the same way as the pieces won't sit flat on each other. The easiest way is to mark the

inforcing screws or dowels that may be needed, drilling pilot holes first.

Making cross halving joints
The difference between cross halving joints and corner halving joints is that you cannot remove the waste using only a saw. You have to make a 'housing' and for this you need a chisel (see Chapter 1 pages 22 -23 and also pages 62 -65).

Saw down the width lines to the halfway mark and make additional saw cuts in between to break up the waste — these can be the same width as the chisel blade to make chipping out easier. Grip the work in a vice, or on a bench hook, and now use the chisel to remove the waste. This is done in four stages. Guiding the chisel blade bevel uppermost with one hand and striking the handle with the palm of your other hand — for this job your hand is better than a mallet — reduce the edge of the timber nearest to you to a shallow slope ending a fraction above the halfway line. Don't try to remove all the wood in one go or it will split. Remove just a sliver at a time.

MAKING MITRES

1 With square or rectangular wood, cut ends absolutely square and stack to form a right angle. Then mark the inner and outer corners on both pieces.

2 Carry lines down each edge with knife and try square, and score a line between corner marks to create an angle of 45°. Shade waste in pencil.

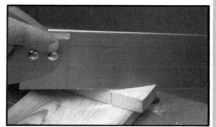

3 Press the wood against the bench hook and keep the saw at a shallow angle. Cut the diagonal, using the line on the edge to keep the saw vertical.

THE SIMPLE MITRE

1 *The ends of two battens are cut to 45° and, when fixed together, make a 90° angle in this simplest of mitre joints, ideal for picture framing.*

2 *With thick timber frames, use corrugated steel fasteners driven into the back of mitre joints, where they will not be seen from the front.*

3 *Another method of strengthening a fairly thick mitre joint from behind is to pin triangles of plywood across the corner, out of sight.*

4 *Ready-made angle brackets with pre-drilled, countersunk screw holes make a quick, rigid and hidden fixing for two mitred battens in a frame.*

point of the mitre (the corner point) and then to use a simple *mitre block* to cut the angle. A mitre block not only helps you support the piece of wood (like a bench hook) but also has saw cuts at 45° in the back face to guide the saw. Then you only have to line up the mitre point on the wood with the saw now set at the correct angle. You can make a mitre block yourself — see *Ready Reference*.

Mitre aids
There are other devices available to help you cut mitres accurately. A proprietary *jointing jig*, for example, guides the saw either at right angles or at 45°; a *mitre box* is like a mitre block but has an extra side so that the whole length of the saw is kept in line.

Without these devices, getting the angles right isn't easy — but if necessary you can use a bench hook, driving in two nails so the wood is held against the block and the line of cutting is free of the bench hook. This is not as easy as using one of the other methods. Mark the wood so you know the sawing line, then place it in the mitre block , box or jig, to line up with the appropriate groove to guide the saw. If the wood you are cutting is very thin, put some blocks of scrap wood under the device to bring it up to a reasonable height. Insert a tenon saw into the guide slot and, holding it level, saw away.

There are only two things that can go

wrong. If the block is old, the 'guide' cut may have widened, resulting in an inaccurate cut. A larger tenon saw may help, but really the only answer is to hold the saw as steady as possible. The other common error when cutting mouldings and the like is to cut two mitres the same — that is two right-handed or left-handed angles, instead of one of each. This can be avoided by always marking the waste on the wood, and checking that the saw is in the correct guide slot before you begin.

Clean up the cut ends with glasspaper, taking care not to alter the angle, and glue and cramp the joint together. For frames, special mitre cramps are available, but you again make up your own. From scrap wood, cut four L-shaped blocks, and drill a hole at an angle through the point of each L. Feed a single piece of string through the holes of all four blocks, position the blocks at the corners of the frame and tie the string into a continuous loop. To tighten up, twist the string around a stick, and keep twisting the stick to draw the blocks together. You can then wedge the stick against the frame to stop it untwisting until the adhesive has set.

There are three ways to strengthen mitres – with timber connectors, plywood triangles or metal angle repair irons. For frames they should be fitted from behind, either by gluing, or gluing and pinning (see the photographs above).

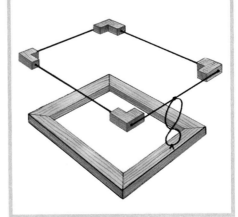

MAKING JOINTS WITH DOWELS

Called wood pins or pegs, dowels are lengths of hardwood with an important role to play in simple carpentry. They can be a decorative part of joints made with them, or be there for strength alone. Few tools are needed but the secret of success lies in using them accurately.

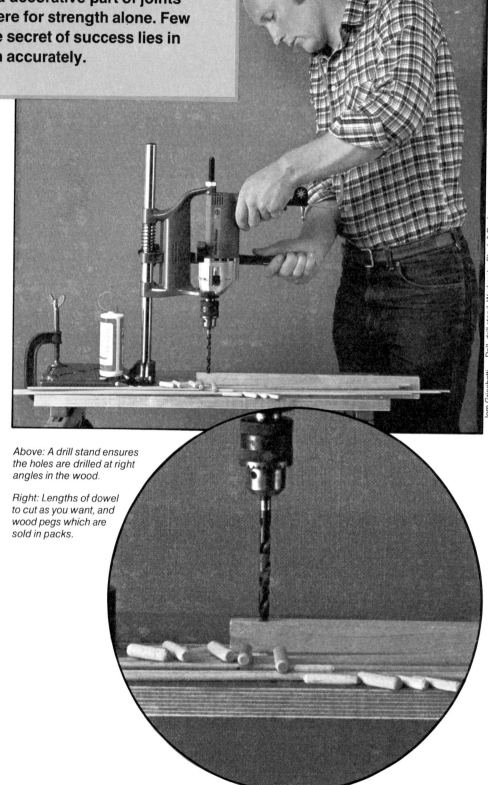

Above: A drill stand ensures the holes are drilled at right angles in the wood.

Right: Lengths of dowel to cut as you want, and wood pegs which are sold in packs.

There are two basic ways in which you can use dowels in woodworking joints. You can drive a dowel through such joints as a half lap instead of using a nail or screw, or you can use them to make joints in their own right by drilling holes in one piece of wood, glueing in dowels, and then slotting these into corresponding holes in the second piece.

The dowel joint proper is used mostly in furniture making where it provides a neat joint of great strength without intricate cutting and without the need for unsightly reinforcement. Dowels can also be used to repair furniture.

In any joint, the size of the dowel is very important. Use a small one in a big joint and it won't have sufficient strength; use one that's too large and the holes you drill to accommodate it will weaken the wood. Ideally you should choose dowels which are no more than one third the thickness of the timber into which they will be fixed.

The thickness of the wood must be considered, too, for the dowels must have sufficient space between them and at each side otherwise when they're hit home or pushed into their corresponding holes the wood will split. So follow the carpenter's 'one third rule' and mark the width as well as the thickness into three (ie, a 9mm/⅜in dowel will need at least the same amount on both sides of it). And don't forget that planed wood can be up to 5mm less all round than the dimensions you ordered, and three into this size might not give you enough room for a successful joint.

Types of joints

There are different types of dowel joint. The simplest and easiest to make is the *through* dowel joint in which the dowel peg passes right through one piece of timber and into the other, sometimes passing through this as well if it's thin enough. Because in either case the ends of the dowels show, they are often used as a decorative feature of the article you're making.

If you don't want the ends of the dowels to be seen, you must make a *stopped* joint. In

Jem Grischotti   Drill, drill stand, Workmate: Black & Decker

JOINTS MADE WITH DOWELS

The through dowel joint ready for assembly. The dowels are firmly embedded in one piece and will pass right through the other.

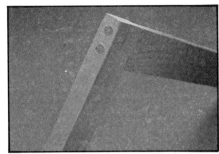

When assembled the through joint shows up the dowels. Cut them a little longer so after cramping they can be planed flush with the wood.

The stopped joint has dowels in one piece which will go into the other far enough to ensure rigidity but won't be seen on the other side.

A close fit for the finished stopped joint. When drilling the holes they should be slightly deeper than the dowel to hold any excess adhesive.

Mitred dowel joints can be tricky to make as you can't use the 'pin' method (see next page) for marking up because of the 45° angle.

The hidden strength in this joint is the two different lengths of dowel. Very effective for frames where you don't want reinforcement to be seen.

A halving or half lap joint made at a corner can either be glued and screwed or, if it will be on show, made secure with dowels which fit into holes placed like spots on a dice.

The completed dowelled halving joint gives one overall look of wood. The same effect can be achieved by topping countersunk screws with dowel pellets cut from an offcut of the wood.

Jem Grischotti

READY REFERENCE

BUYING DOWELS

Dowel lengths from timber merchants are sold in these diameters:
● 6mm (¼in)
● 9mm (⅜in)
● 12mm (½in)
Larger diameters – 16mm (⅝in) and 19mm (¾in) – can be softwood rather than hardwood.

TIPS TO SAVE TIME

● Buying grooved dowel saves you having to groove it yourself.
● **Pre-packed dowels** are bought in packs containing short lengths of diameters such as 4mm, 8mm and 10mm. They are fluted (finely grooved) and the ends are chamfered.
● **Dowel pellets** finish woodwork where screws have been countersunk. They should fit the hole exactly but be fractionally deeper so they can be planed back when the adhesive has set. Buy pre-packed, or cut your own from offcuts using a special plug attachment for an electric drill.

TOOLS

● **try-square and marking gauge** are essential for accurate marking up
● **electric drill** held in a drill stand for perfectly plumb holes
● **mallet** for tapping in the dowels
● **block or ordinary plane** for finishing a through joint
● **cramp** to hold the joint until the adhesive has set

CHAMFER DOWEL ENDS

If cutting your own dowels rub the cut ends with medium-grade glasspaper to give a gentle chamfer (it makes the dowel go in more easily).

Apply woodworking adhesive to the meeting faces of the wood as well as brushing or squirting it into the holes.

MARKING UP

1 *With wood that's rectangular or square in section, use a marking gauge to make the central line on the edge where the dowels will go.*

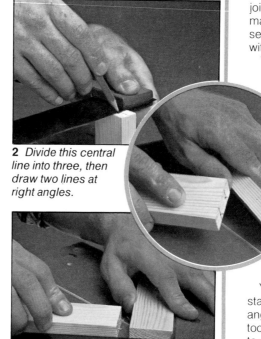

2 *Divide this central line into three, then draw two lines at right angles.*

3 *Lightly tap small panel pins into the wood at the two centre points. Snip off their heads leaving about 3mm (¹⁄₈in) protruding.*

4 *Holding the second piece of timber firmly against a bench hook or edge of the try-square, press the pins in to mark the drill positions (inset).*

Jem Grischotti

this the peg doesn't go right through either piece of timber. This is perhaps the most common dowel joint.

Joint shapes
Dowels can be used to make joints of various types, including L-joints, T-joints and X-joints between rails or boards, and three-way joints between rails and posts, as in furniture-making. They can also be used to reinforce edge-to-edge joints between boards, for example when making a drawer.

Cutting dowels
Cut dowels to length with a fine-toothed tenon saw, holding the dowels in a bench hook or a vice. For through joints, cut one dowel slightly longer than the combined thicknesses of the timbers, so that the ends can be trimmed flush after the joint is assembled. For stopped joints, cut the dowels slightly shorter than the combined depths of the holes into which they fit, and lightly chamfer the ends using glasspaper, a chisel or a proprietary dowel sharpener (which works just like a pencil sharpener).

Dowels need a shallow groove cut in their sides to allow excess adhesive to squeeze out as the joints are assembled. With much

practice you can do this with a chisel or tenon saw (having cramped it lengthways in a workbench), but it is probably easier to buy grooved dowel in the first place – in lengths you cut to size yourself, or for small jobs as pre-packed pegs. If buying pegs make sure you choose ones that correspond with the bit size for your drill.

Marking hole positions
First, use a try-square to check that the meeting faces or ends of the timber to be joined are cut perfectly square and are of the same thickness. You can then mark the positions for the dowel holes. Set a marking gauge to half the width of the timber, and mark a line down the middle of the end of one length of timber. Determine exactly where on this line the centre of the holes will be – the ideal is that they should be from 25mm (1in) to 50mm (2in) apart and never nearer than 19mm (¾in) from the edges. Using a try-square, draw lines across the gauge line to mark the exact centres of the holes.

To mark matching holes in corresponding positions on the second piece of timber use the following method to ensure accuracy. Drive small panel pins into the first piece at the positions you've marked for the holes.

Leave the pins slightly proud of the surface and snip off their heads with pliers. Bring the two pieces of wood together in the correct joint position, and the heads of the pins will mark where the holes are to be bored in the second piece of timber. Remove the pins with pincers before drilling.

Where you are joining two horizontal rails to an upright at a corner, you should stagger the holes, otherwise the dowels will clash inside the upright.

Cutting holes
Holes for the dowels can be made either with a hand drill or an electric drill. In each case, obviously, the bit used must match the diameter of the dowel. The main difficulty is that you must ensure the bit is truly at right angles to the timber you are drilling, or a dowel that protrudes from one hole will not fit snugly into the hole in the matching timber.

You can use an electric drill held in a drill stand to guarantee that the bit is truly at right angles to the timber. Or where the timber is too large for this you can use a dowelling jig to ensure accuracy. Where you are cutting a through dowel joint, you can avoid this problem by cramping both pieces of wood together in a vice and boring through both.

For stopped joints, the hole you bore should be slightly deeper than the depth to which the dowel penetrates, to leave a small reservoir for any excess glue that is not squeezed out along the groove. A depth gauge ensures this. Various types for both hand and electric drills are available but you can improvise by making your own. Either stick a bit of tape on the bit's shank, carefully positioned so that the distance between its lower edge and the end of the drill exactly equals the depth of the hole required. Or you can take a length of timber – 25mm (1in) or 38mm (1½in) square according to the diameter of the dowel – and bore a hole right through its length. Cut this timber to length so that when it is slipped onto the bit's shank, the part of the bit left protruding will cut a hole of the right depth. In both cases you should take your measurement to the cutting end of the drill only – not to any threaded or shaped lead-in point.

For a stopped dowel joint, drill holes so the dowels will penetrate each piece of timber by between one-half and two-thirds of the timber's thickness.

Fixing and finishing dowels
Always check first that the joint is a good fit and is accurately square before applying PVA adhesive. You can then squirt adhesive into the holes, but since you risk applying too much this way, it is better to brush the

DRILLING HOLES

1 *To ensure that holes will be in exactly opposite positions on a through joint, drill both pieces of wood at the same time.*

2 *The depths you have to go to for a dowel joint can be marked on the bit with a piece of tape, allowing a little extra at both ends for glue.*

3 *Another way of making sure you don't go too deep is by making a depth gauge from a scrap of timber. Or you can buy a proprietary gauge.*

4 *A dowelling jig has holes for different sized bits. When you cramp it over the wood use spare timber to prevent the screw marking the wood.*

adhesive onto the dowel before tapping it into place with a mallet — you can use a hammer but you should protect the dowel with a block of wood. You should also apply adhesive to the meeting faces of the timber.

The glued joints should be cramped until the adhesive has set.

With through joints and halving joints, you now saw off the bulk of the protruding dowel

and use a block plane to trim the end flush. You can use an ordinary plane for this, but it must be set for a very fine cut. Smooth off any remaining roughness with glasspaper.

If using dowel pellets, hit them into place over the countersunk screws (with the ones you've cut yourself make sure the grain follows that of the wood). Plane off excess after the adhesive has dried.

MAKING THE JOINT

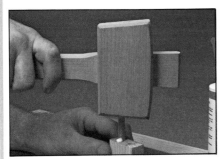

1 *First check that the dowel fits snugly, but not too tightly. Then apply adhesive and gently tap it into place with a mallet.*

2 *After cramping to allow the adhesive to set, finish off a through joint by planing away the excess along the side of the wood.*

Dowelling jig: Buck & Ryan Jem Grischotti Block plane: Stanley Tools Jem Grischotti

READY REFERENCE

RULES FOR DRILLING HOLES
● make them the same diameter as the dowels
● they should be a little deeper than the dowel's length
● slightly countersink these where the pieces of wood meet

TIP: DOWELLING JIG
With a drill use a dowelling jig so the holes will be straight and square.

WHAT CAN GO WRONG?
The most common problems are:
● the dowels being too tight. Forcing the joint together causes the wood to split – so always check the fit first
● the joint being forced out of alignment because the holes were drilled out of line with one another – always check the alignment before finally applying the adhesive

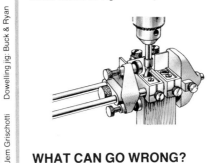

MITRED DOWEL JOINTS
● use a mitre box for accuracy
● place mitred pieces together in a cramp and mark them at the same time
● the dowel at the outer corner should be shorter than the one at the inner corner

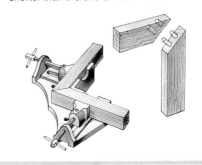

MAKING HOUSING JOINTS

If you're putting together a bookcase or installing shelves in any other sort of furniture, then housing joints are the ones to use for attaching the shelves to the uprights. Here's how to make them.

Housing joints are very useful in constructing drawers, door frames and partition walls, among other things: but they're indispensable for fixing shelves neatly into uprights. The joint gets its name because the end of the shelf fits into a square-bottomed channel or 'housing' across the upright. A basic housing joint is as simple as that, and very easy to cut and assemble. What's more, it's ideal for supporting the weight of a shelf and its contents – it resists twisting, and it looks much more professional than the metal brackets or other fittings which can do the same job.

Such fittings are readily available and often easy to use, but if your design is modern, they'll tend to spoil its clean lines; and if it's traditional, they'll naturally be inappropriate. They will never give the unobtrusive and craftsmanlike finish which you can obtain from carefully designed and made housing joints.

Jem Grischotti

Types of housing joint
There are a few variations, and each has its own purpose. A 'stopped' housing joint is completely invisible; you can't see the connection between shelf and upright at all, because (unlike the basic 'through' housing joint) its housing stops about 20mm (¾in) short of the front of the upright. You can also cut out a step in the front of the shelf to allow it to fit flush with the upright just as in a through housing joint, and so get the best of both worlds.

A 'barefaced' housing joint is a little more complicated. You still slot the shelf into the upright – but this time you also cut away a step or 'rebate' across the end of the shelf to form a sort of tongue (with one 'bare face'). So the housing into which it fits has to be correspondingly narrower than the shelf thickness. This type of joint is used at corners, where you can't cut an ordinary housing; and its stepped shape helps to keep the structure rigid. It can also be used with the rebate in the upright where you want unbroken woodgrain across the top surface of the horizontal.

Strongest of all is the dovetail housing joint. For this one, the housing has sloping (undercut) sides, and the end of the shelf is shaped to fit – which means it can't be pulled out sideways. This is an attraction where you expect furniture to come in for rough treatment, (eg, being dragged across the floor). However, it's tricky to cut without power-tool assistance, and in practice the do-it-yourselfer will seldom find it really necessary.

It's worth saying here that even the best-made housing joint is only as strong as the shelf. If you're planning shelf storage, you have to think about what the shelf is made of, its thickness, its length and how much weight you want it to carry. A thin shelf bends easily, and it's unwise to try to span a gap of more than 1,200mm (4ft), at the very most, without some support in the middle. Even then, a full load of books will cause sagging.

Making a housing joint
Even with hand tools, housing joints are among the easiest to cut. For a basic through housing joint, you don't need to touch the shelf at all. You just mark out the position of the housing in the upright, cut down the housing sides with a tenon saw, and pare

away the waste with a chisel and wooden mallet (see pages 54 -57 for details). The only difficulty, as in all carpentry, is to make sure that your marking, sawing and chiselling are always careful and accurate.

A stopped housing takes a little longer to cut, but only because you need to hollow out its stopped end first, to make sawing easier. You may also need to remove a small notch or 'shoulder' from the shelf, which is easily done with a tenon saw and perhaps a chisel too.

For a barefaced housing joint, the housing is cut in the same way as a basic housing. Cutting the rebate in the shelf is another job for tenon saw and chisel.

Using power tools
A power router is an integral tool with a chuck that accepts a wide range of special bits for cutting grooves and mouldings quickly and accurately. It saves a lot of time when making housing joints, and eliminates both sawing and chiselling. Or you can use a circular saw, setting it for a very shallow cut and running it across the upright where you want the housing to be – first clamping on a batten to act as a guide. Because the saw-

BASIC HOUSING JOINT

1 Use your knife and try-square to square a mark across the inner face of the upright where the top of the shelf is to go.

2 Measure up the full shelf thickness with a carpenter's rule or a flexible tape measure. As always, try for absolute accuracy.

3 Mark this distance on the upright, working down from the first line to give the housing width; square the mark across in pencil only.

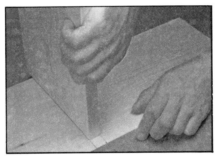

4 Place the shelf between the two lines to check them. If necessary, re-draw the second. When that's right, go over it with knife and try-square.

5 Use a rule to set your marking gauge to ⅓ the thickness of the upright, which is the usual depth of a housing for a strong and rigid joint.

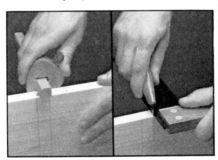

6 With the gauge, mark the housing depth on the upright's edges. Then use a knife to square the marks for the housing sides to depth across the edges.

7 When cutting the sides to depth, cramp on a batten to prevent the saw from wandering sideways.

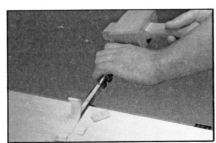

8 Remove the waste with a chisel, working from both ends on long housings. Pare along the sides if necessary to clean them up.

READY REFERENCE

WHICH HOUSING GOES WHERE

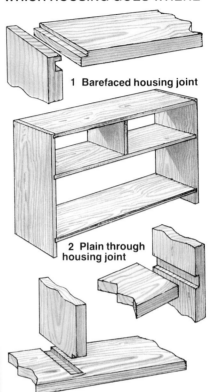

1 Barefaced housing joint

2 Plain through housing joint

3 Stopped housing joint with shoulder

THE TOOLS YOU'LL NEED

A tenon saw: for cutting the sides of housings, rebates and shoulders.
A bevel-edged chisel: the same width as the housing, plus a wooden mallet.
A hand router: is useful for smoothing the bottom of the housing.
Marking gauge, knife, pencil and try-square: for accurate setting-out.

POWER TOOL OPTIONS

A power router: ideal for cutting all types of housing quickly and easily.

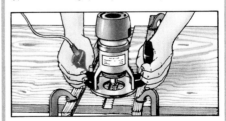

A circular saw will cut an ordinary housing very well – but you'll need to make several passes with it across the timber to cut the housing.

Jem Grischotti

STOPPED HOUSING WITH SHOULDER

1 *After marking out the housing on the upright (except on the front edge), mark where it stops, about 19-25mm (³/₄-1in) inside the front edge.*

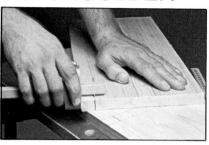

2 *With the marking gauge still at the same setting, mark the shoulder depth across the shelf end and a little way down each of its faces.*

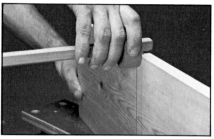

3 *Set the gauge to ¹/₃ the thickness of the upright, and mark the housing depth on its back edge only. Bring the side marks down to meet it.*

4 *Use the same setting to mark the shoulder width on the front edge and both faces of the shelf, meeting the marks you've made for the depth.*

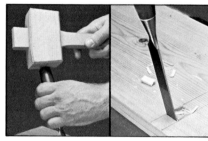

5 *Roughly chisel out the first 25mm (1in) or so of the stopped end of the housing – across the grain and up to the sides, then back towards the end.*

6 *Cut the sides of the housing with a tenon saw. You'll need to use short careful strokes so as not to bang against its inner end.*

7 *Clear out the housing with a mallet and chisel, inching forwards at an angle if the chisel won't reach all the way in when held flat.*

8 *Saw down into the front edge of the shelf until you reach the marked depth of the shoulder, being careful not to overshoot.*

9 *Chisel into the endgrain to remove the waste and complete the shoulder; or you can use a saw – but again, don't cut too deep.*

blade is narrower than the housing you're cutting out, you'll need to make several parallel, overlapping cuts.

Putting it together

When you assemble the joint before gluing, to see if it fits, you may think that it's too tight and you need to pare away wood from the housing or the shelf.

But be sure not to overdo this – and be careful where you remove it from. A shaving off the wrong place can allow the end of the shelf to rise or fall so that it's no longer level.

If, on the other hand, the joint turns out to be very loose, you'll need thin slivers of wood or veneer to pack it out.

For maximum tightness, strength and squareness, a housing joint should really be glued, then cramped together while the adhesive sets. Where a shelf or shelves fit between a pair of uprights, as usually happens, your best plan is to glue and cramp the whole structure up at once, so as to get it all square in one go. Use sash cramps (long bars of steel with two adjustable jaws) and simply place the structure between them, with the shelf running along their length, and blocks of scrap wood positioned on the outside of the uprights to protect them from the pressure of the jaws. You'll probably have to borrow or hire the sash-cramps. When using them, you need to

check the structure constantly for squareness, as cramping, unless done correctly, can cause distortion.

You can always reinforce a housing joint by nailing through the outside of the upright and into the endgrain of the shelf, concealing the heads by punching them in and plugging the holes with wood filler.

On the whole, screws are best avoided, since they grip badly in endgrain; but for a chipboard shelf you can use special chipboard screws – or ordinary wood screws each driven into a special plastic plug, or 'bush', which is pressed into a pre-drilled hole in the end of the shelf. You can disguise screwheads with plastic covers.

BAREFACED HOUSING JOINT

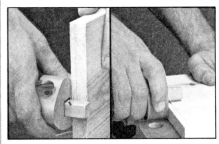

1 At ⅓ the shelf thickness, mark the rebate depth along its end and across its edges; likewise mark across the upright's edges and inner face.

3 Saw out the rebate depth across the shelf with a tenon saw, using careful strokes to keep it the right side of the line.

5 Measure the full shelf thickness and set your marking gauge to that measurement by holding it against the rule.

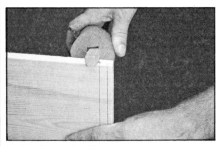

7 Mark the depth of the housing on the back edge of the upright, only ⅓ of the way across: any further and you'll weaken the joint.

2 At ⅓ the upright thickness (very likely the same as the shelf thickness), mark your rebate width across the top face and both edges of the shelf.

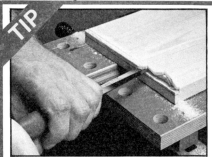

4 Chisel out the rebate width along the endgrain. You'll get a more accurate result if you do it in several goes rather than all at once.

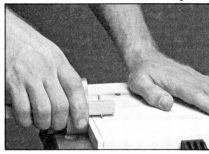

6 Pressing the gauge against the end of the upright, mark across its face and edges where the bottom of the shelf will be positioned.

8 Cut the housing just like the basic one, taking care not to break off the end. After gluing, nail through into the tongue for extra rigidity.

READY REFERENCE

TIPS FOR BETTER HOUSINGS

● a cramped-on batten is useful as a saw guide
● a third saw-cut down the centre of a wide housing will help the removal of waste

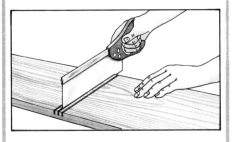

● for short housings in narrow wood, set the piece on edge and chisel vertically for greater accuracy

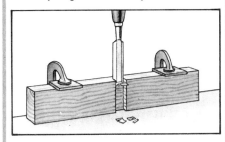

● use a rule or try-square to check that the housing has a level bottom

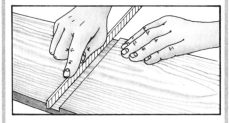

● for pairs of uprights, use the housings in the first to mark out those in the second; this will ensure a level shelf

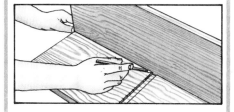

● a chipboard shelf can be secured with chipboard screws driven into special plastic plugs.

Jem Grischotti

MORTISE & TENON JOINTS

Mortise and tenon joints are indispensable if you're making furniture that's both strong and good-looking, and are particularly useful for making the most popular pieces of furniture – tables and chairs.

Take a piece of wood, shape the end to form a 'tongue', then fit the tongue into a matching slot in the side of another piece, and you've made a mortise-and-tenon joint.

The tenon is the tongue and the mortise is the slot, and the joint has proved its usefulness over centuries in all kinds of wooden frameworks because of its strength and resistance to movement. It's the best joint for fixing horizontal pieces of wood – 'rails' – into uprights such as table and chair legs.

Once you've got the knack of cutting it cleanly, you've mastered a joint which will stand you in very good stead. Whenever you're joining two lengths of wood in a T or L shape, and you want something stronger and more elegant than a halving joint, go for a mortise and tenon joint. The only time it won't work is on thin, flat pieces – boards, planks and panels: use housing joints instead.

There are numerous types of mortise-and-tenon joint at your disposal. Think carefully about the job the joint has to do before deciding which to use.

Choosing the right joint

A *through tenon* passes right through the mortise piece (which makes it easier to cut the mortise). Because you can see its endgrain, it's used in rougher work or as a decorative feature. It can also be wedged from the outside for strength and/or visual effect.

A *stub tenon* is one which doesn't pass right through, but fits into a 'blind' mortise – a hole with a bottom. The most familiar kind, especially in furniture, has shoulders all round which conceal the joint.

A *barefaced tenon* has the tenon cut with only one side shoulder instead of two – useful if the tenon piece is already very thin; or the tenon may be reduced in width by having edge shoulders cut in it – see *Ready Reference*.

A *haunched tenon* is a compromise often used at the corner of a frame to keep it from twisting. The haunch – an extra step between the tenon and the piece it projects from – can

be square or sloping. A sloping haunch is hidden and easier to cut – see *Ready Reference* again.

A *double tenon* is just a pair of tenons cut on one piece of wood – used if the piece is very wide and you don't want to cut a single enormous mortise to take one wide tenon.

An *offset tenon* is simply one which isn't in the centre of the tenon piece.

Making the joint

Let's assume you're making a basic stub tenon joint. It doesn't really matter whether you start by making your mortise or your tenon; the important thing is to get them to fit together. However, cutting the tenon first means you can mark off the mortise from it, possibly getting a better fit. This is easier than the other way round. Either way, play safe by making the tenon a little too large (or the mortise a little too small), rather than the reverse. You can always cut off a bit more.

Marking and cutting the tenon

Begin by scoring round the tenon piece with a knife and try-square to mark the length of the tenon, using the width of the mortise piece as a guide. A through tenon should be a little bit over-long to allow for planing it flush to give a neat finish; a stub tenon should go about halfway through, and be about 3mm (⅛in) shorter than the mortise to leave room for any excess adhesive.

A mortise gauge is very useful for the next stage. Choose a mortise chisel which has a blade about one third the thickness of the tenon piece (under rather than over, though you can use a wider one if the tenon piece is

READY REFERENCE

WHICH JOINT IS WHICH

A through tenon goes right through the mortise piece. A **stub tenon,** on the other hand, fits into a stopped mortise. Either sort can have shoulders cut away on one, two or three sides to form a **barefaced tenon.**

The idea of a **haunched tenon** – with either a square or sloping haunch – is to help prevent the pieces from twisting in relation to each other.

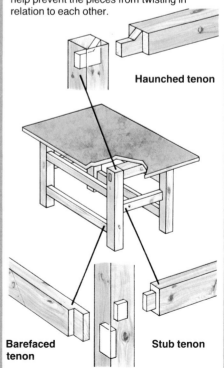

Haunched tenon

Barefaced tenon

Stub tenon

MARKING THE TENON

1 *Lay the mortise piece on the tenon piece and mark where the tenon starts. Leave a through tenon over-long, as shown, for later trimming.*

2 *If you're making a stub tenon, it'll be easier to mark the tenon length if you lay the tenon piece on top of the mortise.*

3 *Square the mark round all four sides of the tenon piece by scoring across them with your marking knife against a try-square.*

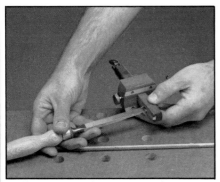

4 *Set your mortise gauge to the exact blade width of your mortise chisel, or to the diameter of your drill auger bit if you have one available.*

5 *Use the gauge to score out the tenon width down the sides and across the end of the piece, stopping at the length marks you have already made.*

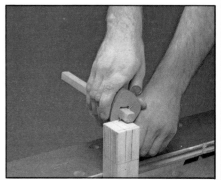

6 *If you are cutting edge shoulders as well, use an ordinary marking gauge to score lines the other way for each of the shoulders in turn.*

Jem Grischotti

much thinner than the mortise piece), and set the gauge's twin spurs that distance apart. Then set the stock so as to place the resulting 'tramlines' in the centre of the timber thickness – unless you're deliberately off-setting the tenon – and try it from both sides, adjusting the position of the stock till the two sets of tramlines coincide.

Now you can score the edges and end of the tenon piece to mark where the tenon will be cut. If you don't have a mortise gauge, use an ordinary single-spur marking gauge and mark the tramlines separately.

For a straight tenon, that's all the marking-up you need. If you're cutting shoulders in the width as well, set a marking gauge to one sixth the width of the tenon piece and mark down both faces and across the tramlines on the end.

If you're including a haunch, use the gauge to mark its width across the end and down the faces; then mark its depth with a knife and try-square. For maximum strength, the haunch should be not more than one third the tenon's width, and its depth not

more than one quarter the length (or 12mm/½in long, whichever is smaller). We will be dealing with these joints in more detail in another section.

To cut a tenon you need, not surprisingly, a tenon saw. All you have to do is grip the piece upright in a vice and saw down each side of the tenon; then lay the wood flat and saw off the shoulders. The vital thing is always to keep your saw-cuts on the waste side of the lines.

Marking and cutting the mortise
At this stage, you can lay the tenon on the mortise piece and mark the mortise length on it. Then score its width with the gauge.

To cut the mortise, cramp the timber in position. If working near the end of a piece, leave extra length – a 'horn' which you saw off later – to prevent the wood from splitting as you chisel into it. If you have a carpenter's brace or a power drill, you can start by drilling holes close together along the length of the mortise. Make quite sure you keep the drill vertical – a drill stand will help.

Then chop and lever out the waste with the mortise chisel, and cut the recess for any haunch. Lastly, clean off the sides and ends with a bevel-edged chisel.

If you have no drill, use a mortise chisel by itself, keeping the bevel away from you and working from the centre of the mortise towards the ends – stopping just short of them so as not to bruise them when you lever out the waste before going deeper. On a through mortise, chisel halfway and then work from the other side. Clean up with a bevel-edged chisel.

Assembling the joint
Now you can fit the pieces together. Don't be tempted to force them, or you may split the wood; if the joint is impossibly tight, carefully shave the tenon with a chisel and glass-paper checking all the time. When it's a neat, close fit, glue it, cramp it and leave it to set.

Ideally, you need sash cramps – long steel bars with one fixed head and another which you tighten (see pages 80-83 for more details) – plus scrap wood to protect the work.

CUTTING THE TENON

1 *After marking off the waste areas, clamp the piece upright and start to cut the tenon. Be sure to keep the saw on the waste side of the lines.*

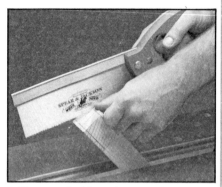

2 *You may find it easier to work accurately if you clamp the piece in the vice at an angle of about 45° while you saw down for the next few strokes.*

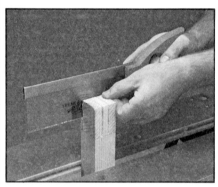

3 *Finish off the cut with the piece upright again. It's easy to overshoot when sawing along the grain, so be careful as you approach the depth marks.*

4 *Make identical cuts along the grain, down to the same depth marks, for each of the edge shoulders if you have marked any.*

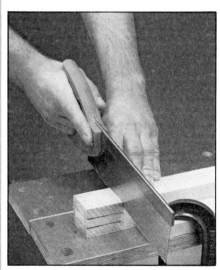

5 *Firmly hold or clamp the piece down flat on the workbench as you cut away each of the tenon's face shoulders by sawing across the grain.*

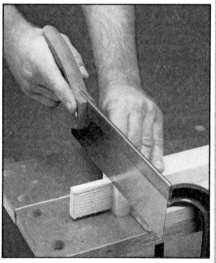

6 *Lastly, turn the piece over on to its side and make similar cross-cuts to remove the edge shoulders, if any are included. This completes the tenon.*

READY REFERENCE

STRENGTHENING THE JOINT

For extra strength and decorative possibilities, consider wedging or pegging the joint once it's fitted. Hardwood wedges go either into previously made saw-cuts in the end of a through tenon (A), or into the mortise above and below it (B). The mortise needs to be slightly tapered. Pegging is done with one or more dowels inserted into holes drilled sideways through the joint.

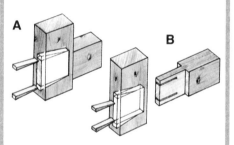

TIPS FOR BETTER JOINTS

● a through tenon should be cut too long, and made flush once the joint is assembled
● some people find it easier to start cutting the tenon while holding the piece upright, then to re-position the wood and saw at 45°, and to finish off with it upright again
● set your mortise gauge from the exact width of your mortise chisel
● if mortising near the end of your timber, leave it over-long to prevent splitting, and cut off the extra bit later
● to keep drill or chisel vertical, stand a try-square on end beside the tool as you're working

● leave it till last to pare down the mortise ends, so as not to risk bruising them while levering out the bulk of the waste
● to stop yourself drilling too deep when starting a mortise, fit a depth stop (an item you can buy) or wrap masking tape round the bit as a depth indicator.

Jem Grischotti

MARKING AND DRILLING THE MORTISE

1 If you're working near the end of the mortise piece, mark off a short length or 'horn' as waste, for removal once the joint is assembled.

2 Lay the tenon on the mortise piece, allowing for any horn, and mark there the tenon's width.

3 Square these two length marks across the inner side of the mortise piece.

4 With the gauge at its existing setting, score down the mortise piece, between the last two marks, to give the mortise's width.

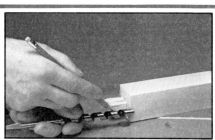

5 For a stub mortise-and-tenon joint, mark out the tenon length on your drill bit, if you have a bit of the right diameter.

6 Drill holes to remove the bulk of the mortise. For a stub joint the tape at the mark on the bit warns of the depth.

CHISELLING OUT THE MORTISE

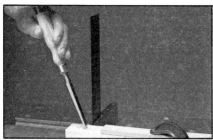

1 Instead of drilling, you can chop and lever out the waste with a mortise chisel, starting halfway down the length of the mortise.

2 Work along to its ends as you chisel deeper. For a through mortise, chop halfway through, then work from the other side of the piece.

3 For a stub mortise and tenon joint it pays to mark off the length of the tenon on the chisel as a depth guide, just as you would for a drill bit.

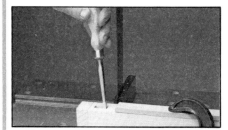

4 Then you can wind sticky tape round it next to the mark, again as a depth indicator, for use when you chisel out the bottom of the mortise.

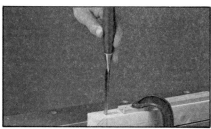

5 After removing most of the waste, use a bevel-edged chisel to pare down each end of the mortise, shaving off any irregularities.

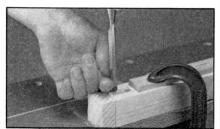

6 Work on the sides likewise. As you're cutting along the grain, you'll need greater care, to avoid splitting out more wood than you want.

ASSEMBLING THE JOINT

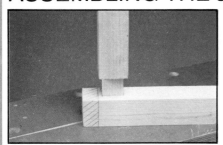

1 Try the pieces together to see if they fit – but without forcing the tenon all the way in. Carefully sand or pare away as needed.

2 A through joint can be strengthened with small wedges cut from scrap hardwood and inserted in or next to the tenon after assembly.

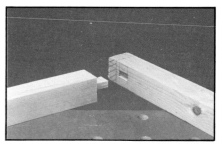

3 A stub joint will need to be glued, and cramped. If working at a corner, leave the horn on until this is done.

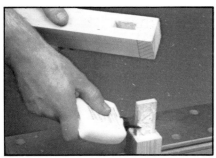

4 For either type, start by spreading adhesive all over the tenon and shoulders. Use a wet rag to wipe off any excess after assembly.

5 Once the through tenon is fully home, insert any wedges you are using and drive them carefully into place with a wooden mallet.

6 To get wedges tight, you'll probably need a piece of scrap wood to help drive them fully home past the projecting end of the tenon.

7 Saw off the excess length of the tenon and any wedges so that they're almost flush with the surface of the mortise piece.

8 Lastly, turn the assembly round and complete the operation by planing across the end of the joint to give it a smooth finish.

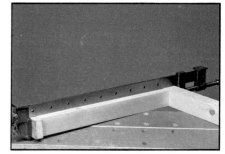

9 A wedged joint can now be left alone while it sets, but any other (whether it's through or stub) will need cramping during this stage.

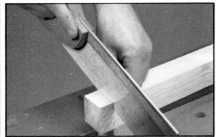

10 After the adhesive has set, saw off any horn that you may have been leaving at the end of the mortise piece while making the joint.

11 Now plane the end you've just sawn, to get it smooth. Work inwards, as shown, to avoid splitting from the mortise piece.

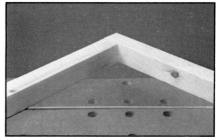

12 The finished mortise-and-tenon joint is both strong and neat. A corner version is shown here, but a T shape is equally possible.

MAKING DOVETAIL JOINTS

Dovetail joints are not only beautiful, they're very strong. Once you know the right way to cut them, it only takes practice to get a good fit every time.

Most pieces of wooden furniture are built as either frames or boxes. The mortise and tenon, as the principal framing joint, is common in chairs and tables. But in box construction the dovetail has traditionally reigned supreme.

True, modern storage furniture often uses screws, dowels, assembly fittings, and edge joints cut with power tools. But you only have to look at a set of dovetails to see that they make the perfect corner joint between flat timbers such as box sides – including the top and side panels of furniture 'carcases'.

In fact, dovetails are impossible to pull apart. That's why they're found joining drawer sides to drawer fronts and sometimes backs. Every time you open a drawer, you're trying to pull the front off – and the dovetail joint withstands this tendency as no other joint can. Note, however, that it only locks in one direction. If you use it the wrong way round where its strength matters, its unique properties are wasted.

There's one other major point to remember Chipboard is far too weak a material in which to cut dovetails – although, at a pinch, they'll work in plywood and good-quality blockboard.

The dovetail joint is always admired and even respected. But there's really no mystery about it. While no one could pretend that well-fitting dovetails are easy for a beginner to cut, the only secret of success is practice; and you'll find things go a lot more smoothly if you stick closely to the time-tested procedure described here.

Anatomy of a dovetail joint

Dovetails themselves are fan-shaped cutouts in the end of one of the pieces being joined – fan-shaped, that is, when you look at the face of the piece.

The sides of each tail slope along the grain at an angle of between 1 in 5 (for a 'coarse' but strong joint, suitable for softwood and man-made boards) and 1 in 8 (generally considered the best-looking, and usually used with hardwoods). If you make them any coarser, they may break; any finer, and they may tend to slip out under strain.

Between the tails, when the joint is assembled, you can see the 'pins' cut in the other piece. These, of course, follow exactly the same slope or 'rake' as the tails – but across the endgrain, so you can only see their true shape when looking at them end-on. Note that there's always a pin at either end; this helps to secure both pieces against curling up.

The spacing of the tails is another factor in the joint's appearance. In general, the wider they are (and therefore the further apart the pins·are) the better – but this too affects the strength if you overdo it.

Marking out the tails

The first step in making a dovetail joint is to get the ends of both pieces square (they needn't be the same thickness). Particularly if it's your first attempt, you may find it wise to leave a little extra length as well – say a millimetre or two.

After that, it's customary to start with the tail piece (which is the side, not the front, in the case of a drawer). First decide on the slope of your dovetails – say 1 in 6 – and mark it out on a scrap of wood or paper. That's just a matter of drawing two lines at right angles to each other, then making a mark six units along one, and another mark one unit up the other. Join up the marks with a diagonal, and set a sliding bevel to the same slope.

Now you need to work out where each tail should come. However, there's no need for fiddly calculations. First decide the width of

READY REFERENCE

WHAT IS A DOVETAIL JOINT?

A dovetail joint consists of 'tails' on one piece and 'pins' on the other. When they're fitted together, the joint is completely inseparable in one direction (shown by an arrow). It's very strong the other way too.

The contrast between endgrain and face grain (especially if the two pieces are of different woods) can also make an attractive decorative feature.

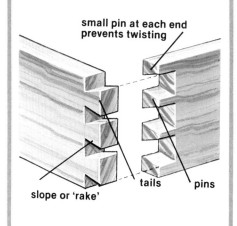

small pin at each end prevents twisting

slope or 'rake'   tails   pins

MARKING OUT THE TAILS

1 Plane both pieces to exactly the same width, and check that the ends are dead square. Correct with a block plane if necessary.

2 Square the end pins' width along the tail piece, then slant a measure between the lines to give handy divisions for the pin centres.

3 Use a gauge to extend these centre marks from the slanting line down to the end of the piece, where the tails will be cut.

4 Make another mark 3mm (¹⁄₈in) either side of each centre mark. This will give you the widths of the tails at their widest.

5 Set a sharp marking gauge, or preferably a cutting gauge, to the exact thickness of the pin piece or a bit more – but no less.

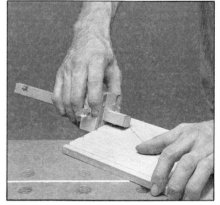

6 Score a neat line all round the end of the tail piece with the gauge. It's usual to leave this visible in the finished joint.

7 Set a sliding bevel (or make a card template) to a slope of 1 in 6 – ie, six units in one direction and one unit in the other direction.

8 Use the bevel or template to mark out the slope of the tails, working inwards from the marks which denote the tail widths.

9 Square the width marks across the end of the piece, then mark the slope again on the far side with the bevel or template.

TYPES OF DOVETAIL JOINT

Coarse and fine dovetails
For general work, tails and pins are equally spaced and steeply raked (below left) – unlike fine work (below right).

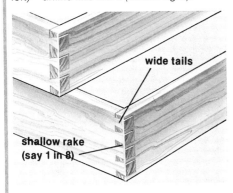

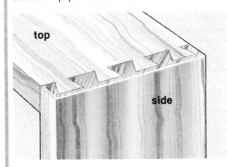

Carcase dovetails
A coarse dovetail joint traditionally joins sides to top on solid timber cabinets. An added top panel hides it.

Lap dovetails
Concealed by an overlap, unlike through dovetails (shown in Ready Reference*), these are traditional in drawers.*

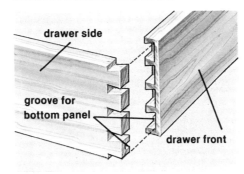

Framing dovetails
A large dovetail can provide useful strength in a frame where its locking properties are especially vital.

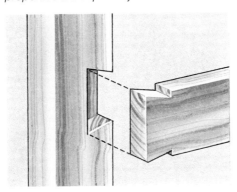

Dovetail housings
The dovetail housing is the odd man out – it's not a corner joint. The tail runs across the width.

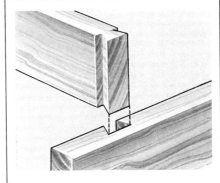

Cut like other housing joints (see Housing joints, pages 62 -65), it can be plain (above) or barefaced (below). The latter will usually do.

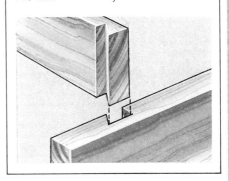

---

the pin at each end, and square that along the grain. Then place a tape measure diagonally between the squared lines, and swing it round to give a figure easily divisible into equal parts. Mark off these equal divisions, and square them along to the end of the piece. These are the centres of the gaps between your tails.

Then make a mark 3mm (⅛in) either side of each centre mark, and draw a line sloping inwards from it along the face – using the sliding bevel as your guide. Square these marks across the end, and then repeat them on the other face.

Lastly, set a marking or cutting gauge to the exact thickness of the pin piece, and scribe a line all round the end of the tail piece. If you've been allowing for extra length, add that to the scribed thickness. This will make the tails slightly too long; when the joint is complete, trim them flush with a block plane.

At this stage, a very wise precaution is to hatch in – or mark with an X – all the bits you're going to cut out.

Cutting the tails and pins
The next essential is to have the right saw. An ordinary tenon saw is too heavy; you need the lighter version actually known as a dovetail saw, or the still finer gent's saw. But even one of these, especially if new, will have too much 'set' – the teeth will project too far sideways, giving too wide and inaccurate a cut. You can remedy this by placing the blade on an oilstone, flat on its side, and very lightly rubbing it along. Do this once or twice for each side.

To make your cuts, cramp the tail piece in a vice. (If making, say, two identical sides for a box, you can cut more than one piece at the same time.) Align the timber so that one set of sloping marked lines is vertical. Cut along all these, one after the other, before tilting the piece the other way and cutting those on the opposite slope.

Saw immediately on the outside of each marked line, and begin each cut with the saw angled backwards, steadying its blade with your thumbnail. Once you've got the cut

established, tilt the saw forwards to make sure you're keeping to the line on the other side. Lastly, level the saw up as you finish the cut. Whatever you do, don't cut down past the gauged line!

The next step is to use your gauge to mark the thickness of the tail piece in turn on the pin piece.

A neat trick follows. Hold the pin piece in a vice, and cramp the tail piece over its end in exactly the intended position. Then, inserting the saw in the cuts you've just made, use it to score corresponding marks on the endgrain of the pin piece. Square these across its faces.

At this point you can remove the waste from between the tails. Begin by sawing out the little piece next to each of the two outer tails; then use a chisel. (Some people like to get the bulk of the waste out with a coping saw first.) Drive the chisel down into the face each time, keeping well in front of the gauge line, then tap the blade into the endgrain to get the chips up and out. Turn the piece over and do the same on the other side.

CUTTING THE TAILS

1 Cramp the tail piece at an angle, so that each set of sloping marks is vertical in turn. This makes it easier to saw straight.

2 Use a dovetail saw or at least a small tenon saw. Rub it on an oilstone (once or twice for each side) to reduce the 'set' and so give a fine cut.

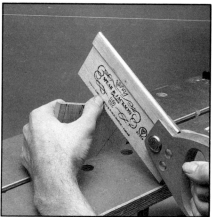

3 Place the saw exactly on the waste side of the line, steadying it with your thumbnail; begin the cut with it slanted back towards you.

4 After a few strokes, slant it forwards. Check you're cutting straight on both sides. Level up to finish – and don't cut too far.

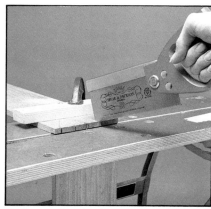

5 Cramp the pin piece upright, cramp the tail piece over it, place the saw sideways in the cuts and score the pin piece with it.

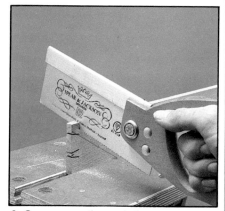

6 Saw across the grain to remove the small waste piece next to each of the two outer tails. Again, keep the saw outside the gauge line.

7 Between each tail, chop about halfway through, well outside the gauge line. Then tap the chisel in from the end, flicking out the waste.

8 Turn the piece over and do the same again. Then work back towards the gauge line on each side, with the chisel slanted inwards.

9 Finish by paring exactly to the line on each side – though you can still slant the chisel to 'undercut' for an easier fit.

COMPLETING THE JOINT

1 With your gauge at the exact thickness of the tail piece or a little more, scribe a line all round the end of the pin piece.

2 Square along from this gauged line, on each side, to the ends of the slanting lines you've scored across the endgrain with the saw.

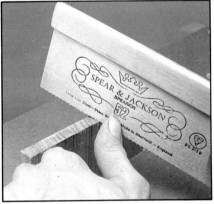

3 Make all the saw cuts at one angle first, then those at the other – their edges exactly on the outsides of the lines, as before.

4 After chiselling out the waste between the pins as for the tails, pare down the inside edge of each tail a little, for a smooth fit.

5 Fit the joint together halfway (but no further), keeping the pieces square to each other. Note any places where it sticks.

6 Holding the chisel blade, carefully shave where needed. Glue and cramp the joint, and plane the endgrain flush if necessary.

Lastly, place the chisel against (not over) the gauge line and pare away the rest. It's sensible to angle the tool inwards from each side, so that you actually 'undercut' – ie, cut beyond the line, but only inside the timber where it won't be seen. This helps to ensure the joint goes all the way home.

Saw out the pins as you did the tails. Again, the crucial thing is to cut immediately on the waste side – so that the outer edge of the saw teeth touches the line. If anything this is even more important now, at the pin stage, because you won't be able to make any further adjustments if the pins are loose between the tails.

Lastly, chisel out the gaps between the pins. Here too the procedure is similar to that for the tails.

Putting it together

Before you try assembling the joint, pare away any remaining unevenness which might make things difficult – being quite sure not to overdo it. You can even carefully shave the inside edge off both sides of each tail (especially the outer ones). This will be hidden after assembly.

Now comes the nerve-racking part: fitting the pieces together. At first, don't attempt to force them more than halfway, because dovetails fitted more than once become slack. See how well they go home, separate them, and make further adjustments with a chisel.

Then put some adhesive between the pins, and tap the tails right in. That's it. If it's a good joint, congratulations. If not, your next will be better, and the one after that better still – as long as you rely on sharp tools and gentle, accurate cutting. Hurry and force will only cause imprecision and heartbreak.

Lap dovetails

'Through dovetails', described above, can be seen from both sides. They look fine in most circumstances – especially since the modern tendency is to make a feature of them, using them in preference to hidden versions.

However, there is one variant worth knowing. In 'lap dovetails', only part of the endgrain on the pin piece is cut away to form pins; the rest (say one-third of the thickness) is left to overlap and thus hide the endgrain of the tails. For this reason, lap dovetails are traditional in fitting drawer-fronts.

When marking them out, you have to remember not to score a gauge line round the outside of the pin piece, and to allow for the lap thickness when gauging for the tails and pins. Cutting the pins is likewise a bit more difficult. However, mastery of through dovetails will give you the confidence to tackle lap dovetails, and thus expand your range of techniques still further.

SHAPING WOOD AND BOARDS

There's more to woodwork than straight lines. Even everyday jobs often call for accurate curves. Here are the methods for marking them, and the tools and techniques for cutting them.

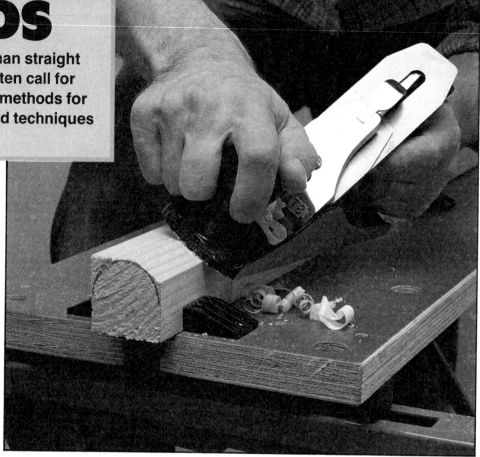

When tackling carpentry jobs, people tend to think in straight lines and angular shapes. This is partly because you buy wood off the shelf in straight lengths – and, of course, that's often how it's needed. It also results partly from modern attitudes to design.

However, it's not the whole story. Curves are often a practical necessity – for example, when you're cutting panelling to fit round skirting boards. And, of course, they can be most attractive. If you leave curves out of account when designing furniture and fitments, your work can begin to look unnecessarily stark. You can buy curved mouldings, but you may well want shapes which these can't provide, or to put curved edges on flat boards – whether solid or man-made.

Marking out

Before you cut shapes, you'll usually need to mark them out. This needs a bit of thought.

If you're scribing round an obstacle such as a skirting board or pipe, the problem takes care of itself. But if you're using a shape of your own devising, there's no reason why you shouldn't draw it freehand. If you draw it onto thin, stiff card, rather than directly onto the work, and cut it out with a sharp knife, you can use this template to reproduce the shape any number of times.

A symmetrical shape (one which is identical on either side of a centre line) is very difficult to draw out accurately. Instead, make half a template, with a straight side corresponding to the shape's centre line. Draw this centre line on the workpiece, and use it to position the template. Then draw round one side, flip the template over, and draw round the other to create a perfect mirror image.

When using templates, bear in mind that the line you draw round the edge is unlikely to be quite accurate. When cutting, allow a margin of error for smoothing down to the exact shape afterwards while checking against the template.

The shape you want may well be a circle or part of a circle. For small, non-critical jobs such as rounding corners (especially where you need an exact quarter- or half-circle), you can always draw round something of the right

size – say a coin or a plate. But on the whole the best method is to use a pair of compasses. The trouble is that, unless you have a large 'beam compass', the maximum radius of the instrument may be too small for the curve you want.

In that case, you can improvise. One option is to use a length of string, tied to a round nail or panel pin tapped in at the centre of the intended circle, with a pencil tied to the other end. This is simple, but its snags are that it can be difficult to set to an exact radius, that the string tends to wind round the nail, the pencil or both, and that you may have trouble keeping the string taut and the pencil vertical.

The second possibility is to use a timber slat with two small holes drilled in it, distant from each other by the radius of the circle you want. You drive your nail or pin through one, and insert the pencil point through the other. This works well enough, except that the pencil lead tends to break.

Cutting shapes in plan

There are two types of curve: simple and compound. Compound curves – such as you might find on a shaped chair leg – go in two directions at once, and so require shaping which is more complex than just cutting.

Simple curves go in one direction only. However, this can be either 'in plan' (looking from above) or 'in section' (looking end-on or sideways). If you cut a circle from a piece of plywood, that's in plan. If, instead, you round over the board's edges, you're changing the section. If you take, say, a timber floorboard, and cut bits out so it fits round pipes, you're working in plan. But if you make a tongue or groove along one edge, you're modifying the section. This distinction is important because the tools and techniques you use vary in each case.

Shapes cut from flat boards – that is, in plan – usually demonstrate simple curves at their most straightforward. Unless you own a bandsaw, they're generally best made with a powered jigsaw (see pages 42 -44).

There's no special knack to using this tool. You just have to make sure you've fitted the appropriate blade for the material and finish (finer teeth give finer cuts), and that it's long enough to cut right through the material. You'll need a special narrow 'scroll-cutting blade' to get round very tight curves – of less than, say, 25mm (1in) radius.

Where the shape is a cut-out, so that you can't start the cut from the edge of the material, drill a hole first (well to the waste side of

MAKING A CUT-OUT

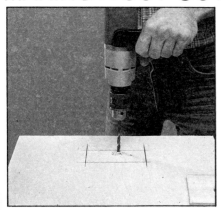

1 Mark the shape accurately and drill a hole inside the line, using a bit whose diameter is greater than the width of your jigsaw blade.

2 Insert the jigsaw (or padsaw) blade, press the switch and start cutting. For square corners, continue right to the end of the marked line.

3 Then draw the saw back and turn the corner. Do this all round, then reverse it and remove the waste piece from each corner.

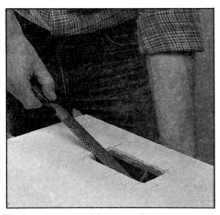

4 A rasp is good for rounding over edges, especially where you can't get a plane in. Lift the tool up between forward strokes.

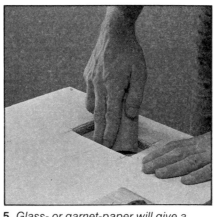

5 Glass- or garnet-paper will give a smooth finish after rough shaping. Use a coarse or medium grade first, then a fine grade for finishing.

TIP

6 A file, whose teeth are finer than those of a rasp, will give a smooth finish to corners where sanding proves to be too clumsy.

SHAPING CONVEX EDGES

1 In the absence of a jigsaw, an ordinary panel or crosscut saw will do fine. Make a straight cut that just touches your marked line.

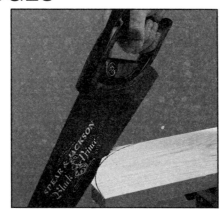

2 Make similar cuts as necessary to create shallow corners all along the length of the curve – rounding it as much as possible.

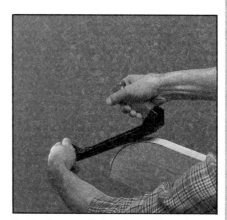

3 Finally smooth the shape down to the exact profile. A Surform (provided the blade is in good condition) will do this very efficiently.

your marked line) and insert the blade through it to begin the cut.

A coping saw (see pages 10 -11), with its narrow, swivelling blade, is the traditional way of cutting out flat shapes. Unlike the jigsaw, it will only work up to a certain distance in from the edge – determined by the distance from its blade to the back of its frame. A fretsaw, lighter in construction but otherwise similar, is deeper in this dimension and so will cut further from the board edge.

A coping saw, too, is only useful on thin timber and boards. If the material is much over 12mm (½in) thick, you'll find that the narrow blade makes for very slow going ... and frequent breakages.

If no jigsaw, coping saw or fretsaw is available, you can often obtain just as good a result – on convex curves at the edge of the workpiece only – in another way. First use a tenon, panel or circular saw to make successive cuts which take the shape as near to the curve as possible (on small pieces, a chisel will do the job just as well – an action known as 'paring'). Then round it off to the exact profile with a Surform or rasp (see pages 20 -21), and finish with abrasive paper. Use a coarse grade of paper first, to get the right shape, then a finer one for finishing off. A drum sander will give even quicker results.

This method is also handy when the material is too thick for one of the specialised saws anyway. But, if you need a concave shape, you'll have to look further. The answer may be to make a number of parallel cuts inwards as far as your marked line, using an ordinary saw, before carefully taking the waste out with a chisel.

This will leave you with a fairly rough finish. Neither a bench plane nor a Surform (unless it be the cylindrical type) will work on concave surfaces, so you need another tool. This can either be a half-round rasp, followed by a half-round file for smoothing, or else a tool called a spokeshave. This is a type of plane, with a handle at either side, and a very short heel-to-toe length which means it can effectively take smooth shavings off all but the tightest curves.

Changing the section

At its simplest, working in section is just a matter of chamfering edges and rounding them over. The former can, of course, be done with a plane. You can often do the latter with abrasive paper, provided you don't want too much of a curve.

If you do, it's back to the plane. Here again, you start by making more and more flat surfaces. In other words, plane off a square corner to make two flatter corners; then plane off each of those to make two still flatter ones; and so on. This way you can obtain an almost perfect curve, to which you can easily give a final rounding with abrasives.

Obviously, you'll be relying mainly on your eye to achieve smoothness and evenness along the length of the piece. But it's wise to check the uniformity of the result with a card template, cut to the exact profile you need and fitted over the piece. If there are gaps between the template and the material, you know you have more shaping to do.

There will be times – for example, if you're rounding over the edges of a cut-out section – when you can't get a plane into the space available. Here the answer is a rasp, which is far more manoeuvrable and removes material quickly, plus a file (with its finer teeth) for finishing. See pages 20 -21 for more information on these tools.

Making concave curves in section is a practical impossibility without a power router or sepcialised hand plane – though small lengths might be tackled with a gouge (see pages 22 -23).

Compound curves

Naturally enough, the techniques for making compound curves combine those for making curves in plan with those for shaping sections.

The simplest compound curve is just a matter of rounding over an already curved edge. Again, you can sometimes use abrasive paper alone for this, with a file coming in handy for awkward corners. But to remove substantial amounts you'll need a rasp or Surform.

Concave shapes present more problems. The inside of a bowl, for example, has a concave curve in both directions. Unless you have a lathe, the only way to work such a shape is with a gouge.

A shape which is concave in only one direction, and convex in the other (like, say, the waist of an hourglass), is easier, because you can use a half-round rasp or a cylindrical Surform. If the concave curve is especially deep, you may need to go back to the trick of making parallel saw cuts and chiselling out the waste – but this time working in two successive directions. This will give you two concave surfaces at an angle to each other. To make a rounded shape, you need only remove the corner with a half-round rasp, cylindrical Surform, or spokeshave.

However, if you're working any compound curve over a considerable distance, neither a rasp nor probably a Surform will give you the clean action you need for a smooth, accurate finish. Especially on shapes which are partly concave, your only option is the specialised tool for the purpose – namely the spokeshave.

Even a power router (to be dealt with in other sections) may not be equal to the job. As in all shaping work, the only really essential requirements are a good eye, a steady hand and a bit of practice.

MAKING COMPOUND CURVES

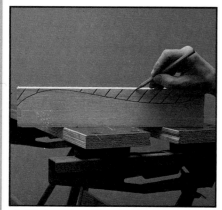

1 First mark out the shape on one surface, and cut it out. A small bandsaw (see pages 42 -43) is the ideal tool for this job.

2 Then, using the available flat surface, mark out the same curve again – but this time at right angles to the one you've just cut.

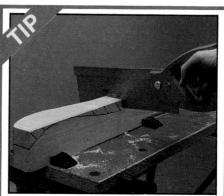

3 Without a bandsaw, you can tackle the curve (especially if it's concave) by first making a series of saw cuts in as far as the line.

ROUNDING IN SECTION

1 Mark on the end of the piece the shape you want, then plane it to make two or three flat edges which approach that intended curve.

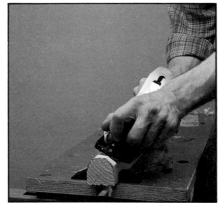

2 Next, remove the corners between these surfaces, again with a smoothing or jack plane, to create a series of even flatter angles.

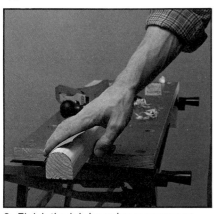

3 Finish the job by using a coarse or medium abrasive paper to round off all the remaining angles and give a smooth curve.

4 Test the result with a piece of card in which you've cut out the profile, and make adjustments with a plane and glasspaper.

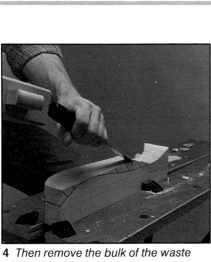

4 Then remove the bulk of the waste with a chisel – always cutting 'downhill' to avoid digging into the timber by accident.

5 A curved angle will remain between the two cuts. Round this over with a spokeshave and then glasspaper for a true compound curve.

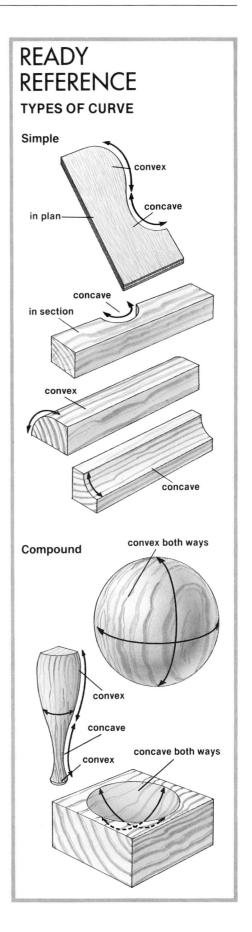

READY REFERENCE

TYPES OF CURVE

Simple

convex

concave

in plan

concave

in section

convex

convex

concave

Compound

convex both ways

convex

concave

convex

concave both ways

GLUING AND CRAMPING WOOD

Assembly is one of the most important techniques in carpentry. In fact, you need to know how you're going to put each job together even before you make the parts.

If you want a timber joint that's permanent, rigid and invisible, glue it together. True, furniture can often incorporate screws and assembly fittings in all their different varieties. But these may obstruct clean lines or free access, and lack strength. In such circumstances you need adhesives.

Even decorative and semi-decorative items which don't have to bear much load – such as beading and architraves – may still need to be glued as well as nailed or pinned. But it's free-standing wooden objects – chairs, tables, sideboards – which especially need glued joints to help them resist the stresses they suffer from all directions. A dining-chair, for example, will be dragged across the floor forwards, backwards and sideways, sat on, stood on, leant on, tipped back and lounged in, so that the legs, back and seat joints are forced apart.

However, although modern adhesives are often stronger than the timber they join, you can't expect them to do all the work. You'll always get more strength from cutting a proper joint, as well as gluing it, than from just butting two pieces of wood together with adhesive in between. The point to remember when designing glued joints is that the larger the area the glue is spread over, the better it will hold.

Likewise, you can't fall back on adhesives to make good a joint which you haven't cut to a tight fit – although some adhesives do have the ability to fill smallish gaps.

Modern industrial adhesives come in a great many formulations and have many different properties, but two types – PVA and urea-formaldehyde (UF) – take care of most do-it-yourself needs. Broadly speaking PVA is used for timber indoors and UF for timber outdoors.

Cramping

Cramping (another word for clamping) goes hand–in–hand with gluing. Unless the joint is nailed, pinned or screwed as well, you'll need something to hold the structure together until the adhesive hardens. Nails or pins driven in halfway and later removed are a simple form of cramp. So are heavy weights; but you often need greater

pressure than these can provide, and to be able to exert it in two or three different directions at once (for example, along the length and across the width of a box). Here, G-cramps will be adequate for most small jobs and sash cramps for most large jobs but in unusual situations, you may have to improvise and use whatever arrangement seems to grip most firmly.

There are at least two approaches to the problem of holding together a square or rectangular framework if sash cramps aren't available. One is the mitre cramp (see pages 56 -57 for details). This consists of four blocks, each with a right-angled notch cut in it, which fit over the corners and have a cord passing through them to pull the frame together. The other method is to use wedges. For example, place the frame between two parallel battens, each firmly fixed, and drive in pairs of wedges to

tighten it up against them. Alternatively, fit a second frame over the one you're assembling, and use wedges between the two.

Working in stages

In order to ensure the squareness of a frame, such as a window-frame, or a box, such as a freestanding cupboard made from panels, you'll need to glue and cramp the whole thing in one operation. Sometimes, however, you'll be able to glue components or sub-assemblies (individual frames or boxes) separately and join them together later.

A chair, for example, often consists of two identical side-frames, joined to each other with cross-rails at front and back. Each frame would comprise two uprights (the front and back legs), and two connecting rails – one at seat height and the other at calf height.

The best way to work would be to glue them and leave them to set completely. Then take both frames, insert the cross-rails and glue and cramp this bigger assembly in the same way. To break the job down methodically into steps like this is far more sensible than trying to assemble the whole chair in one go. If you try to do so, you'll give yourself a lot of trouble, because you'll be working in at least two directions at once. However, as furniture is three-dimensional, awkward assembly procedures are sometimes unavoidable.

Often you'll need to sand and perhaps stain certain components before assembly, since it may be impossible afterwards (as, for example, with the inside of a box).

Successful assembly

When gluing, the secret is to have everything ready beforehand. First you should knock the structure together 'dry' (unglued) and make quite sure it all fits. (Tight joints shouldn't be forced all the way home at this stage.) Lay all the cramps you need in position, adjusted to size, with enough spare room to insert whatever you're glueing. Have a wooden mallet handy to tap pieces gently into position if necessary. Be clear about the order of assembly, so that you won't be left with a part that you can't insert into what you've already glued. Once the adhesive is applied and starting to set, you'll have no time for last-minute searches for protective blocks or a wet rag to mop up excess adhesive.

You need only coat one surface, unless you're using a contact adhesive, but do it thoroughly. When you've finished, leave everything to set in a place where no one will move it, knock it or kick it. In cold weather, wood adhesives take longer to set, so make sure the environment is warm too.

THE GOLDEN RULES

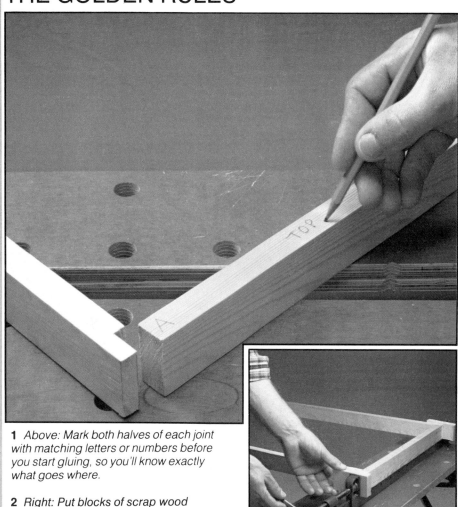

1 *Above: Mark both halves of each joint with matching letters or numbers before you start gluing, so you'll know exactly what goes where.*

2 *Right: Put blocks of scrap wood between the jaws of the cramps and whatever you're assembling. That way you can't damage its surface.*

3 *Arrange cramps so that joints are tight and square. With box structures, long protecting blocks cramped at both ends spread the pressure evenly.*

4 *Check constantly for squareness throughout the process of assembly, and make any corrections before the adhesive has set.*

5 *Always wipe off excess adhesive straight away, while it's still runny – don't forget inside corners.*

USING CRAMPS

Cramping up a box

A box or 'carcase' made of panels or boards (below) is more difficult to cramp than a frame; ideally you need four sash cramps, but improvising cramps (see right) may be an easier solution. When the carcase is assembled, check that it is perfectly square. As an alternative to measuring the diagonals, you can use a 'squaring rod' – a slim piece of softwood with one pointed end. Mark the length of one diagonal on it and check this against the other diagonal.

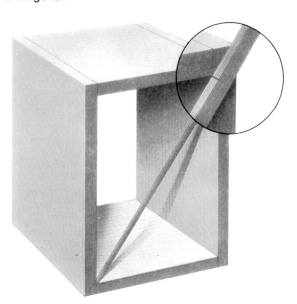

Cramping edge joints

If you are using natural timber and want a wide surface such as a table top (below), you will have to join individual planks edge to edge, either as butt joints or using tongued-and-grooved timber. Set the sash cramps as shown here to hold the planks tightly together; note that they are fitted alternately above and below the assembly to distribute the stresses more evenly and lessen the risk of curvature across its width. Use a straight-edge or metal ruler to check that the assembly is perfectly flat across its width before leaving it to set. You may have to remove slight surface irregularities later with a power sander.

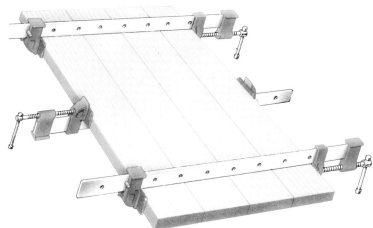

Cramping awkward pieces

G-cramps with their ball-and-socket feet are ideal for cramping assemblies that are not meant to be square. With an assembly such as this, use a sash cramp to hold scrap wood against the ends of the lower piece of wood. Then the upper piece is prevented from sliding down the 'slope' as the two G-cramps are tightened.

To cramp in a triangular reinforcing block, such as the one shown between a table top and leg, use a second block. Stick brown paper tape to that with PVA adhesive. Cramp the assembly and leave it to set. Then release the cramp and knock off the second block, soaking off any remaining paper if necessary.

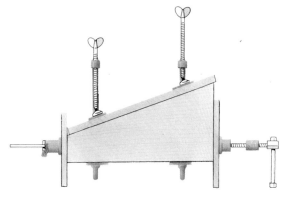

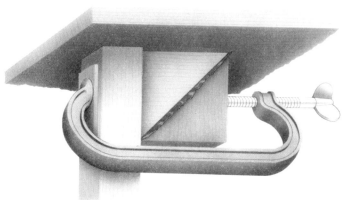

USING CRAMPS
Cramping up a frame

1 *Whenever you are cramping up a frame (eg, a pair of chair legs with their connecting rails), use sash cramps as shown here to hold the joints tightly together. When you have cramped the frame, check that it is perfectly square by measuring the diagonals. If the two measurements are not exactly the same, undo the cramps and adjust the assembly until they are. Replace the cramps and check the squareness again before leaving the frame to set.*

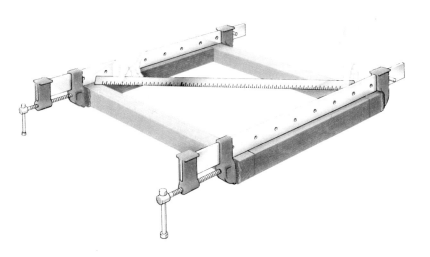

2 *If an assembly is out of square (because of inaccurately-cut joints, for example), you may be able to correct the problem by setting the cramps at a slight angle to the frame sides. The effect of this is to pull the frame back square. Cramp battens against opposite sides of the frame, and tighten the cramps gradually until the diagonals measure the same. Leave to set.*

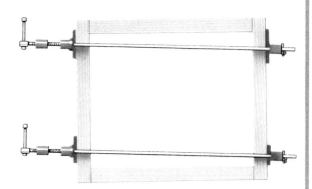

3 *If the assembled frame is twisted out of true (below), use G-cramps and battens as shown to cramp the frame to a flat surface. Check that the cramping has not forced the frame out of square, and leave to set.*

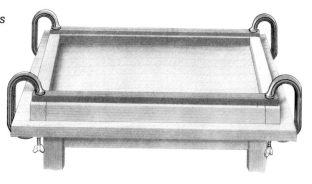

READY REFERENCE

TYPES OF CRAMP

Cramps used for glued joints are usually metal, with jaws which are tightened by a screw action.

G-cramps are the most common and will take assemblies of up to 305mm (12in).

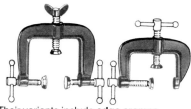

Their variants include **edge cramps,** which exert pressure in two directions at right angles to each other and are useful for fixing edging materials, and **quick-release cramps,** which can be re-adjusted more speedily than ordinary G-cramps.

Sash cramps have two heads – one fixed (but adjustable like a vice) and another which can be pegged into any of a number of positions on the sash bar according to the size of the job. Their capacity is up to 1370mm (54in), although larger versions are available. They can also be extended by bolting two bars together with their movable heads re-moved. Assembly of any box or furniture carcass usually requires several sash cramps. Cramp heads are also available for fixing to suitable lengths of wood 25mm (1in) thick – a cheaper alternative.

CHAPTER 4

USING POWER TOOLS

Power tools take all the hard work out of woodworking and
allow you to achieve highly professional results as well.
Using them is largely a matter of common sense,
particularly in the vital area of safety, but there are plenty of
tricks and tips you need to know to get the best out of them.

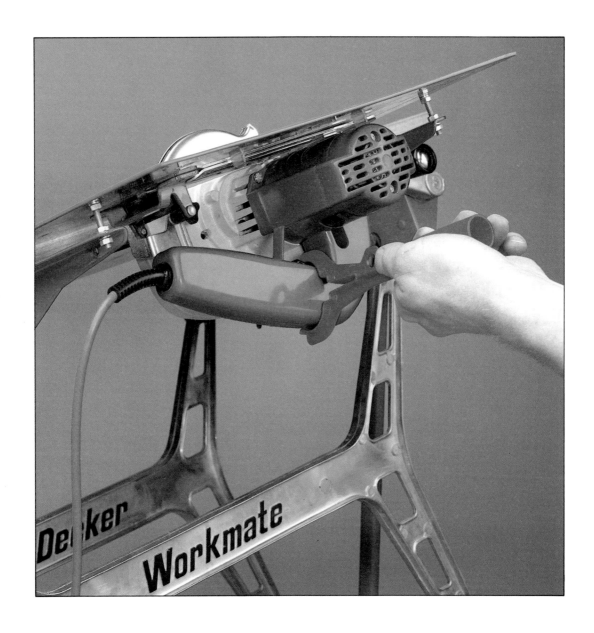

USING DRILL STANDS & JIGS

An electric drill is the one power tool you need for almost every job – be it building, plumbing, electrics, decorating, home repairs or, of course, woodwork. Here's what it does and how to use it.

In do-it-yourself work, you won't get far before you have to start drilling holes. That means a drill, fitted with a drill bit.

Often, of course, you can drill holes with hand tools (see pages 24-26). But they won't always serve the purpose. For one thing, they're relatively slow. And for another, they only really work in timber and boards. For masonry and concrete – as with the average wall fixing – a power drill is the only answer.

Which drill?

Electric drills vary a lot. The more advanced and powerful models incorporate all sorts of special features. Before spending money, however, you ought to think fairly hard about which of those you actually need.

Firstly, power is important. A high-powered drill will tackle large and/or deep holes, especially in hard materials, with greater ease, for longer periods and with less strain. Look at the wattage. 350 is low, 750 is enough to tackle any job.

Secondly, drills are single-speed, two-speed, three-speed, four-speed – or variable-speed (multi-speed); variable-speed drills run at anything from 0 to maximum rpm according to the pressure you put on the trigger.

The point is that you ideally need a very low speed for drilling hard materials such as steel, glass and concrete, and a high one for clean holes in timber; single-speed drills only give you a compromise.

The advantage of the variable-speed type is that you can start a hole very slowly indeed, for accuracy in hard materials, and then speed up without stopping to change gear from one speed to another. Or you can keep it extra-slow – essential for screwdriving (with a screwdriver bit) and for the largest holes in the very hardest materials. Some two-, three- and four-speed drills have variable-speed (or 'acceleration') control in each of their gears.

A further refinement is electronic feedback control, which keeps the tool running at the same speed even if the bit meets a sudden obstacle.

Another very useful feature is hammer or percussion action – available in addition to ordinary rotary drilling, never on its own. This makes the drill deliver rapid hammer blows into the material as it turns, and it's essential for all work in concrete, stone and hard masonry. Percussion attachments are available for ordinary rotary drills.

What's more, it's worth finding out which other attachments can be fitted to the drill concerned. There is a vast number, and they form an excellent way to get more use out of your drill – provided it has the power and compatibility (including the ability to run at high speeds). You'll find details of them on pages 39-41.

The chuck is the 'nose' of the drill. Its jaws are tightened onto the bit (or the spindle of the attachment) with a chuck key, supplied with the drill. The chuck size, ranging from 10 to 13mm (⅜ to ½in), denotes the maximum diameter of the bit shank which can be inserted.

Drill bits

However good your drill, you still need the right bit for the job in hand.

The standard bit for use in wood, steel, aluminium and just about anything except masonry, concrete and stone is the twist bit, often called the twist drill (see page 25) – a cylindrical steel bar with spiral 'flutes' cut in it to remove the waste material.

Although the carbon (as opposed to high-speed) steel version is only strong enough for wood, the twist bit was really developed for metalwork. It's the only power drill bit which will make small-diameter holes; but others, which have points at the tip to take them through the grain, are more suited to woodwork. Most of these are quite short.

The spade, flat or speed bit is a good general-purpose wood bit, which comes in diameters up to 39mm (1½in). It only works at high speed. Its long point is very useful for drilling at an angle; however, it can be a liability if it threatens to break right through the wood when you don't want it to.

You can also get spade bits consisting of a single shank and interchangeable tips.

The dowel bit has the flutes of a twist bit, but these are shaped differently to get rid of wood chips more quickly. It also usually (though not always) has a small lead point, and a tip whose outside edges dig into the timber. This combination makes for great accuracy and straight drilling. Its main use is for dowelling. Usual diameters are 6, 10 and 13mm (1/4, 3/8 and 1/2in).

You need an end mill for making large, flat-bottomed holes in wood. Its principal use is in making the recesses for concealed hinges. However, it's not easy to use accurately without a drill stand (see below).

The hole saw is for cutting accurate holes right through sheet materials; you'll probably require one when fitting pipes into a cold-water cistern. It consists of an ordinary twist bit for starting the hole, plus a collar which fits round it and accepts one of a set of circular toothed blades.

All but the smallest screws require pre-drilled pilot and clearance holes, and in many cases the screw head is flush with the surface (in a countersink) or below it in a counterbore – pages 34 -35. This usually means drilling the pilot hole with one twist bit, changing that for another and drilling the clearance hole, and lastly changing that for a countersink bit (to drill a countersink) or a still larger twist bit (to drill a counterbore).

However, you can get special types of bit which perform all these operations in one go for a given length and gauge of screw. The drill and countersink bit (pictured on page 25), which has a twist in it, finishes by countersinking. The drill and counterbore bit, also known as the combination drill bit, screw-sink or Screw-mate, is flat; either it makes a counterbore, or it can be stopped when its spurs have cut into the surface just enough for the screw to countersink itself. The only problem is that you need quite a few such bits to deal with all the screw sizes you re likely to use.

The plug cutter cuts neat cylindrical pellets of timber which are used as plugs to conceal counterbored screw heads.

The router drill bit can be used as a drill, a rasp – or even a saw or router bit, for cutting straight lines and shapes.

Masonry bits are needed for concrete, stone and hard brick. The commonest type of masonry bit now has flutes shaped like those of a twist bit. All masonry bits can be recognised by the tip, which is a flat insert of tungsten carbide – an exceptionally hard metal – protruding on either side. They come in a great range of lengths (from about 85mm/3 3/8in to 375mm/15in), and also of gauges – ie, tip diameters. The latter run from No. 6, at 4mm (3/16in), to No. 38, a massive 38mm (1 1/2in) in diameter. Oddly enough, the numbering doesn't go in even steps.

For hammer drilling, make sure you get a percussion bit, not a rotary bit. 'Universal' bits are suitable for both uses. For holes over 15mm (5/8in) in diameter, drill a 6mm (1/4in) or 10mm (3/8in) pilot hole first, to make things

USING A DRILL STAND

1 Before using a drill, always close the chuck jaws over the bit shank by hand, and then tighten them fully by turning the chuck key.

3 If drilling right through a piece, you should always place scrap wood under it to protect your bench or stand and to make a cleaner hole.

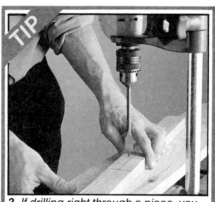

5 Press down the lever in order to check the depth to which the bit will drill. Adjust the drill's height in the stand if necessary.

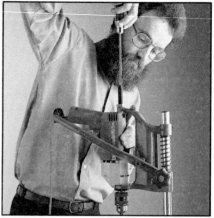

2 Tighten the clamp to make sure the drill is properly gripped in the stand, so that it can't possibly work loose and cause an accident or damage the workpiece.

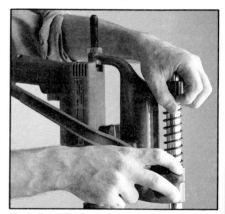

4 Adjust the height of the drill in the stand to roughly the position you want. Make sure the bit can't descend far enough to foul the base.

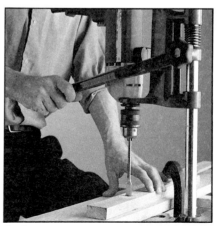

6 Cramp your piece or pieces accurately in position, switch the drill on for continuous running, and press the lever down fully to drill the hole.

USING A DOWELLING JIG

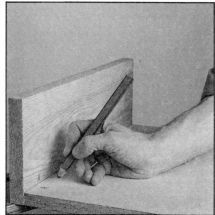

1 *Mark both the pieces to be jointed so that you know which way round they go – otherwise you might drill through the wrong face.*

2 *Separate both pieces with the spacers provided and lay one on top of the other. You must be sure to align it exactly in position.*

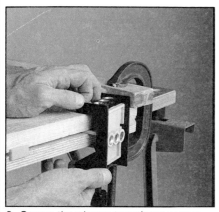

3 *Cramp the pieces together on your table or bench, fit the dowelling jig in position over the edges of both, and tighten its clamping screw.*

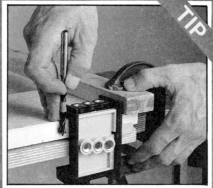

4 *Place adhesive tape or a depth stop round the bit, to ensure you drill deep enough for the dowels but not so deep that they disappear.*

5 *Drill vertically through whichever hole suits the board thickness and bit diameter, then through the corresponding horizontal hole.*

6 *Glue the dowels into one piece, then fit both pieces together after gluing the rest of the joint. Use a wooden mallet for assembly if necessary.*

easier when you insert the bigger bit.

Lastly, the glass drill or spear point drill – as its names make clear – is a bit with a point shaped like a spearhead, designed to make clean holes in glass. When using it, make a 'pool' round the spot with plasticine or putty, and fill that with water as a lubricant.

Basic drilling techniques

Power tools make drilling a simple operation. However, a few tricks will solve common problems and give you better results.

A starting hole locates the point of the bit and stops it wandering. In wood and other softish materials, you can make one with a bradawl; in brickwork and similar materials, try tapping in the tip of a masonry nail. In metal, use a pointed, hand-held tool called a centre punch, again hit with a hammer.

While drilling, withdraw the bit every so often (especially in brick and concrete) to remove debris, thus speeding up the job and preventing clogging and excessive wear.

Keeping the drill straight is often difficult, too. Unless you use a drill stand (see the step-by-step photographs) your best bet is someone else who can tell you what you're doing. The snag isn't so serious with spade bits, because you can easily tell if you're drilling straight just by checking whether the bit is cutting a complete circle as its edges first touch the wood surface.

Another problem is ragged edges and splintering in timber where the bit emerges on the far side. Avoid these either by drilling first from one side till the point (if any) emerges, and then turning it over to drill from the other – or by placing the workpiece on a backing of scrap wood or board and drilling right through into that.

Better still, cramp the scrap wood in place. In fact, you should always hold movable workpieces firmly when drilling; not only does this make for accuracy, it's also safer, because it avoids any risk that the piece will spin round uncontrollably if the bit 'snatches'.

Precision drilling

Drilled holes often have to be an exact depth. The simplest way to ensure this is to wrap adhesive tape round the bit at the appropriate place and use that as an indicator. However, you can get plastic or metal 'depth stops' which fit round the bit and physically prevent you from drilling deeper than you want. Alternatively, you can improvise a depth stop from a piece of wood. (The drill and countersink bit incorporates its own.) Some drills include a 'depth gauge' in the form of an adjustable rod projecting forwards past the chuck.

A drill stand holds a power drill rigid and exactly vertical, while lowering it to a precise depth by a simple lever action when drilling. This helps a great deal when accuracy is

POWER DRILL BITS

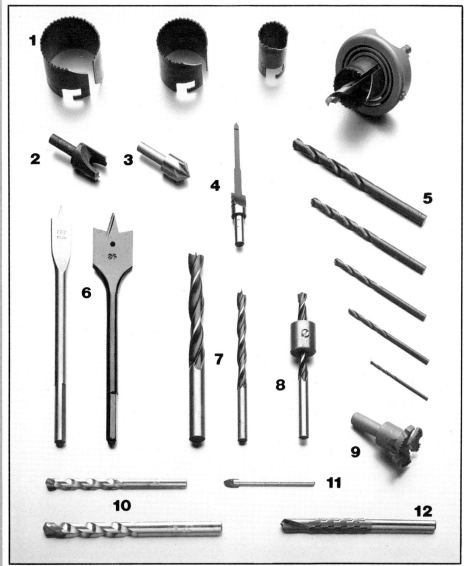

1 Hole saw and cutters
2 Plug cutter
3 Countersink
4 Drill and counterbore bit
5 Twist bits
6 Spade bits
7 Dowel bits
8 Dowel bit with depth stop
9 End mill
10 Masonry bits
11 Glass bit
12 Router drill bit

READY REFERENCE

USING A PLUG CUTTER

1 Counterbore the screw hole to a slightly shallower depth than that of the plug cutter. (Unless using a twist bit, do this before drilling pilot or clearance holes.) Insert the screw. **2** Cut a plug from matching timber. **3** Use a screwdriver or chisel to snap it off and lever it out. **4** Insert the plug, and plane it flush. The chamfer eases insertion.

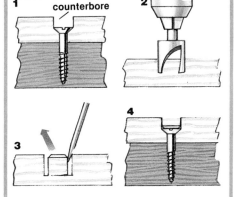

DRILLING FOR WALL PLUGS

1 Drill a clearance hole the same size as the screw shank in the timber you're fixing. **2** Mark the wall through the hole with a bradawl. **3** Remove the timber and drill the wall with a masonry bit. Make the hole slightly too long for the plug. **4** Insert the plug and screw the timber in place.

Alternatively, you can drill a hole in the timber big enough to pass a masonry bit through, and drill through that. This ensures the holes will line up – but you'll need big screws, or washers, because the hole in the timber is extra-large.

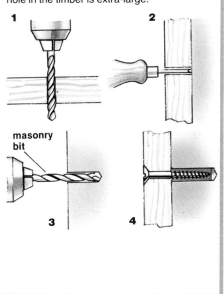

important – eg, in furniture making. A drill stand removes a lot of the snags from, say, drilling a neat series of holes before cleaning them up with a chisel to make a mortise. It should be clamped to a table or workbench, and its accuracy will be further improved if you arrange some form of fixed guide or 'fence' against which the work can be firmly aligned (and if possible cramped) while you're drilling.

Dowelling (see Chapter 3, pages 58-61) is another operation where accuracy matters but is hard to achieve. The main problem lies in getting the holes to line up exactly, as they must. One of the several patterns of jig (the word refers to any device which helps when machining or assembling a particular workpiece) is very useful here. In fact, even when using dowel bits, it's almost indispensable – because it supplies the accuracy which, for all the advantages of power drilling, is the hardest thing to achieve.

USING SHAPING CUTTERS

Shaping cutters provide an easy way to turn your power drill into a more sophisticated tool. Using them well takes a little know-how, plus some practice.

The main function of a power drill is, of course, making holes; that's what it's designed for. But it does have other uses.

For one thing, you can get any number of attachments – see pages 39 -41 – to turn it into something different altogether: a paint stirrer, for example, or a jigsaw or hedge trimmer. To fit many of these, you first have to remove the drill chuck.

But there's another range of items which, in a less radical way, greatly extend the possibilities of your drill as a woodworking machine: namely shaping cutters. These simply clamp into the chuck jaws, like bits; however, you run them along the timber or board, not just vertically into it.

In most cases, you also need a 'shaping attachment' to act as a guide for effective cutting; but a drill stand (see page 86), plus a proprietary or home-made 'shaping table', is best of all.

Drills versus routers
There is, of course, another power tool which is especially designed for this type of work – that is, the router. Routers (dealt with at length in Chapter 5 on pages 114 -128) are more versatile, and more effective because purpose-built. Shaping attachments and tables are largely restricted to edges and other narrow work-pieces. What's more, a router's speed of rotation is seven or eight times that of the average drill, so it gives faster, cleaner cuts.

Drill-mounted cutters, however, compensate for lack of speed by having more cutting edges. They fall into two main categories. The conventional pattern usually has nine or so cutting edges, compared with two on the average router bit. The rasp type has (as its name implies) a great many individual teeth instead. Most router bits, in fact, won't work in drills, as the slow speed won't allow them to clear out the waste material.

Conversely, you must never use a drill cutter in a router. It's highly dangerous, because drill cutters are only made of ordinary tool steel, which may break up into flying pieces at the high speeds used in routing However, such steel is relatively cheap, and its softness means that drill

cutters (unless they're the rasp type) can be sharpened at home.

Router bits, on the other hand, are made from special 'high-speed' steel – often tipped with tungsten carbide for longer life – or wholly from tungsten carbide. This increases their cost, and the tungsten-carbide types can only be sharpened by specialists.

Lastly, a router costs money – which is only well spent if you use it a lot. This may not happen unless you do fairly complex woodwork. Drill cutters, in contrast, fit a tool which most people already have. So they're a sensible solution for the do-it-yourselfer who usually works with off-the-shelf mouldings and simple hand-shaping techniques, yet occasionally needs something more elaborate.

A shaping table (above), with a drill stand, gets the best from shaping cutters.

Normally you slide the workpiece past the plywood 'fence' while the drill cuts. For mortising, clamp the piece as shown, and slide the table to and fro.

What drill cutters do
Each main category of cutter (edged or rasp-toothed) has a similar range of shapes.

You can make rebates with a drum-shaped *cylindrical* or *trimming cutter*; its rasp versions are called *heavy-duty cutters* and *housing mills*. Small rebates can be tackled with a *straight cutter*, primarily designed for making grooves. Or you can cut a rebate in two passes with a *slotting* or *slit-saw;* turn the piece through 90° after the first cut.

Narrower grooves require a *straight-face cutter* (known as a *groove cutter* and *combi-cutter* in its rasp versions) or the still finer *slotting cutter,* which is a smaller and slightly thicker version of the slotting saw. A *concave* rasp cutter makes a rounded groove.

USING A HAND SHAPER

1 Insert the shank or 'arbor' of the shaper into the drill chuck, and tighten it up very firmly – just as you would with a hole-drilling bit.

2 Hold the chuck steady with the key, fit the cutter without its shank, and tighten that too. (Rasp cutters thread on before you fit the shaper.)

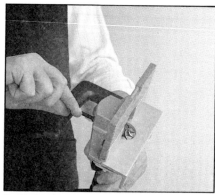

3 Fit the fence into position, adjusted to the width you require, ready for a test cut. On some models, the fence is already part of the shaper.

DOVETAILING WITH A DRILL

1 Fit the dovetailing attachment, including cutter, into the chuck, and tighten it – in the same way as you fit a hand shaper.

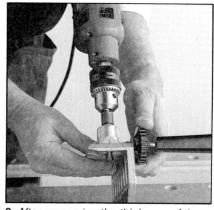

2 After measuring the thickness of the pin piece, set the attachment to the same dimension, using the gauge markings on the dovetailing jig.

3 Clamp the jig over the pin piece, and locate the attachment in the first slot. Switch on, and push it along each slot to mill out the pins.

5 Using the jig as a guide, mark a pencil line across the end of the other piece – the one in which you'll be cutting out the tails.

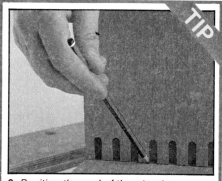

TIP

6 Position the end of the pin piece against this line (keeping the edges of both pieces flush) and mark the position of one of the pins.

7 Clamp the jig over the tail piece, aligning the marks on the jig with the mark you've just made, and mill out the tails: this time vertically.

4 *Set the drill for continuous running, and make the cut by carefully pushing the tool along – aligning the workpiece in the angle of the shaper.*

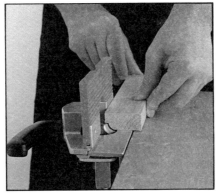

5 *Alternatively, this type of shaper can be mounted on a bench with two screws. To cut, push the work past the cutter with both hands.*

4 *On wide pieces, you use all the slots, then simply re-clamp the jig further along to repeat the procedure once or even twice.*

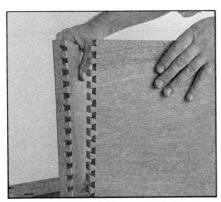

8 *The result should be a set of cleanly cut dovetails – evenly spaced, so that they line up accurately between the pins and form a tight joint.*

SHAPING TABLES

1 *Adjust and tighten the fence so the cutter projects the required distance into the workpiece, and fix the drill at the right height on its stand.*

2 *Switch on and make a test cut. For safety pull, rather than push, as you finish off. The cutter shown here mills out a projecting tongue.*

If you need a tongue, you can of course make a pair of rebates, one in each edge. But it's quicker and far more accurate to use a *tongue cutter*, which does this in one go. It's available in sizes corresponding to those of straight-face, groove and combi-cutters, so the tongue will automatically fit the groove.

Shaping edges – often purely for decoration – is another principal use of cutters. *Rounding-off, chamfering* or *angle* (45° or 75°), *coving, beading, hollow beading* and *convex cutters* each do what their names imply, and do it fast and neatly.

The rasp range offers two further cutters. The *dovetail groover* makes short work of a very good joint, the otherwise laborious dovetail housing (see page 73); and the *dowel mill* – also usable for rebating and other jobs – functions rather like the conventional plug cutter (see page 88). It has the unique ability to cut a projecting dowel in the end of a piece of timber, as well as a matching hole.

As with router bits, you can produce all sorts of compound shapes by using different cutters one after the other. Some cutters, too, can be aligned so as to make tenons and/or halvings.

Lastly, a few other shaping bits – unlike the two main ranges – are used freehand. Ordinary 'rotary' and 'profile rasps' – usually cylindrical, conical or spherical ('ball-ended') – are for rough shaping work. So are 'rotary files'. The 'drill saw' (another word for the router drill bit shown on page 88) makes slots. The 'hole enlarger' or 'enlarging mill' is just that. And 'mounted stones' (often available in miniature versions) are small rotary grindstones, useful for intricate contours.

Setting up the job

Except when using the freehand bits just mentioned, there are two principal ways of mounting drill cutters.

The first employs the shaping attachment, or hand shaper. This gadget fits directly into the drill chuck, and receives the cutter in turn. (In the case of rasp cutters, this order is reversed – but not all cutters are threaded to fit the shaper.) The shaper is made so you can hold it in one hand, with the drill in the other, and keep its fence and back plate, or its rotary guide, against the workpiece so the cutter runs straight and true. It has the advantage that you can take it to the workpiece if necessary.

At least one model of shaper can be mounted on a bench too. This means you can push the work past the cutter, rather than the other way round, using both hands for control and therefore accuracy. Moreover, some types of shaper have a special guide to replace the fence when you're profiling a curved edge. (So do some shaping tables.)

The second method is to place your drill in

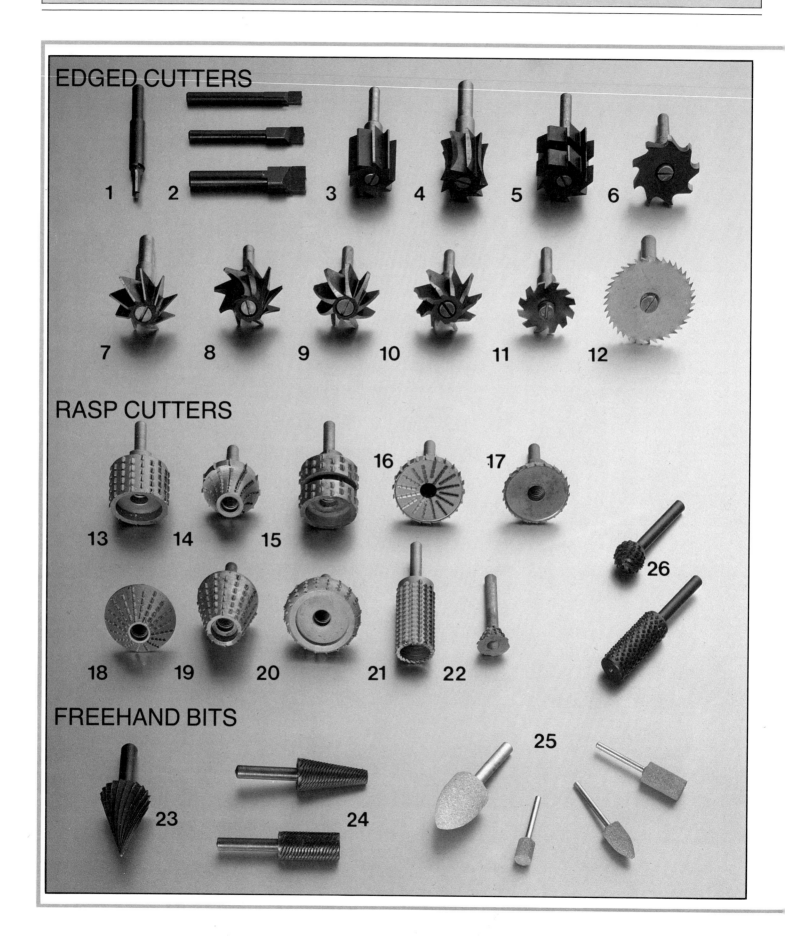

EDGED CUTTERS

1 2 3 4 5 6

7 8 9 10 11 12

RASP CUTTERS

13 14 15 16 17

18 19 20 21 22 26

FREEHAND BITS

23 24 25

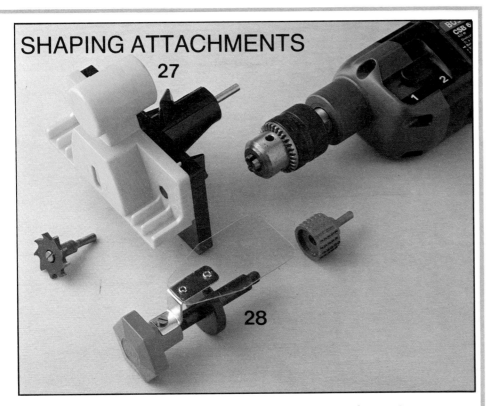

SHAPING ATTACHMENTS

Drill-mounted shaping bits

Edged cutters
1 *Straight cutter*
2 *Mortise cutters*
3 *Cylindrical cutter*
4 *Rounding-off cutter*
5 *Tongue cutter*
6 *Straight-face cutter*
7 *Chamfering cutter (45°)*
8 *Rounding-off cutter*
9 *Coving cutter*
10 *Hollow beading cutter*
11 *Slotting cutter*
12 *Slotting saw*

Rasp cutters
13 *Heavy-duty cutter*
14 *Convex cutter*
15 *Tongue cutter*
16 *Combi-cutter*
17 *Groove cutter*
18 *Angle cutter (45°)*
19 *Angle cutter (75°)*
20 *Concave cutter*
21 *Dowel mill*
22 *Dovetail groover*

Freehand bits
23 *Hole enlarger or enlarging mill*
24 *Rotary files*
25 *Mounted stones*
26 *Rotary rasps*

Shaping attachments

Shaping attachments or 'hand shapers' are really nothing more than guides for running the cutter accurately against the workpiece, and sometimes vice versa.

One type (27) works on the same principles as that shown on pages 90-91 (photographs 1 to 5). The sharper fits directly into the drill chuck, and accepts a conventional (edged) cutter, without its shank. You adjust the distance the cutter sticks out from the back of the attachment, and also the vertical position of the fence – thus altering the depth and width of the cut respectively.

While all shapers are mainly for working on, or close to edges, this type can also be used to make a groove or housing across a wide, flat board. Use a straight cutter and clamp on a batten to act as a guide.

The second type (28) is for use with certain rasp cutters, which are fastened into the chuck and screwed onto the shaper. The rotary guide disc is moved along the shank and fixed to set the depth of cut. You keep its rear face pressed against the workpiece.

To reduce the width of cut, clamp a batten against the workpiece at the appropriate height, so that the disc rolls along it as you work.

a stand, and use a shaping table. The latter is basically a flat surface across which you can slide the work. It's fitted with an adjustable fence: this can be moved sideways towards or away from the cutter, depending on the width of cut you want, and locked in position before starting work.

The stand itself enables greater variation and quicker adjustment of the depth of cut than is possible with a shaper. Its instant lever action is essential for certain operations – such as mortising. This can be done with *mortise cutters* or *slot mortising bits* by first drilling a row of holes, then sliding the piece to and fro while continually deepening the cut. Some shaper tables slide bodily from side to side, within limits set by you, while the workpiece is clamped on top – thus making the job even easier.

Another useful device is a dovetailing jig. This is an angled piece of metal incorporating rows of slots, which you can clamp over the edges of timber or boards. Fitting your drill with a dovetailing attachment (a type of shaper) and a special cutter called a dovetail bit, you simply use the attachment and jig as guides to mill out tails and then pins (see pages 71-75).

Because the cutter revolves, the slots between the pins have rounded ends. In a through dovetail joint (for which the bit is too short unless the pin piece is very thin) this produces gaps which are visible from outside, and therefore unacceptable. In lap dovetail joints, they still show from inside. What's more, tails and pins have to be exactly the same size. In other words, the dovetail attachment is no craftsman's tool – but it does speed things up.

Using drill cutters
There are three vital things to remember when using shaping cutters in your drill.

Firstly, always work in the right direction. The cutting edges must revolve into the workpiece. With a hand-held shaper, this means moving the tool along in the same direction as the cutter is turning; with a fixed cutter, you move the work into it – in the opposite direction. (None of this applies when making grooves.)

Secondly, keep the speed up. Though designed to work efficiently at much slower rates than router bits, drill cutters still need the maximum possible rpm for a smooth finish.

And, thirdly, the secret of using any machine is not to ask too much of it. You should learn to tell by sound and feel when you're trying to work too fast or remove too much in one go.

The answer is to make the cut in more than one successive pass, going a little deeper each time. This technique makes light work of even fairly hefty cuts – and it ensures that, despite their limitations, drill cutters can still be a very handy addition to your toolkit.

USING CIRCULAR SAWS

The circular saw cuts natural timber and man-made boards accurately. It's an indispensable tool for all types of woodwork – as long as you know how to get the most out of it.

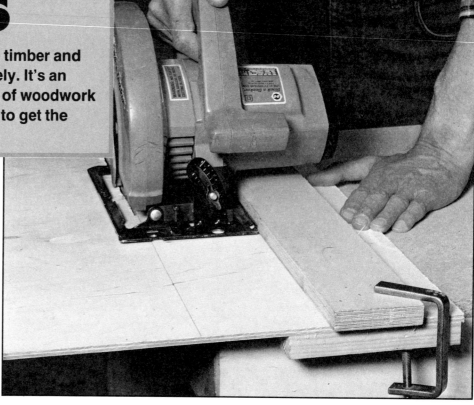

Circular saws do nothing that hand tools can't do, but they do the job much more quickly. This eliminates much tiring work – which in many cases also means greater accuracy, especially for the beginner. They're particularly useful for cutting man-made boards, because of the long cuts involved.

The one thing of which you must be constantly aware is the need to work safely. But that, of course, is a matter of developing good habits.

Choosing a saw
Circular saws are available either as integral units on their own, or as attachments for power drills; each type has its advantages. There's also a range of sizes and power outputs which demands careful consideration before buying. And there's a special blade for every purpose. See pages 42-44 for more details).

Circular saw drill attachments are often satisfactory for general use, and fairly cheap. Naturally, however, this depends on the power of the drill itself – and that's unlikely to be enough if you do a great deal of sawing, or if you frequently use hardwoods. There's also the fact that the attachment has to be removed if you want to do any drilling, and must then be replaced afterwards.

If you do get a saw attachment for your drill, remember one thing. Unlike integral circular saws, most drills can be locked in the 'on' position so that the drill is rotating even if it is unattended – in a saw bench, for example. Never do this while the saw attachment is fitted. You *must* always be able to stop a saw in an emergency by simply lifting your finger from the trigger.

Integral saws (those with their own motors) are rated according to size and power in a quite complex way. The lowest-powered, with a motor of 300-450W, will generally accept blades 125mm (5in) in diameter and will be capable of making cuts up to 30mm (1³⁄₁₆in) deep. The highest-powered saws have motors around 1000W, use 180mm (7in) blades, and can make cuts to a depth of 60mm (2³⁄₈in).

What you should check before you choose a saw is whether its vital statistics suit your

likely use of it. Saws vary considerably in their maximum and minimum cutting depths – and these will be reduced if you're cutting with the blade at an angle.

The larger and more powerful the saw, the faster it will cut. This may not be all that important unless you make constant use of it. You may get good value from a cheaper saw, and some people find the larger ones daunting. But there's always the risk of burning out the motor on a low-powered saw by overloading it (ie, trying to cut too fast, or through material that's too tough).

The anatomy of a saw
On almost all types of circular saw, the blade cuts on the up-stroke. It's attached to the drive shaft or 'arbor' with a bolt fitted with a washer.

The top of the blade is protected by a permanent safety guard; the bottom (protruding) part has a spring-loaded guard which recedes automatically as the cut progresses, and springs back as you finish. This sprung guard may be made of either metal or plastic. If at any time you intend to cut metal or masonry, choose a saw with metal guards, which can't come to any harm from flying fragments, etc; plastic ones may crack or chip.

The depth of cut (ie, the amount by which the blade protrudes through the bottom of the saw) is adjusted by a calibrated knob on the side of the machine, raising and lowering

KNOW YOUR SAW

A circular saw is an indispensable tool, especially for cutting up man-made boards quickly and easily. You'll find it's not at all complicated to use, once you know your way round it. Very useful features are the depth adjustment, which regulates how far the blade protrudes downwards, and the angle adjustment, which enables you to cut with the blade at a slope (eg, for mitres).

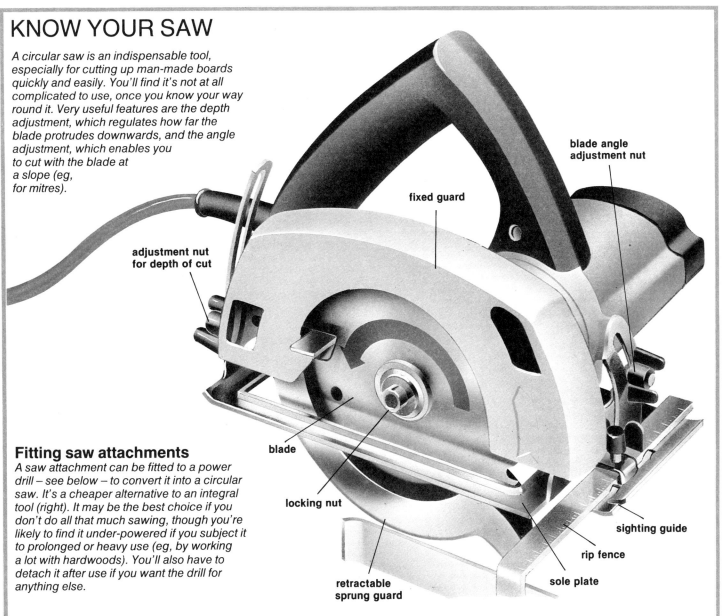

blade angle adjustment nut

fixed guard

adjustment nut for depth of cut

blade

locking nut

retractable sprung guard

sole plate

rip fence

sighting guide

Fitting saw attachments

A saw attachment can be fitted to a power drill – see below – to convert it into a circular saw. It's a cheaper alternative to an integral tool (right). It may be the best choice if you don't do all that much sawing, though you're likely to find it under-powered if you subject it to prolonged or heavy use (eg, by working a lot with hardwoods). You'll also have to detach it after use if you want the drill for anything else.

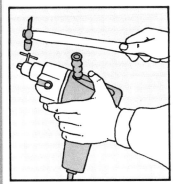

1 *Remove the chuck from the front of the drill, inserting the chuck key and tapping it with a hammer if necessary.*

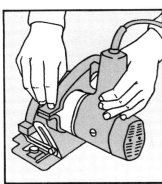

2 *Locate the saw attachment over the front of the drill, and tighten any fixing nuts which are provided.*

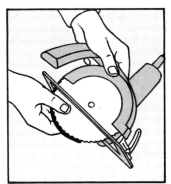

3 *Fit the blade, together with the retractable lower guard, into position over the shaft of the drill.*

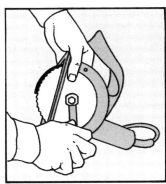

4 *Add the nut which holds the blade in place, get it finger-tight by hand, and finish tightening it up with a spanner.*

the body of the saw in relation to the sole plate (the saw's flat base). This depth should be slightly greater, by a millimetre or two, than the thickness of the material to be cut; if the blade protrudes too much, it will cause splintering.

There's also a second knob for angling the blade, usually adjustable in 5° steps – but you'll need to double-check with a protractor to guarantee accuracy, and make test cuts in scrap wood. Bear in mind that you'll also need to increase the cutting depth to allow for the cut being at an angle.

Circular saws use a detachable rip fence to guide the saw when making long, straight cuts parallel to the edge of the workpiece (eg, when 'ripping' – that is, cutting solid timber lengthwise). This is a T-shaped piece of metal; the 'leg' is fitted to the sole plate so that it sticks out to one side, while the cross of the T locates over the edge of the material you're cutting.

Some saws are also fitted with a 'riving knife' behind the blade, which keeps the cut open to prevent the saw from sticking.

Fitting the blade

Using a circular saw is extremely simple once you know your way around it and have practised a bit and gained confidence.

Fit the blade with the power off and the saw resting safely on the workbench. Be sure that the blade is the right way round and is properly centred on the spindle. Then jam it in place. Most blades have holes in them through which you can put a screwdriver blade for this purpose; otherwise, insert a piece of wood between the teeth. Start the fixing bolt on the thread with the utmost care – you want it to be a tight accurate fit to avoid accidents. Don't forget the washer, either.

Making a cut

Before you switch the mains power on, check that the retractable safety guard is working smoothly.

Always make sure, too, that the piece of wood you're cutting is securely clamped, either in a vice or with G-cramps. Don't work along long unsupported runs of material; clamp the other end as well, if necessary, to stop the piece wobbling about. And check that there's nothing beneath the work to get in the way of the saw. In a situation like this, it's all too easy to cut through your workbench by mistake, so beware.

Don't start the saw and then present it to the workpiece. It could jump back at you. Instead, rest the sole plate of the saw flat on the work and line the blade up, but keep it just a few millimetres back from the actual start of the cut. Then press the trigger and wait for a moment for the saw to reach full speed. Holding it firmly, advance it to the start of the cut.

SETTING UP AND BASIC CUTTING

1 *Fit the blade and jam a piece of wood between the teeth to stop it moving. Some blades have holes for you to insert a screwdriver instead.*

2 *Tighten the blade nut very firmly indeed with a spanner. It's absolutely vital that it shouldn't come loose while you're cutting.*

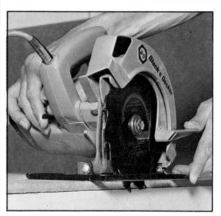

3 *Adjust the height of the saw's body in relation to its sole plate, so the blade just protrudes through what you're cutting.*

4 *Line the saw up so the blade is on the waste side of your cutting line. A mark or cut-out on the front of the sole plate will guide you.*

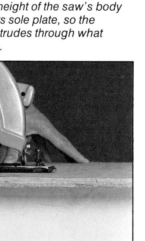

5 *Draw the saw back, still keeping its sole plate flat on the surface. Press the trigger and let it reach full speed before starting to cut.*

6 *As you move the saw forward, the guard is pushed up from the back. It springs back down to cover the blade when the cut is finished.*

USING A GUIDE BATTEN

1 *To cut timber lengthwise, or remove any narrow strip parallel to an edge, fit the fence the required distance from the blade and tighten the screw.*

2 *While cutting, make sure the fence stays flat against the edge of the material so you end up with a straight, parallel cut.*

3 *Where a rip fence is too short, use a batten instead. First measure from the side of the saw teeth to the edge of the sole plate.*

The motion of the blade itself will help to draw the saw forward: don't force it, because that will strain the motor and may snag the blade, causing kickback – though most modern saws do have a slip clutch to prevent this kind of trouble.

At the end of the cut, switch off the saw and let the blade stop before removing it. Otherwise you'll cause splintering (always a problem with circular saws).

Using a guide batten
There will often be times when you want more accuracy than you can get from cutting freehand, yet the rip fence is no use, because your intended cut is either too far from the edge or not parallel to it.

In such cases the answer is to cramp a batten across the surface of the material you're cutting, so that you can keep the sole plate of the saw against it while sawing, thus maintaining a straight line. If you fix it to the part you want to keep, rather than on the waste side, you'll make it impossible for the saw to wander into the wrong area; the worst than can happen is for it to deviate onto the waste side, so that the workpiece will require trimming afterwards.

The batten needs to be thin enough for the body of the saw to pass over it. Also ensure that you position it accurately so that the blade cuts exactly down the waste side of the cutting line you've marked otherwise you'll simply be making more work for yourself.

Cutting joints
Jointing boards (for example, when you're making box furniture) always demands thought and care. The circular saw is a great help here, because it can cut three types of joint: mitre, rebate and housing.

Cutting a mitre (ie, a mitre in the thickness of a board, rather than across it – see photograph 2 on page 98) is simply a matter of setting the blade accurately to an angle of 45° from the vertical. The great thing about the mitre is that it hides the end grain of both pieces, and this makes it very useful in furniture construction, especially where man-made boards are used. However, in freestanding structures it needs some reinforcement, such as plastic jointing blocks.

CUTTING REBATES AND HOUSINGS

1 *Using the rip fence, cut along the inside of the marked rebate first. Set the depth of cut to less than the material's thickness.*

2 *Make parallel cuts to remove the rest, moving the fence in each time, and clean up the finished rebate with a chisel if necessary.*

3 *Make a housing in a similar way. Cut its sides first, then remove waste from the middle of the housing with successive parallel cuts.*

4 *Align a straight piece of timber or plywood parallel to the cutting line, distancing it from the line by the amount you've just measured.*

5 *Cramp the batten on and hold the saw against it as you cut. If it's fixed to the workpiece, not the waste, you can't cut too much off.*

A rebate can be cut by using the rip fence, set very close in and adjusted for successive parallel cuts until you've made the required 'ledge' across the edge of the piece.

Parallel saw cuts also make housings and grooves (for example, to take the ends of shelves). The rip fence may be too short for use here, so you may need a batten instead; re-locate it for each individual cut.

Using a saw table
So far we've dealt with using a portable circular saw freehand. However, professional woodworking shops possess larger circular saws ('bench saws') which are mounted in fixed units. The advantage of fixed saws is that you have both hands free to guide the

work into the blade. That, plus a flat surface on which to rest the work, means greater convenience and accuracy.

While full-scale purpose-built home bench saws for the keen do-it-yourselfer are available, there's a cheaper alternative. You can mount your portable circular saw in a bench – basically a table with a hole in it. The saw is fixed underneath the bench so that the blade sticks up through the hole. The bench can be either bought (see pages 42 -44), or home-made from timber and man-made boards.

All saw benches are fitted with adjustable fences for accurate cutting, whether parallel to an edge or at an angle. Perhaps their only drawback is that the exposed blade makes them more dangerous than portable saws.

MAKING ANGLED CUTS

1 *To cut at other than 90°, adjust the angle of the sole plate in relation to the blade. Degree markings are calibrated on the fitting.*

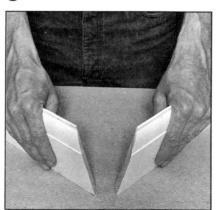

2 *A circular saw with the blade set at 45° is ideal for cutting mitres in skirting boards where they join at external corners.*

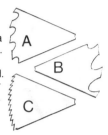
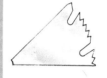

USING A SAW TABLE

Mounting your circular saw in a saw table opens the way to better, more accurate woodwork. Here's the principle, plus the tricks you need to know to get the most out of the set-up — and to use it in safety.

In general, fixed machines do harder and more precise work than the corresponding portable power tools.

Of course, there are times when you have to take the tool to the job – when the workpiece is immovable, or too big to handle. Otherwise, however, a fixed arrangement makes it easier to set the tool up for accurate work, and usually makes it quicker to repeat the same operation.

For example, a drill mounted in a stand will make an entire series of truly vertical holes to a given depth, without variation. A router in a table makes light work of repetitive cuts. And the circular saw is no exception to the rule.

But remember one thing. If you're careless or ignorant or both, the circular saw mounted in a table is dangerous. See *Ready Reference* for the specific safety points of which you must constantly be aware.

What is a saw table?
A circular saw table is a simple affair. It has a flat, rigid top, with a slot near the middle through which the blade sticks up, the saw itself being securely fastened upside-down to the underside. If the table is bought rather than home-made, the mountings will probably be specifically designed for certain models of saw. Before you buy, check which one will suit your saw.

Remember, too, that the saw will need to run continuously without your finger on the switch. Most types do have such a facility. But it's better still to fit a socket outlet to the table edge, and plug the saw into that. Then you can clamp or tape the saw's own switch in the 'on' position, and rely instead on the control that's within easy reach. In an emergency, it could be a blessing.

The top will be on legs, or some other firm structure. Solidity, in fact, is the prime requirement for any machine table, for reasons both of safety and of accuracy. However, no proprietary saw table for the home user is big enough to let you man-handle standard-sized sheets of board across it accurately. You'll either have to use the saw hand-held, or employ special trestles or other supports to stop the workpiece from tipping over.

On the saw table, just as on the portable saw, you can adjust the depth of cut – it should be only a little greater than the thickness of the material; you can also tilt the blade to give bevelled cuts (the slot in the table must be wide enough to allow this to happen).

If possible, too, the table must be fitted with a guard, supported above the blade.

Lastly, it must incorporate two fences – one for ripping and one for crosscutting. You generally use only one at a time.

Using the rip fence
The rip fence runs parallel to the blade. It's fitted so that it can be slid from side to side, but it must be secured in position before you make a cut.

When 'ripping' – cutting along the grain – you set the fence at a distance from the blade which corresponds to the width of the piece you want to end up with, and hold the piece against the fence while feeding it into the blade. This technique is equally good for cutting man-made panels lengthwise.

Ripping requires even more care than circular sawing in general. An essential accessory here is a 'riving knife' – a wedge-shaped piece of steel behind the blade, whose function is to ensure that the cut doesn't close up again, causing the blade to

snatch the piece and fling it back at you. It's vital to keep the piece on the move, and well under control. At the end of a cut, you should always use a push stick – notched at the end – to propel the work past the blade, thus saving your fingers from risk of severe injury.

You can also use the rip fence to cut grooves, tongues and rebates. You simply make a series of parallel cuts, shifting the fence each time, until you've removed the waste. A handy accessory for this is a pair of 'wobble washers' – bevelled washers fitted on either side of the blade, which make it wobble slightly from side to side and thus give a wider cut. For tongues and rebates, another method is to make two cuts at right angles to each other (four, in the case of a tongue).

On many models of saw table, the rip fence is rather short for accurate joint cutting. It may be a good idea to extend it with a wooden batten, screwed on to the existing fence and perhaps also clamped to the table at the far end.

Using the crosscut fence
The crosscut fence works in a different way. Used for cutting lengths of timber across the grain, or man-made boards in their shortest dimensions, it stands at right angles to the saw blade.

SETTING UP AND RIP CUTTING

1 Mount the saw in the table according to the manufacturer's instructions, and ensure all the fixings are absolutely tight so it can't move.

2 See that the riving knife is positioned correctly – ie, just clear of the blade – and fasten the blade guard securely in place as well.

3 Adjust the depth of cut via the fitting on the saw; the blade should project through the workpiece by about 5mm (³/₁₆in). Then lower the guard.

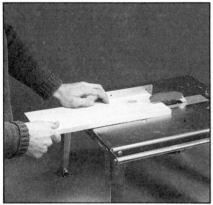

5 Switch the machine on, let it reach full speed, and feed the workpiece firmly into the blade, keeping it against the fence all the time.

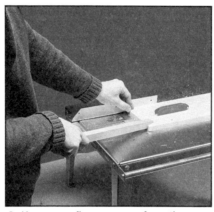

6 Keep your fingers away from the blade, and use a push stick to finish off the cut. Stand to one side of the saw in case it throws a piece back at you.

7 Push the pieces clear of the blade (note that the rip fence stops level with it, in order to allow this) and switch the machine off.

9 Clamp the batten to the table at the other end so it can't bend. For a rebate, simply push the piece along the batten and over the blade.

10 Then reset the depth if necessary, turn the piece round and make the second cut. You'll usually need a push stick to finish this type of cut too.

11 For a tongue, make two rebates with four cuts. You'll need a wider fence for stability when feeding wide pieces through the saw on edge.

4 *Fit the rip fence, and measure between that and the saw teeth for the width of cut you want. Make test cuts on scrap wood to check it.*

8 *To cut rebates, tongues and grooves, you remove the guard and riving knife. Screw a flat, straight batten to the front of the rip fence.*

12 *Make a groove in the same way, re-setting the fence if you need more than one cut. Here, a third cut will clear the centre of the groove.*

You position it at the front of the saw, hold the workpiece against it with both hands in such a position that the required amount will be cut off, and slide the fence and workpiece together past the blade so that it makes the cut.

It's important, of course, to be able to crosscut pieces to a specific length. However, because of the shape of the saw teeth, it's not always easy to measure exactly where the cut will come. You can use trial and error – but the 'error' may ruin your work!

For a single cut, one solution involves screwing a longish wooden batten to the main crosscut fence – useful anyway as a lengthening device. Push both forwards so that the saw blade just marks the batten. Then pencil-mark your workpiece where you want the cut, line this mark up with the saw-mark in the timber batten, push the whole lot forwards and make the cut.

There are two very neat ways of making repeated cuts to the same size. One is to clamp a timber stop block to the crosscut fence in such a position that, when you push the rear end of the workpiece up against it, the front end will be cut off accurately when you slide the fence forwards.

Secondly, you could set the rip fence to the required distance from the blade, and push the front end of the piece against it, so the rip fence acts as a stop. But this would be risky, because the cut-off piece might catch in the gap between blade and fence, and be hurled out. The safe variation is to clamp or screw a block to the rip fence – or even the table – well in front of the level of the blade, and butt the workpiece against the face of that before sliding it forwards to be cut.

This second method restricts the length of the workpiece. The waste – the part you're holding against the fence – can be longer. With either method, use a scrap piece to make test cuts while setting up.

The tenon and halving joints are the two joints you can make with the crosscut fence. For tenons, it's extremely difficult to hold the piece vertical accurately and safely when cutting along the grain; so your best plan is to remove the waste with a series of parallel cuts across the grain, with the tenon passing over the blade. Ideally, use wobble washers too. The depth of cut should, of course, equal the intended shoulder depth of the tenon. For halvings, the principle is similar.

The mitre fence

The crosscut fence is sometimes called a mitre fence because, apart from cutting ends off square, it's also adjustable to any angle – being used in exactly the same way to make mitred and other non-right-angled cuts.

The only thing you have to watch is that the workpiece doesn't 'creep' along the fence as you're cutting it, producing a distorted result.

USING THE CROSSCUT FENCE

1 With the crosscut fence fitted, the basic action is to hold the workpiece against it, and slide both forwards past the blade to square off the end.

2 For an angled cut, swivel the fence round and tighten the knob to secure it at the angle you want, using the gauge marks on the fence as a guide.

3 To stop the workpiece accidentally moving along the fence as you cut, stick on a piece of sandpaper. Double-sided adhesive tape is ideal.

5 To cut a single piece off at a particular point, first screw a batten to the crosscut fence so that the batten projects past the saw blade.

6 Then push the fence forwards until the saw blade cuts into the batten – just far enough to make a 'kerf', but not all the way through it.

7 After having marked up the workpiece for the cut you want, switch the machine on and line the pencil mark up with the kerf in the batten.

9 Alternatively, for cutting to length, you can screw on a 'false fence' instead, and cramp on a stop block at the required distance from the blade.

10 Then hold each piece against the fence so its end butts against the block, and make the cut. You can repeat it exactly on other pieces.

11 Another trick for repeat cuts is to cramp a block to the table (or the front of the rip fence) at the required distance, and butt each piece against that.

4 When making the cut, you just hold the piece firmly against the fence and push both of them forwards past the blade in the usual way.

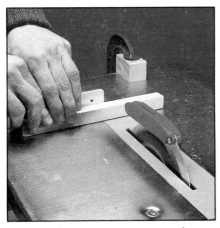

8 Hold the workpiece firmly in position against the batten, and push the fence forwards so that you cut through the two pieces at once.

12 Then, being sure not to move the piece along the crosscut fence, feed it forwards to make the cut. This way, the waste is the part you're holding.

CUTTING JOINTS

1 To cut a halving, cramp a stop block to the crosscut fence as well as at the other side. Remove the guard and riving knife, and make the first cut.

3 Remove the waste with repeated intermediate cuts, still using the crosscut fence. Clean the cut up later with a chisel if necessary.

5 Moving the timber back a little each time, make repeated cuts to get rid of the waste while still holding the piece against the crosscut fence.

2 Line up the second cut by butting the piece against the other block, then make it in the same way. This will give you the two ends of the halving.

4 To cut a tenon, use the rip fence as well. Set it for the tenon's length, and make the first cut with the end of the piece butted against it.

6 Finish by turning the piece over and repeating the procedure, after adjusting the depth of cut if necessary. Then use a broad chisel to make a clean joint.

TOOLS FOR WOODTURNING

Woodturning demands not only a lathe but a good set of cutting tools – chisels, gouges and scrapers. Here's how to choose them, use them and sharpen them.

To understand woodturning more fully (see pages 107 -112) you need to be familiar with the tools for the job. They fall under three main headings: chisels, gouges and scrapers.

Chisels

Turning chisels are used only on spindle work (pages 109 -111). Unlike ordinary chisels, they're bevelled on both sides.

By far the commonest and most useful pattern is the **skew chisel**, with its angled tip. It has four main uses:
● making convex curves which have a relatively small radius
● cutting decorative rings
● neatly squaring and cleaning up endgrain
● giving a clean finish to a cylinder after roughing it out with a gouge (see below).

You introduce it to the workpiece at a slight angle (looking from above as well as sideways) and lower the handle, pivoting the blade on the tool rest so the tip rises till it cuts. Usually you use it on edge – cutting with the heel, and making sure the toe is well clear of the work so it can't dig in and tear a chunk out. (The exception is in cleaning up a cylinder, when you use it almost flat, pointing in the direction

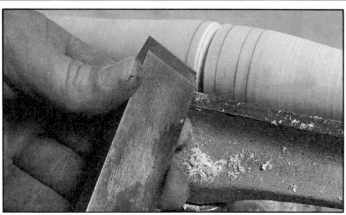
● *Cutting a decorative ring with the skew chisel*

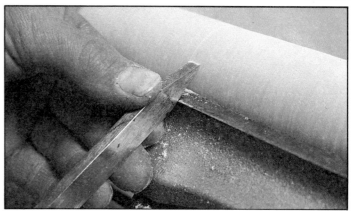
● *Using the parting tool to cut in deeply*

● *Rounding an edge with the spindle gouge*

● *Turning a cylinder with the roughing-out-gouge*

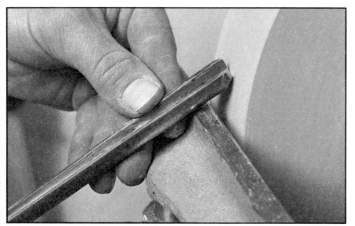
● *Truing a bowl with the narrow deep-fluted gouge*

● *Finishing a bowl with the bullnosed scraper*

you're working but with the toe away from you.)

Square-tipped chisels are also available but not so generally useful as the skew pattern.

The parting tool is a thick, narrow chisel, held square to the work when seen from above. You push it into the wood horizontally. Once it's entered, you again tilt it by lowering the handle, so the edge slices rather than scrapes. This will make a faster, cleaner cut, and keep the tool sharp for longer. Wiggling it slightly from side to side may also speed things up.

Used on edge, the parting tool will cut V-shaped rings round the piece. Used flat, it rapidly cuts in deeply. This is ideal when you want to establish a diameter to cut to (page 1691). In addition, when you finish a piece you often need to cut the ends square while it's still on the lathe. Use the parting tool to reduce the tail end to about 6mm (1/4in) in diameter. Then support the revolving work loosely in one hand; holding the tool in the other, cut right through it at the drive end. The piece will stop dead in your hand. Remove it, and cut off the tail-end stub with a tenon saw.

Gouges

Shallow-fluted gouges have rounded ends and are usually narrow. Known as **spindle gouges**, they're used for curves in spindle work, both concave and sometimes convex. Wide ones will only tackle shallow curves, and have limited usefulness.

Deep-fluted gouges, which have square ends, come in two types. Wide ones are called **roughing-out gouges** and always used for the initial conversion of wood to a cylindrical shape. They're also better for gentle curves than shallow-fluted gouges. Narrow ones are used for almost all face-plate work (page 112) except final scraping.

Gouges are always allowed to rub against the work before you raise the handle to an angle at which the tool just starts cutting – but no further. The roughing-out gouge is usually held square to the work, or nearly so; spindle gouges are pointed in the direction you're moving them.

Gouges are used constantly for straight cuts – you just move them sideways with even pressure. To make a curve with a roughing-out gouge, you vary the pressure. To do so with a spindle or narrow deep-fluted gouge, roll the tool over or use a scooping action (both while still resting it on its bevel), depending on whether you want a convex or concave shape.

Scrapers

Easiest of all to use are scrapers. Beginners may be tempted to rely on them completely, for they're simply held horizontal and square to the workpiece, and moved sideways. However, chisels and gouges give a cleaner, faster cut, and scrapers are

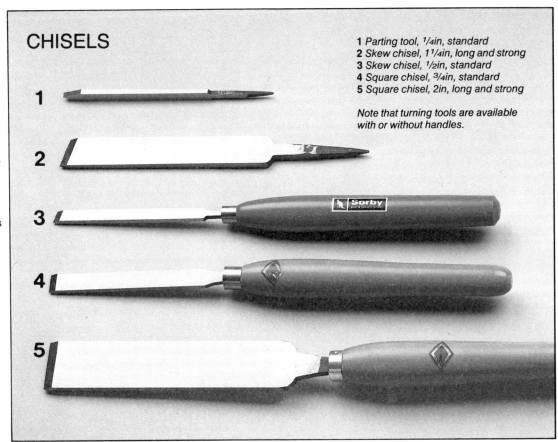

CHISELS

1 Parting tool, 1/4in, standard
2 Skew chisel, 1 1/4in, long and strong
3 Skew chisel, 1/2in, standard
4 Square chisel, 3/4in, standard
5 Square chisel, 2in, long and strong

Note that turning tools are available with or without handles.

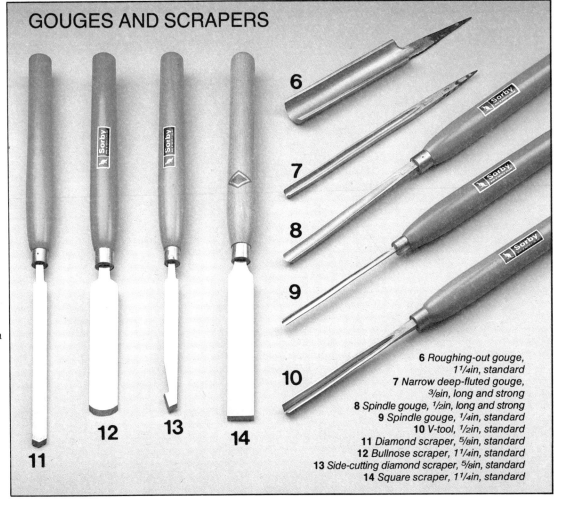

GOUGES AND SCRAPERS

6 Roughing-out gouge, 1 1/4in, standard
7 Narrow deep-fluted gouge, 3/8in, long and strong
8 Spindle gouge, 1/2in, long and strong
9 Spindle gouge, 1/4in, standard
10 V-tool, 1/2in, standard
11 Diamond scraper, 5/8in, standard
12 Bullnose scraper, 1 1/4in, standard
13 Side-cutting diamond scraper, 5/8in, standard
14 Square scraper, 1 1/4in, standard

best reserved for their own particular job: producing a fine finish on face-plate work after you've shaped it. They're ideal for this, and keep subsequent sanding down to the minimum.

The most often used scraper has a round-nosed ('bullnosed') end, but others are available with square ends, pointed ends, and only one side curved. People often grind the tips of scrapers to their own particular requirements.

Tool sizes
All turning tools come in three grades. The small ones available from do-it-yourself shops are useful for experimenting on a drill lathe attachment, but are too insubstantial for serious work on a bigger machine.

'Standard' tools, on the other hand, are fine for most purposes. But best of all is the variety known as 'long and strong'. You can buy just the blades, and turn the handles yourself – a very satisfying way of gaining good practice. Alternatively, the tools are also sold complete.

In each individual grade and pattern there are several sizes. Some are much more useful than others. A good selection, made from experience, is the following.

For **spindle** work:
● a 32mm (1¼in) deep-fluted (roughing-out) gouge
● one 6mm (¼in) and one 13mm (½in) shallow-fluted (spindle) gouge
● a 32mm (1¼in) skew chisel
● a 10mm (⅜in) parting tool.
For **face-plate** work:
● a 10mm (⅜in) deep-fluted gouge
● one 19mm (¾in) and one 32mm (1¼in) bullnose scraper
● a 32mm (1¼in) square scraper.

Such a set would do very nicely for almost any job; but you could undertake excellent small work with much less – even ordinary and woodcarving chisels. As always, it's a question of assessing your needs – and your means.

Accessories
To set up any job for spindle turning, you need a two- or four-pronged drive centre, plus a fixed or revolving tail centre (page 1689). These are usually supplied with the lathe.

Not supplied, but pretty essential, is a pair of outside callipers. You set these to the diameter you want (eg, when copying) and use them for checking your work, as in photograph 5 on page 110. Inside callipers have a similar use in face-plate turning, for gauging internal diameters.

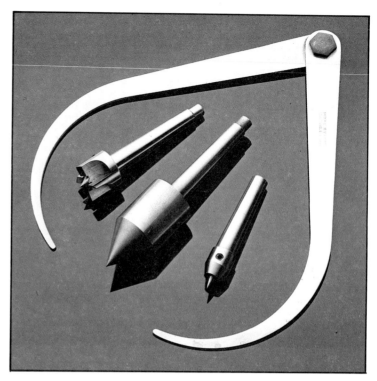

ACCESSORIES
Outside callipers, plus (top to bottom);
● *Four-pronged drive centre;*
● *Revolving tail centre;*
● *Fixed tail centre, ring or cup type*

hints

A Chisel
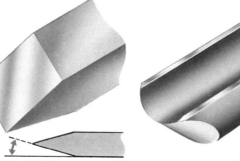
about 15°

B Spindle gouge
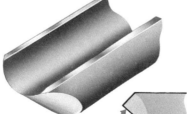
about 40°

C Deep-fluted gouge
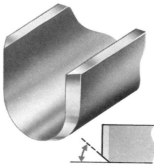
about 40°

D Scraper

about 80°

Woodturning tools require care in sharpening – especially as they often come from the factory only roughly ground. Gouges, in particular, may need re-shaping.

Additionally, turning tools come in for heavy wear in use, so they need sharpening constantly – often in the middle of a job.

All turning tools are honed on the ground bevel, not at a different angle as is usually the case with other woodworking tools. In fact roughing-out gouges are often used without being honed at all.

Refer to Chapter 10, pages 180-187 for information on sharpening techniques and

materials. Unless you have purpose-built equipment such as a powered bench grinder or whetstone (see also page 186), your main alternatives will be oil- or waterstones and abrasive sheets – the latter either in the form of pads for manual sharpening, or glued to discs for mounting in a power drill.

If you use a stone, or stones, you may find it sensible to keep one for chisels and square scrapers and one for gouges and bullnose scrapers, since curved tools tend to wear a stone unevenly and thus make it useless for flat bevels.
● *Chisels are bevelled on both sides at about 15° to the horizontal*

(A). The action of sharpening is similar to that used for an ordinary chisel.
● *Gouges require varying treatment. Spindle gouges (B) should have nicely rounded tips (viewed from above); roughing-out gouges, on the other hand, and usually narrow deep-fluted gouges are ground square (C).*

Both types are bevelled at 40° or so; but their different tip shapes, combined with their different flute depths, demand different sharpening techniques. Shallow-fluted gouges should be twisted bodily, so that the whole of the wide bevel comes into contact with

the abrasive. Deep-fluted gouges require only a wrist action.

When honing a gouge, work on the bevel first. Then remove the resulting burr from the inside of the flute with a slipstone (see pages 180-184), placed absolutely flat in the hollow.
● *Scrapers are bevelled at 80° (D). Ideally, the edge should be 'turned over' after honing, in the same way as that of a cabinet scraper. You rub a smooth steel rod – eg, a screwdriver shank – hard along the sharpened edge, to make a burr which will stick up proud of the flat side. It's this burr which does the actual cutting.*

BASIC WOODTURNING TECHNIQUES

Using a lathe isn't the most essential skill in woodwork. But it can prove extremely useful – for example when making repairs – and it's highly enjoyable (not to say addictive) to work with into the bargain.

A woodworking lathe is a machine which revolves a piece of timber at 600 to 2000rpm – either between two centres (spindle turning) or fixed at one side only (face-plate turning). Unlike all other woodworking machines, it doesn't cut. You shape the timber yourself by hand as it revolves, using a variety of steel tools.

It's the combination of the lathe's speed and your own handling of the tools, plus the instantaneous appearance of professional-looking, symmetrical shapes, which gives woodturning its tremendous fascination.

In addition, it offers the only practical means of making certain types of article. Spindle turning produces basically cylindrical objects: chair legs and stretchers, balusters, newel posts, table legs, tool handles etc. Faceplate turning produces basically round objects: bowls, plates, lamp-bases, eggcups and similar items.

How does a lathe work?

In spindle turning, the lathe's left-hand centre – that in the 'headstock' – is driven by the motor; the other is fixed to the 'tailstock', which slides along and locks in the required position to hold the work. Both are removable, and are usually just a push fit into tapered holes.

The drive centre has a point in the middle, and either two or four prongs to grip and turn the workpiece. The tail or 'dead' centre just has a point; in a 'revolving centre', this is mounted on bearings, whereas a fixed centre needs a dab of grease to cut down friction.

In face-plate turning, the work is held on a single revolving centre, often projecting from the left-hand side of the headstock for 'rear' or 'out' turning, which accommodates larger pieces and allows more freedom to work effectively.

You fix the wood onto a metal disc (the face plate) – usually with four screws, but there are other ways. For instance, you can screw a second block of wood to the face plate, and glue the workpiece to that with a piece of newspaper between the two glued faces. After turning, you remove the block (the glue will split on the paper line) and clean up the bottom of the piece with a plane.

Alternatively, there are various special chucks, for both spindle and face-plate turning.

In both types of work, your next step is to adjust and secure the tool rest as close as possible to the workpiece without actually touching it. It should be in line with the lathe centres, if not slightly higher, and for spindle turning it should also be parallel to the work.

Once all is set, you start the machine, hold the appropriate tool firmly on the rest, and bring it into action at the correct angle to shape the timber as required.

Choosing a lathe

Lathes come in a great many shapes and sizes, from drill attachments to huge cast-steel monsters.

For spindle turning, the important measurement is the distance between centres. For face-plate turning, it's the maximum diameter and depth of disc which can be worked. The former dimension is known as the 'swing'.

A good lathe should ideally
● measure 750mm (30in) between centres;
● accept a disc 300mm (12in) in diameter by 100mm (4in) thick;
● have a motor of not less than ⅜-½ HP;
● have a variable-speed mechanism (slower speeds being used, among other things, for pieces with larger diameters);
● be fixed onto a very sturdy base.

However, such a machine can be expensive, and is by no means vital for the beginner who wants to try his hand and find out if he has an aptitude for woodturning. The alternative is a small bench-mounted lathe driven by a portable power drill; there are several makes on the market, and you can probably pick up a secondhand one quite easily. It will have limited power and capacity, and will probably be restricted to spindle turning, but it will still be capable of good work if you set it up correctly and securely.

Materials for woodturning

There's no single ideal timber for turning. Any wood can be used. Although certain timbers do work better than others, some of the more difficult ones will give a very good finish if worked with the correct tools, properly sharpened.

Ordinary pine, preferably of 'best joinery' quality, free of knots and defects, will turn well with extremely sharp tools. Even if you can't get a very good finish straight 'from the tool', you can soon remedy that with abrasive paper. However, pine lacks the strength and rigidity needed for things like the thin sides of large bowls.

The common hardwoods such as beech, oak, ash and mahogany all turn well both in spindle and face-plate work. Particularly good are elm, sycamore and yew.

PARTS OF A LATHE

A lathe may be either a fairly small drill-mounted attachment, or a free-standing integral machine like the one pictured here. Even the latter isn't as expensive as perhaps it looks. You can choose from a wide range of models.

The fixed headstock, with its electric motor, is also a gearbox; often you can change speeds by moving the drive belt from pulley to pulley. Protruding from its right-hand side is the 'drive centre' for spindle or face-plate turning; the centre at

the left (not present in drill attachments) is especially for face-plate work.
The tailstock slides along the 'bed' before being secured in position, and is then further adjusted to grip the workpiece tightly.

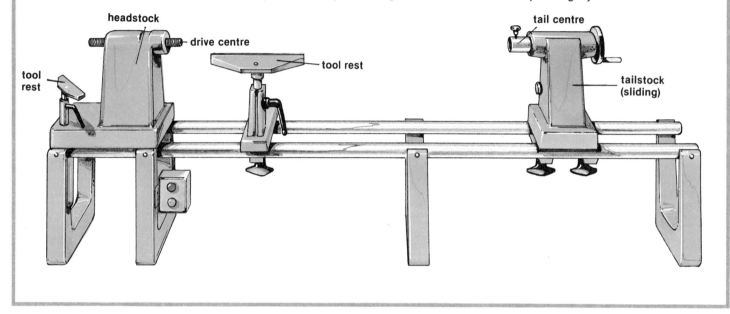

In addition, timber can be turned at any stage of dryness. If you get hold of a nice piece of 'green' (freshly cut) wood, you can use it for a bowl. It must be free from defects and 'heart' (the centre of the tree). Cut it roughly to a disc, then mount it on the face plate and roughly shape and hollow it, leaving a wall thickness of about 13mm (½in). Now the timber can dry out much faster, especially if it's kept in an airing cupboard for about three months. During this time it will distort – but, once dry, it can be remounted on the lathe, re-turned and finished.

If you want to use the piece for spindle turning, make it as near cylindrical as possible by splitting with an axe, turn it to a perfect cylinder with a deep-fluted 32mm (1¼in) gouge – see photographs – and store it till dry before use. Waxing the ends will help to stop it drying out too fast and thus splitting.

Green timber is a pleasure to turn because it cuts so well when you use sharp tools, producing heaps of curly streamers. Just to put such a piece between centres and turn it down to nothing is great fun and invaluable practice.

First things first
In fact, before attempting any job on your new lathe, it's a good idea to put a piece of scrap wood on the machine, turn it to a

cylinder and experiment with using all the different tools. Even if it's just 50x50mm (2x2in) softwood, you'll begin to get a feel for the whole procedure. This will undoubtedly prevent frustration and save you from wasting good timber. There's only one way to learn and improve in turning, and that's to practise as much as you can.

The lathe is a very safe machine if used with care, respect and patience. However, the following safety precautions must not be ignored:
● always tie long hair back and up. Never wear any loose or dangling clothes – ie, scarves, baggy sleeves. You'll be working close to the machine, and if any of these things get caught you can kill yourself quite easily
● before starting the machine, revolve the workpiece by hand to make sure it spins freely without obstruction
● for spindle work, always check that the tailstock is up tight
● check that the tool rest is securely fixed
● always place the tool on the rest before presenting it to the wood – never the other way round, or it will be violently snatched
● wear goggles when roughing out an uneven piece of timber
● always be patient and wait for the machine to stop before you detach the work. Avoid grabbing it to slow it down.

● never use blunt tools; always maintain a keen edge
● control tools firmly and manipulate them carefully, especially in face-plate work, to avoid digging in.

Starting work
Using the lathe is almost wholly a matter of knowing exactly how to handle the tools concerned – gouges, chisels and (for face-plate work) scrapers. All these are shown and described in action on pages 104 -106, as well as in the photographs here.

Very commonly, turning jobs involve copying – either for repair purposes, or in order to produce, say, four identical legs. Two things help here. One is to place the pattern in front of you so you can see it while you're turning. The other is a pair of callipers, which you can set to the exact diameter (or diameters) of the pattern and use for constant checking.

When you've finished the actual cutting, you can not only sand your work while it's still on the lathe, but even rub on finishing treatments such as french polish and wax if you run the machine slowly.

Turning is a craft in its own right, with many more aspects than we can detail here. For anyone who's seriously interested, there are many books about it, and short beginners' courses are widely advertised in woodwork magazines.

SPINDLE TURNING: SETTING UP

1 Cut a length of square timber at least 6m (¼in) larger each way than your intended diameter, and 25mm (1in) too long. Mark diagonals on both ends.

2 Use a pair of compasses to draw the largest possible circle on each end of the timber, centring it on the intersection of the diagonals.

3 Until you've gained some experience, it's easier to plane off the four edges before turning, making a roughly octagonal section.

4 Position the drive centre in the middle of one end and tap it hard. If you're using a metal hammer, a wooden block will protect the centre.

5 Repeat more gently at the far end. If using a fixed tail centre, give the wood a spot of grease or a rub with a candle to reduce friction.

6 Insert the drive centre into the headstock. Its spike and prongs should fit into the dents you made in the timber when tapping the centre home.

7 Fit the tail centre into the tailstock, slide the latter along, secure it where you need it, centre the workpiece at both ends and tighten up.

8 Secure the tool rest on the left (if you're right-handed), parallel to and level with a line between the centres. Check that the work revolves freely.

9 Start work with the roughing-out gouge. Place it on the rest, roughly square to the work but tilted by 30° so the wood just rubs its bevelled tip.

SPINDLE TURNING: ROUGHING DOWN

1 Raise the tool's handle towards the horizontal, so that the edge starts to cut into the revolving wood. Keep the gouge at that angle whenever you work.

2 Move the gouge repeatedly along the rest from left to right (if you're right-handed), twisting it slightly but applying even forward pressure.

3 When you've removed the flat surfaces from that part of the piece, move the tool rest along, secure it and repeat the procedure on the other half.

4 After checking that the resulting cylinder is even, set callipers to about 1.5mm (¹⁄₁₆in) more than the widest diameter of your finished piece.

5 Use the parting tool (lowering the handle from level till it cuts) to make a series of rings down to your intended diameter. Check each with the callipers.

6 With the roughing-out gouge again, bring the cylinder down to that diameter by cutting it level with the bottoms of all the rings.

READY REFERENCE

TOOLS FOR TURNING

Pages 104 -106 give full details of the various hand-held cutting tools used in woodturning. Here's a brief guide to what they do:

Chisels are used only in spindle work, mainly to give a clean finish but also for tight convex curves. The skew chisel (A), with its angled tip, is the commonest. The parting tool (B) is a type of chisel usually used for cutting deeply into the workpiece, and right through it altogether when finishing a job (hence its name).

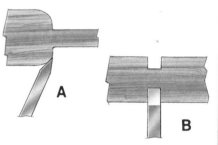

Gouges can be shallow- or deep-fluted. Narrow shallow-fluted gouges (spindle gouges – C) are used in spindle work. Wide deep-fluted gouges (roughing-out gouges – D) are for spindle work too; narrow ones (E) are for face-plate work, such as bowl turning. The latter requires a fair bit of skill.

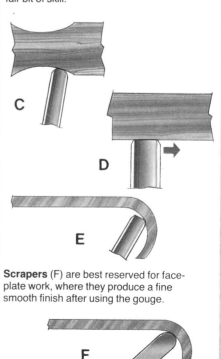

Scrapers (F) are best reserved for face-plate work, where they produce a fine smooth finish after using the gouge.

SPINDLE TURNING: SHAPING AND SANDING

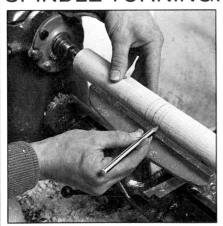

1 Revolve the wood and mark with a pencil the centre lines of any hollow grooves and/or raised 'beads' you want to run round the piece.

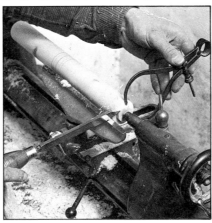

2 Set the callipers to the finished diameter of each end of the piece, and use them for checking as you cut the ends down with the parting tool.

3 Use the roughing-out gouge or a spindle gouge (again from left to right) for the main curve. Check against any piece you're copying, or use a template.

4 Begin each groove with the skew chisel, lowering its handle to cut. Make two straight, angled cuts for a V-shaped groove. Use the heel of the tool.

5 This chisel is also ideal for rounding over the edges of grooves; twist it while cutting. Make sure its pointed toe doesn't dig into the work.

6 You can also use a 6mm (¼in) spindle gouge for rounding-over, as well as general shaping. As with all gouges, you raise the handle till it cuts.

7 A spindle gouge has a deep, curved bevel. For tight curves, use that as a guide while carefully angling and twisting the tool in your fingers.

8 When you've got the shape you want (the pencil marks should still show) remove the tool rest and hold glasspaper to the work – underneath, for safety.

9 Follow coarser with finer grades, and use folded sheets for crevices. To avoid scratches, don't move the abrasive too quickly from side to side.

FACE-PLATE TURNING

1 For a bowl, cut a rough disc (eg, with a jigsaw). Then plane one side flat – often best done across the grain with a sharp plane. Sand it now too.

2 Fix the face plate very securely to the smooth side of the disc (eg, with short screws). For smooth turning, centre it as exactly as possible.

3 Fit the face plate to the headstock, fix the tool rest near the disc's edge, level a 10mm (³⁄₈in) deep-fluted gouge to cut, and pass it across the edge.

4 After making the edge perfectly flat and circular with even strokes, use the same gouge to shape the outside of the bowl as you require.

5 Re-adjust the tool rest and flatten the disc's face with even strokes across it, again using a fairly narrow deep-fluted gouge – from right to left.

6 Hollow the bowl with the same gouge, working into the centre. On the first cut, beware of skidding; after that, the cut timber will support the tool.

7 Continue hollowing wider and deeper, angling and twisting the gouge as necessary. Check you're not cutting too far through the bottom of the bowl.

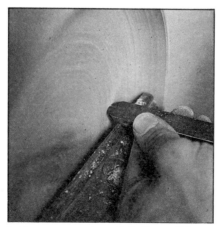

8 Use a scraper (usually bullnosed) for a fine finish. Hold it square and level, and pass it from side to side. Angle a small scraper into the corner if necessary.

9 Continue scraping till the bowl is exactly as you want it. Then stop the lathe, remove the face plate, detach the bowl and fill any screw holes in the base.

CHAPTER 5

USING A ROUTER

The power router opens up whole new areas to the home woodworker,
enabling special effects to be created that were formerly
the province of the fully-equipped carpentry shop.
By choosing the right cutters and using some simple jigs and guides,
you can save money by shaping your own mouldings.

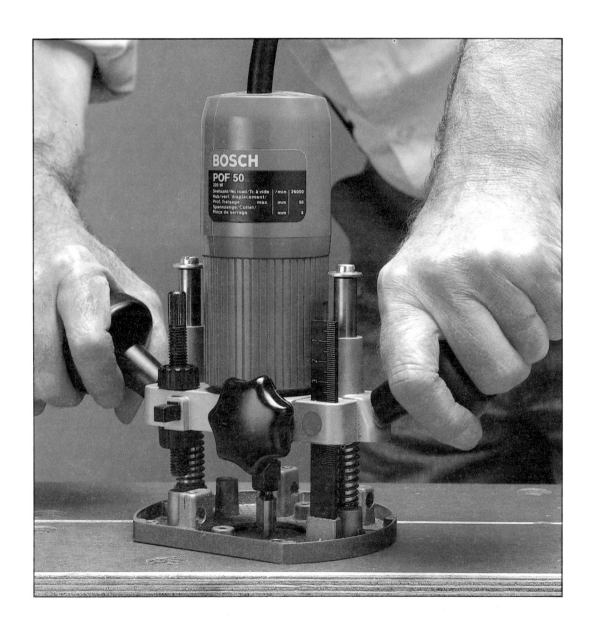

SETTING UP AND CUTTING GROOVES

The router is the ultimate portable power tool. Almost all the jobs it tackles are difficult or impossible with any other machine.

The power router is both beautifully simple and outstandingly versatile. As on all power tools, its heart is an electric motor which turns a spindle. Its most important feature, however, is the motor's very high speed – between 18,000 and 27,000 rpm, compared with the maximum of 4000 rpm given by power drills. This is what allows it to handle such an enormous variety of grooving, rebating, shaping and other cutting jobs in wood, plastic and even soft metals.

A router's power is from 300 to 2000W. Naturally, the more powerful models are meant for professionals and are more expensive. The power sets strict limits on the amount of material you can cut away without overloading the motor. A 300W model will make a groove 6mm (¼in) square in one go, whereas a 600W motor allows a 10x6mm (⅜x¼in) groove.

This means that some jobs take a bit longer with a low-powered machine, because you need to make two or three passes (adjusting it for a deeper cut each time) instead of just one or two.

At the end of the spindle is a 'collet chuck', into which you fit the bit (also called a cutter), very much as you fit a drill bit into a drill chuck. A collet chuck, however, is tightened with a spanner – while you hold the spindle steady with a tommy bar, another spanner, or a locking switch. Collets are made in three main sizes, to accept bits whose shank diameter is ¼, ⅜ or ½in.

The 'overhead router' used in industry is a fixed machine, suspended in a large stand – like an enormous drill stand, but fastened to the floor – and lowered onto the workpiece with a lever. On the portable router, however, the motor (complete with spindle) is mounted in a frame or 'carriage' with handles, in which it moves up and down as you adjust it. This frame has a flat base, through which the bit projects to make the cut. In operation you generally rest the base on the workpiece, and move the machine along bodily – though you can fix the machine and move the workpiece instead.

The general principle is the same as when using shaping cutters in a power drill: see pages 92 -93 for more details. But the router is far easier to handle (though larger models can be quite heavy), and it's capable of harder and more efficient work because it's purpose-built.

The plunging router

Portable routers are either fixed-base or plunging models. A fixed-base router is lowered into the material with the bit already protruding from the base, after you've got it to project the required amount by adjusting the height of the motor in the carriage.

With a plunging router, on the other hand, the motor is on sprung mountings, and this means you set the projection (ie, the depth of cut) in two stages. First you lower the motor until the bit just touches the workpiece, and you rotate one of the handles to lock it in position. Then, on most models, you simply adjust the height of the depth bar – a sliding or threaded vertical rod fixed to the side of the motor – so that, when you 'plunge' the motor right down to cut, the lower end of the rod will meet the base of the carriage and prevent your going any deeper than you want. Lastly, you turn the handle the other way to release the motor so that it springs right up, back to its original position.

That done, you're ready to start cutting. This is a straightforward matter of positioning the router where you want it, switching on, and pressing down fully on the handles to plunge the rotating bit into the workpiece.

KNOW YOUR ROUTER

To get the best from a power router, you need to know how to set it up for the cut you want. This is a typical 'plunge' model – so called because of the sprung mountings, which make for safety and accuracy. You position the router before pushing down to start the cut – and let the motor spring up again as soon as you've finished.

All these router bits (cutters) will make grooves – and shape edges (see pages 119 -123). Some, like 10, give varied profiles.

KEY
1 Straight: one-flute (veining)
2 Straight: two-flute
3 Groove and chamfer
4 Radius (veining)
5 Core box, radius or half-round
6 V-carving or V-groove (veining)
7 V-groove and chamfer
8 Panel raising
9 Chamfer
10 Ovolo
11 Pointed round or quarter-round
12 Pointed ogee
13 Ogee (end cutting)
14 Panelling
15 Classic

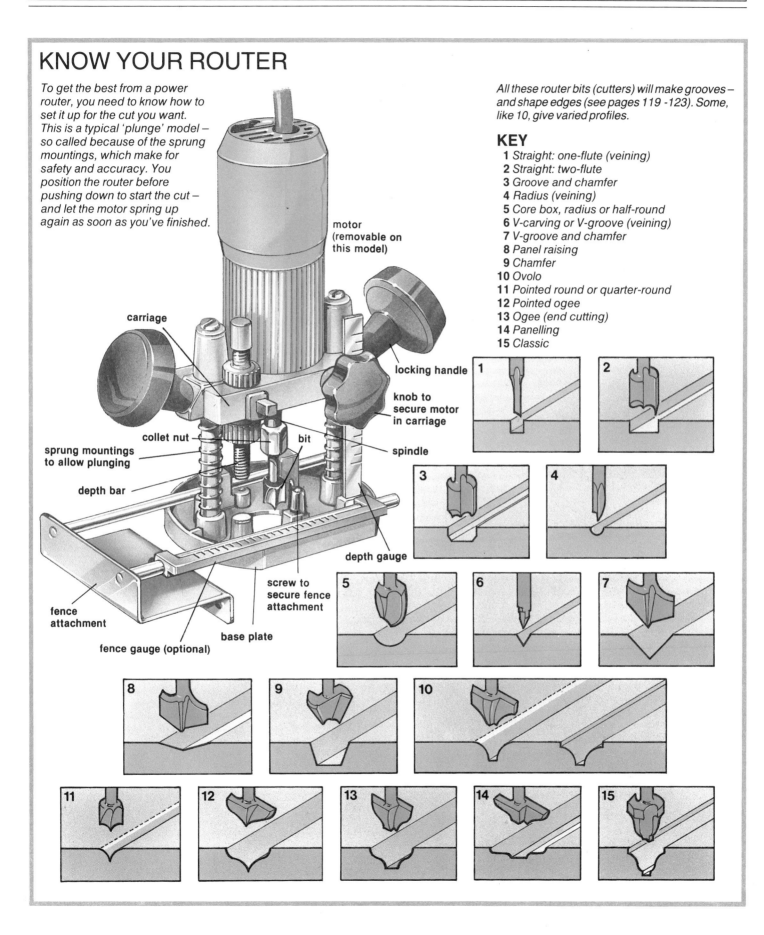

carriage

motor (removable on this model)

locking handle

knob to secure motor in carriage

collet nut

bit

spindle

sprung mountings to allow plunging

depth bar

depth gauge

screw to secure fence attachment

fence attachment

base plate

fence gauge (optional)

Then you turn the handle again to lock it there, before running the tool along to do the actual job. When you've finished, you just use the handle to unlock it, allow it to spring back up, and switch off.

The plunging router's sprung action makes it safer than the fixed-base type, and also ensures that the bit always enters the work at exactly 90°.

Using a router

If the sound of a router motor drops from a high-pitched whine during a cut, you're probably trying to work too fast – or cut too deeply. The harder the material and the wider the bit, the slower and shallower each cut will have to be to avoid straining the motor. The general rule is to cut no deeper than the diameter of the bit.

A smell of burning, on the other hand, may mean you're cutting too slowly. The important thing is to acquire a feeling for the tool's natural cutting rate. It shouldn't take long.

But either of these symptoms may denote a blunt bit instead. So may a 'furry' finish (although that's common on moist wood anyway), or difficulty in pushing the router along. And remember that, as with any other tool, the texture of your material matters. In solid timber, the grain may dictate the direction in which you have to move the machine for a clean cut.

As for safety, remember that a power router runs at a tremendous speed. Treat it with respect. Wear goggles to protect your eyes from whirling dust. On a plunging router, always release the lock after a cut to let the bit spring up out of the way. Unplug the machine whenever you're not using it – and keep it in a cupboard. If stored on a shelf, it could fall off; and, if you leave it on the floor, wood chips and other debris may get into the air intake.

Router bits

Router bits come in an extremely wide range of shapes – from straight bits, which are for grooving, to angled and curved patterns, plus a number of others. Not only knowledge but also imagination is required to exploit them to the full, for just about all can be used in several different ways; and of course you can use more than one in succession for creating compound shapes – see below.

It's also important to know what they're made from. Although special drilling bits have been designed for use with plunging routers, no bit or cutter of ordinary steel should ever be used in a power router, because the high speed will very likely smash it to pieces. Proper router bits are made, instead, of high-speed steel (HSS) and tungsten carbide (TC).

HSS bits are cheaper, and fine for working softwoods and fairly soft plastics. Their draw-

SETTING UP FOR A CUT

1 *With the machine unplugged and the motor removed from its carriage if possible, steady the spindle with the tommy bar.*

2 *Insert the shank of the bit into the collet, tighten the nut as far as you can by hand, and then finish securing it with a spanner.*

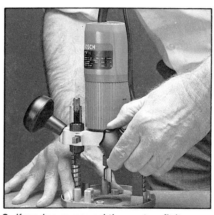

3 *If you've removed the motor, fit it back into the carriage now, and tighten it up firmly with the knob or other fastening provided.*

4 *'Plunge' the motor down in its carriage till the bit meets the surface on which the machine is standing, and lock it there with the handle.*

5 *Adjust the depth bar until the gap below it roughly equals the depth of cut you want – ie, the amount the bit should project. Release the lock.*

6 *Plunge the bit below the surface through a convenient hole, use the gauge to check the depth, and let the motor spring back up.*

ROUTING GROOVES

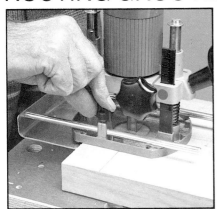

1 *Set the fence attachment so that, with the fence against the edge, the groove will be in the position you want. Mark the groove out first if you like.*

2 *Switch on, plunge into the workpiece some way along the groove, and lock the handle when you've reached the full pre-set depth.*

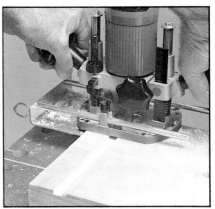

3 *Move the router along, still holding the fence firmly against the edge – especially at the end. Then return across the piece to complete the groove.*

4 *Repeat the procedure after doubling the depth of cut. Sometimes a cut takes three passes, depending on the machine, the material and the bit.*

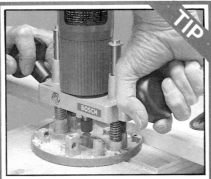

5 *If grooving across the middle of a piece, you may have to abandon the fence attachment and instead cramp on a straight batten as a guide.*

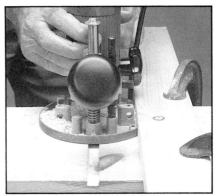

6 *A router will cut through knots and other blemishes without difficulty – provided you keep its cutting speed up, without dawdling.*

back is a tendency to blunt quickly, which is greatly accelerated if they're used on harder and/or more abrasive materials. However, by the same token, they're soft enough to sharpen at home – if you know how. Not only must the front of each cutting edge be dead flat and smooth; there must also be a 'clearance angle' of at least 15° between its back and the circle made by the bit as it rotates.

For chipboard, plywood and blockboard (all of which contain synthetic resins), as well as for plastic laminates and glass-reinforced plastics, you need TC bits. They're even a good idea for use on hardboard and hardwoods. Their higher initial cost – and they can be very expensive – is often outweighed by their much longer life. Usually they consist of TC tips (cutting edges) brazed onto steel bits – but you can get bits made from solid TC. For eventual sharpening, TC and TC-tipped (TCT) bits must go back to the manufacturer or another specialist firm.

Remember that a router is only as good as its bit. If you find you have a blunt one, don't just go on using it and hoping for the best – see that it's sharpened. What's more, bit shanks should be kept smooth and undamaged to avoid damaging the collet when you insert them.

Routing grooves

Cutting grooves across the face of timber or boards is a fine example of a task which is as trouble-free with a router as it's demanding by hand.

Even the marking-out process (see Housing joints, pages 62 -65) is simpler, because you need only indicate where one side of the groove is to go. In some cases you can even omit marking-out altogether, because the essential thing in all routing work (except for a very few truly freehand applications) is to make sure the tool is properly guided anyway: see *Ready Reference*.

The simplest method of doing this is to use a fence attachment. This is very similar to the rip fence on a circular saw: in other words, it's a removable metal fitting which locates against the edge of the workpiece, and thus keeps the router on a parallel course. It's important that the edge should be reasonably straight in the first place – in other words, that there should be no bumps or hollows which are pronounced, and/or which run for any distance. However, if there are only small unevennesses, the fence attachment will actually bridge the defects and allow a straight groove despite a less-than-perfect edge.

You can extend the fence attachment, too, by screwing to it a piece of timber or board about double its length. This is very useful when the groove runs right out at one side of the material, because you can 'follow through' with it, still keeping it pressed against the edge as the cut finishes – thereby preventing

7 *Grooves needn't have square bottoms. Different-shaped bits produce a whole variety of profiles, many of which are extremely decorative.*

8 *Grooving with a shaped bit can produce a panelled effect. Sharp corners will always occur where the grooves cross each other.*

the tool from suddenly slipping, as it can easily do with an ordinary fence.

Better still, you can also cramp a straight-edged piece of scrap material (an 'overcut board') beyond the workpiece and level with it, and simply continue the cut into that. This will not only prevent a ragged end to the cut, especially when working across the grain, but also provide additional support for the fence and so help to ensure an absolutely parallel groove.

Some manufacturers supply a special guide roller or extra fence plates, to enable the router to follow edges which have fairly gentle curves. These are screwed to the main fence attachment. However, edges which have sharp concave curves, or are otherwise too elaborate, will rule out such devices.

Even if you want a straight groove, the fence attachment itself will be no use if the edge is curved or angled, or if you're working

too far in from the nearest parallel straight edge. In either of these cases your best plan is to cramp on a straight, solid guide batten parallel to your intended groove, and run the machine against that. The batten must, of course, be at such a distance that the bit will run along your mark. That means the distance from the edge of the router base to the centre of the bit, minus half the bit diameter.

It also helps if the batten overhangs at both ends, so you can keep the router pressed against it when entering and leaving the cut. The idea is, once again, to avoid swinging off course.

If you're cutting a whole set of housings, you can even add a T-piece to the end of the batten. Apart from forming an overcut board, this will enable you, without effort, to locate the batten squarely every time. Moreover, when you've continued a groove through into the T-piece, you'll be able to use it as a guide mark for aligning subsequent cuts (see *Ready Reference*).

If possible, fit your router with a straight bit whose diameter equals the width of the groove you want. In the case of a housing, this will be the thickness of the piece being housed (usually a shelf).

With a light-duty router, start by setting the depth of cut at about 2 to 3mm (1/16 to 1/8in), and remove that much again with each subsequent pass; in other words, double the setting for the second pass and treble it for the third. That way, three passes will cut a housing 6 to 9mm (1/4 to 3/8in) deep. In chipboard, don't go deeper than half the board's thickness, in case you weaken it too much.

Some routers have a 'rotary turret stop', which is simply a means of pre-setting the depth bar for three different heights. This allows you to change the depth of cut for the second and third passes merely by rotating the device to the next setting, without having to stop and adjust the tool.

Rotating bits mean that all routed internal corners will be rounder, however slightly (the radius depends, of course, on the bit diameter). The ends of stopped housings are no exception; you'll either have to chisel them square, or round the edges of the housed pieces to match. The latter operation, however (see pages 119 -123), is simply another straightforward cut in the router's repertoire.

Shaped grooves

A groove needn't be square-bottomed. There are a number of graceful shapes for decorative work. You can create panelled effects, too (although grooving in man-made boards will, of course, expose the core).

Moreover, even simple combined cuts – for example, a rounded groove 15mm (5/8in) wide superimposed on a deeper square groove 10mm (3/8in) wide – can look very good.

READY REFERENCE

GUIDING THE GROOVE
A long strip of timber or plywood screwed to the fence attachment (A) makes it easier to keep the router steady as you finish a cut.

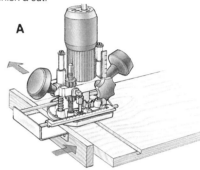

An **overcut board** (B) achieves the same result by supporting the fence (short or long), and also prevents splintering at the end of cross-grain cuts.

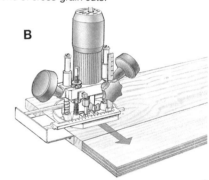

A **T-square guide** (C) is ideal for repeated grooves which are too far from a parallel edge for a fence attachment to be useful. After each cut, you un-clamp it and reposition it for the next groove. The T-piece, if accurately fitted, ensures instant squareness, and acts as an overcut board; the groove routed in it aids alignment with your marked groove position.

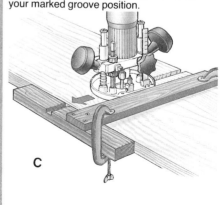

PROFILING & BOX JOINTING

Once you've grasped the power router's basic workings, you can move on from making simple grooving cuts to the vast possibilities of edge profiling, box jointing and other techniques.

After cutting housings and other square or shaped grooves (see pages 114 - 118), the use of the router that next springs to mind is usually shaping edges.

That may sound unimportant, but it covers a tremendous range of jobs, both functional and decorative. The router will cut any number of ornamental mouldings (eg, ovolo, ogee) along the edges of tabletops, shelves, skirting-boards and the like – and indeed make lengths of moulding, such as architrave or staff bead, to your own design from the timber of your choice, as an alternative to buying them off the shelf. It will also produce straightforward rebates, plus bevels and chamfers at various angles; trim off overhanging edges of plastic laminate after it's been glued down; and, very importantly, make a whole variety of joints which involve grooved, tongued and rebated edges.

Bits for edging
The first step, of course, is to choose the right shape from the range of bits available. All grooving bits (see page 115) can be used for edging, and there are also several for edging alone. Rebates, for example, can be cut either with an ordinary two-flute bit, or a special wide rebating bit. Other edging bits include rounding-over, coving, ogee and a number of others. Any router supplier should be able to give you further details, or tell you where to find them.

Each individual router bit will produce cuts of different shapes, depending not only on its profile and size but also on your depth setting. In the case of edging, you can also vary the shape according to the width of cut – ie, whether the bit just skims the edge or bites deeply into it.

Guiding the cut
There are two main ways of profiling edges with a router. One is to use the fence attachment – if necessary with accessories for following curves. The other is to fit a 'self-guiding' bit.

As when grooving, working with the fence attachment is a simple matter of keeping it pressed firmly against the edge of the material. In this case, that's the self-same edge in which you're making the cut – therefore the fence must be right underneath the router base, on or near its centre line.

A self-guiding bit has its own built-in guide, in the form of a pin – like a small extra shank, but at the opposite end – or else a roller bearing. This guide is in addition to the cutting edges and almost always below them. You keep it pressed against the workpiece (whether straight or curved) in exactly the same manner as a fence attachment, thus ensuring a uniform cut all the way.

Self-guiding bits involve no cumbersome setting up, unlike the various types of fence. They will also follow the tightest curves, and even go round corners. Their corresponding snag is that they reproduce any bumps or hollows in the original edge, to a greater extent than fence attachments do. On blockboard, for instance, the guide will wander into any exposed voids between the core battens. So, if you can't get your edge absolutely true and smooth, it's best to stick with the fence attachment – or, still better, a guide batten clamped across the work. A template (see pages 124 -128 for details) is another possibility.

A guide batten (or template) is also needed if for any reason you have to cut away the whole of an edge, rather than just part of it, since there will be nothing for a guide pin or bearing to run against when using less than the bit's maximum width of cut.

READY REFERENCE

GROOVING EDGES
If you use an ordinary one- or two-flute bit for edge grooving (A), the router must run along the edge. So you'll need extra material on each side to prevent the machine tilting over.

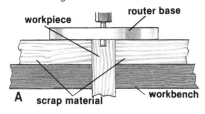

If you use an arbor and groover (B), the router runs over the face, so it will be steadier. This method also lets you position the cut more accurately, since you use the depth adjustment.

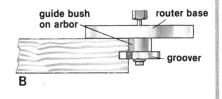

ROUTER BITS FOR EDGING

Some bits (1-5) must be used with a fence attachment, guide batten or template.
1 *Dovetailing*
2 *Edge-rounding*
3 *Double edge-rounding*
4 *Staff bead*
5 *Tongueing for staff bead*

also cuts groove 1

2   3

4   5

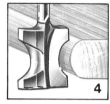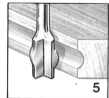

Others have a guide pin or bearing, whose size (6-9) varies the cut.
6 *Rounding-over (large pin)*
7 *Ovolo or corner round (small pin)*
8 *Ovolo or corner round (small bearing)*

9 *Rounding-over (large bearing)*
10 *Rebating (pin)*
11 *Chamfering (pin)*
12 *Coving (pin)*
13 *Roman ogee (pin)*

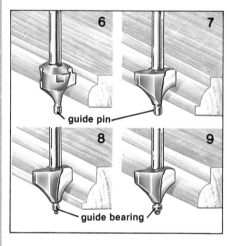

6   7

guide pin

8   9

guide bearing

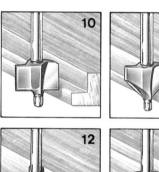

10   11

12   13

There are also special bits for trimming plastic laminates.
14 *Pierce and trim*
15 *90° trimmer (self-guiding)*
16 *90° trimmer*
17 *90° trimmer with guide bearing*
18 *Bevel trimmer*

The pierce and trim bit (14) drills through the laminate, then cuts it away cleanly. This is useful if you've laminated over an internal cut-out, for a sink in a kitchen worktop, for example.

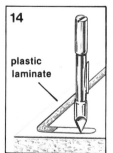

14

plastic laminate

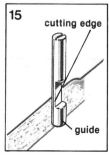

15

cutting edge

guide

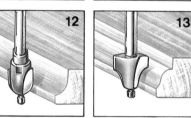

18
17
16

PROFILING EDGES

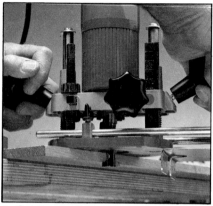

1 *Set the depth for the exact edge profile you require (see page 114). The bit shown inserted here is known as a staff bead cutter.*

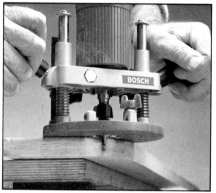

5 *When cutting, keep the guide pin pressed against the edge. That way, the bit will follow the edge even if it's curved or has corners.*

Bits with roller bearings, as opposed to pins, are very expensive, and so only worth getting if you'll be using them a great deal. Their advantages are that the bearing, unlike a pin, won't burn or mark the edge, and that you have only to change the bearing in order to vary the width of the cut (and thus its shape).

In all edging work it's important to remember that routers can usually only do their job properly if they're fed (moved along the workpiece) against the rotation of the bit – ie, so that the bit's cutting edges are always travelling into the cut rather than away from it. Remember that the bit rotates clockwise if you're looking from above at a router pointing downwards. The same principle applies if the router is fixed in position – see pages 124 -128.

You can in fact work the other way, eg, for a clean cut in difficult grain. But care is needed in order to prevent the bit from 'snatching' uncontrollably.

2 *If you're not using a self-guiding bit – see below – slide the fence attachment in and adjust it for the precise width of cut.*

3 *With the router plunged and locked at the pre-set depth, switch it on and make the cut. Always 'feed' it so the bit rotates into the work.*

4 *A self-guiding bit lets you do without a fence, because it has its own guide pin (like the one shown here) or roller-bearing guide.*

6 *A rounding-over bit like this will also give a 'stepped' moulding: you just have to set it for a deeper cut (see no. 10, page 115).*

7 *A coving bit gives yet another edge profile. Simply stopping a cut short always produces a nicely rounded end like the one shown here.*

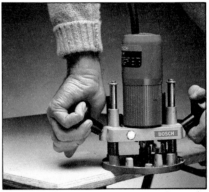

8 *A chamfer bit puts a neat angle on the edge. A guide pin, like a guide bearing, enables you to follow corners as well as curved edges.*

Routing joints

When you make box furniture from man-made or solid timber, one of your prime considerations must naturally be how to joint it. In the ordinary way, this isn't an easy decision. Butt joints are weak, and almost any form of strengthening (nails, screws, timber strips or even assembly fittings) is bound to show – inside the cabinet, if not outside.

The professional answer is to use a joint which doesn't need reinforcement, and it's here that power tools come into their own. The router, in particular, is ideal when you want a rebate in one or both pieces. You can match a rebate in one piece with a groove in the other, to form a barefaced housing joint – see pages 62 -65. And one of the stongest joints available (though it's not for corners, and not for chipboard) is the dovetail housing. This is very easily made by using a dovetail bit – set to a uniform depth – to cut both the groove and the sides of the matching tongue. You'll need the fence attachment, and maybe a guide batten for the groove. For a tongue of exactly the right width to fit the groove, careful alignment is required. Remember, too, that the 'undercut' dovetail shape means you can't plunge into the work.

Any kind of tongue-and-groove joint, in fact, is a natural for the router. If you're grooving an edge, make sure that the machine is properly supported so it can't tilt while cutting. This may mean clamping additional pieces on either side of the work. It's better, however, if you're doing a lot of edge grooving, to use an arbor with a groover fixed over it. An arbor is a separate shank, often with a guide bush or bearing, that fits into the collet. A groover is like a circular-saw blade but smaller, and with fewer and thicker teeth. The advantage of this arrangement is that you can run the router base over the face of the work, as with most edging jobs, and thereby gain stability.

A matching tongue can usually best be formed by cutting two rebates.

Trimming plastic laminates

Before fixing a sheet of plastic laminate to a panel sub-surface, you'll naturally try to cut it to approximately the right size, aiming to trim the slight overhang once the sheet is stuck down in position.

Laminates are exceptionally hard, and therefore not really suitable for shaving with a hand plane. A router, however, makes light work of the job. You'll need a tungsten carbide (TC) bit, solid or tipped, to avoid rapid blunting. Special trimming bits are available; some make right-angled cuts, some make bevelled cuts at various slopes, and some provide a choice between the two. Several are self-guiding – and, to make the work even easier, there are bits which will trim

ROUTING BOX JOINTS

1 *For a dovetail housing, start by cutting the groove. Use a dovetail bit – and don't plunge into the material, or you'll spoil the job.*

2 *Clamp the other piece on end, with scrap wood either side. Without changing the depth of cut, set the fence and mould one side of the tongue.*

3 *Re-adjust the fence to cut the other side. Keep the scrap edge on your left – ie, against the direction in which the bit rotates.*

6 *Clamp the other piece on end and make an identical cut; if using a fence, don't change the setting. Use scrap timber to steady the router as you work.*

7 *When you fit the pieces together, the cuts should match exactly. You may need to fix lipping to conceal the exposed core of a man-made board.*

8 *For edge grooving, a slotter on an arbor makes it easier to keep the tool steady, since it still rests on the face. The guide bearing follows the edge.*

laminate from both faces of a panel at once.

Even when using a TC bit, make sure the laminate doesn't overhang by more than about one-third of the bit diameter, otherwise you'll cause unnecessary wear. Varying the depth setting, too, will spread the wear more evenly along the cutting edges.

Unless you're using a self-guiding bit, you'll need to set up the fence attachment for the job. What's known as a 'fine screw feed' – available on some machines – is very useful here, as for many other tasks. It's a mechanism that adjusts the fence attachment more precisely than you can manage when you just slide it over and tighten the screws.

If the panel's edge is lipped with laminate too, it's best to trim that before laminating the top surface – so that any marks left by the bit will only mar the top of the base board, to which the laminate has still to be fixed, rather than the plastic finish itself. Marks on the edge lipping will be much less obvious.

You needn't turn the router on its side for this, as long as you're using a bit with a 'bottom cut' – namely cutting edges at the bottom as well as on each side. At least one router manufacturer supplies a special 'sub-base' accessory to act as a guide for this particular operation.

Occasionally, you may have already cut holes in the base board (eg, for an inset sink and taps) before laminating it. If you fit a 'pierce and trim' bit, you can then drill through the laminate – and trim it exactly to follow the shape of the cut-out, because the bit is self-guiding, with the pin being aligned for this purpose.

Cutting circles

A unique feature of the router is the ease with which it will make a perfect circle. Most models come with an accessory which acts like the point of a pair of compasses. You use it as a pivot while you swing the machine round.

This way you can employ the various grooving bits to make any number of patterns which depend on circles or parts of circles. If you take enough passes at successively greater depths, you can even cut right through the material – producing, for example, a perfectly circular table-top or bread-board. Such a job is almost impossible with hand tools alone.

Freehand routing

It's also possible to use a router completely freehand, without any sort of fence or other guide at all. This happens mainly when you're 'carving' or 'engraving' lettering or other patterns on a flat surface, and it needs a bit of practice. A light machine is easiest to handle on this type of job. The usual bits for the purpose are 'veining' bits (see page 115), which have very small diameters and square, V-shaped or rounded ends.

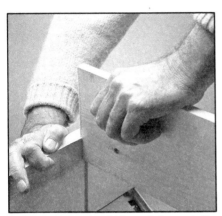

4 *The tongue should be a tight push-fit in the groove. Cut it too thick, if anything: you can always re-set the fence and make it thinner.*

5 *For a double rebate joint, set a two-flute or rebating bit to a depth of half the board thickness before cutting. The bit used here is self-guiding.*

9 *A loose tongue, usually of thin plywood, is often useful. If necessary, widen the groove by making a second cut, slightly higher or lower.*

10 *When grooving the second piece, be sure to keep it the same way up, for perfect alignment when you glue the tongue into position.*

As with all other routing techniques, your best plan is simply to make a few test runs on scrap timber and board to see what effects you can obtain, before applying your ideas to an actual project.

Setting up a job
As a matter of fact, the use of a 'test piece' is absolutely standard practice in professional woodworking shops. In general, power tools are capable of very fine adjustment, and among do-it-yourself models this is especially true of the router. An alteration of even a milli-metre or so in the setting – up, down or sideways – will usually have a noticeable effect when you come to do the actual machining.

Indeed, in the timber trades 'setting up' a tool quite often takes longer than the job itself. This preparation time isn't wasted; on the contrary, it's essential for a trouble-free result. The care you invest in choosing the right bit,

setting the depth, adjusting the fence, and so on, will always be repaid with better finished work.

Router safety
Despite its extremely high speed, the portable router in normal use is probably less danger-ous than a circular saw. Plunge routers score in this respect because the bit retracts.

However, you need to get into the habit of only plunging immediately before cutting, and always letting the motor spring back immediately afterwards. Don't lay the machine down, either upright or on its side, while it's still plunged – and certainly never, ever, if it's switched on too. That would mean either a hole in your workbench, or a horribly danger-ous exposed bit.

While cutting, keep both hands on the tool, and feed it in the right direction when doing edging jobs. Lastly, when changing bits, pull the plug out.

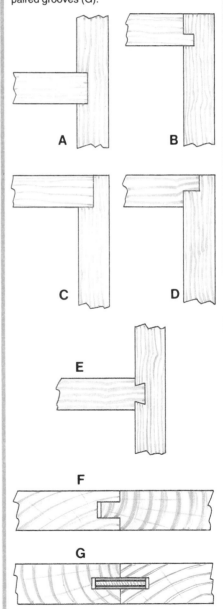

USING JIGS, TEMPLATES AND SPINDLES

Earlier articles on using a router have dealt with basic techniques. To exploit your machine to the full, it's also well worth knowing some of the methods professionals use for speed and accuracy.

The advanced uses of the router fall under three main headings. You can use special jigs and templates; you can mount it for use as a 'spindle'; and you can mount it in a stand.

Using a jig

What marks out a good wood machinist is largely his inventiveness in using jigs and templates – devices for guiding the cutter or blade accurately through, into, along or round the workpiece and vice versa. The clamped-on betten, which guides the router to cut a straight grove (see page 117) is a very simple jig, but the same principle is used for all others.

Suppose, for a start, that you want a wide groove, but have no bit large enough. You merely clamp battens on both sides, instead of just one, and move the router from side to side as well as forwards.

You can extend the batten principle to cut joints, too. If you want a number of identical halvings, it's usually a simple matter to clamp all the pieces side by side, fix battens across them, and move the router between these as if making a groove – cutting all the halvings at once. This ensures speed, plus (if you've set the job up correctly) total accuracy.

Similarly, suppose you want a recess – eg, for a flush handle in a sliding door. Trying to make this freehand is most unwise, because you're unlikely to cut accurately all the way round. Even if you manage it once, you'll never repeat the trick – as you might need to if you were fitting a pair of handles.

The solution is, of course, a jig: in this case, a 'box guide', the equivalent of four straight battens to guide the tool round the four sides of the recess. These pieces should be positioned and joined so that, when the router base is run against them, the bit will cut round the line you require. The box guide must therefore be bigger than the recess you want, so the base fits inside with room to manoeuvre.

You'll also need a means of locating any jig firmly and accurately. For small jobs, cramps are probably most efficient. In general, too, jigs and templates should be fairly heavy and substantial. That way there's less risk of slipping and harming the work or yourself.

A BEDSIDE CABINET

Almost all the joints in this unit are cut with the router, like the shapes at the bottom – see photographs. The groove in each front leg stops above the mortise.

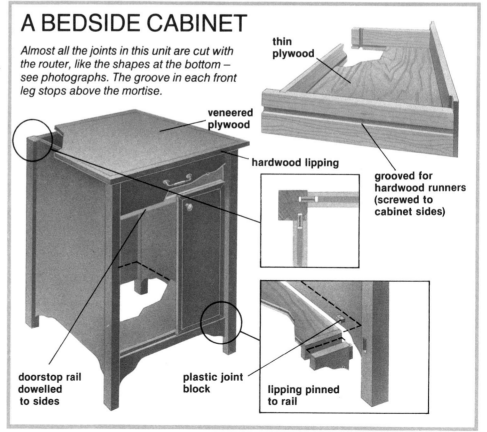

thin plywood

veneered plywood

hardwood lipping

grooved for hardwood runners (screwed to cabinet sides)

doorstop rail dowelled to sides

plastic joint block

lipping pinned to rail

A ROUTER TABLE

Made of chipboard, plywood or blockboard, and jointed with screws and/or plastic blocks, this table serves for a spindle (below) or for an 'overarm router' set-up (see Ready Reference).

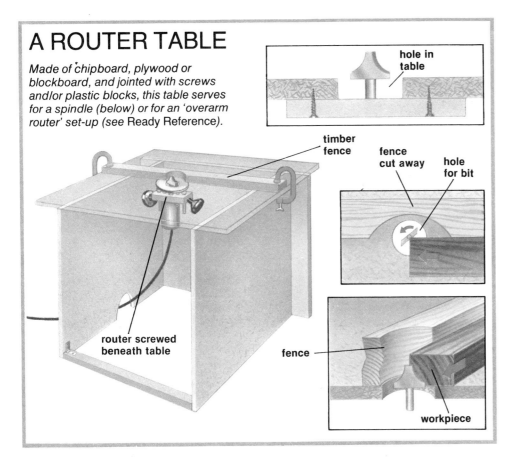

hole in table

timber fence

fence cut away

hole for bit

router screwed beneath table

fence

fence

workpiece

READY REFERENCE

THE OVERARM ROUTER

One way of making a router table is to fit the machine into a drill stand. Lower it, and push the work under the bit – usually against a fence.

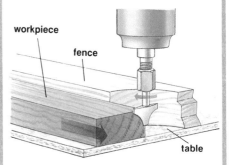

workpiece

fence

table

USING TEMPLATES

With a hand-held router, you fit a template guide to follow a jig or template which will produce the required shape. The template needs to be a different size from the workpiece. To find out by how much (A), subtract the bit diameter (B) from the outside diameter of the guide (C). Make the template thicker than the amount the guide protrudes from the router base to allow the guide to slide easily.

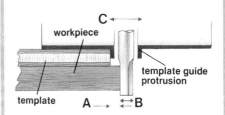

C

workpiece

template guide protrusion

template   A →   ⇄ B

On the overarm router, templates are used with a guide pin, centred under the bit. A pin and bit of the same diameter (1) let you make the template the same size as the workpiece. Otherwise make the template smaller (2) or larger. The pin can be made of hardwood or steel. A hardwood pin lets you do without a packing piece, allowing the bit right down to meet the pin.

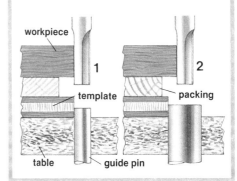

workpiece

template

1

packing

2

table   guide pin

The template guide

When the router is guided by its base, you have to allow for as much as half the base diameter when making the jig or positioning your guide battens. This is no good for fine work, especially where curves are involved. The answer there is a 'template guide'. This is a small metal plate with a sort of funnel in the middle. The plate is screwed across the hole in the router base, so that the funnel fits over the bit like a sleeve and projects in the same way as the bit does.

You can then guide the router by running the side of the funnel along the edge of a jig, which is often a flat pattern or 'template' of plywood (or a harder material) cut to the desired profile. The workpiece – often cut roughly to shape already – is fixed under the template with cramps, pins or double-sided adhesive tape, so that the bit cuts into or through it as the router is guided along. The template must be thicker than the funnel is long, so the guide will slide easily.

When making a template (see *Ready Reference*) for use with the hand-held router, you have to allow for the difference between the diameter of the bit and the outside diameter of the funnel. If you subtract the former from the latter and divide by two, you'll know how much smaller (or larger) the template should be than the piece you want to end up with.

Templates are useful whenever you want to repeat a special shape. You'll get perfect copies – provided the template doesn't include any concave curves whose radius is smaller than that of the funnel, because the template guide won't follow them. The results, of course, depend on the accuracy of the template. To make it, use the shaping tools demonstrated in Shaping wood, pages 76 -79.

Self-guiding trimming bits (see Router bits, page 120) are also useful for template work. While the ball-bearing guide runs along the template, the cutter cuts the workpiece. The template goes on top of or underneath the piece, depending on the position of the bearing.

Such bits do away with the template guide, and – provided the bearing is the same size as the cutter – they let you make the template the same size as the final shape. In fact, you don't need a template as such. You just make the first piece the right shape by hand, and use that instead.

The template guide itself has other uses than for making repeated shapes. It can be used for recessing, if you make a jig on the lines described, and for mortising, because a mortise is simply a deep, narrow recess.

Lastly, it can be used for dovetailing – in conjunction with a dovetail bit, plus a dovetailing jig which you clamp over the

USING A SPINDLE

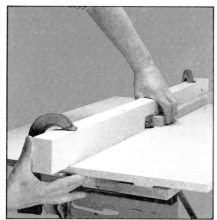

1 *With the bit poking up through the table, move the cutaway fence over it, and cramp it tightly in position to give the width of cut you need for the job.*

3 *For stopped cuts (those which don't continue right along the piece) cramp a block of timber to the fence as a buffer in the position you want.*

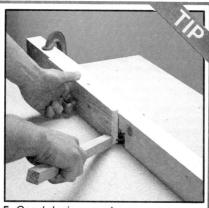

5 *Good design may let you re-use a setting for several cuts. This is a drawer side. When ending a cut, it's often safest to use a push stick.*

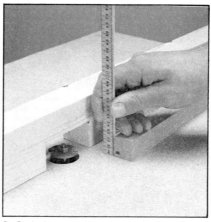

2 *Switch on and push a test piece into the bit, holding it against the fence. Then check the depth and width of cut, adjusting either or both if necessary.*

4 *When you're sure the setting is right, switch the router on again and push each workpiece carefully past the bit with both hands to make the cut.*

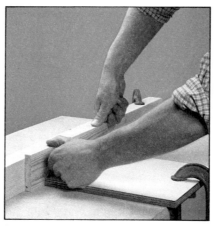

6 *Another way of holding thin workpieces safely against the bit is with a straight board, cramped to the table so the pieces can just be pushed past it.*

workpieces. The procedure is very like dovetailing with a power drill, as shown on pages 90 -91. And you can use the same jig with a straight bit (in a router or drill) to cut finger joints.

The spindle

As already hinted, you can turn the portable router into a fixed machine. This is especially convenient for small workpieces – or long, narrow ones such as lengths of moulding – where it's hard to support the tool properly.

In a 'router table', as the fixed set-up is called, the machine may point upwards or downwards. Some manufacturers supply mountings in which it points sideways. The first arrangement is known as a spindle. You can buy a ready-made table for this, or make one from timber and boards – see illustration on page 125. The essentials are solid construction, and a flat top. The router is secured to the underside of the top, with its bit sticking up through a hole. Use wood or chipboard screws – or, better still, machine screws in threaded bushes.

You'll also require a timber or plywood 'fence' along which to slide the work past the bit. Ideally this should itself be mounted to slide back and forwards, so you can vary the width of cut more easily, but it can be clamped on. It should be cut away, in width or thickness, at the point where the bit emerges through the table. You can adjust the depth of cut (ie, the amount the bit protrudes) on the machine as usual.

When using a spindle, safety should never leave your mind. Don't switch the router on until you're sure that both it and the fence are firmly fixed in position. Make sure you feed the workpiece against the rotation of the bit – ie, from right to left – or it may kick back at you. Always hold it firmly on course; this is important for accuracy as well as safety. And **keep your hands clear of the rotating bit at all times.** At the end of a cut, it's often better to push the workpiece through with a stick, while still holding the already machined end with your other hand.

The 'overarm' router

The alternative to a spindle is to mount the router in a stand, just like a power drill (removing it from the carriage first if necessary). This makes an 'overarm' router. Here too you'll need a table; the photographs show a ready-made pattern, but again, you can improvise if you prefer. You'll also require a removable fence.

Apart from all everyday jobs, the overarm router will tackle mortising, like a drill in a shaping table (see page 93). Tenoning is possible on either type of table (though it's usually more accurate on a spindle). You just fit a large straight bit and run the workpiece over (or under) it, end-on to the fence;

MORTISING AND TENONING

1 For mortising with a hand-held router, first screw the metal 'template guide' into position in the router base. Its 'bush' projects below the base plate.

2 Allowing for the size of the guide, make a jig for it to follow when cutting. This should locate over the workpiece to give the cut you want.

3 Cramp the workpiece and jig together. Fit a straight bit (ideally one which is the same width as the mortise) and place the router on the jig.

4 With the template guide against the side of the jig, switch on, plunge and cut – still keeping the guide pressed against the jig's side and ends.

5 You'll end up with a round-ended mortise. A bit which was smaller than the mortise width would need a jig with four sides for an accurate groove.

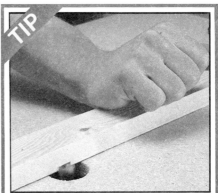

6 Use a spindle for routing tenons. Fit a wide straight bit, adjust it for the tenon shoulder depth and push the timber fence gently over it.

7 Clamp the fence at the right width of cut. Short tenons need only one cut on each side. Use a broad push block to keep the piece square to the fence.

8 Re-adjust the depth of cut (but not the fence). Then turn the piece on edge and cut each of the edge shoulders in turn in the same way.

9 Round the corners of the tenon with a chisel, and try it in the mortise for fit. If necessary, re-adjust the spindle slightly and re-cut the tenon.

then turn the piece over to cut the other side – plus any edge shoulders. If the diameter of your bit is smaller than the length of the tenon, you'll need two or more passes. Set the fence so that you'll have cut the full length of the tenon by the time you're holding the piece up against it.

On any router table, you can make repeat shapes by removing the fence and using a template (you don't need a template guide). Again, you can use a self-guiding trimming bit. On the overarm router, however, there's an alternative – namely, to fit a guide pin. The guide pin is simply a cylindrical length of steel or even hardwood – or maybe a round-headed screw – driven into the table top with its centre exactly beneath the cutter's centre. It sticks up so you can run the template against it, lowering the router to cut the work-piece at the same time. A packing piece between workpiece and template helps ensure that the bit doesn't meet the guide pin.

In all template work (except on the spindle), you can cut internal as well as external shapes. You can shape, for example, the inside of a frame as well as the outside. The guide pin will do nicely for this. What's more, you can use the pin for recessing. Suppose you want to make a small box from a piece of solid hardwood, by recessing out the inside. You just make a template to the same size and shape as the recess, fasten the wood on top of it, and place it over the pin. Then you switch on, lower the router into the piece, and move the template and workpiece to and fro until the recess is hollowed out. The sides of the template will come up against the pin and stop you cutting too far.

If the template matches the shape you want, and the guide pin's diameter matches that of the bit, you'll get exact copies. If you vary the size of the pin (see Ready Reference) or bit, you'll get a shape that's larger or smaller – just as if you vary the size of the template instead.

The possibilities don't end there. For example, if you nail a board to the table and rotate it, you can cut a circle whose radius is the distance between the nail and the outside edge of the bit. It's simple enough – if you've got the imagination!

The router lathe
Perhaps the most ingenious appliance for routing is the router lathe. A do-it-yourself version of the automatic lathes now used in industry, this lets you make and shape cylindrical pieces.

You secure your length of timber – initially square in section – between the 'stocks' at each end, and fit your router to the carriage which slides on rails above it. You turn the work with a hand crank while the bit, often shaped, makes the cut. The router can also move along simultaneously at a pre-set rate, giving spiral cuts.

USING TEMPLATES

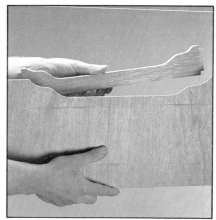

1 Template work is one use of the overarm router. Shape the workpiece roughly, then fix it over the template – eg, with double-sided adhesive tape.

2 When cutting, hold the template against the guide pin. If the pin is wooden, lower the bit into it – you need no packing between template and workpiece.

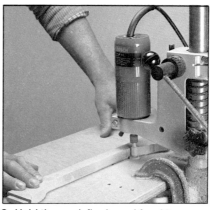

3 Hold the work firmly and feed it against the bit's rotation. Note that a larger guide pin means a smaller template (and vice versa).

4 With larger pieces, it's easier to fix the template on top, and cut with a hand-held router – plus a template guide with which to follow the shape.

5 The cabinet's legs are joined to the sides and back with plywood tongues in routed grooves. The shaped template is used for sides, back and lower rail.

6 Routed grooves also take the drawer runners and bottom, and join its sides and back. Rebates are routed in the front to accept the sides.

CHAPTER 6

WOODWORKING EQUIPMENT

There are a number of simple pieces of equipment
you can make yourself as aids to successful woodworking,
ranging from a simple bench hook or saw horse
to a sturdy yet inexpensive workbench.

MAKING AIDS FOR WOODWORK

There are countless devices for making woodwork quicker and easier, and the short time it takes to build them will be amply repaid. Here are some of the most useful.

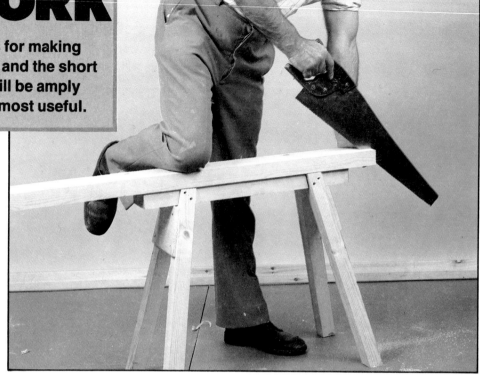

Traditionally, woodworkers made a great many of their own tools. Not only did this cost less, and assure each man of a high-quality item that would exactly suit his individual requirements. Perhaps more importantly, it would never have occurred to him not to.

With the rise of industry, fairly comfortable, durable and accurate tools have become ever easier to obtain ready-made. Today it's usually the craftsman or enthusiast who takes the trouble to create his own tools, and even he often limits his efforts to the simpler items such as marking gauges.

However, although every tradesman nowadays buys his tools, or at least the great majority of them, the spirit of self-reliance shouldn't be abandoned. It's still very necessary – particularly because standardised production tends to mean that the unusual items gradually slip out of sight.

What's more, practically every job with hand or power tools, no matter how simple it may be, demands a bit of improvisation – even if that only consists of sawing off a block of softwood to use with your pencil when scribing, or making a notched push stick for safety on the table saw or spindle.

Woodworking devices, therefore, come under any number of headings. There are aids for marking-out, especially on awkward shapes; aids for clamping work of various configurations for various purposes, and specifically for steady and accurate sawing, planing and drilling – square, or very often at an angle; and aids for power tool work. Some of these last, commonly known as jigs, are discussed in the sections dealing with power drilling, routing and sawing.

It's impossible to generalise, because the ends and means differ so much in each case. Nevertheless, one sign of a good worker is the ability to think of – and if necessary to build – short cuts to good results.

Making a saw horse

There are certain appliances which even the beginner can, and most often does, make himself without much difficulty.

Perhaps the chief of these is the saw horse. This consists of a horizontal piece of wood on four legs, and it's the time-honoured device for resting lengths of timber at a convenient height for sawing – either along it or across it.

Even if you have a Workmate (see page 29), you'll still find a saw horse invaluable for supporting the far end of a long piece, or of a panel. Besides, it's a lot lighter, and thus more portable.

The principle is simple enough. The only tricky part of its construction is ensuring that its legs are angled correctly for stability. They should be splayed away from the vertical in two directions instead of just one, and this demands some careful marking-up. However, the technique isn't difficult once you know how it's done – see the photographs on pages 133 -135.

Bench hook and other devices

The little gadget known as a bench hook is as outstandingly simple as it's useful – see also page 51.

It's just a small piece of board with a batten screwed across its top at one end, and another across its underside at the other end. The latter hooks over the near edge of the bench, and you hold the wood against the former while sawing. That way the workpiece doesn't shift, and you get a square cut.

A shooting board performs a similar function when you're planing sides and edges. Again, our photographs show its construction and use.

see also page 51; see page 29; on pages 133 -135

READY REFERENCE

PLANING BOARD

It's often hard to hold small pieces for face planing. But this bench aid clamps the timber more tightly as you push.

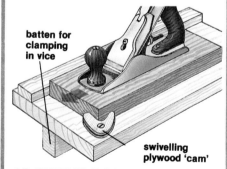

batten for clamping in vice

swivelling plywood 'cam'

ADJUSTABLE SQUARE

A snag with fitted shelves and cupboards – eg, in alcoves – is that walls are seldom square to ceilings, floors or other walls. Fit this tool in the corner, tighten it, and mark even wide panels at the angle it gives.

A BENCH HOOK

1 Glue and screw a batten to the underside of the base, so that the completed device can be hooked over your workbench or held in a vice.

2 Glue and screw a stop block onto the other side at the far end. Hardwood is the best material for this (and for the base as well), but softwood will do.

3 To use the bench hook, hold it firmly against the edge of the bench, and anchor the workpiece securely against the stop block while you're cutting.

MAKING A SHOOTING BOARD

The idea of a shooting board is to achieve square sides, edges and ends on your workpieces when planing. On a right-handed board like this one, you steady the piece with your left hand and hold the plane with your right.

*The board's primary use is for planing endgrain – see **5**. It's not meant for face planing. When you're planing along the grain, as in **4**, you need a particularly firm grip on the workpiece.*

*The main variant is the mitre shooting board, which has its stop block (see **2**) screwed on at 45° instead of 90°, with the end cut off at the same angle. It's used for 'trueing up' mitred pieces for an absolutely clean joint, eg, in picture-framing.*

For efficiency, a shooting board must be accurately made.

1 Make the basic board from two flat, straight pieces as shown, glued and screwed together. The edge of the upper piece must be at exactly 90°.

2 Inset the stop block slightly, insert one screw through it, and get it dead square to the fence. Then drill for the other screw, and drive it in.

3 A batten glued and screwed to the underside of the base enables you to clamp the shooting board in a vice or Workmate; stability is essential.

4 When using the board, hold the workpiece firmly against the stop. It's also very important to keep the plane absolutely flat on its side.

5 The shooting board's main use is in planing endgrain, when you can most easily keep the workpiece securely up against the stop block.

Aids for making mitres

Turning out good mitre joints (see Chapter 3 pages 54-57) can be demanding – especially since their main use is in decorative work, such as picture-framing and fitting architraves, where any gaps are all the less desirable. Fortunately, there are several devices to help you.

The mitre shooting board is a variant of the ordinary shooting board; its stop block is at 45° (or any other angle you like), so you can trim endgrain accurately.

Cutting accurate mitres in the first place, particularly in large pieces and shaped mouldings, isn't always straightforward. The sensible plan is often to buy a mitre box, with ready-made guides. This must be wide enough for your piece to lie flat on the bottom. For small sections, you need only make a mitre block (page 57), which is a type of bench hook.

The shooting board, bench hook, mitre box and mitre block can all be gripped in the Workmate for greater stability. On the mitre box, make one of the sides wider than the other, so it projects below the base and can be held between the vice jaws. The shooting board will need a batten screwed to its underside for the same purpose.

When using a mitre box or block, you have only to indicate the position of the cut on the workpiece, in order to align it in the appliance, rather than go to the trouble of marking round it. The saw will follow the angled cuts in the box or block, rather than your marks.

However, if you haven't got (and aren't in a position to make) one of these two saw guides to a suitable size, a mitre template (shown in the photographs) makes light work of marking up even complicated mouldings – for which a mitre or combination square, being basically flat, is no use.

Sensible rules

In general, appliances and jigs should be made from tough, stable materials.

While a bench hook for everyday use need only be of softwood, it will give longer service if its base and stop are from a hardwood such as beech or oak. For the base, plywood is an alternative.

For mitre boxes and templates, hardwood is essential. In softwood, the guide cuts in a mitre box will widen so quickly with use as to defeat the whole purpose. A hardwood or multi-ply template or square of any kind also has a longer life.

It goes without saying that accuracy is vital, too. On a shooting board, for example, all the components must be dead square to one another, since the idea is to produce more precise work, not to reproduce errors. When making such appliances, you must always be sure to check your work at every stage to avoid trouble.

MAKING A MITRE TEMPLATE

1 Glue and screw together two pieces of planed hardwood at right angles to each other as shown. Position both screws near the centre of the joint.

2 Carefully mark two opposite diagonals of 45° across one piece, and square them across the other piece. Keep the marks clear of the screws.

3 Clamping the device with the diagonals on top, saw right through both pieces on your marked lines. Check constantly that your saw is upright.

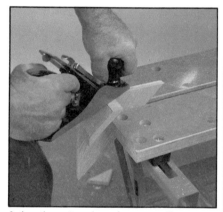

4 Lastly, set a plane for a very fine cut and carefully shave the ends smooth. Check the angle with a combination or mitre square.

5 When mitring two lengths of moulding, mark the plain (unmoulded) width of one on the other, leaving a little waste at the end of the piece.

6 Then position your template with its slope across the marked lines, and use its right angle to mark where the cut should extend to on the moulded part.

MAKING A SAW HORSE: 1

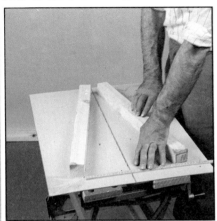

1 Cut four legs of 50x50mm (2x2in) planed softwood, about 625mm (25in) long; angle each pair equally, their lower ends 150mm (6in) from a centre line.

2 Cut a suitable length of 75x50mm (3x2in) planed timber for the top, position it squarely across the tops of both legs, and mark round it.

3 Square across the inner face of each leg from the lowest point of this marked outline, and make a mark on the far edge of the timber.

4 Measure down 10mm (³/8in) from this mark, and make another one next to it. This is necessary to obtain the correct double slope for the legs.

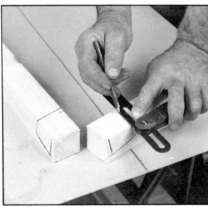

5 Set a sliding bevel to the angle from the bottom of the outline to the lower of your two marks, and use it to pencil a line across each leg.

6 Returning to the marked outline of the top on each leg, measure and mark 13mm (¹/2in) in – at top and bottom – to give the actual depth of the cutout.

7 Join these marks, and extend the line right to the end of the leg to make cutting easier. Then mark in or label the waste areas of wood.

8 Square this new depth mark at right angles across the end of the leg, and continue marking in the waste areas clearly to avoid mistakes.

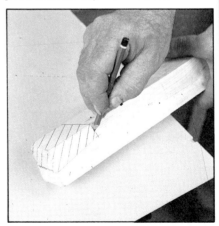

9 Mark across the far side of each leg with the sliding bevel as shown; for the longer line, take the setting from the near side. Then mark in the waste.

MAKING A SAW HORSE: 2

1 Clamp each leg firmly and make the first cut – across the grain. Note that the saw is tilted, as well as being angled across the workpiece.

2 Clamp the leg nearly upright, so that your depth mark is vertical, and carefully saw along the grain. Check your cut for accuracy as you work.

3 Hold each leg in turn firmly against the top piece, and mark its position on the side only, making sure that it's pointing the right way.

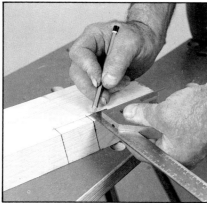

4 Square each of these lines inwards to a depth of 13mm (1/2in) on top and bottom, and join them up. A combination square is ideal for this.

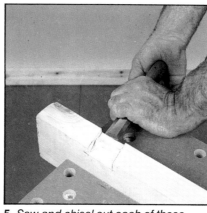

5 Saw and chisel out each of these angled halvings across the grain. Begin by tilting the chisel upwards, then level it off to finish the job.

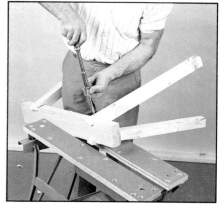

6 Glue and screw each of the legs into position after drilling countersunk holes. Plane all their protruding ends flush with the top later on.

7 Set the sliding bevel to the angle at which the legs splay sideways from the top. Check with it that this angle is the same on all four legs.

8 Then use it to mark up timber or plywood braces. Cut these and screw them on right under the top, adjusting skewed legs if necessary.

9 Get the saw horse level, chocking it up as needed, and scribe all round each leg with a piece of wood about 19mm (3/4in) thick. Cut to your marks.

BUILDING A WORKBENCH

Make no mistake: if you're serious about woodwork, a proper bench is a must. Here's how to design and build one which will perfectly suit all your needs – without spending a fortune.

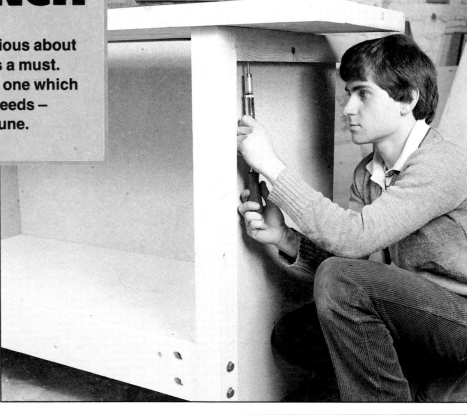

Apart from experience, the two most vital factors in efficient woodwork are sharp tools and a sturdy bench.

The bench provides a focus for your activity – an area in which you can give your full attention to the job in hand. A bench that rattles and bends under pressure, or has an uneven surface, upsets concentration.

So good work demands a good bench: and that means one which will recede into silent, unobtrusive reliability.

Deciding dimensions

If you're making a bench, the first consideration is its overall size. That depends on several things.

The first is your own height. Traditionally, the work surface was positioned at the level where your knuckles hang with arms relaxed. Nowadays, however, portable power tools have removed some of the need to bring a lot of weight to bear over the bench, and knuckle height is too low for any but the most arduous planing. It leads to back strain from bending, and eye strain from peering at fine detail.

Wrist height is a better bet – but, if you have a clear idea of the type of job you intend doing, take that into account too. Fine, delicate work could mean raising the top by another 75mm (3in) or so.

Similarly, the size of your anticipated jobs will affect the size you make the top. But remember that 'junk expands to fill the space available' and avoid a needlessly huge work surface, which will only become cluttered with half-finished jobs and un-cleared-up tools, as well as wasting valuable storage space in the room.

On the other hand, it's best to include a flat surface at least 485mm (19in) wide, in case you want to stand chairs on it.

Basic construction

The traditional cabinet-maker's bench was mortised and tenoned throughout. But there are less laborious ways of providing equal (or even greater) rigidity.

Strong legs are still necessary, especially at the front, to withstand hammering. In our design the front legs still receive tenoned cross-bearers for the top at either end, plus a very substantial front rail lower down. But the main stiffening comes from large panels of thick chipboard at the sides and back, plus a very useful chipboard shelf. These are screwed and preferably glued into rebates in the framing, and to each other via substantial battens. This completely stops the bench from 'racking' – distorting into a diamond shape – in either direction.

If you want to be able to dismantle your bench (a facility well worth considering in case you move your home or workshop), you can omit adhesive, and bolt the front rail into the legs instead of tenoning it; see the photographs, page 138, and illustrations.

Useful details

A modicum of woodworking experience suggests several other features.

If you incorporate a thick top (at least 25mm/1in when using softwood), you can leave out the customary upper front rail. This arrangement has the great advantage that you can slip G-cramps quickly and easily over the front edge.

The solid timber work surface itself is needed for firm cramping, and to absorb the odd chisel blow or other impact. You can, of course, extend it right to the back of the bench. But this costs more, and the usual design provides a 'tool well' along the back – a shallow recess in which to place the items immediately required during a job.

MAKING A STURDY BENCH

This workbench is extremely strong and stable. Yet it's made from cheap materials, and you need only two proper joints – the mortises and tenons which connect the top of each leg to the corresponding side rail.

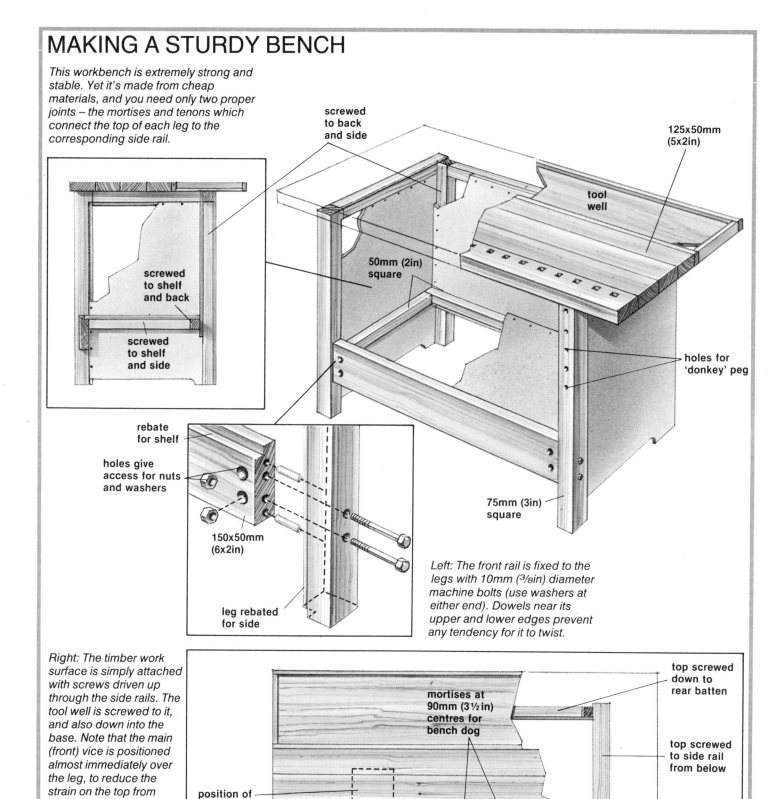

screwed to back and side

125x50mm (5x2in)

tool well

screwed to shelf and back

screwed to shelf and side

50mm (2in) square

holes for 'donkey' peg

rebate for shelf

holes give access for nuts and washers

150x50mm (6x2in)

leg rebated for side

75mm (3in) square

Left: The front rail is fixed to the legs with 10mm ($^3/_8$in) diameter machine bolts (use washers at either end). Dowels near its upper and lower edges prevent any tendency for it to twist.

Right: The timber work surface is simply attached with screws driven up through the side rails. The tool well is screwed to it, and also down into the base. Note that the main (front) vice is positioned almost immediately over the leg, to reduce the strain on the top from hammer blows.

mortises at 90mm (3½ in) centres for bench dog

top screwed down to rear batten

top screwed to side rail from below

position of main vice

position of leg

position of end vice

MAKING THE BACK AND SIDES

1 Begin by cutting away the lower edge of each side panel to within about 75mm (3in) of the rear. This will make the bench more stable.

2 Cut 75mm (3in) square planed timber for legs and side rails. Rebate each to the board thickness (18mm/¾in), cut mortises and tenons, and glue up.

3 Glue and screw each panel into the rebates; then glue, cramp and screw on a full-height upright batten, just inside the rear edge.

4 Glue and screw a similar batten to the back panel – flush with its top edge, but short by exactly its own thickness at either end of the board.

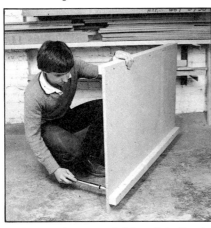

5 Glue and screw a full-length batten to the back panel's inside face, at the height where the shelf will rest (remember the panel doesn't reach the floor).

6 Stand the back and sides upside-down, and screw through the back into the battens on the sides. Always screw through chipboard into wood.

The well helps to keep the bench tidy, and its drop of 18mm (¾in) or more below the main surface prevents its contents from sticking up far enough to dent or obstruct the movement of workpieces. A really useful detail is a large hole in the corner of its base; this allows shavings and other debris to be swept onto the floor, where you can clean them up far more easily.

Various work-holding devices in and on the worktop are also essential. Foremost among these is the bench vice (see pages 1078-9). A small but critical point concerns its siting; it should be as near as possible to the appropriate leg (the left leg if you're right-handed) so that downward blows are transmitted more or less directly down the leg rather than causing the top to spring.

If you're planing a long piece in the vice, a 'donkey' helps a great deal by supporting the far end. This small peg fits into any of a row of holes in the front of the opposite leg.

The 'end vice' is invaluable for holding long boards flat on the bench. It can take the form of an ordinary steel vice, bolted to the right-hand end of the top. You insert only one wooden jaw instead of the usual two, after cutting a mortise in its top edge to line up with a series of other mortises along the bench top. A pair of 'bench dogs' (see Ready Reference) grip the work: you fit one in the jaw mortise, and the other in one of the bench mortises. Some vices already incorporate a steel dog of their own.

Constructional materials

The traditional timber for workbenches is beech – very dense, hard-wearing and 'stable'. This last quality, its lack of susceptibility to shrinkage and swelling, is useful in a precision work-surface.

Buying beech, however, means planing rough-sawn planks. This will give you an excellent bench – but it's arduous and difficult. Mahogany, also very stable, is a good substitute, which is often obtainable ready-planed. The obstacle in this case is cost.

Softwood, the cheapest alternative, will be quite serviceable provided you use large enough sections; 75mm (3in) square planed is the minimum for the legs.

Don't use man-made board for the top. The veneers on plywood and blockboard are too easily damaged, and the resin in chipboard will blunt cutting edges.

For the structural panels, use 18mm (¾in) chipboard – ideally a high-density (750kg per m³) flooring grade. Paint it with a gloss finish so you can wipe off spilt glue more easily. For the same reason, give the work surface several coats of Danish oil, well rubbed in and buffed down. This is particularly important because lumps of dried glue are sure to dent your work. What's more, it can be quickly renewed when necessary.

COMPLETING THE BASE

1 Rebate the front rail, and mark dowel centres near the top and bottom of each end. Drive in pins at those positions, and cut off their heads.

2 Work out where your bolts will come (between the dowels) and drill large holes through the rail so you'll be able to insert nuts and washers.

3 Cramp the rail in position without adhesive, and drill bolt holes. The pins will meanwhile mark centres for matching dowel holes in the legs.

4 Un-cramp the assembly, and finish drilling the bolt holes in the rail if necessary. Then remove the pins and drill dowel holes in the rail and legs.

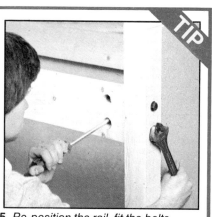

5 Re-position the rail, fit the bolts (each with washers at both ends) and tighten up. Use a screwdriver to jam the nut as you turn each bolt head.

6 Screw battens across each side, their tops level with the rear batten and the bottom of the rebate in the front rail. Then cut the shelf and screw it down.

ADDING THE TOP

1 Drill mortises for bench dogs in one of the top pieces, aligning them as on page 134. Drill them out first, then pare them square with a chisel.

5 Use a jigsaw or hand saw and chisel to cut away the front of the top to take the inner jaws (both metal and timber) of the front vice.

9 Screw the end vice on in a similar way, again cutting out the bench top and fitting a packing block underneath. Fit only an outer jaw this time.

AND FITTING THE VICES

2 Glue the pieces together for the top – dowelling or loose-tongueing them if you like. Afterwards plane the surface flat and sand it smooth.

3 The tool well is just a shallow box of 50x25mm (2x1in) planed timber and thin plywood, with a hole for sweepings. Rebate the bottom in if you like.

4 Position the top, and drill and screw up into it through the side rails. Screw the tool well onto it sideways, and down into the rear top batten.

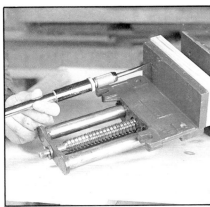

6 Cut and plane two wooden jaws, and screw one to the inner metal jaw. Hardwood wears best. Make the jaws too high and plane flush.

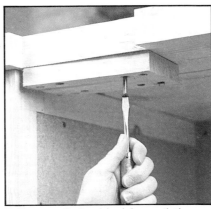

7 Screw a timber block beneath the worktop so the top of the vice will be just below that of the bench, to save tool edges from impact damage.

8 Coach-screw the vice to the block. Then insert the outer wooden jaw, tighten the vice, and screw that jaw into place through the metal jaw.

10 Square pencil lines across the wooden vice jaw from the last mortise in the worktop. Remove the jaw, and cut a square groove down its outer face.

11 Replace the jaw so that the groove forms a mortise. You can then grip workpieces between two dogs – one in a bench mortise, one in the end vice jaw.

12 Drill holes in the adjacent leg, making the top one level with the steel rods in the front vice. A 'donkey' peg then helps support long pieces.

CHAPTER 7

CHOOSING AND USING OTHER TOOLS

Maintaining your home means that you'll need a range of tools
for jobs other than woodwork. These are likely to include
working with bricks and blocks, making electrical and plumbing repairs
and decorating walls, ceilings, doors and windows.
Choosing the right tool is the first step to doing a thorough job.

MASONRY TOOLS

The term 'masonry' can mean anything from a brick or piece of stone to a complete wall, so it is important to be specific when choosing the right tool for a cutting or shaping job.

The hardness of the material to be worked is, perhaps, the most important consideration when choosing masonry tools. Some stone-cutting tools are designed for use only on relatively soft stones such as sandstone, and to use them on a hard stone like granite could cause damage to the tool or workpiece. Most 'brick' tools are intended for use on ordinary, relatively soft bricks and tend not to cope with hard engineering bricks, which have to be treated more like hard stone. Some are tempered just to cut brick and nothing else, whereas others may cut a variety of materials; it is important to check. When dealing with mixtures of materials, the general rule is to pick a tool that will handle the hardest element in the mixture.

Cutting and shaping tools

The commonest tools for cutting and shaping masonry of all types are cold chisels. There are several general-purpose and specific versions.

The **flat-cut cold chisel** is frequently used on masonry for splitting, chopping out, cutting chases and, occasionally, rough shaping. Like the rest of the cold chisel family, it is a hexagonal steel bar with a cutting tip formed at one end – in this case a straightforward wedge-shaped tip a little wider than the bar. The other end has chamfered edges to prevent chipping when struck with a heavy hammer.

The **cross-cut cold chisel** also known as the Cape chisel, has a cutting edge very much narrower than the bar from which it is made, allowing it to cut slots and grooves with great accuracy.

The **half-round cold chisel** is a variation of the cross-cut chisel and may also be known as the round-nosed chisel. It has a single cutting bevel ground into the tip to produce a semi-circular cutting edge. Used mainly for cutting grooves, it can produce rounded internal corners as well.

The **diamond-point cold chisel** is yet another variation of the cross-cut chisel and is sometimes known as the diamond-cut chisel. It has a diagonally-ground single cutting bevel. Use it for making V-shaped grooves and neatly angled internal corners.

The **plugging chisel** is otherwise known as the seaming chisel or seam drill. It has a curious slanting head, and is used for removing the mortar pointing in brickwork. Two types are available: one with a plain head and the other with a flute cut into the side to help clear waste material.

The **concrete point** is a fairly rare cold chisel that tapers to a point rather than a normal cutting edge and is used for shattering concrete or brickwork in areas previously outlined with a flat chisel.

The **dooking iron** is intended for cutting holes through brickwork and stone. This extra-long, flat-cut cold chisel has a narrow 'waist' let into the bar just behind the head to help prevent waste from jamming it in the masonry.

The **brick bolster** has a extra-wide, spade-shaped head and is designed to cut bricks cleanly in two. Most have a 100mm (4in) wide cutting edge, but other widths can be found, and care should be taken not to confuse these with other types of bolster chisel such as the mason's bolster (see below) or even the floorboard chisel. They are not tempered in the same way and may be damaged if used incorrectly.

The **mason's chisel** comes in two varieties. Narrow versions look like ordinary cold chisels, but the wider versions are more like brick bolsters. They are intended for general shaping and smoothing of stonework. The very narrow types (sometimes called edging-in chisels) are used to make a starting groove for a bolster when splitting large blocks and slabs.

The **mason's bolster** is a much tougher tool than the brick bolster, being designed for use on stone or concrete. Use it to split blocks and slabs, or to smooth off broad, flat surfaces.

Breaking tools

When it comes to breaking up solid masonry, heavier-duty tools are needed. The **pickaxe**, usually known simply as a pick, is the tool most people think of for breaking up masonry. It has a pointed tip for hacking into hard material and a chisel or spade tip for use on softer material such as ashphalt. In practice, though, you may find it easier merely to crack the masonry with a sledge hammer (see below) and then use the spade tip of the pickaxe to grub out the debris. Neither tool is worth buying, hire them instead.

The **club hammer** is a double-faced hammer used for breaking up masonry and for driving chisels and bolsters. It is also known as the lump hammer.

The **brick hammer** is designed specifically for driving cold chisels or bolsters when cutting bricks. It has a head that incorporates a chisel end for trimming the brick after it has been cut.

The **sledge hammer** is used for directing heavy blows at masonry in order to break it up. For light work, it should be allowed to fall under its own weight, but for more solid material, it can be swung like an axe.

Electric hammers and hydraulic breakers

If you have a lot of demolition work to do or have to break through thick concrete, it is possible to hire an electric hammer to do the job. This will come with a variety of points and chisels.

If no electricity supply is available, then you can hire a hydraulic breaker which is powered by a small petrol driven compressor.

Saws for masonry

For cutting blocks and slabs, or even masonry walls, a hand or power tool can help to achieve a neat finish.

Although the **masonry saw** resembles a normal woodworking saw, its extra-hard tungsten carbide teeth and friction-reducing PTFE coating are capable of slicing through brick, building blocks and most types of stone.

A large two-man version, which has a detachable handle at one end so that an assistant can help pull the saw through, will even cut through walls. Unfortunately, with the exception of small **chasing saws** used to cut electric cable channels in walls, using masonry saws is very hard work.

The **cut-off saw** is just another name for a heavy-duty circular saw which may be electrically or petrol driven. The key to cutting masonry, though, is not so much the power of the saw as the special cutting wheel – a rigid disc of tough abrasive that grinds its way through the stone. Various grades are available to match the material being cut.

Such saws are professional tools that can be hired if there is sufficient work to warrant it, or if a particularly deep cut is required. However, if you already own a circular saw, you should be able to buy a masonry cutting disc for it. Take care, though, to get the right grade for the job.

The **angle grinder** is usually used to cut and grind all types of metal – pipes, rods and sheets. However, fitted with the appropriate stone-cutting disc it can also be used to make cuts and shallow channels in brick, stone and concrete. It is extremely useful for cutting earthenware drainpipe sections.

Tools for drilling holes

When drilling holes in masonry of any type, it's vital to use a drill bit or other tool that is specially hardened to cope with the task. Never attempt to use ordinary twist drills.

Masonry drill bits allow you to drill into brick, stone, mortar and plaster with an ordinary hand or electric drill. Each has two small 'ears' at the end to help break up the waste, and is tipped with tungsten carbide.

Special long versions and extension sleeves are available for drilling right through walls.

Core drill bits are used for boring large-diameter holes – up to 50mm (2in). The bit is a hollow tube that cuts out a 'plug' of material much like a woodworking hole saw. A reduced shank allows it to be fitted into a normal drill chuck.

One thing that masonry drill bits cannot cope with is hard aggregate, such as that found in concrete. One solution is to break up the aggregate particles with a **jumping bit** as they are met. This is a hole boring tool that is driven in with a hammer and twisted by hand at the same time. Sometimes the bit is mounted in a special holder and is interchangeable with bits of different sizes. The **star drill** is a heavier-duty one-piece relation of the jumping bit, and has four tapered flutes to clear debris as the drill is hammered into the masonry.

Electric percussion drills look like normal electric drills and are used in the same way, but there is an important difference. While the drill bit rotates it is hammered in and out, offering the benefits of the twist drill and jumping bit in one.

If you intend buying such a tool, make sure the hammer action can be switched on and off as required and that it has a strong steadying handle. Also, check that it is powerful enough for your needs. This may be indicated by the wattage of the motor or by the chuck size; generally, the larger the chuck capacity, the more powerful the drill.

Make sure that any bits you use with the hammer action are designed for such use, since otherwise they may shatter.

Finally, remember that safety goggles or glasses are essential when using masonry tools.

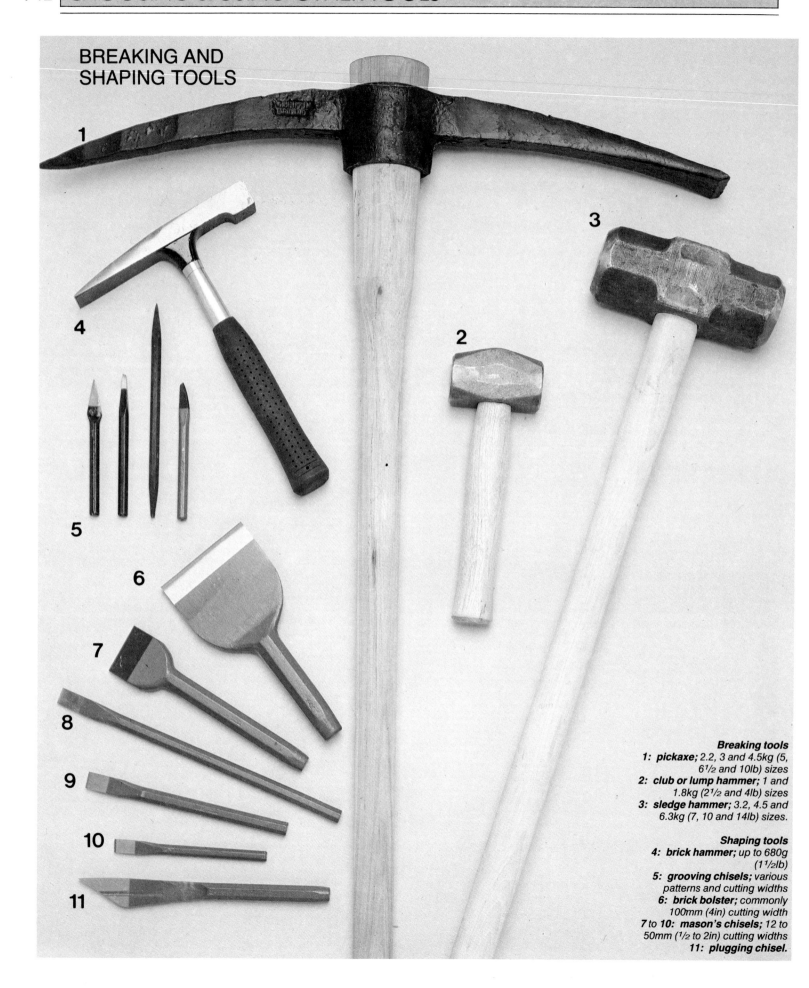

BREAKING AND
SHAPING TOOLS

Breaking tools
1: pickaxe; 2.2, 3 and 4.5kg (5, 6½ and 10lb) sizes
2: club or lump hammer; 1 and 1.8kg (2½ and 4lb) sizes
3: sledge hammer; 3.2, 4.5 and 6.3kg (7, 10 and 14lb) sizes.

Shaping tools
4: brick hammer; up to 680g (1½lb)
5: grooving chisels; various patterns and cutting widths
6: brick bolster; commonly 100mm (4in) cutting width
7 to 10: mason's chisels; 12 to 50mm (½ to 2in) cutting widths
11: plugging chisel.

CUTTING AND DRILLING TOOLS

1: *masonry saw* with tungsten carbide-tipped teeth

2: *angle grinder* with masonry cutting discs

3: *interchangeable cutters* for jumping bit (4); diameters match screw gauges

4: *star drill;* diameters match masonry bolt sizes

5: *jumping bit* holder and cutter

6: *hammer-action drill* with depth stop, plus masonry drill bits

7: *circular saw* with masonry cutting disc.

PAINT BRUSHES, ROLLERS AND PADS

You can put paint onto the many surfaces of your home in several different ways, using brushes, rollers, pads or even spraying equipment. Choosing the right tool is a major step on the route to success.

It's unlikely you will not at some time or another have wielded a paint brush, but you may not be aware of the range available.

Types of brushes
Brushes are the most versatile paint applicators; a good set will cope with almost every painting requirement and if looked after properly will last a lifetime. Different types include:
Flat paint brushes: also known as varnish brushes, these are used to apply solvent-based paints and varnishes where a high quality finish is required. They are made from natural or synthetic bristles, or a mixture of the two, fixed to a wooden or plastic handle with a ferrule, usually made of steel. The most commonly available sizes are: 12mm (½in), 25mm (1in), 38mm (1½in), 50mm (2in), 62mm (2½in), 75mm (3in) and 100mm (4in) wide but 6mm (¼in), 16mm (⅝in) and 19mm (¾in) versions are also to be found. The bristles are tapered so that when they are loaded they give the brush a sharp 'cutting edge'.

Cutting-in brushes: sometimes called window brushes, these are flat paint brushes that have the ends of the bristles angled to make it easier to 'cut in' accurately when painting to a line on window frames or other areas.

Radiator brushes: are used for painting awkward areas such as behind radiators. They have a flat paint brush head between 25 and 50mm (1 and 2in) wide, with a long, bendable wire handle emerging at right angles from the side. A short wooden handle is fixed to the end of this so the brush can be easily held.

Angle brushes: have a solid handle about 300mm (12in) long from which the head emerges at an angle of between 30° and 45°. Some have a flat head about 38mm (1½in) wide; others have a round head between 6mm (¼in) and 19mm (¾in) wide. They are also used for painting awkward corners but are less versatile than radiator brushes.

Stencil brushes: are designed for the stippling action needed to produce a crisp outline when painting through a stencil. They have a short, round wooden handle and short, stiff bristles tightly bunched to give a round head between 6mm (¼in) and 60mm (2⅜in) in diameter.

Sash brushes: are specially shaped for painting window frames but a standard 12-25mm (½-1in) wide flat brush will do equally well.

Wall brushes: these are for painting walls with emulsion paint and are often called emulsion brushes. They are extra large, flat paint brushes, normally 100, 125, 150 or even 175mm (4, 5, 6 or 7in) wide, but the bristles tend to be coarser and do not have the same degree of tapering; and the handles are usually stronger and more crudely shaped. Though many have steel ferrules, better-quality brushes have ferrules made from copper so they don't rust when used with water-based paint.

Choosing brushes
To meet all your painting requirements you'll have to get several brushes. A set of flat paint brushes is a must for gloss work; you'll need a 25mm (1in) wide brush, a 50mm (2in) wide brush and also one which is 75mm (3in) wide. These should enable you to cope with most situations, but if you intend doing lots of fiddly, very precise work, get a 12mm (½in) brush as well. A radiator brush will be useful too; it takes time getting used to but saves you the trouble of removing the radiators when you want to paint the walls.

If you don't intend to do a great deal of painting you can make do without a cutting-in brush. Given care and patience, you can achieve the same results using a 25mm (1in) flat brush. But to complete the set, buy a wall brush, though you must make sure it's not too big. While it may seem that the larger the brush, the faster you will get the job finished, in practice, brushes larger than 100 or 125mm (4 or 5in) wide are too tiring on the wrist to use for any length of time.

Regarding quality, unless you're going to do a great deal of painting it's not worth investing in really top-quality brushes.

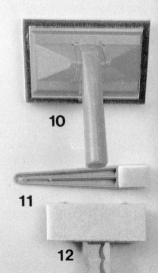

Types of brushes
1 emulsion brush

Flat brushes of various sizes
2 75mm (3in) brush
3 50mm (2in) brush
4 25mm (1in) brush
5 15mm (½in) brush

6 sash brush
7 cutting-in brush
8 angle brush
9 stencil brush

Paint pads
10 standard pad
11 small (wand) pad
12 edge pad

Professional quality brushes in mint condition may not, in fact, be suitable; for example, a flat paint brush of this quality has very long bristles so the brush can hold a lot of paint, increasing the time during which you can work before it needs to be reloaded. But a professional decorator would not normally use a brush like this for finished glossy work; instead he would break the brush in (ie, wear down the bristles slightly) by using it to apply undercoats before using it for gloss paint. For the occasional decorator, therefore, a brush with a shorter, cheaper bristle is preferable. However, don't make the mistake of buying too cheap a brush, unless you intend to throw it away when you have finished.

Check that the brush you buy has a reasonable thickness of bristles in the head. (If you open up the bristles, you'll often find a wooden wedge bulking out the head but this is not necessarily a bad thing unless the wedge is very large.) Purely synthetic bristles are all right for wall brushes but they tend not to make a very good brush for gloss work. Finally, make sure the bristles are secure and that the brush has a firmly fixed ferrule. A few loose bristles are inevitable, even in a good brush, but a poor brush will moult at an alarming rate when you run your fingers through it. Many top-quality brushes will have the bristles bonded securely into the ferrule with two-part adhesive, which forms a solid block and minimises bristle loss.

Types of paint rollers

Paint rollers are less accurate than brushes and you will have to use brushes along with them for any precise work. But they cover surfaces much faster and are ideal for painting large, uncomplicated areas.

A roller consists of a metal frame containing the roller mechanism with a handle fitted to one end and a roller sleeve on the other. They come with a special tray in which you load the sleeve with paint. Most rollers are 175mm (7in) wide, though larger and smaller versions are available.

The cheapest type of sleeve is made from foam. There are sleeves made from other materials: mohair sleeves which have a fine, short pile; sheepskin or synthetic fibre sleeves with a longer pile; and embossed rollers for use with textured paints.

There are also special paint rollers with a very slim sleeve for painting behind radiators and ones with two or more narrow rollers fitted on a flexible axle for painting pipes. For painting ceilings and high walls you can buy an extension pole which screws into the end of the roller handle, but it's cheaper to improvise an extension by fitting a broom handle or a length of 25mm (1in) thick dowel.

Choosing roller sleeves

When buying a roller, watch out for a cheap flimsy frame which won't last long or too large a frame which can be tiring to use. Choosing the sleeve for a roller is, however, the most crucial factor.

● Before using a brush, especially a new one, 'flirt' the bristles through your fingers and 'strop' the brush head in the palm of your hand, to remove any dust and loose bristles.

● When loading a brush, never dip it into the paint too deeply or it will work up around the base of the bristles, dry, and shorten the brush's useful life. Make sure only the end third (or less) of the bristles enters the paint.

● Soak a new fibre roller sleeve in soapy water for a few hours before you use it. Then run the roller (without any paint) over the wall to dry it out. This will make sure you get rid of any loose fibres from the sleeve.

● Never overload a paint roller and never work it too briskly across the surface you are painting. If you do, paint will fly off in all directions, spattering you and areas you don't want covered in paint.

● Hold a brush round the ferrule rather like a pencil, when using it. This gives more control than if you clench your fist round the handle.

RIGHT

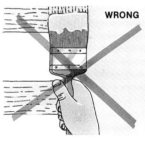

WRONG

Foam sleeves tend not to last long and can be difficult to clean. They can also be splashy in use and paint can drip from the ends if too much pressure is applied or the sleeve is overloaded with paint. That said, they are suitable for use on smooth or slightly textured surfaces. Sheepskin sleeves are expensive but worthwhile where you are dealing with a very rough surface and need a very hardwearing roller. As for the rest, you should aim to get a sleeve with the correct length of pile. When considering coverage, choose short-piled sleeves for smooth surfaces and long-piled sleeves for rough surfaces. But if it's a really good

Rollers
1 short-pile sleeve
2 long-pile sleeve on handle
3 sheepskin sleeve
4 radiator roller
5 extension for handles
6 foam-sleeved roller in tray

finish you're after, short-piled sleeves tend to give better results, though a lot here depends on the type of paint: sleeves made from natural materials work best with solvent-based glosses; synthetic sleeves are best with emulsions.

Paint pads

Paint pads consist of a square or rectangle of short pile fibre (synthetic or mohair), usually backed with foam, attached to a metal or plastic plate and handle. They come in a range of sizes varying from 62mm (2½in) up to 187mm (7½in) wide. You can also buy special edging pads for cutting in between walls and ceilings and at corners; these have small guide wheels which run against the surface you are not painting. And there are very small pads (often with a flexible handle) for precision painting such as in crevices and behind radiator pipes and other hard to get at areas.

For high walls and ceilings, pads are available with a socket to which you can fit a broom handle. By providing you with the extra reach you need, this cuts out the need for ladders.

Pads are sold with special trays (narrower and deeper than a roller tray) for loading them with paint, some trays have a grooved roller for transferring the paint to the pad you are using.

You can use paint pads with all commonly available paints (though thixotropic paints must first be thoroughly stirred to destroy the jelly texture). They are not particularly expensive but many are sold as complete sets which may be inconvenient if you want only one size as a replacement.

Paint sprays

Another way of applying paint is to use a paint spray. Gloss paint is available in aerosol form but, since it is very expensive, it is only worth using on small jobs such as repainting a wicker chair (where it's ideal for all the nooks and crannies) or to spruce up an old domestic appliance. For larger areas you can use a spray gun. This consists of a compressor (usually electric) connected to a paint reservoir and nozzle; you squeeze a trigger to apply the paint. These have the limitation that, for interior use, you would have to spend a great deal of time masking off areas you don't want painted, so it's better to use them for exterior work such as painting the outside walls of the house. Because of their restricted usefulness it's worth hiring a spray gun rather than buying one. When hiring, make sure the paint reservoir is neither so large as to make the gun too heavy, nor so small that you are forever refilling it. Also check that the gun is suitable for use with the type of paint you have in mind. Exterior paints sometimes contain fibre or granular 'filler' and not all guns are able to cope with this kind of solid matter. Usually a special nozzle must be fitted.

Pressurised paint systems

A recently developed product is the pressurised paint system. This consists of a container into which you fit special tubs of paint; an ordinary soda syphon bulb then provides the pressure to force the paint along a flexible tube to the painting head, which may take the form of a flat brush, a paint pad or a roller (these are interchangeable). The paint flow is controlled by a push-button in the head.

This method is a lot less messy than painting with conventional equipment but it's expensive and you can only use the type of paint recommended by the manufacturer of the machine.

Care of equipment

If you want your painting equipment to last you will have to look after it properly, which means you must clean it after use.

Where brushes are concerned, you should work the brush over several sheets of clean newspaper to remove as much paint as possible, then work it up and down in the appropriate solvent (white spirit for most solvent based paints, water for emulsions) changing this frequently to remove the remaining paint. Make sure when you do this that the solvent is worked right up to the point where the bristles are set into the brush.

When you reach the point where no amount of working in solvent appears to remove any more paint, wash the brush out in warm, soapy water (to remove the last vestiges of paint and solvent) and pat dry with a clean cloth. Mould the bristles into their correct shape, then wrap the brush head in paper secured around the ferrule with a rubber band before storing it away. The paper both absorbs residual moisture and helps the bristles keep their shape to prolong their useful life.

Clean roller sleeves in the appropriate solvent, too, but do not leave them to soak in solvent or they may be damaged. Rinse them well and dry them away from direct heat. Paint pads can be cleaned in a similar fashion; again, prolonged immersion in cleaning solvents may cause damage by lifting the pad away from its handle.

Cleaning obviously takes time and if you intend to stop work for only an hour or two and then restart, merely wrapping the brush, pad or roller tightly in polythene will mean it's ready for use when you want it. If, however, you are leaving the paint applicator overnight, it's worth cleaning it out properly. Don't simply leave it standing in solvent until you are ready to re-use it. The solvent in the bristles or fibre will ruin your work when you re-start unless you clean it out.

To store equipment after it's dried out, it's best to hang brushes on nails through holes drilled in the top of the brush handle and store roller sleeves and paint pads securely in polythene bags.

Other paint applicators

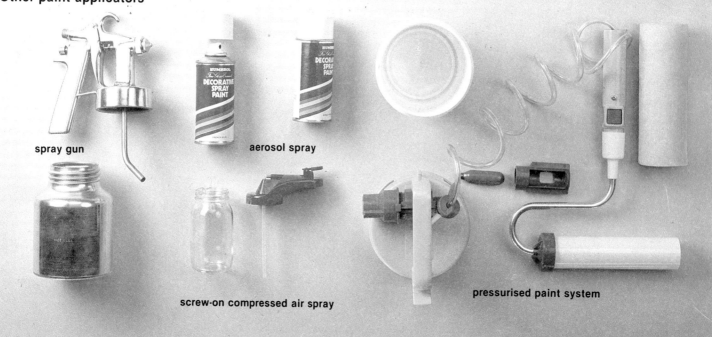

spray gun

aerosol spray

screw-on compressed air spray

pressurised paint system

TOOLS FOR ELECTRICAL JOBS

Electrical work, like so many other jobs about the home, can be carried out more successfully and more quickly if you have the right tools to hand. Here is a selection of what you will need for installation work, and also to enable you to cope with emergencies.

To carry out electrical work properly without causing damage to cables and other household fittings, you'll need to have the right tools for the job. Most DIY enthusiasts will already have many of the tools needed for such heavy work as raising and replacing floorboards and chopping out chases in walls to bury cables. Very often the car tool kit will produce spanners for dismantling appliances when renewing flexible cords or heating elements.

Nevertheless, if you are contemplating carrying out your own electrical installation work, you should assemble a tool kit to cope with all the jobs you are likely to encounter. That way not only will you find the work much easier, but you'll also be able to ensure that the final result reaches a professional standard that will give you great satisfaction.

Screwdrivers
A minimum of three straight-tipped screwdrivers is required: a small, thin-bladed electrician's screwdriver for reaching shrouded grub screws in electrical fittings; and medium and large size normal screwdrivers. A selection of crosshead screwdrivers may also be helpful in dealing with Pozidriv and similar screws.

There are two other screwdriver types which you may find useful: a ratchet screwdriver with a chuck to accept a range of different driver bits, and an offset screwdriver. The latter is a simple steel bar, the ends of which are bent at right angles and terminate in a straight tip at one end and a crosshead tip at the other. It is ideal for reaching awkward screws, particularly when servicing electrical appliances.

Bradawls
A bradawl is needed for piercing holes in timber and plaster to mark the position of fixing screws for appliances and their mounting boxes or brackets.

Pliers
Pliers are among the essential tools for electrical work. They are used to grip and bend wire, and to hold small items such as nuts and washers in confined spaces.

Electrician's pliers are similar to engineer's pliers but have insulated handles suitable for working with voltages of 240 volts or above. However, remember you should never carry out any work on an installation unless the power has been turned off, so the presence of insulated handles is only an extra safeguard.

Complementing the standard electrician's pliers should be a pair of long-nosed pliers, which may also be obtained with insulated handles.

SPECIALIST TOOLS
There are a number of specialist tools which are essential for any electrical installation work. These will enable you to get perfect results with the minimum of effort.

KEY
1 *Torch*
2 *Flooring saw*
3 *Floorboard chisel*
4 *Adjustable wire strippers*
5 *Side cutters*
6 *Long-nosed pliers*
7 *Snub-nosed pliers*
8 *Joist brace*
9 *Continuity tester*
10 *Neon screwdriver*
11 *Ring-main tester*
12 *Screwdrivers*

SPECIALIST TOOLS

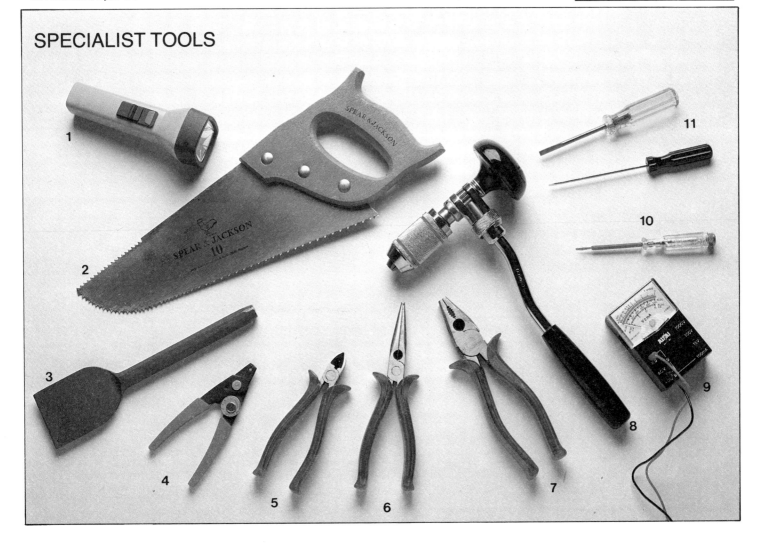

GENERAL-PURPOSE TOOLS

Cutters and strippers

Small side cutters are used for cutting the ends of fuse wires when rewiring circuit fuses, and for trimming cable and flex cores when making connections. The jaws are shaped to get close in to the work and still allow knuckle room to grip the handles.

A pair of wire strippers of the adjustable type to fit the various sizes of insulated conductor will permit the insulation to be removed efficiently without damaging the conductor itself. Also available is a cable stripper which will remove the outer sheathing of a cable without cutting into the insulation of the conductors inside. This is much safer than using a knife.

Handyman's knife

If you can't get hold of the type of cable stripper mentioned previously, a handyman's knife will do for trimming the insulation and cable sheathing, providing it is used carefully. Also, it it useful for trimming floor coverings when lifting and replacing floorboards.

Grips and wrenches

Where metal conduit, armoured and mineral-insulated cables are used, an adjustable spanner will be needed. A companion tool is the locking wrench which also has adjustable jaws, but they can be locked on to the workpiece to apply great pressure, leaving the hands free.

Hammers

Ideally, your tool kit should include three types of hammer, and you may already have some of them. A claw hammer is used for general work, a pin hammer for fixing cable clips and a club hammer for driving cold chisels.

Chisels

A selection of cold chisels will make installing cable runs and mounting boxes easier. A short, sharp, small-diameter chisel should be used for chopping out cable chases and recesses in plaster. Deeper recesses in brickwork and masonry can be cut with a thicker 150 to 200mm (6 to 8in) long chisel. A longer (at least 300mm/12in) thin chisel is ideal for cutting holes through brick walls.

The electrician's bolster chisel is useful for lifting floorboards; you drive it between the boards to split off the tongues and then lever them upwards. The wide blade spreads the load.

Since a certain amount of wood cutting is involved in laying cables beneath floors, a set of general-purpose wood chisels will also prove to be invaluable.

Saws

Various types of saw are needed in electrical work since metal, wood and plastic need to be cut.

For cutting plastic trunking, floorboards and other timber, you'll need a tenon saw.

Cutting down into floorboards and removing the tongues when lifting boarding can be done with a special floorboard saw. This has a curved blade, allowing the waste material to be cleared quickly from the groove the saw cuts, and so reducing the likelihood of damaging adjacent woodwork when cutting across a board. The tip of the back edge of the blade is set at an angle with cutting teeth to allow cuts to be made right up to a skirting board without the handle fouling the wall.

A padsaw is useful for cutting timber in confined spaces and for making holes in ceilings to accept mounting boxes for light fittings.

Metal fittings and large cables, including the armoured variety, may be cut with an adjustable hacksaw, which will take 200 to 300mm (8 to 12in) long blades. Finally, small sawing jobs and shortening fixing screws can be carried out with a junior hacksaw.

Your tool box (above) should contain many general-purpose tools that will help you with your electrical jobs, as well as being useful for other repairs. Screwdrivers, chisels, drill bits and saws are all vital. In addition, it's a good idea to keep a number of spare electrical accessories in case of an emergency.

Drills

A hand drill should be available for light drilling of plastic or thin metal, and can also be used for drilling small holes in brickwork and masonry.

Alternatively, a power drill is a better bet providing, of course, that you already have a live circuit from which to operate it. Pick one with a large chuck capacity, and give serious consideration to buying a drill with an optional hammer action, which will be a great help when drilling into masonry.

Drill bits

A set of masonry drill bits is necessary for drilling brickwork. If you have a power drill with a hammer action make sure the drill bits are suitable for this; not all are.

For drilling holes in metal and plastic boxes, a selection of high-speed twist drills is a must.

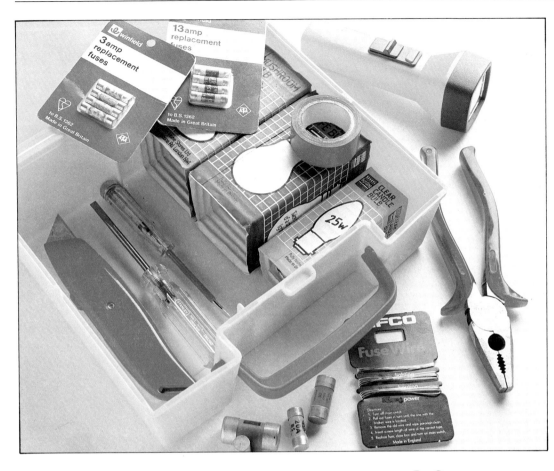

AN EMERGENCY TOOL KIT

Even if you're never likely to carry out any electrical installation work in your home, you're sure to have to cope with running repairs to your system when things go wrong. So you can find the tools and materials you will need when the lights go out, buy a small box and assemble an emergency tool kit you can keep near to the fuse board so you can always find it when you need it. Include a torch, a pair of pliers, a handyman's knife, a couple of screwdrivers, some PVC insulating tape and fuse wire or replacement fuses of appropriate types. It's also worth adding two or three spare light bulbs. Label the box, and always replace any components of the kit if they are used.

Emergency procedures

Before dealing with any repair, make sure that the circuit is safe to work on. If a fuse has blown, you should turn off the mainswitch and identify which circuit it is. Remove the fuse carrier and renew the wire or cartridge, or reset the MCB. Never undertake any work with wet hands and always make sure that you have sufficient light by which to see.

Hand brace and bits

Most general wood-drilling jobs can also be accomplished with a conventional carpenter's ratchet brace and a set of auger bits. However, drilling through joists often presents problems due to their close spacing. A special compact joist brace is made for this purpose and has a ratchet lever immediately behind the chuck.

Measuring tape

A retractable steel tape is essential for the accurate positioning of switches and other accessories. A 3m (10ft) one will do for installation work, but a longer one will be useful when estimating cable runs.

Plumb bob

The position of vertical runs of cable can be determined accurately with the aid of a plumb bob and line. It can also be used to carry a draw wire down into a hollow partition where it can be hooked out at the switch position.

Spirit level

Switch and accessory boxes need to be level, and a small spirit level is ideal for setting them correctly.

Soldering iron

For servicing and repairing electrical appliances, you will need a soldering iron to unsolder and remake connections. You should

keep a supply of flux and solder with it. For more information see pages 161 -162.

Testers

Two testers that every home electrician should have are a neon tester (usually in the form of a small screwdriver) and a continuity tester.

The neon tester is used to determine if a terminal is live. Place the tip of the tester blade on the terminal and a finger on the metal cap at the end of the tester's handle. This completes a circuit, causing a neon bulb in the handle to light if there is power. A built-in resistor prevents electric shocks.

Battery-powered testers are relatively cheap to buy. The most popular type has metal probes, and such a device will test cartridge fuses and other conductors of low resistance, continuity being indicated by a positive meter reading. Some models double as mains testers.

High resistance items, such as light bulbs and heating elements, should be checked with a special high-resistance tester.

Another useful tester takes the form of a 3-pin plug and is used for checking the cable connections at a socket. It has neon indicators to show whether the socket is wired correctly, has faulty earth, live or neutral connections, or reversed live and neutral connections.

hints

● When lifting a floorboard, lever the end clear of the floor and lay a long cold chisel across the adjacent boards to support it in this raised position. Continue levering, moving the chisel as you go, until the board can be removed.

● A flooring saw with its specially shaped blade will allow you to cut through floorboards right up to skirting boards without the handle touching the wall. It may also be used for cutting through the tongues of T & G boarding.

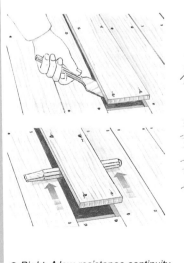

● Right: A low-resistance continuity tester can be constructed using a 4.5V bell battery, a torch bulb, MES lampholder and insulated wire for leads.

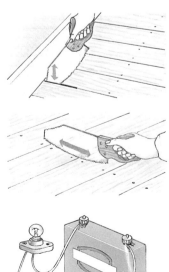

TOOLS FOR PLUMBING JOBS

You should always check you've got the right tools to hand before starting any work, and plumbing is no exception. Here's a list of the ones you're most likely to need, plus some essential items to help you cope with emergencies.

Anyone living in a fairly modern – or modernised – house with copper or stainless steel water supply pipes and a plastic waste water system can carry out all routine plumbing maintenance and repair work with only a minimal tool kit. In fact, many of the tools required for plumbing work will already be part of the general household or car tool kit. But, if you plan to do a lot of plumbing work you'll need a few specialised tools.

Before buying any expensive new tool ask yourself how often you will need to use it. If the honest answer is 'not more than once a year' then you should seriously consider hiring it instead.

Spanners
You'll need a couple of adjustable spanners for tightening up compression fittings – one to grip the fitting steady while you use the other to tighten it up. You'll need them for many other types of fittings too.

A useful tool which can make life easier is the 'crows-foot' spanner. It's used to undo the virtually inaccessible back-nuts that secure bath and basin taps in position. Unless you have a lot of room beneath the taps you'll find it almost impossible to undo these nuts with an ordinary spanner.

Wrenches
Only wrenches are capable of gripping and turning round objects such as pipes. There are two types used in plumbing. The pipe wrench looks like an adjustable spanner but its lower jaw is able to pivot slightly, and both jaws are serrated. As you use it, the lower jaw is able to open just enough to grip the pipe, then, as you turn it, the serrations dig in, pull in the jaws and grip even tighter. The harder you turn, the tighter they grip, so they're suitable for really stubborn jobs. Wrenches will only work in one direction; if you turn them the wrong way the jaws won't grip and the pipe will slip round.

The lockable wrench is slightly different. You adjust the jaw separation with a screw, then close them round the pipe, squeezing the handles to lock them on tightly.

Pipe cutters
You can cut pipes with a hacksaw quite successfully, but if you plan to do a lot of plumbing work you should consider buying a pipe cutter. The pipe is placed between two hardened rollers and a thin cutting wheel; the tool is then rotated round the pipe while the cutting wheel is screwed down into the metal. A pipe cutter always produces a perfectly square and smooth cut – there is none of the rough metal burr that you'd get with a hacksaw. Yet it does round the end of the pipe inwards a little and the metal flange must be removed with a reamer which is usually incorporated in one end of the tool. Since pipe cutters need to be rotated round the tube they can't be used to cut existing pipes fitted close to a wall. So you will need a hacksaw as well.

Pipe benders
Sharp bends in pipe are easiest to make with capillary or compression fittings. But you can bend pipe by hand it you want, and you'll have to if you want shallow curves. Copper pipe with a diameter of 22mm (¾in) or less can be bent using bending springs or in a bending machine. The purpose of both springs and bending machine is to support the walls of the tube so that they don't flatten or wrinkle inside the curve as the bend is made. A bending spring supports the tube internally, while the bending machine supports it externally. As you're unlikely to want to bend copper pipe that often, these are tools it's best to hire when they're required.

Thread sealers
Jointing compound and PTFE tape are both used to make a watertight – and gas-tight – seal on screwed

fittings. Jointing compound is a sticky paste which you smear round the thread, and PTFE thread sealing tape is wound anticlockwise round the male fitting before the joint is assembled.

Asbestos gloves
If you're using a blowlamp and doing a lot of soldering then you'd be wise to invest in a pair of asbestos gloves. Copper pipe conducts heat very efficiently so the gloves could prevent many burnt fingers.

Torch
Very often you'll need to work at the back of sinks and baths or in dark, awkward corners in the loft, so a torch is essential. Change the batteries as soon as the bulb dims.

Tape measure
You'll need a tape measure for accurate cutting of lengths of pipe and for positioning taps and fittings in the right place.

Files and steel wool
A file is essential for removing burrs left by a hacksaw. Emery paper and steel wool are both used to clean the ends of copper pipe ready for making soldered joints. They're also used to roughen plastic pipe to provide a key for adhesives.

Blowlamp
Unless you plan to use compression fittings for all your plumbing work you'll certainly need a blowlamp. See pages 152 -153 for information, but in most cases, a small blowlamp operating off a disposable canister of gas is easiest to use. Don't forget to keep a spare canister in your tool kit; they have a habit of running out at the most awkward moments.

Other tools
Apart from the tools described above, you'll also need a power drill for drilling holes for fixing screws and pipes, a set of screwdrivers and a pair of pliers.

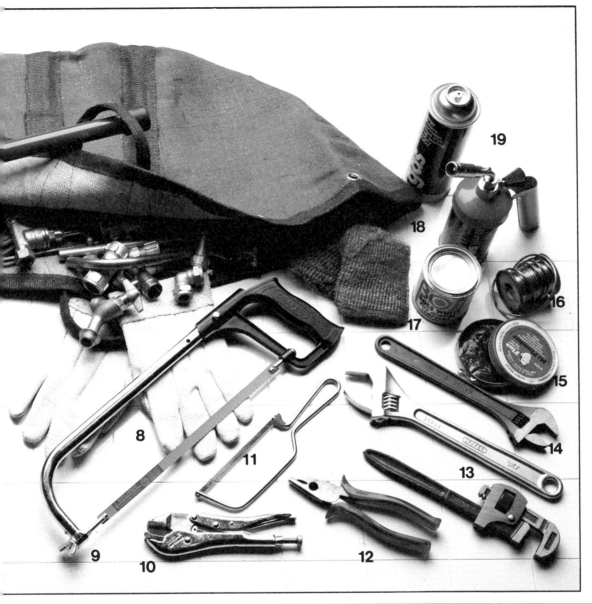

KEY

Tools for major plumbing work

 1 *crows-foot spanner (one end for bath taps, the other for basins)*
 2 *pipe bender and formers for 15 and 22mm pipe*
 3 *retractable tape measure*
 4 *wheeled pipe cutter*
 5 *bending spring (available in 15 and 22mm sizes)*
 6 *half-round file*
 7 *screwdrivers for slotted and cross-point screws*
 8 *asbestos gloves*
 9 *hacksaw with spare blades*
10 *lockable wrench*
11 *junior hacksaw*
12 *pliers*
13 *pipe wrench*
14 *adjustable spanners*
15 *flux paste for soldered capillary fittings*
16 *solder in coil form for end-feed capillary fittings*
17 *jointing compound (and/or PTFE tape) for threaded connections*
18 *wire wool pads*
19 *butane or propane blowlamp with replacement gas canisters.*

In addition to the tools and items of equipment mentioned above, you are also likely to need:
● *power drill with a selection of different sized masonry, twist drills and wood-boring bits*
● *pipe clips in 15 and 22mm sizes*
● *wallplugs (the stick type that you cut to length are the most economical)*
● *screws for mounting pipe clips, radiator brackets and so on*
● *a torch*
● *a bag to carry everything round the house in.*

AN EMERGENCY PLUMBING KIT

There's really no point in assembling a full plumbing tool kit if you never intend to do any plumbing work. But emergencies can always happen so it's wise to keep a small tool kit to hand to stop an accident turning into a disaster. This should include an adjustable spanner, a locking wrench, a screwdriver and a pair of pliers, plus equipment to cope with bursts and leaks.

If you hammer a nail into a pipe you can easily make a quick repair with a two-part pack of epoxy resin sold especially for plumbing repairs. The adhesive and hardener are worked together in the hands and the material is moulded round the hole. This makes a permanent repair for small holes or leaking joints, but a larger hole is repaired more securely by cutting out the damaged section of pipe and

inserting a straight compression coupling. So keep at least two of these in your tool kit – one each for 15mm and 22mm pipe.

Keep some penetrating oil for freeing jammed stop-valves or corroded nuts and, of course, an adjustable spanner to undo the latter. You'll also need a selection of tap washers – one for each type of tap, and some O-rings for the ball-valve. A few spare olives are always handy – compression fittings can be reused but you need a new olive each time. For clearing blocked waste pipes you'll need a 'force cup' or sink waste plunger, and a piece of flexible wire for clearing out blocked pipes and drains. Finally, mini-hacksaws are so cheap it's worth keeping one specially for your emergency tool kit – plus a packet of assorted spare blades.

BLOWLAMPS

Blowlamps and blowtorches are an essential part of a tool kit. They may look somewhat frightening to use, but they are surprisingly versatile tools used in plumbing work for making solder joints and more commonly in decorating for paint stripping.

Many people are wary of using a blowlamp or blowtorch. They tend to forget that the modern versions work off a gas canister, and are safe and easy to operate. Instead they associate them with the old paraffin models which generally didn't have a good reputation even though this was largely unfounded. Admittedly they were somewhat messy to use, but they were only dangerous if they were operated incorrectly. The horror stories of lamps exploding usually resulted from somebody doing something foolish like filling them with petrol. But all that is now a thing of the past.

The gas blowlamp
This is the modern counterpart of the old-fashioned paraffin blowlamp and on the face of it it's not so very different – it's still basically a fuel tank (the gas cylinder) and burner unit. But it's the details that make all the difference.

Instead of paraffin in the fuel tank, it contains gas (either butane or propane, or occasionally a mixture of the two). Because the gas is pressurised it is in liquid form and this allows more fuel to be stored in a small container. Depending on the model, these range in size from 150 to 450g (the weight of fuel they contain), so bearing in mind that some jobs burn more gas than others, you can usually work for an hour, and sometimes as long as two, on one container of gas. When the canister runs out, you just unscrew it, throw it away and screw in a new one. Furthermore, as some canisters are self-sealing, you can remove it before it is empty enabling you to transfer it to some other gas burning appliance – a camping stove for example. Finally, because it's the pressure inside the canister that keeps the fuel liquid, there is no need to preheat the lamp in order to begin the process of vaporisation. The fuel vaporises naturally as soon as you release the pressure by turning on the control valve.

The burner assembly also contains a lot of improvements. It comprises a valve to break the seal of the gas canister and to control the flow of fuel, plus a control knob that allows you to turn the flame up

or down as easily as the flame on a gas cooker. Most brands offer a choice of nozzles you can fit to the burner to give different types of flame according to the job in hand (see below).

Modern blowlamps are extremely safe. Quite apart from the fact that most of the dangers associated with the traditional blowlamp are eliminated by the gas blowlamp's design, that other risk of knocking the blowlamp over when it is still alight is also taken care of on most models. The blowlamp simply turns itself off automatically if it finds itself at a dangerous angle.

The gas blowtorch
In principle a blowtorch is exactly the same as a blowlamp. But in contrast to the blowlamp, it has a separate burner unit that's linked to a large refillable gas cylinder via a flexible rubber hose. When the gas has been used up you simply trade in the old cylinder for a new one. Propane is commonly available, which is better than butane for use outside in cold weather because butane will not vaporise at temperatures below 0°C. What's more, the tool is far more powerful, producing a hotter flame which can be useful for certain jobs.

A blowtorch is better when working into tight corners. The reason is that with the burner on the end of a flexible hose, the part you actually bring to the job is smaller than the blowlamp.

Blowlamp or blowtorch?
So what is the best tool to buy? The first thing to decide is what you are mainly going to use the tool for, and how often. In all probability it'll be for paint stripping, and perhaps occasionally soldering work.

Consequently, on the face of it, a small handheld blowlamp is the most sensible choice. It's widely available, relatively inexpensive to buy, and reasonably easy to use. And the small disposable containers are obtainable in DIY shops and stores selling camping equipment. If you're going to use the tool only rarely then this is the tool for you. But if you intend to do a lot of work in this line, then a blowtorch is a much more sensible investment. And if you're a

borderline case, then go for a blowlamp; you can probably hire a blowtorch from a local tool hire shop when you need it.

Nozzles
Whether you are using a blowlamp or blowtorch, you can improve its versatility by buying a few specialist nozzles. These simply fit over the standard burner, or replace it, and alter the shape of the flame the blowlamp or blowtorch produces. You'll find quite a collection on the market, each varying in detail, so ensure that the one you buy is compatible with your particular blowlamp; that means buying the same brand. There are, though, a few general types worth pointing out. There are burners that give a medium sized flame for general work – this is the type often fitted as standard when you buy a blowlamp

or blowtorch. There are burners that give large flames for big jobs, and burners that produce small, thin flames for delicate work. In addition, you'll find flame spreaders – sometimes called fantails or fishtails – which produce a broad flat flame for paint stripping. And there are even burners with a built-in copper soldering iron bit so you can carry out soft soldering.

Solder and flux
Solder, an alloy of tin and lead, is used to join metal to metal. First of all the surfaces have to be cleaned of metal oxide with flux, which otherwise would inhibit the final bond. They are then heated with a blowlamp and the solder held against the join. As it melts it flows between the metal surfaces and binds them together when it cools and solidifies.

BLOWLAMP SAFETY

Below: The hot air stripper has been specifically developed to strip paint. Unlike the blowlamp and blowtorch it is electrically driven and blows out a stream of very hot air which softens the paint so that it can be scraped from the surface. It is somewhat heavy to use, but it is cleaner and you don't have to worry about replacing a gas cylinder.

THE RANGE OF EQUIPMENT

Blowlamps (1 to 4) come in a range of sizes. The smaller versions are more wieldy but the gas cylinders will need replacing more frequently. The larger lamps use larger cylinders which make them heavier to use. Most lamps are fitted with a standard nozzle (7) but smaller heads (5 and 6) give a narrower flame. A flame spreader (8) is ideal

for paint stripping and there's a soldering iron attachment for soldering work (9). Solder is available either on a reel or in stick form. Use a blowtorch (10) instead of a blowlamp if you have a lot of work to do. The torch connects to a large gas cylinder via a flexible hose; so you don't have to hold the cylinder while operating the torch.

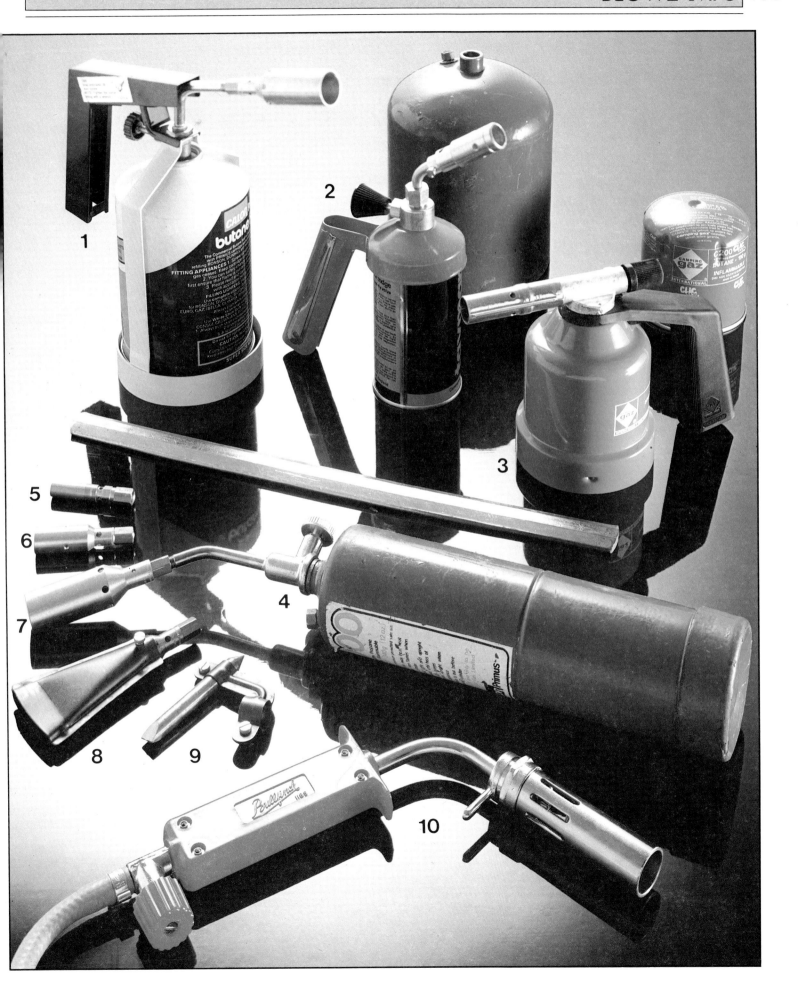

SPANNERS, BOLTS AND MACHINE SCREWS

Manufacturing industry uses a host of different screw fasteners. Sooner or later you'll come across them in repair or maintenance work and you'll need to know what they are, where they're commonly used, and how to turn them.

SELF-TAPPING SCREWS

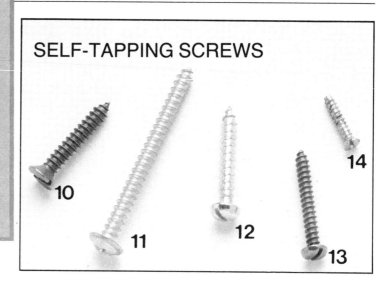

F or most do-it-yourselfers the world of self-tapping screws, machine screws and bolts is uncharted ground, for they belong mainly in industry. But you'll meet them in even simple repair jobs – and bolts are widely used on heavy timber construction, especially outdoors.

These fasteners come in an awesome variety of shapes and sizes. Even with a helpful hardware merchant, you need to know a little about what you're seeking.

Fasteners

● **Self-tapping screws** are the closest to wood screws. Pointed or nearly so, they can often be mistaken for (and if necessary used as) chipboard screws, because they have a fairly shallow and widely-spaced thread extending right up to the screw's head.

They tap (thread) their own way in, like wood screws – although pilot and clearance holes are needed.

There are two types: thread-forming and thread-cutting.

Thread-forming screws are either the pointed type AB (10 to 13) – mostly used in sheet metal and soft plastic – or the blunt-ended type B (14), for thicker materials. Both make a thread by distorting the edges of the pilot hole.

Thread-cutting self-tapping screws have flutes or channels across the thread, which remove the material rather like a drill bit as they're driven in.

In sheet metal, self-tapping screws are also used with **spring**

steel fasteners. These are clips, placed (like a nut) on the other side of the sheet to hold the screw tight.

Self-tapping screws are driven with screwdrivers. Their heads can be slotted or recessed, and they come in gauge numbers very like those for wood screws.

● The **machine screw**, used only in metal, is also threaded up to the head, but it's not tapered. It has more closely-spaced threads than the self-tapping screw, and needs a matching thread in which to engage – either in a tapped (already threaded) hole in the component you're fixing to, or in a nut.

Ordinary machine screws are driven with screwdrivers. A second type, the **set screw** (3), has a hexagonal head and so needs a spanner to tighten it. **Socket screw** heads (4) have a hexagonal recess for an Allen key (see pages 14 -15).

● A **bolt** is a machine screw with an unthreaded shank. It passes right through the components to be joined, and is fastened with a matching nut.

The usual bolt for carpentry is the **coach** or **carriage bolt** (15). Its domed 'cup square' head has a square collar round the neck, which digs into the timber and stops the bolt revolving as you tighten the nut. (Coach bolts are also found threaded up to the head – 16.) Since bolts make a very strong fixing, they're handy in woodwork where appearance isn't crucial, and where jointing is difficult or inappropriate.

Machine bolts have a hexagonal (20) or square head, though you

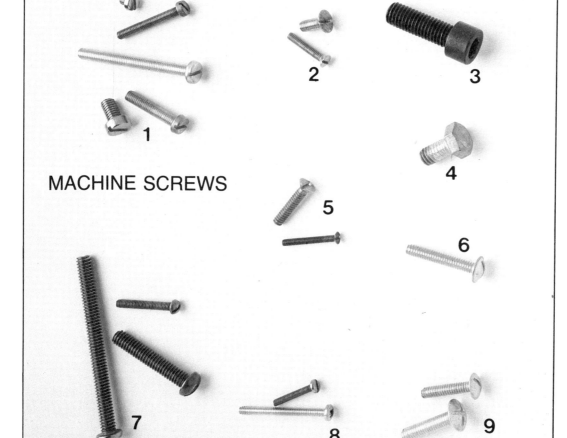

MACHINE SCREWS

Machine screws
1 *Cheese-head*
2 *Raised (countersunk) head*
3 *Set screw*
4 *Socket screw*
5 *Countersunk*
6 *Flange-head*
7 *Round-head*
8 *Pan-head*
9 *Mushroom-head*

BOLTS

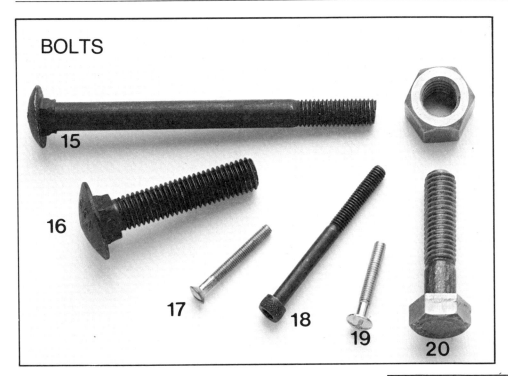

Self-tapping screws
10 *Type AB, countersunk*
11 *Type AB, flange-head*
12 and 13 *Type AB, pan-head*
14 *Type B*

Bolts
15 and 16 *Coach bolts*
17 *Countersunk bolt*
18 *Socket screw*
19 *Mushroom-head bolt*
20 *Machine bolt*

Nuts
21 *Square nuts*
22 *Locking nuts*
23 *Plain hexagonal nuts*
24 *Wing nut*

Washers
25 *Plain washers*
26 *Gripping washers*

can find bolts turned with a screwdriver (17 and 19). Socket screws also come with unthreaded shanks (18).

● **Nuts** are essential for fixing bolts, and can also be used on machine screws. They may be hexagonal (23) or square (21). Cheaper 'flat' nuts are cut from sheet metal.

Locking nuts won't come undone in use. Some require a split pin, and others (22) lock automatically by means of a spring or other feature.

The familiar **wing** or **butterfly nut** (24) is ideal where you need only a finger-tight fastening, plus release by hand.

Dome nuts have one end closed off with a decorative dome.

● With bolts, machine screws and nuts, **washers** are almost always a good idea, and often essential. They spread the pressure, which helps prevent damage to the surface while improving grip.

Washers come in many sizes and materials (25). You generally have to specify the inside (hole) diameter, not the overall diameter.

Special gripping washers (26) are often used in metalwork. Some are **toothed** (inside or outside); **split washers** are like a coil from a spring, and grip by pressing against the surfaces above and below them. So do **crinkle washers**, which are wavy in profile.

● Getting the right bolt, machine screw or nut is quite complicated. Apart from length, you have to consider thread shape, thread diameter and (on set screws and machine bolts only) head size.

There are at least nine different **thread shapes**, mostly incompatible but impossible to tell apart by eye. Three are now

internationally recognised: ISO Metric ('coarse', which is commoner, plus 'fine' in many varieties); ISO Unified Coarse (UNC); and ISO Unified Fine (UNF). The last two – sometimes known as ISO Inch – come in Imperial units. Fine threads are shallower and more closely spaced, and offer more grip.

You'll also meet British Association (BA), British Standard Whitworth (BSW or 'Whit') and Fine (BSF), and perhaps American National Coarse (ANC) and Fine (ANF).

All bolts and machine screws are known by **thread diameter**. ISO Metric coarse ones have an M and the diameter in millimetres – eg, M3.5, M6. Unified ones smaller than ¼in have a number from 12 – the largest – down to 2, which is 2mm in diameter. Over 6mm they're called by actual sizes; so are the BSW and BSF types – a ⅛in diameter BSW bolt or machine screw is '⅛W'. BA sizes rise from a tiny 15BA to 0BA – the largest at 6mm (¼in) in diameter.

Square and hexagonal **head** (or nut) **sizes** are important, because you need a matching spanner. A spanner should always be a perfect fit, otherwise you'll round off the bolt head or nut and make it impossible to turn properly.

The crucial point is that an ISO set-screw or machine-bolt head is known by its actual size – the distance between opposite flat sides (A/F, for 'across flats') – while on other types the head size is known by the thread diameter. For example, an M8 bolt takes a 13mm (½in) spanner, but a ¼W bolt takes a ¼in spanner. The modern practice has one big advantage – you can tell which spanner you need by just measuring.

NUTS

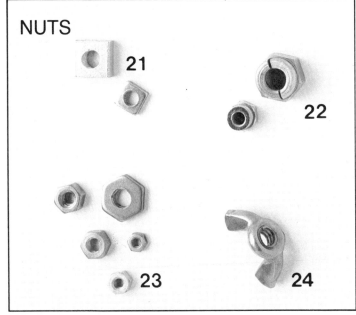

WASHERS

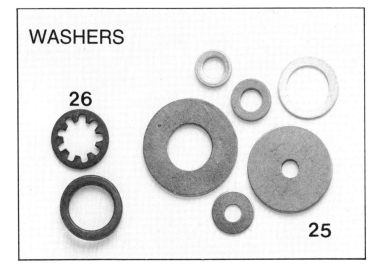

Spanners

Nuts, set screws and machine bolts need spanners to turn them. While screwing on a nut, you'll need a second spanner to hold the screw or bolt head steady.

● The **open-ended** or **C spanner** (2) is the commonest, and best for awkward situations, because it needs access to only two flats. And its head angle means you don't need much turning room to bring the next two flats round.

Its three main variants are **single-ended**, **double-ended** (2) and the double-ended **obstruction spanner**. This last has one head at a greater angle, so it's even better for confined spaces.

● **Ring spanners** (3) let you exert greater force than with an open-ended spanner, yet with less risk of slipping, because they completely enclose the screw head, bolt head or nut. However, they must be lowered into position, accurately located, and re-positioned after each sweep.

Most are **offset spanners** (3) – double-ended, and with the shaft cranked slightly to clear obstructions and leave room for your hands. Plain double- and single-ended types are mainly for heavy work. **Multiple ring spanners** (5) have up to five different rings at each end. The **split ring spanner** has a section out of the ring so it can be slipped on like an open-ended spanner. This weakens it slightly, but it remains less prone to slipping than an ordinary spanner.

In each case there are two head styles. A six-point ring spanner, with its six-sided hole, will only fit hexagonal heads and nuts. The twelve-point version fits square ones too.

● The **combination spanner** (1), despite its grand title, just has a ring at one end, and the other end open. Both heads are the same size: the open end gets the nut or set screw in position fast, and you use the strength of the ring for final tightening.

● The **box spanner** (6) is a tube with shaped ends. Turning force comes from a tommy bar passed through holes in its sides. If you don't place the bar centrally, or if you use an over-long bar, you risk distorting the tool or damaging whatever you're tightening.

For frequent use, go for either the more substantial solid box spanner, or the box spanner's close relative the **socket spanner.**

● The latter has a twelve-pointed recess. The turning power is provided by various lever handles – including ones with ratchets – which fit into the socket head. The socket part comes in several sizes, often sold as **socket sets** with handles.

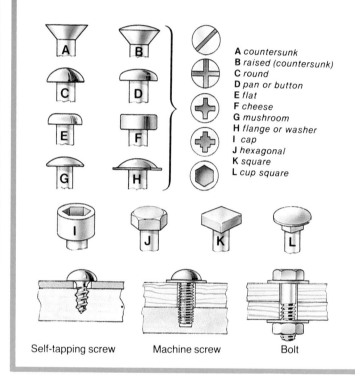

Self-tapping and machine screws have a host of head shapes (A to J). Most are slotted or recessed for screwdriving (D is flatter when slotted) – but some machine screws, called socket screws, have a hexagonal recess for an Allen key. The cap head (I) belongs only on socket screws.

The hexagonal head (J), turned by a spanner, is found on set screws (another type of machine screw) and machine bolts. The square head (K) belongs on machine bolts. The cup square head (L) belongs on coach bolts, it has a square collar round the neck and is used in woodwork.

A *countersunk*
B *raised (countersunk)*
C *round*
D *pan or button*
E *flat*
F *cheese*
G *mushroom*
H *flange or washer*
I *cap*
J *hexagonal*
K *square*
L *cup square*

Self-tapping screw   Machine screw   Bolt

SPANNERS

All the basic types of spanner are shown here. However, if you do a lot of work with nuts, bolts and machine screws – eg, on your car – you may want to invest in a socket set, described above.

1 *Combination spanner*
2 *Open-ended spanner*
3 *Ring spanner*
4 *Crescent adjustable spanner*
5 *Multiple ring spanner*
6 *Box spanner*

● If you don't want to buy a full set of conventional spanners, an adjustable spanner is a must. It fits almost any size of nut, set screw or bolt – square or hexagonal. The **crescent spanner** (4) is perhaps the commonest type. All are open-ended, with one jaw fixed and one adjusted via a screw mechanism. The jaws, like those of an open-ended spanner, are usually at 15° to the shaft.

Though there's an upper limit to each adjustable spanner's capacity, don't imagine that the biggest is always the most versatile. Choose according to your average needs. Beware, too, of loose jaws.

Finally, don't confuse the adjustable spanner with the **pipe wrench**. Although some adjustable spanners are called wrenches, like the **monkey wrench** with its 90° jaws, the pipe wrench makes a mess if used to grip nuts, set screws or bolt heads. Its job is to turn cylindrical objects. It only works in one direction.

CHAPTER 8

WORKING WITH METAL

**Being able to cut, drill, bend and join metal
opens up a field of creative workmanship as well as allowing you
to carry out a wider range of maintenance and repair jobs.
A few basic tools and some easy-to-master techniques
are all you need to get started.**

TOOLS FOR SIMPLE METALWORKING

Many metalworking jobs round the home can be handled with tools from your existing toolkit. But it's worthwhile having a few of the more specialist tools to hand and these can be acquired as and when you need them.

Metalworking isn't something you need do very often round the home. Apart from the plumbing, there is very little in the way of metal that you are ever likely to want to repair or alter. But if you don't have at least a few metalworking tools, then, sooner or later, you are almost certain to find yourself stuck, frustrated and annoyed, in the middle of what you thought would be a ten minute job. It may be a simple repair that you

just cannot do for the want of a spanner. It may be something you've bought that will not fit unless you file a bit off. It could even turn out to be something as elementary as the need to saw off and drill out a rusty old screw.

The type of tools you'll need all depends on the level of work you want to tackle. You should have one group for very basic, almost rough and ready jobs, and another for more precise and complex work.

The basic tool kit is extremely basic, and, when using it, you'll find yourself constantly having to dip into your carpentry tool box to fill in the gaps. It contains no measuring or marking tools, for example. The more advanced kit, on the other hand, gives you the proper tools for the job – tools that are specifically designed for accurate metalworking. Even here, though, you will find that some of them have 'general tool kit' equivalents, and so, unless you intend to take up serious craft metalwork or amateur engineering, it is not worth buying the second kit all in one go, just for the sake of being 'correct'. Instead, look at these specialist tools as possible additions to the basic tool kit. Buy them only when you need them, either because you genuinely cannot do a particular job without the specialist tool, or because the specialist tool will make the job that much simpler.

THE BASIC TOOL KIT
Ball-pein hammer
With its hardened steel face, this is better suited to bashing metal than the average woodworking hammer. What's more, you will find the ball-pein end useful for some shaping

jobs – it's actually designed for roughly shaping rivet heads. A good hammer will have an ash or hickory shaft, and the choice of head weights ranges from 114g to 1.3kg (4oz to 2lb 14oz). For general work, go for a head weight between 340 and 680g (12 and 24oz).

Engineer's pliers
For cutting wire, bending rods, and miscellaneous rough gripping, these are actually electrician's pliers without the insulated handles, so you may prefer to get the latter and kill two birds with one stone. They have serrated jaws to give a good grip, with a semi-circular serrated notch in each face to accept rods. Closer to the pivot are two scissor-like blades for cutting thin wire, and level with the pivot are two notches used for cropping thicker wires. Sizes range between 125mm (5in) and 250mm (10in), though you are unlikely to need anything larger than 180mm (7in). But choose the size you feel is most comfortable to use.

Hacksaws
The obvious use for this tool is to saw through metal. Choose one with a comfortable pistol grip handle,

THE BASIC TOOL KIT

KEY

1 *Steel rule*
2 *Double-ended scriber*
3 *Long-nosed pliers*
4 *Vernier calipers (slide calipers)*
5 *Pocket punch*
6 *Centre punch*
7 *Wing compasses*
8 *Engineer's try square*
9 *Cold chisels*
10 *Pipe cutter*
11 *Cut-off disc*
12 *Soft-faced hammer*
13 *Jigsaw with metal cutting blade*
14 *Ring spanner*
15 *Fixed spanners*
16 *Wire brush drill attachment*
17 *Wire brush*

SPECIALIST TOOLS

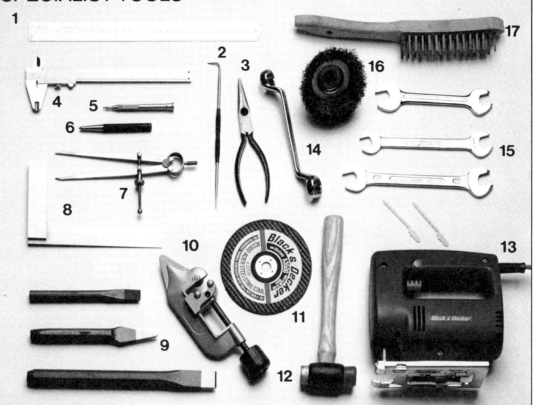

and an adjustable tubular steel frame so that it can accept blades of different sizes, the usual range of blade sizes being 200mm (8in), 250mm (10in) and 300mm (12in). Get a selection of flexible steel blades with hardened teeth. The most important thing here is the blade's coarseness, expressed as the number of tooth points per inch (ppi) – the fewer points per inch the coarser the blade. The most common sizes are 14, 18, 24 and 32 ppi. As a general rule, use the one that will keep at least three teeth in contact with the work. It's preferable to use fine blades for hard metals and coarse blades for softer metals (the latter clog less easily).

Junior hacksaw or mini-hacksaw

In addition to the standard-sized hacksaw, it is worth having a smaller version for fine work and for getting into awkward corners.

The junior hacksaw looks very like its big brother. None of them is adjustable and many types don't even provide a means of tensioning the blade, relying instead on the sprung steel rod frame to do the job. Normally 150mm (6in) long, they are primarily used for fine work, so there is little or no choice over the type of blade. In most

KEY

1 *Hacksaws*
2 *Tension file*
3 *High speed twist drills*
4 *Ball-pein hammer*
5 *Combination spanner*
6 *Adjustable spanners*
7 *Stilson wrench*
8 *Mole grips*
9 *Engineer's pliers*
10 *Flux*
11 *Soldering iron*
12 *Solder*
13 *Blowlamp*
14 *Abrasive paper*
15 *Steel wool*
16 *Files*
17 *File card*

cases, it's a 32 ppi blade or nothing.

Mini-hacksaws, on the other hand, are for more general work. Made from plastic and about 200mm (8in) long, they are really nothing more than a holder for standard hacksaw blades which makes them very handy, if only as a way of using up good blades that you have snapped.

Tension file

A very thin, flexible file, this is fitted into a hacksaw blade and is used to enlarge holes and cut slots where a round file or even a needle file would be too big.

Adjustable spanners and wrenches

For turning nuts and bolts, these can be adjusted to suit a range of sizes, which makes them almost equivalent to an all-in-one spanner set – almost, because individual fixed spanners tend to work better. You'll find a number of different designs available and usually a choice of sizes. Something in the middle of the range is probably most useful, but remember for many jobs you will need two – for example, you need one to hold a bolt head and another to tighten up the nut. For more information, see pages 154 -156.

Files

These are used for shaping and smoothing metal. There are many different shapes to choose from,

each available in varying degrees of coarseness. But you will find that a second-cut (that is, medium-coarse) half-round file is a good jack of all trades. In addition, consider getting the coarser flat bastard file for rough, fast shaping, and a second-cut round file for removing burrs from the insides of pipes.

File brush

This is worth having if you do a lot of filing. It's simply a specially-designed fine wire brush used for removing metal waste that has clogged up the teeth of a file.

Twist drills

For drilling holes in metal, make sure you get the high speed variety and not the cheaper carbon steel types, even though you may be using them in a hand-drill rather then with an electric drill. When drilling some kinds of metal you may have to lubricate the drill to stop it overheating. For convenience, buy a set with a range of sizes – normally between 1.5 and 10mm in diameter.

Abrasives

For metal, use either a silicon carbide abrasive or an emery cloth. The former lasts longer, and is also useful in decorating for rubbing down paintwork and so on. The latter, although slow cutting, and with a relatively short life, is better for polishing hard metals. Choose a selection of grades in both.

Steel wool

This is another useful abrasive that really comes into its own when cleaning metals prior to painting or soldering. A medium/fine grade will cope in the majority of situations.

Solder and flux

Soldering offers perhaps the simplest way to join most metals, but it is important to use the right solder and the right flux for the job (see pages 161 -164). The most convenient form to keep in your tool kit is multi-cored solder wire – as the wire contains its own flux. For large scale work, however, buy the solder in stick form, and the flux as a liquid or paste. It works out cheaper.

Blowlamp or blowtorch

To make a soldered joint you need something that will heat the metal and melt the solder. For relatively large jobs where delicacy isn't important, use a blowlamp or a blowtorch – the same one used for paint stripping. Ideally choose one with a selection of nozzles. The standard nozzle will do for most work, but in some situations a fine nozzle is a must. Some models also include nozzles with a built-in soldering iron, these tend to be rather brutal instruments, and are totally unsuitable for electrical work. (See pages 152 -153).

Soldering iron

For delicate soldering and electrical work, use an electric soldering iron.

hints

● Use slide calipers to check the external and internal diameters of a pipe. Make sure you set the jaw at the widest point and read the relevant measurements on the correct scale.

Vernier calipers (illustrated) are the most advanced form of calipers, and you can make very accurate readings simply by turning the fine adjustment nut.

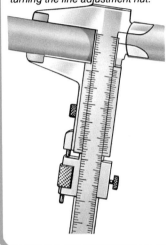

● Use a scriber to mark a cutting line on metal, with a steel rule or engineer's try square to act as a guide. When marking the line, draw the scriber towards you and angle it slightly towards the rule at the same time, as this will make for greater accuracy and prevent the point from skipping off course.

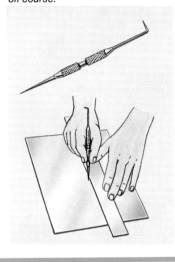

● The main use for wing dividers is to scribe arcs and circles. Set the radius of the arc by holding the dividers against a steel rule and turn the adjusting nut to open or close the arms to the measurement required. Centre one of the legs on a punch mark and pivot the other leg on this. To make a clean line, lean the dividers slightly in the direction of rotation and turn them round with a steady hand.

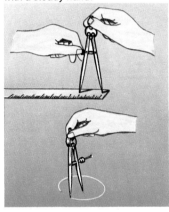

● When using an engineer's try square to mark a line at right-angles to a straight edge, make sure the stock is held firmly and squarely against the edge. In principle, it is the same as a carpenter's try square.

● Hold a dot or centre punch at a slight angle so you can see to position it accurately over the point to be marked. Bring the punch upright before striking it firmly with a hammer.

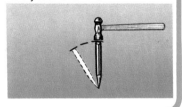

There are many different types offering a variety of features (see pages 161 -162).

SPECIALIST TOOLS
Steel rule
For more advanced metalwork, accuracy is very important, and steel rules are more accurate than most other kinds. Choose one around 300mm (12in) long with a metric and imperial scale, the latter going down to at least 1/64in.

Slide calipers
This is a really specialist piece of equipment for measuring internal and external diameters up to about 81mm (3⅜in). Be warned, though, most metal versions are frighteningly expensive.

Engineer's try square
Used in the same way as a carpenter's try square, the engineer's version with its all-metal construction is simply more accurate. It often has a notch cut into the stock just below the blade, to accommodate any burrs on the metal which may otherwise lead to inaccurate readings.

Scriber
A scriber is used for marking up metal. It leaves a fine scratch in the surface, and so is much more accurate than marking with a pencil. There are three common types – the pocket scriber, the single point scriber, and the double-

ended scriber. The last one is the most versatile.

Wing compasses and spring dividers
These are basically heavier, more accurate versions of the sort of dividers found in school geometry sets - the compass with two points and nowhere to put the pencil. They are used both to scribe arcs on metal, and to step off measurements, the latter being more accurate than transferring dimensions with a rule.

Dot punch, prick punch and centre punch
The dot punch is used to make tiny dents in metal as a means of marking out. Its main jobs are accentuating lines drawn with a scriber – you tap out a row of dots along the line – and to mark hole centres. A centre punch is essentially a dot punch with a blunter point. It is used to enlarge the dent left by a dot punch to accept the tip of a drill, though, unless you want to be really precise, you can actually use the centre punch to mark the hole centre in the first place.

Grinder
Fitted with a grinding wheel, this power tool is useful for reshaping and sharpening badly damaged tools such as chisels, plane irons, and screwdrivers. Fitted with a wire brush wheel or a buffing mop, it can

also be used for polishing. You can also get a grinding attachment for your electric drill.

Soft-faced mallet
A soft-faced mallet is intended to shape sheet metal and not to hit nails. Depending on the material you are working on you can fit the appropriate faces to the head. These are made of rubber, coiled rawhide and copper, for example.

Long nosed pliers
Also known as needle-nosed pliers, snipe-nosed pliers, and radio pliers, these are for more delicate gripping jobs than ordinary engineer's pliers, and for snipping fine wire using the pair of side cutters. They are also better at reaching into awkward corners.

Cut-off discs
A particularly tough abrasive wheel, the cut-off disc is the metalworking equivalent of the circular saw blade. The majority are intended for use with large purpose-made 'cut-off machines' and heavy-duty circular saws. However, smaller versions are available for use with do-it-yourself circular saws and circular saw drill attachments.

Cold chisels
These are for roughly shaping heavy metalwork. Various forms are available, most being designed for particular jobs such as cutting grooves.

Saw blades for jigsaws
Although an ordinary hacksaw is best for most jobs because of the degree of control it offers, if you have a lot of rough sawing to do and you possess a powered jigsaw, consider fitting it with a special saw blade for cuting metal. These are available to suit most models.

Fixed spanners
Available in many different forms and many different sizes, you can buy these either singly or in sets. They are rather more efficient than adjustable spanners, but the sets tend to be very expensive so they are worth getting only if you do a lot of mechanical repair work.

A pipe cutter
This cuts pipes more neatly than a hacksaw and does the job much quicker, so it's worth getting if you do a lot of plumbing. Some have a reamer for cleaning burred edges.

Wire brush drill attachment
Available as a round brush with the 'bristles' pointing forwards, or as a disc with them arranged around the edge, this does the same job as a hand wire brush, but, when fitted to an electric drill does it faster, and with a lot less effort.

Wire brush
Again, this is used for cleaning metal. It will remove the bulk of the dirt, rust, or whatever, to leave the surface ready for finishing with wire wool.

SOLDERING IRONS

Soldering is a way of making effective and lasting metal to metal joints. A modern soldering iron makes this all the easier. There is a wide range of models and accessories available.

There are two methods of making a soldered joint: one is hard soldering, for which you'll need a blowlamp or blowtorch, and the other is soft soldering which requires use of a soldering iron.

With hard soldering, the pieces of metal to be joined are heated so that when solder, a soft metal with a low melting point, is applied to them it will melt and bond them together. This is obviously a fairly brutal and inaccurate method that is really only suitable for plumbing or where the appearance of the items to be joined does not have to be maintained. Soft soldering is more common for electrical or electronic

work where accuracy is vital. A soldering iron is used to melt the solder so that it flows into the joint. That way the pieces being joined are barely heated at all, which is, of course, important when there are delicate electronics at hand, or when you're trying to join insulated wires, for example.

What is a soldering iron?

The traditional soldering iron is now as rare as the paraffin blowlamp. It consisted of a copper bit rivetted to a long steel shaft that was fitted with a wooden handle. Admittedly the copper bits came in various designs, but apart from that they were fairly unsophisticated tools. Because the only way to get them working was to heat up the bit over a gas stove or with a blowlamp, the person using them had very little control over the actual bit temperature. This made them

highly unsuitable for use in delicate jobs. And, because you had to hold them by the wooden handle, they were difficult to use with any kind of precision. It's hardly surprising, then, that they have now almost totally disappeared, to be replaced by the modern electrical soldering iron.

The majority of modern soldering irons are designed primarily for use in electrics and electronics, a fact reflected by the features they offer – namely accuracy, precise temperature control and efficiency. A typical iron consists of a plastic handle so shaped that you get maximum control by holding it like a pencil between forefinger and thumb. A copper bit, often plated with chromium or some other metal to prolong its life, extends from this and is brought up to working temperature by means of a small electric element contained within the body of the tool. This means not

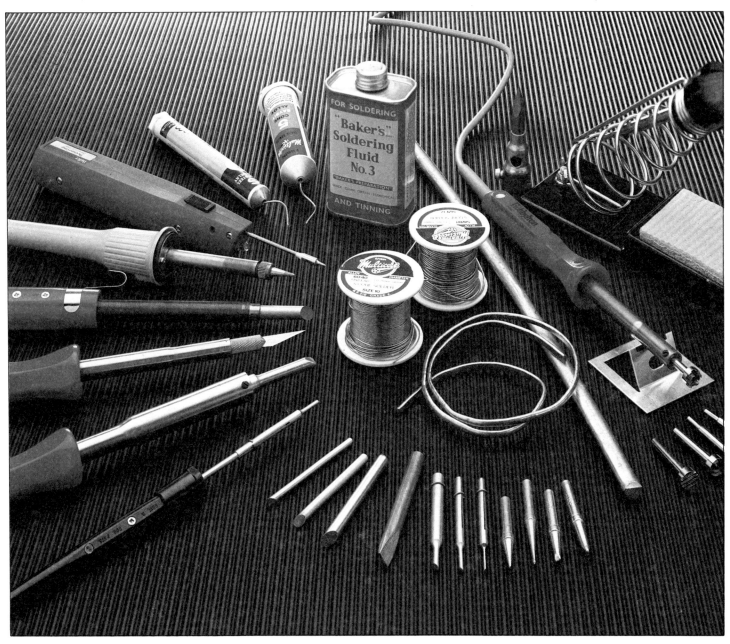

only that the temperature of the bit can be very precisely controlled, but also that you can work more or less continuously without having to stop to heat up the bit – as was the case with the old-fashioned type of iron.

Choosing an iron

There is a wide range of soldering irons on the market and which you use depends largely on the job you're going to do. The most basic iron, as described above, is sometimes known as a 'simple stick'. This will heat up once it's been plugged into an ordinary socket outlet and is likely to be sufficient for most small jobs around the home.

Cordless soldering irons are extremely useful if you are working away from a mains supply – on your car, for example. However, the amount of work you can do in any one spell is limited by the life span of the rechargeable batteries. These can normally be recharged overnight, and most models are supplied either with a charging unit or charger plug. However, a point worth noting, and bearing in mind as you work, is that the batteries will be ruined completely if they are allowed to run out.

Soldering guns are usually more powerful than other irons and consequently heat up in a matter of seconds. Although they have to be plugged in to the mains, the element is only active when the trigger is pulled – which means that it's significantly safer should the iron ever get dropped or be left lying around while still plugged in. With some irons it's possible to control the temperature of the bit by varying the power going to the

element. This is normally done through a control on an isolating transformer that comes with the iron and is called a soldering station.

For those jobs that are difficult to get at or require particularly delicate work, some manufacturers produce miniature soldering irons for extra precision. They come with very fine bits, which means they are perfect for work on electronic circuits.

For general soldering you should just make sure that the iron is powerful enough to do the jobs. A power rating in the region of 60W is about right and it will cope with general repairs and a certain amount of electrical work. However, for delicate electronic work this will certainly be too powerful and you could cause a lot of damage to your circuit boards. The answer is to use one rated at only 15W.

Bits for irons

Whichever type of iron you decide upon, you'll find a variety of interchangeable bits that could go with it. It's likely that you'll already be familiar with the pencil bit which is frequently fitted automatically to irons and is suitable for most electrical jobs. Sometimes referred to as flat or double flat bits, they are sized according to their tip diameter which can range from 1.2mm (³⁄₆₄in) to 8mm (⁵⁄₁₆in).

Oval tapered bits are also fairly common, and like pencil bits are classified by tip diameter, although large sizes are often referred to by their weight. Tapered bits are really all-purpose bits; the flat wide section will heat up a broad area, while its edge can be used on seams. Finally, a pointed bit is perfect for doing accurate

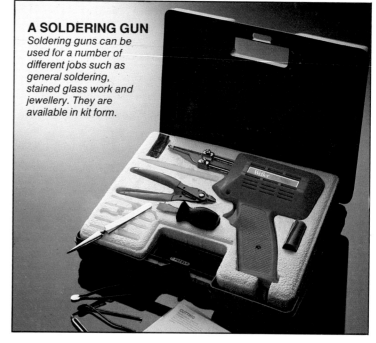

A SOLDERING GUN
Soldering guns can be used for a number of different jobs such as general soldering, stained glass work and jewellery. They are available in kit form.

'spot' soldering, while a hatchet bit is designed specifically for soldering seams.

When selecting a bit it is, of course, important to make sure that your iron is sufficiently powerful to heat it up – otherwise you won't be able to melt the solder. And if a bit is too small for the iron it will lose heat very quickly. To help prevent this, bits are usually given a power rating which should correspond with that of the iron itself.

Replacing a bit is usually straightforward. However, it's worth remembering that some models have their bits attached with split pins, which can be awkward to remove, and others with grub screws. So, if you envisage changing your bit frequently it's a good idea to go for an iron that makes this as easy as possible.

Selecting solder

Although not technically correct, you won't go far wrong if you think of solder as a sort of metallic glue that needs the heat from a soldering iron to make it work. It is this soft metal – usually a mixture of tin, lead, copper, zinc, silver, antimony or bismuth – which actually joins the two items. Soft solder, which is the sort you'll probably be using, is normally based on lead and tin, but invariably traces of other metals will be present to improve the solder's performance.

To make things easy, solder is normally described according to the work it does. So you can ask for plumbers' solder, tinmen's solder or electricians' solder. It comes in one of two forms – stick or wire. It's unlikely you'll have to deal with stick solder as it's used only for large jobs. Wire solder should be

perfectly adequate for your needs and is extremely easy to handle. It is available in small dispensers containing about 2m (6ft), or in bulk on reels. These reels range in size from around 2.4m (8ft) up to 159m (about 500ft).

In addition to its convenience, wire solder usually contains its own flux which removes any oxide from the metal. The flux is liberated as the solder melts, and so saves you the trouble of applying it separately – which could be awkward.

However, if you are soldering a large joint you might well find it easier to use solder that doesn't incorporate a core of flux. In this case the flux will have to be applied separately. This will keep both surfaces clean, as well as helping the solder to stick properly. Flux is usually available in tins.

Stand up for safety

When buying your soldering iron, it's worth laying out a little bit of extra money to get a stand. That way there is less chance of you accidentally burning yourself, your carpet or whatever surface you're working on when you put down the iron. You'll certainly find a stand convenient, and it's worth making sure that the one you buy incorporates a bit-wiping pad. This is merely a small piece of sponge, but if you keep it damp while you're working you can use it to remove excess solder and clean your bit.

If, for some reason, you decide that you don't want a stand, and in some circumstances it would prove redundant – when you're working on your car, for example – you should make sure the iron you use has a hanging hook; that way you can at least rest it safely while you're doing a job.

SOLDERING EQUIPMENT: KEY

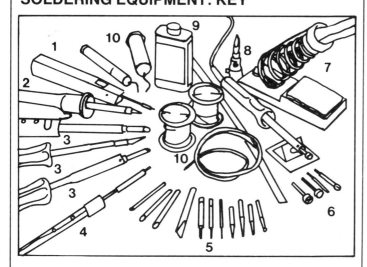

1 Rechargeable iron	6 Woodburning kit
2 Electronic iron	7 Bench holder
3 Simple stick iron	8 Blowlamp bit
4 Mini iron	9 Flux
5 Replacement bits	10 Solder

DRILLING, CUTTING & BENDING METAL

Drilling, cutting, shaping and joining pieces of metal may not be skills you will want to use every day, but they will prove invaluable for many jobs around the home.

Although many people will steer clear of attempting fabrication or repair work in metal, there is no reason for any competent DIY enthusiast to do so. Here we describe these basic skills; techniques for joining metal will be covered on pages 168-172. The tools you need are shown on pages 158-160.

Guarding against injury
Safety is an important consideration when working with metal because the tools and materials used are hard and sharp and can easily cause nasty injuries. Therefore, you must take steps to avoid accidents.

In particular, do not wear loose clothing when using powered metalworking tools like grinders; roll up your sleeves, remove your tie, tuck long hair under a hat, and wear stout shoes. Wear safety spectacles when carrying out any job, such as drilling or grinding, where pieces of metal may fly about. Whenever possible, wear thick leather gloves.

Marking the workpiece
Mark any straight cutting or bending lines with a rule or try-square and a scriber. To ensure accuracy, hold the scriber so that its point is tight to the edge of the rule or square. You can make the scribed line show up more clearly by applying a coat of engineer's blue to the workpiece before starting, but if this is not available you could use a felt marker to apply a coloured finish roughly where the marks are to be scribed.

Positions for drilling should be marked with a scribed cross, and dimpled with a centre punch to prevent the drill bit wandering. Similarly, use the punch to provide a location for one point of a pair of dividers when marking curves or circles.

Drilling holes in metal
Always use high speed steel (HSS) drill bits when drilling metal; for large holes in sheet metal, tank cutters or hole saws can be used. However, if the latter are not available, mark the circumference of the hole with dividers and then drill a series of small overlapping holes just inside this mark. Known as chain drilling, this method will allow you to

MARKING OUT

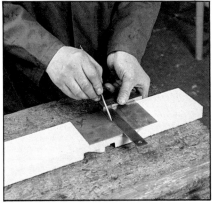

1 *Mark cutting lines on the workpiece with a try-square and scriber. The latter provides a permanent mark that will not rub off with handling.*

2 *Use a centre punch to mark drill centres, providing a start for the bit and preventing it wandering. Place the punch carefully and strike it with a hammer.*

DRILLING HOLES IN SHEET METAL

1 *Clamp the workpiece securely in a vice or to the bench. This will prevent it from being snatched and spun round dangerously by the drill bit.*

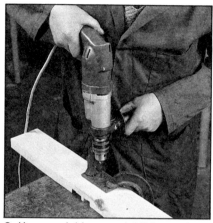

2 *Use a variable-speed drill for working with metal, selecting a high speed for small-diameter holes and a slow speed for large holes.*

3 *To help dissipate heat as you drill, lubricate the bit with oil when drilling cast iron or mild steel; use paraffin if working with aluminium.*

4 *Thin sheet materials are best drilled when clamped to a piece of scrap wood. Drill right through the workpiece and into the wood for a clean hole.*

5 *Never attempt to drill a large-diameter hole in one go. Centering the bit will be difficult and the job hard work. Drill a small pilot hole first.*

6 *If you need to drill matching holes in two plates, carefully align the plates and clamp them down before drilling through both at once.*

7 *Use hole saws at slow speed or in short bursts to prevent overheating. Screws either side of the workpiece prevent it from twisting.*

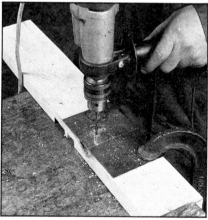

8 *Cut-outs can also be made by drilling a series of small holes. If the holes don't quite overlap, break the intervening metal.*

9 *After drilling, you will find a small lip of metal, or burr, around the edge of the hole. Remove this by twisting a much larger bit in the top of the hole.*

tap out the centre of the waste metal, leaving the edges to be cleaned up with a file.

It is advisable to use a power drill when drilling metal. Ideally, this should be supported in a vertical drill stand. Use a high speed for small-diameter holes and a low speed for large diameter ones.

When drilling thin materials, you can ensure a clean hole by backing the workpiece with a piece of scrap timber and drilling right through into it. In all cases, clamp the metal firmly to prevent it snatching as the bit breaks through.

Carefully align the tip of the bit with the punched mark and apply a steady force as it begins to cut into the metal. Take care, as excessive pressure will cause overheating and can damage the bit. Lubricating the bit with light oil when drilling mild steel or cast iron will help dissipate heat. Paraffin should be used when working with aluminium, but no lubrication is needed with brass or copper, which are soft and easily drilled.

When drilling a large-diameter hole, use a small-diameter drill first to make a pilot hole. This will assist in centering the larger drill bit. After drilling, deburr each hole.

Cutting metal

Thick metal plates, rods, bars and pipes are normally cut with a hacksaw, while thinner sheet metals are often cut with tinsnips, proprietary cutters, or power tools such as jigsaws or bandsaws fitted with metal-cutting blades.

To start a cut with a hacksaw, grasp the handle of the saw with one hand and position the blade just to the waste side of your cutting line. Use the thumb of your other hand as a guide for the blade as you make a few short strokes. Once the cut is deep enough to prevent the blade skipping across the surface of the workpiece, use your free hand to grip the front of the hacksaw frame. Making sure you are standing comfortably, continue cutting by using the full length of the blade at each stroke, releasing the pressure on the back stroke. Keep the saw horizontal, unless cutting at an angle is the only way you can keep at least three saw teeth in contact with the workpiece. After removing the waste metal, clean up the cut line with a file.

Tinsnips are used just like ordinary scissors, but you must make sure you have the right type for the job, 'universal' being the best since they will cut both inside and outside curves as well as straight lines. They will work on thin sheet metal if it is fairly soft, but they can distort the edge slightly, particularly if you allow the tips of the blades to close completely as you cut.

Proprietary cutters work with a nibbling action and will handle mild steel. Some produce a strip of waste metal, so use them on the correct side of your cutting line. Unlike snips, they won't distort the metal.

Filing for shaping and smoothing

The technique of filing is more difficult than it looks. Clamp the workpiece low in a vice to prevent vibration; ideally, it should be at elbow level. You should adopt a stance like a boxer, facing the workpiece with your left foot forward (if you're right-handed; reverse these instructions if you're left-handed). Hold the file handle in your right hand so that the file and your forearm are in a continuous straight line. Tuck in your elbow and hold the tip of the file with your left hand.

Keeping the file straight, apply even pressure as you push it across the workpiece, releasing pressure as you return it. Your elbow must be in line with the file; if it is above or below, the file will rock and produce a rounded finish. Rubbing the teeth of the file with chalk will help prevent them clogging.

Use a coarse file to remove large amounts of metal, selecting progressively finer grades to obtain a smooth finish. Flat files will handle flat and convex surfaces, but you will need a half-round version for concave shapes. Burrs left after filing can be removed by holding the file at an angle to the edge of the workpiece and working it gently along from one end to the other.

If the workpiece is small enough to be picked up easily, it can be smoothed and shaped very quickly on a grinding wheel. Adjust the gap between the rest and the wheel to about 3mm (⅛in) to prevent small items being snatched out of your hands.

Bending metal over a former

Thin sheet metal steel strip can be bent cold, although bending always sets up stresses in the metal which can weaken it. Therefore, try to limit cold bending to situations where maximum structural strength is not important. To obtain greater workability, particularly with thick sections of metal, heat the workpiece before bending. This technique of softening metal is called annealing. With copper and brass, you should heat the metal to a dull red and allow it to cool slowly; mild steel should be heated to a bright red before allowing it to cool. Usually a blowtorch will give enough heat, but you can also heat the metal on a gas ring or in a coke fire.

Avoid trying to form tight right angles, giving corners a slight radius; this will reduce the likelihood of fracture. You will find the job easier if you shape the metal over a former, such as the edge of a metal vice jaw, a block of steel, or a steel rod clamped in a vice.

Ideally, use a mallet or a soft-faced hammer to work thin sheet materials, gradually tapping the workpiece down over its entire length. Don't try to make the bend in one go, as this will stretch the metal; slowly work it into shape. Thicker steel strips should be worked with a hammer, applying the blows just short of where the metal will bend.

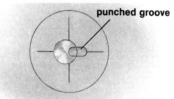
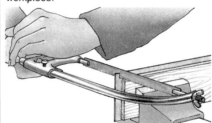
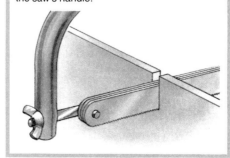

USING A HACKSAW

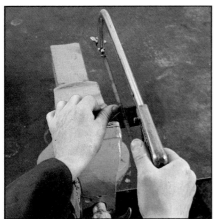

1 When starting a saw cut, prevent the blade from skipping across the metal by guiding it with your thumb. Use a few short strokes to begin with.

2 The blade will become very hot as you saw, and heat may blunt it. Prevent this by lubricating the blade with oil as you would a drill bit.

3 Once you have started the cut, use your free hand to grip the end of the saw frame. Keep the saw horizontal and use the full length of the blade on each stroke.

4 Thin sheet metals will judder as you cut them, causing the blade to catch. Clamping the piece between blocks of wood will absorb the vibration.

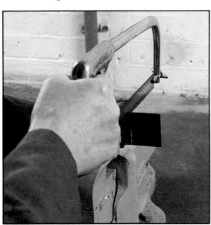

5 If you break an old blade half-way through a cut, start the new blade at the opposite end of the cut line. Being new, the replacement blade will be thicker.

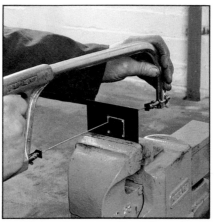

6 When using a saw file, drill starting holes in the workpiece, pass the blade through and connect it to the hacksaw frame before making the cut-out.

USING SNIPS

With the correct tools, cutting sheet metal can be easier than cutting wood. Thin sheets of soft metal such as aluminium, tin or copper, are best cut with tinsnips , and there is quite a variety to choose from. Normal tinsnips cut with a scissors-like action and can be obtained in versions for making straight cuts, or left- or right-handed curved cuts. Take care to buy the right type for the job in hand as curved-blade snips won't cut straight lines, and straight-blade snips won't cut inside curves. If you don't expect to be doing sufficient metal cutting to warrant buying several pairs of snips, you can buy 'universal' snips that will cut both straight lines and curves. When using snips, don't let the blade tips close together as this will distort the edge of the metal.

1 Take small 'bites' with the tinsnips, using them as you would scissors. If you are right-handed, keep the waste metal on the left of the blade, and vice versa.

2 Unless you have a pair of universal snips, use curved-blade snips to make curved cuts. Again, take small bites to keep on the cutting line.

USING A FILE

1 Hold the file so that it is horizontal and in line with your forearm and elbow. Apply pressure on the forward cutting stroke, using the full blade length.

2 Start at one end of a long edge and move the file along as you make the cutting stroke. Point the file in the direction of travel.

3 Draw-file the edge to remove previous file marks, holding the file at right angles to the plate and pushing it along from one end to the other.

4 Remove the inevitable burrs from the corners of the filed surface by holding the file at an angle to the corner and pushing it along lightly.

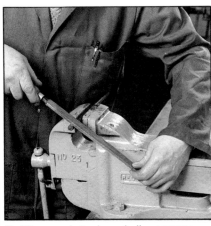

5 File round stock or similar convex surfaces by rocking the file round the piece as you push it forwards on its cutting stroke.

6 To make a concave shape, remove the bulk of the material with a hacksaw and then use a half-round file to dress back the material.

BENDING METAL

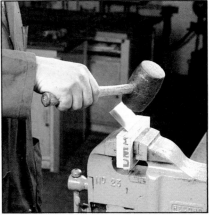

1 Clamp a thin sheet between wooden formers and tap it down with a mallet or soft-faced hammer. Don't try to make the bend in one go.

2 Keep tapping firmly and gently along the line of the bend, working from one end of the sheet to the other until the desired angle is achieved.

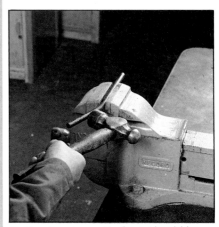

3 Heavier pieces like bars should be clamped in a vice and bent with a heavy hammer. Aim the hammer blows just short of the point where you want the bend.

MAKING JOINTS IN METAL

Although many methods of joining metal can require considerable skill, there are several simple techniques which are easily mastered. They are quite adequate for most home jobs and require the minimum of equipment.

M ost of the metalworking jobs you are likely to be involved in will be limited to the cutting, drilling, shaping and bending techniques described in detail on pages 163-167. However, sooner or later, you will want to join two or more pieces of metal; you may need to repair something or to make something useful (an ash pan, for example). In some cases, you can use an epoxy-resin-based adhesive, providing the item is small or is not required to be exceptionally strong, but there are several other stronger methods of joining metal.

Making seam joints
Folding is a good method of joining thin sheet metals, but although this kind of joint can be quite strong, it is best to reinforce it with solder or an epoxy resin adhesive.

The simplest type of folded joint is known as a groove seam. To make this joint, bend the edge of one sheet at right angles by clamping it between two blocks of hardwood and turning the metal with a mallet. If the metal is easy to work you could hold it on a piece of angle iron and tap it with a hammer. Further bending is achieved by beating the edge down over a length of bevelled hardwood. Finally, the bend is completed by tapping the edge down over a slightly thicker piece of metal. Alternatively, you can use two pieces of the metal you are working with. Prepare the second sheet in the same way.

Hook the two sheets together and set their face sides level by hammering along the length of the seam with a tool known as a groove punch or seaming tool. This has a groove in its face to accommodate the raised seam. You can achieve the same effect by clamping the lower sheet on a flat surface and setting the upper sheet down by placing a length of hardwood on it adjacent to the seam and hammering it flat. To complete the joint, tighten the seam by knocking it down with a mallet.

Making joints with rivets
Permanent joints can be made by riveting, and this techniques can be used on all types and thicknesses of metal; the only requirement is that the total thickness of metal

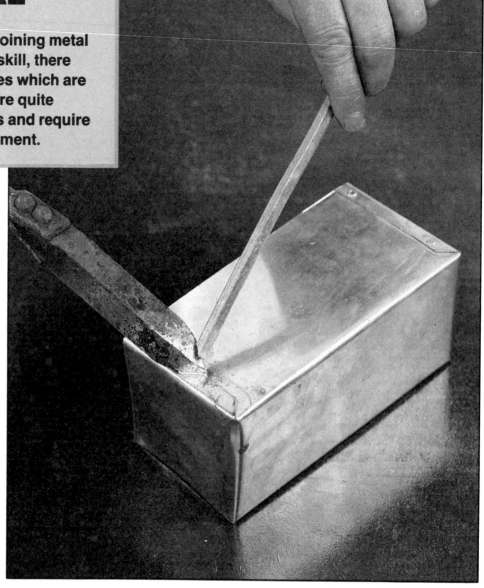

WAYS OF JOINING METAL

Various techniques can be used to join two pieces of metal. When working with thin metal sheet a folded seam is the ideal joint to use. With thicker sheet you could use a solid rivet, or even a blind rivet set in *place with a special gun. If you want to separate the two pieces of metal sometime in the future, use a self-tapping screw or a nut and bolt. Permanent joins can be made using solder.*

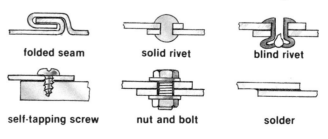

folded seam   solid rivet   blind rivet

self-tapping screw   nut and bolt   solder

MAKING A SEAMED JOINT

1 Use a length of angle iron, or something similar, over which you may make a 6mm (¼in) right angle bend. Clamp the sheet if you can't hold it firmly.

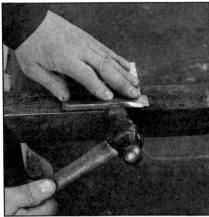

2 Place a couple of strips of sheet metal against the fold to act as formers, and gently tap over the flap again using a hammer, or better still a mallet.

3 Use a plumber's dresser or mallet to 'iron out' the turnover on the strips. For a successful joint it's important that the flat is completely flat.

4 Repeat these operations for the second sheet of metal and then remove the metal strips. Interlock the channels so the seam can't be pulled apart.

5 Use either a seamer or, better still, a groove punch (illustrated) tapped along the seam to lock the joint and to ensure that the two sheets lie in the same plane.

6 Finally, tighten the joint by tapping it with a plumber's dresser or mallet. When the joint is complete there shouldn't be any movement between the metal sheets.

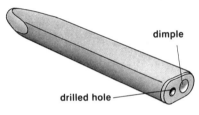
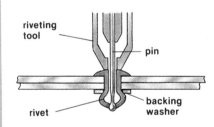
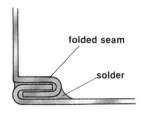

MAKING A BOX SEAM

1 *When making up a box, first mark the cut and fold lines on the sheet metal with a fine felt pen, crosshatching the waste areas to be removed.*

2 *Use snips to cut away the metal not required for making the base, then make the first part of the seam joints by folding in the sheet as described earlier.*

3 *Make a right angle fold in the bottom edge of the side panel and then form a corner. Note the snip in the flap to allow the angled edge to be folded round.*

4 *The side and base sections can now be slotted together. Once in position, use a mallet to firm the base against the flap of the side panel.*

5 *Support the box on angle iron or a piece of hardwood. Use a mallet to fold over the first seam to lock the joint. Then fold in the corner with a seamer.*

6 *Finally, use a mallet to fold over the other seam. Note that the seams are formed on the outside of the box, which then has a 'clean' inside.*

allows the rivet to pass right through. There are two types of rivet: the hand-formed solid type and the 'blind' rivet.

Solid rivets can have round, countersunk or flat heads. They are made from various malleable metals, and it is usual to match the rivet to the metal being joined. The diameter of the rivet shank should be at least as thick as one of the sheets being joined and no more than three times its thickness.

Drill both sheets to be joined so that the rivet shank is a tight fit, countersinking the holes in both sheets if necessary. Push the rivet through both holes and support its ready-made head on a flat plate, or a piece of end-grain hardwood if using a round-head rivet. Tap the plates down so that they are tight together; ideally, use a draw-up tool which can be made by drilling a block of mild steel so that it fits over the rivet shank. Cut the rivet shank back so that the amount pro-

truding is equal to its diameter if using a countersunk rivet, or 1½ times its diameter for a round-head rivet.

To finish the rivet, the exposed shank must be hammered and shaped to match the ready-made head on the other end. Do this with a ball-pein hammer. Countersunk heads should be hammered flush with the surface of the workpiece and any surplus filed off. Round-head rivets should be roughly shaped with the hammer and finished off with a tool called a 'snap' which has a dimple in its face. Place this over the rivet head and hammer down. Combined snap and draw-up tools are available.

Blind rivets are excellent where you only have access to one side of the sheets being joined. Each rivet has a protruding pin which fits into the jaws of a special riveting tool. After pushing the shank of the rivet through the holes in the sheets, close the tool's

handles. This pulls the pin through the middle of the rivet, deforming its back and locking the two sheets together.

If you are likely to dismantle the workpiece at any time, you could assemble it with self-tapping screws or nuts and bolts. Insert self-tapping screws into pre-drilled holes that are slightly smaller in diameter than the screws themselves. Each screw cuts its own thread as it is inserted. Make sure you get the right length as, being hardened, they cannot be ground back or shortened.

Nuts and bolts are suitable where you have access to both sides of the joint, but they tend to be bulky and unsightly. Fit them in holes just big enough to allow the shank to pass through. Using washers beneath the bolt head and nut will help prevent them shaking loose and protect the surface of the workpiece. You'll find more information on pages 154 -156.

HAND-RIVETING

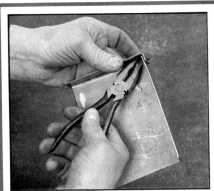

1 *Drill a hole through the surfaces to be joined; the diameter should be the same as that of the rivet. Insert the rivet with pliers in awkward corners.*

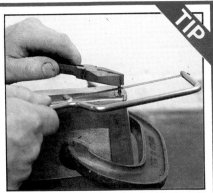

2 *When hacksawing the rivet to length, support the head on the end-grain of a hardwood block and hold the rivet shank securely in pliers.*

3 *Use first the flat face of a hammer and then the ball pein to shape the rivet shank into a dome that joins the surfaces fairly tightly together.*

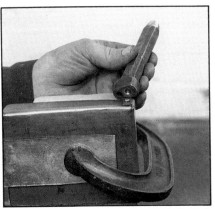

4 *Set the dimple of a rivet punch (snap) over the dome of the rivet and strike it so that the two pieces of metal are squeezed tightly together.*

POP RIVETING

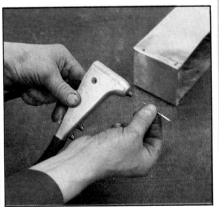

1 *Use a riveting gun when it's difficult to get to the back of the surfaces that are to be joined. First load the special gun with a pop rivet.*

2 *Push the rivet through the pre-drilled hole until the gun butts against the metal. Squeeze the handles together; when the shank breaks away riveting is complete.*

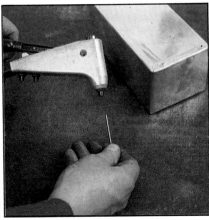

3 *Remove the remainder of the shank from the gun. A neat rivet head is left on the outside of the join, while a short if somewhat ungainly stub is left on the inside where it can't be seen.*

Soldering joints

Soldering is a quick and easy way of permanently joining lightweight pieces of steel, brass and copper. The different methods of soldering and the tools available are dealt with on pages 161 -162.

The first step in soldering is to make sure both surfaces to be joined are a good close fit, and are cleaned right back to bright metal by using a scraper and emery cloth. Similarly, it's important to clean the soldering iron bit with a file. Heat the soldering iron and 'tin' it by dipping the bit in flux and then into the solder so that the tip acquires a coating of solder. If using flux-cored solder wire, simply melt this directly on to the iron's tip.

Apply flux to the two surfaces to be joined and run the soldering iron over them to heat and tin them at the same time. Bring the two pieces together and heat the area of the join with the iron. Apply the solder while continuing to run the iron along the join, using it to rub the solder into a neat joint. You must make sure that the workpiece is hot enough to melt the solder completely; you'll know this as it will run into a very fluid, bright silver puddle. Add sufficient solder to fill the join; it will actually run between the two faces by capillary action. If using an active flux, wash off all traces with clean water to prevent corrosion, and allow the joint to cool before testing its strength.

Until fairly recently soldering irons consisted of a large copper bit that had to be heated manually over a gas stove or blowtorch. Such irons are slightly awkward to use and are not really suitable for delicate work. And if you've a lot of soldering to do then the bit will have to be reheated from time to time. So consider using a modern electric iron instead (see page 172) which is cleaner and easier to handle.

SOLDERING SEAMS

1 Clean the surfaces to be joined using fine-grade steel wool. Then apply flux using either a scrapwood stick or a brush – not your finger.

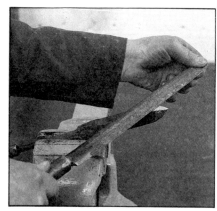

2 Use a second-cut medium file to clean the tip of the soldering iron. You'll find it easier to do this if you first clamp the iron in a vice.

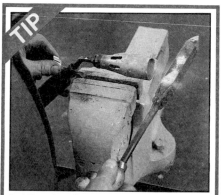

3 Likewise, for ease of working and safety, clamp the lighted blowtorch in a vice and heat the soldering iron until it turns a coppery colour.

4 Dip the tip of the iron into some flux (the liquid sort is best for this) and then coat the tip with solder – a process known as tinning.

5 With thin sheet metal, run the flat part of the tip and not just the point of the iron over the join to heat it; and hold the solder against the opening.

6 Capillary action will ensure that solder is drawn between the surfaces to seal the join. Remove the excess flux and clean the join with steel wool.

Electric soldering irons
The traditional type of soldering iron is a somewhat cumbersome tool to use and nowadays electric soldering irons have largely taken over. They have the advantage that they maintain a constant pre-set temperature and they can be used for accurate and delicate soldering work.

The photograph shows on the left the wide range of irons commonly available. For ease of working these can be held in a bench stand (far right). With some models the bits are interchangeable (see foreground of photograph) which means you don't have to change the iron if you change the type of work you are doing. Special irons are available for craft-work.

For more detailed information on soldering irons see pages 161 -162

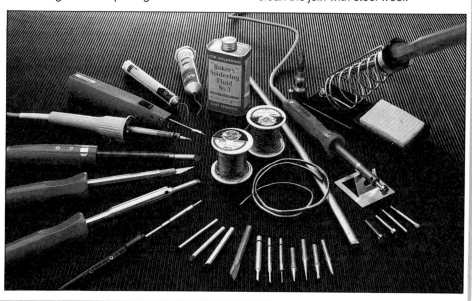

CHAPTER 9

ACCESS EQUIPMENT

For many jobs the right tools are not enough;
you need a helping hand to reach what you're working on
in comfort and safety. Ladders and steps are the answer
in most cases, and a sensible choice of ladder accessories
can greatly increase their versatility.

LADDERS AND STEPS

Ladders and steps are often vital for DIY work yet all but the simplest and smallest represent a considerable financial investment. With some it's simply not worth buying; better to hire when you really need them.

Whether you're buying or hiring a ladder, it's actually the way you use it that matters most. Although they're all designed to do exactly the same job, some give you a lot more flexibility than others – and are also a great deal safer to use.

The traditional ladder was always made of wood. Nowadays, a great deal of thought goes into designing ladders which not only use lighter materials – like aluminium alloys – but also give more flexibility in use. Extension ladders which slide apart or fold up, for example. Or ladders with safety feet, ribbed rungs for better grip and special brackets which can be used as supports for scaffold boards.

All these developments can make using ladders a lot safer, but there's still no substitute for common sense. Some helpful hints are illustrated on the next page. In general, if you're using an old ladder, do check it thoroughly before you start climbing, particularly if it's been stored out of doors.

Single section ladders

Timber versions are often just flat sided pole ladders, though it is possible to get them with square or D section rungs, sometimes in aluminium. Some taper towards the top and, if very long, the stiles are often reinforced with steel cable set into the back. Glass fibre stiles with aluminium rungs are now also available. Aluminium ladders offer the same rung choice as wood, are generally ribbed for extra grip, and come with solid I section or hollow box stiles.

Push-up extension ladders

These are 2 or 3 single-section ladders linked in such a way that, by sliding them over each other and locking them in position with locating hooks, you can vary the ladder's length. This makes it versatile, easy to use, and reduces the storage space needed. Usually each section can be separated for use as a single section ladder. Heights vary but

most 2-section versions have a fully extended height of between 3 and 10.5m (10 and 35ft), though some go as high as 13.5m (45ft). The 3-section models range between 4 and 14.25m (13 and 47ft), though with most manufacturers, 9 to 10.5m (30 to 35ft) is the upper limit.

Rope operated extension ladders are used primarily by the trade. These are extended by using a system of ropes and pulleys and locked with a patent locking device. This makes them a lot easier to use, but does add considerably to the cost. Heights tend to be greater, but most are in the 6 to 12m (20 to 40ft) bracket for 2-sections; 9m to 18.25m (40 to 60ft) for 3-sections.

Series ladders

Normally made of aluminium, a series ladder consists of up to four short, normally about 0.9m (3ft), ladder modules which can be slotted together end to end to produce a 'single section' ladder. Designed as a means of access, not as working platform, for people like surveyors and service engineers, they are compact but expensive.

Roof ladders

Designed to provide access and a safe working platform on a sloping roof, a roof ladder has wheels at the upper end so you can slide it into place without damaging the roofing material and a large hook which locates over the roof ridge to hold it in place. It should also have padded spacing bars to keep the rungs a safe distance from the roof surface, to prevent roof damage, and be made of lightweight aluminium alloy. Old-fashioned 'crawl board' roof ladders are still available, but take skill to be used safely.

Builders' steps

This is the traditional step ladder with a tapering flight of fairly

narrow steps also known as painters' steps. Some have cross-pieces fitted to the back stay, which is then called a trestle back, to take scaffold boards. Most manufacturers can supply steps in heights from 1.25m to 3m (4 to 10ft). These steps are aimed at the trade, are rugged, and cost more than DIY steps.

Platform steps

Much better for the amateur than builders' steps, these have wider more comfortable treads, tend to be more stable, and have a good sized platform at the top on which you can stand, or place tools, paint pots etc. Normally, it is this platform that stops the back stay opening too far. Many have a safety rail. Available in timber, aluminium, or tubular steel (with timber treads), most DIY versions offer platform heights ranging from 0.75 to 2m (2ft 6in to 7ft), but models intended for the trade may reach 35m (12ft) or more.

Combination ladder/steps

By sliding, swinging, and dismantling the two or three sections from which they are made, they can be converted from a simple step ladder into what is essentially a single-section ladder. Many can provide unequal legs for use on stairs, and some can be converted into a trestle platform. They come in aluminium, tubular steel and timber versions.

Trestles

These are not really step ladders, though superficially they look as if they are. Essentially, they consist of a pair of extra wide, extra strong tapering step ladder back-stays, hinged together and fitted with stout cross-rails to support scaffolding boards. They are very useful decorating aids and well worth hiring.

Lean-to steps

These are specially designed for use indoors where access to high shelves, as in libraries, is needed. Usually provided with hand rails, both ends are well protected with rubber stops.

1

2

3

9

Ladders from Slingsby

1 & 2 Single section and
push-up extension ladders

3 Lean-to-steps

4 Builders' steps

5 Platform steps

6 Trestles

7 Combination ladder/steps

8 Series ladder

9 Roof ladder

hints

Ladder safety
Check the condition of rungs and stiles before you start climbing.
● *Make sure that step-ladders have their legs fully extended, and that they're standing on level ground. If they're not, support them with blocks of wood and tie them to stakes or something solid nearby.*
● *When climbing a ladder, always hold on to the rungs, not the stiles. This helps to balance your weight evenly.*
● *Don't climb a ladder carrying awkwardly-shaped or very heavy objects. Haul them up with a rope instead.*

Extending ladders
To extend or open out a two-part ladder stand it against the wall, avoiding any windows or pipes. Then walk it away from the wall to a distance of about one quarter of its length.

Correct positioning
For stability and balance, the foot of the ladder should be positioned at least a quarter of the ladder's height out from the wall.

Securing ladders
Most accidents with ladders are the result of not securing the base properly, or leaning the top against something unstable. Although many modern ladders are fitted with special, non-slip safety feet which provide adequate grip, there are lots of other ways of making sure that a ladder won't slide away.

1 *On a concrete surface, try standing the ladder on sacking.*

2 *On soft earth, stand a ladder on a wooden board with a batten screwed across one side to hold the stiles in place. To make doubly sure the board itself can't move, drive in wooden pegs behind.*

3 *Another way is to position wooden pegs driven in alongside or near each stile, and then tie the ladder to them.*
It's often just as important to make sure the top of the ladder is secure. Never rest the top against anything likely to give way. Guttering will rarely take the

weight of a ladder, and window panes are easily broken, so avoid them completely. Only lean the ladder against solid walls or boards (in awkward situations you can use ladder stays instead – see below).

4 *In some circumstances you have to keep the ladder away from guttering or from overhanging eaves. This is where what's called a ladder stay comes in useful. A ladder stay hooks onto the top rungs and provides an extension bar which*

keeps the ladder itself away from the wall. The bar is usually fitted with non-slip pads to help prevent the whole thing slipping sideways. Ladder stays are available from hire shops.

5 *It makes sense to tie up the top of a ladder, just as you would the bottom. You may be able to open a window and tie up the ladder to the frame, or loop a rope around a screwed-in gutter fixing.*
6 *Against a roof, an alternative method is to screw in a hook to the fascia board and tie the ladder to that.*

Carrying ladders
It's easiest to carry a ladder (even a heavy one) held vertically. Hook one of your hands under a lower rung, and use your other hand over a higher rung to balance it. Although it's also possible to swing the ladder so it rests on your shoulder, it can be very awkward to get it evenly balanced.

Ladder brackets
These are designed to hook over the rungs of a pair of ladders to provide support for scaffold boards – thus creating a simple working platform. Some brackets are adjustable so that the angle can be altered to provide a level support when the ladders are leaning against a wall.

LADDER ACCESSORIES

Ladders have improved over the years so that many former optional extras are now included as standard. But there are still a number of accessories which can help you use the ladder more efficiently and more comfortably.

A simple ladder is invaluable for decorating and repair work (see pages 174 -176) but it can be improved in various ways by adding on a few accessories. It can be made safer by fixing non-slip feet at the bottom and a tie at the top. It can be made more comfortable to use by adding a tool tray and a platform step. And it can be made more versatile by fixing on a stay, or brackets, or by converting it into a roof ladder.

Many of these accessories are available from ladder manufacturers and you may also find them in builders' merchants, DIY stores and hire shops. Do keep safety in mind, though, and think twice about some of the 'novelty' accessories occasionally advertised in magazines. You are, after all, trusting your life to them.

Also take care when using some of the more professional accessories such as the ladder brackets. These are designed for the trade and require a certain amount of skill to use safely. Follow the advice of the supplier and practise setting them up near ground level to start with – only use them at height when you know exactly what to do.

Ladder stay
This is a metal frame that fits over the rungs near the top of the ladder to hold it away from the wall. This protects gutters from the weight of the ladder and makes it easier to reach overhanging features. They are sometimes fitted with rubber pads to protect the wall surface and prevent slipping. If not, you should make up and fit suitable pads yourself.

Tool tray
This is a simple metal tray, usually with a lip to stop things slipping off. Most designs clip onto the side of the ladder and some can be swivelled to compensate for the angle of the ladder; others clip over a rung of the ladder. Some designs fit onto a ladder stay but this obviously fixes the tray's position at the top, which is not always convenient.

Ladder platform
This is a small platform that fits over a rung on the ladder to turn it into a more comfortable step. This is less tiring than standing for long periods on a rung, but the platform can sometimes get in the way when climbing the ladder.

Safety tie
This is a specially designed galvanised steel cleat which clamps onto the ladder or staging to provide a convenient tie-off point for a retaining cord.

Levelling feet
These are fitted to the bottom of the ladder stiles and allow you to extend the length of each stile individually. They are obviously useful on sloping ground and flights of steps. They may be sold singly or in pairs, sometimes with an extra extension piece.

Safety feet
These are rubber or metal feet that you fix to the ends of wooden stiles to prevent slipping and improve safety. There are several different designs, including straightforward grips and suction cups. Since most ladders are now sold with safety feet as standard, you may have trouble buying them separately.

Ladder brackets
Also known as ladder cripples, these are designed to support a pair of scaffold boards between two ladders, thus making a larger and more comfortably working platform. The two ladders can be placed some distance apart which is useful when working over a porch or bay window. Normally they consist of a fixed triangular metal frame that hooks over the rungs of the ladder, but some are adjustable to allow the boards to be held at right angles to the wall irrespective of the ladder's angle. Most designs have provision for a safety bar as well.

Scaffold boards
These are stout wooden boards used on ladder brackets or to bridge between two pairs of steps.

KEY

1 ladder bracket
2 tool tray

Lengths vary from 1.5 to 4.3m (5 to 14ft) with widths of 230 to 300mm (9 to 12in). For safety always use a pair of boards and check with your supplier the safe span – it could be as little as 1.5m (5ft). Also, never be tempted to substitute ordinary wooden planks such as floorboards, as they are not strong enough to be safe.

Batten staging
These are more convenient than individual scaffold boards and generally provide a more stable platform. They consist of a softwood framework topped with wooden slats. Some heavy-duty versions now use aluminium stiles and you may find the cross-members are reinforced with metal tie rods. Most are 460mm (18in) wide and 1.8 to 7.2m (6 to 24ft) long. Unlike scaffold boards, staging does not normally need intermediate supports.

Roof hook
This bolts onto the end of an ordinary ladder to convert it into a roof ladder. It consists of the curved metal section that hooks over the ridge of the roof, and like a roof ladder it is fitted with wheels to make it easier to push the ladder into position.

Butcher's hook and string
The hook can be used to hang tins of paint from a rung of the ladder to leave your hands free. And if you tie a length of stout string to the hook you can haul pots of paint or tools up the ladder once you've reached the top – as long as there's someone at the bottom to help.

hints

Ladder safety
Many safety hints on using ladders were given on page 176. Here is a summary of some of the more important ones.

● *Most accessories can be used only if the ladder is held at the correct angle against the wall. The foot of the ladder should be a quarter of the ladder's height out from the wall.*
● *Check the condition of the rungs and stiles before climbing.*
● *Don't climb a ladder carrying awkwardly-shaped or very heavy objects. Haul them up with a rope instead.*
● *When climbing a ladder, always hold onto the rungs, not the stiles. This helps to balance your weight more evenly.*
● *Always secure the ladder by tying it up at the top or bottom so it can't move or slip.*
● *It's easiest and safest to carry a ladder if you hold it vertically. Hook one of your hands under a lower rung and use your other hand over a higher rung to balance it.*

KEY (continued)
3 ladder stay
4 butcher's hook
5 ladder platform
6 roof hook
7 safety feet
8 levelling feet

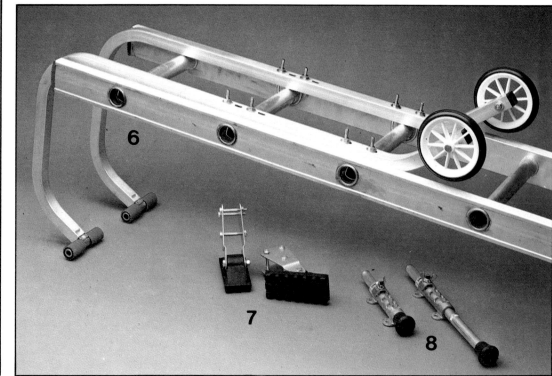

CHAPTER 10

LOOKING AFTER YOUR TOOLS

Good tools are expensive, but will often last a life-time
if they are well looked after. Regular maintenance, sharpening
and adjustment all play their part in keeping tools in perfect order,
and sensible storage helps to protect them when they're not in use.

SIMPLE TOOL MAINTENANCE

Good work needs good tools. But wise purchases must be followed up with care in use, storage and maintenance. These simple pointers tell you what you need to know – especially when it comes to the vital matter of sharpening.

Tools cost money – especially the good ones you need if they're to give hard wear, efficient work and a good finish. It's only common sense to protect your investment by looking after it as well as you can.

General rules
The first and most important principle is, of course, to use your tools properly. In particular, don't make them do jobs for which they weren't designed, because the chances are you'll damage them.

Secondly, clean your tools thoroughly each time you've finished with them. Remove anything that may harbour moisture – including sawdust and shavings. And make sure you get rid of any substance that sets (paint, glue, plaster, cement) before it's too late.

Finally, give some thought to storage (see pages 188 -190). Rust is likely to be your main enemy, so choose somewhere dry. For the sake of wooden components, avoid extreme temperatures too.

If the tools aren't in regular use, it's worth taking extra precautions against rust. Wipe metal parts with a rag soaked in graphite grease or moderately thick, sticky oil.

In most cases, it's better to hang tools up than to keep them in a box. Not only will they be easier to find, and unable to hurt you as you rake through a jumbled heap, they'll also be unable to damage one another. Either way, fit chisel and saw blades with suitable guards (these are easily bought) so they can't become blunted or chipped.

Now let's look more closely at the needs of specific tools.

Hammers
The most important thing with a hammer is a secure fixing between head and handle. If there's any looseness, fit a new handle (page 13). Shape the end of the shaft for a really tight fit in the head, then make a couple of saw cuts along the grain so they'll be at right angles to the length of the head. The depth of these cuts should match that of the wedges; these can be hardwood, or bought ready-made in steel. Tap the head into place, drive in the wedges, and saw and file off any excess for a neat finish.

The next thing to inspect is the hammer's face. If dirty or scratched, it's more likely to skip off nail-heads, so clean it carefully by rubbing it over a sheet of medium-grade glasspaper laid flat. Watch out, too, for chips around the edges of the face. If you find any, you'd do well to throw the hammer away – because, the next time a chip breaks off, your eyes might be in its way.

Screwdrivers
Fortunately, there isn't much to go wrong with a modern cross-point screwdriver. Very occasionally the handle may come loose, which serves you right for buying a cheap one.

The tip of a flat-bladed screwdriver, however, is more vulnerable. If it's twisted, there's not much you can do. If it's rounded, you can file it back square. In itself that isn't very difficult, but it can ruin the temper of the steel, making it more brittle and hence prone to future damage.

Power tools
The main enemy of most portable power tools is dust. Every now and then, clean out the air vents of power drills, circular saws, jigsaws, etc – a vacuum-cleaner with a fine nozzle does quite well unless the dust is caked with grease, in which case you must simply brush out what you can, taking care not to push it further into the works.

For other maintenance, read the instruction books. Unless you're sure you have the necessary know-how, it's unwise to take such machines apart yourself – so present them to the local service agents for annual overhauls instead.

The only other thing to watch for is a damaged flex. Get it replaced immediately.

Drill bits

Even when drill bits are used only in timber, it's surprising how quickly they blunt.

Twist drill bit sharpeners designed for the amateur are available (page 41), in the form of power-drill attachments. A cheaper alternative is the small jig (see photograph 1 on page 184) which enables you to do the job correctly by hand. Thirdly, you can use a powered disc, wheel or belt – see pages 185 -187 for more details.

Other bits must all be sharpened by hand.The efficiency of their cutting depends on the precise shapes of their various points and edges, so it's vital not to alter these.

The basic tool is a 'smooth' file of a suitable shape and size for the sharpening operation concerned, though you can produce an even finer finish with a 'slipstone' – a small hand-held natural or artificial abrasive stone in one of numerous shapes, sometimes lubricated during use (generally with oil).

On spade and dowel bits, just be sure to follow what remains of the existing edges, and remove as little steel as possible. Auger bits are trickier. First make sure the bit really needs attention; many people sharpen them too often. After that, the main rule is to sharpen from inside and underneath – never outside or on top, or you'll upset the cutting action. Make sure both main cutting edges are identical, and avoid touching the lead screw.

A golden rule with all twist, dowel and auger bits is never to continue boring a hole deeper than the extent of the bit's twist or flutes, because the waste won't clear and you'll strain the bit unduly. If you need a hole that deep, keep stopping and withdrawing the tool instead.

Saws

Hacksaws, coping saws and others with replaceable blades are very easy to maintain. You just oil any moving parts regularly, and replace the blade at the first sign of wear.

With the rest – crosscut saws, panel saws, rip saws, tenon saws, etc – you have a choice. If you want to sharpen them yourself, the necessary equipment is available, often in simplified amateur versions. However, you will of course pay a financial penalty if you mess things up. What's more, the risk of that is high because 'saw doctoring' is a complex business. You must not only sharpen the teeth in the fashion appropriate to the particular type of saw, but also 'set' them at the correct angles to the blade.

Unless, therefore, you're really keen – and willing and able to learn from an expert – saw sharpening is best left to the many tool shops and hardware stores which offer such a service. Most manufacturers of good-quality saws will do the job by mail order, too. A bent saw will certainly need to be sent away, as will circular-saw blades.

Chisels and plane irons

If you've been careful not to abuse your chisels, for example by bashing wooden handles with a hammer instead of a mallet, the only regular attention they need is sharpening.

The traditional method of doing this is on a 'stone' – a rectangular block of abrasive material, either natural or artificial. The best natural stones, which come from Arkansas, last a lifetime but are quite expensive; Welsh slate is the main alternative. An artificial stone comprises bonded particles of a man-made abrasive: 'India' stones are of aluminium oxide, 'carborundum' is silicon carbide.

All types of stone come in several grades of texture. A coarse stone works quickly, and is therefore useful if the tool's edge is in bad shape; but you need a fine or at least a medium stone to finish off. Artificial 'combination stones' with one coarse and one fine side are readily available. The finest stones of all are for polishing to a razor edge such as only the specialist craftsman needs.

Stones should be thoroughly soaked in lubricant before use, unless 'factory-sealed'. It's essential, moreover, to flood the surface of the stone with lubricant while sharpening. This prevents it from clogging with its own particles and those of the metal, and stops excessive heat which would weaken the blade. For most stones the lubricant is oil: neatsfoot oil, honing oil and light machine oil (ideally mixed 50/50 with paraffin are all suitable. Welsh slate and Japanese artificial stones, both known for their fast cutting, use water instead.

However, excellent though the best stones are, there's a ready alternative for all everyday purposes, which demands a lot less trouble and expense. You just use a sheet of artificial abrasive (aluminium oxide or silicon carbide) paper; those sold for orbital sanding machines are ideal. Or you can buy the abrasive in cloth-backed form, as a loop (for a sanding drum) or belt, and cut out a suitable piece; the cloth is thicker and less likely to tear. Either way, glue the sheet onto a flat, rigid board.

A grade of about 80 or 100 'grit' is suitable for coarse work, and anything from 120 to 320 for honing: with all abrasives, experimentation will tell you which grade best suits your requirements.

Such a sharpening pad needs no lubricant, because the particles won't break away and clog, and it will simply need replacing when

HAND SHARPENING: PLANE IRONS AND CHISELS

1 To hone a plane iron, place it on the abrasive, flat on its ground bevel. Raise it by another 5° and rub it evenly to and fro, using both hands.

2 Alternatively, fit the iron (or chisel) into a honing guide. Marked on this device is the amount the blade must protrude to give the right bevel.

3 After locking the iron in place, protruding from the guide by the amount you've measured, roll guide and iron back and forwards across the abrasive.

4 After ensuring the honing bevel is even across the whole of the iron, rub your thumb down the back to the edge: a burr should have formed.

5 Lay the iron absolutely flat on its back, and rub away the burr. Check you haven't just bent the burr over: if so, rub the honing bevel again.

6 Hold the cap iron at an angle to the iron, fit the screw into the hole, and slide it back before turning it through 90°. This protects the cutting edge.

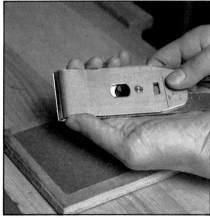

7 Slide the cap iron forwards again till its tip is about 1.5mm from the iron's edge (closer for harder woods and finer cuts) and tighten the screw.

8 A spokeshave blade is hard to grip effectively while sharpening. The best answer is to make a suitable wooden holder with a slot in it.

9 You sharpen a chisel exactly as you do a plane iron, except that if it's narrow you can't keep a thumb at each side to steady it. Instead, work as shown.

it dulls. It won't wear unevenly and have to be re-flattened, as stones do. For artificial stones, that means rubbing them face-down in carborundum powder – with water, paraffin, or paraffin and oil – on a marble slab, paving stone, or piece of glass or hardwood. Japanese water stones use 200 grit silicon carbide paper and water. Natural stones need silver sand and water, on natural stone or marble.

A chisel or plane iron is supplied new with a bevel of 25° ground at the tip. This edge almost always needs honing to a finer finish before use. It's quite possible to follow the same angle, which gives a very sharp though slightly more fragile edge. That way there's no problem about getting the angle right – but you give yourself a fair bit of work, since the 25° bevel is relatively wide.

For quicker sharpening and a more robust edge, the honing angle is usually changed to 30° so that you end up with two bevels. The exceptions are block-plane irons set at a low angle, which are generally ground to 35° and honed to 40°, and curved beading cutters for plough and combination planes, which are always sharpened (with a slipstone) at the ground bevel to preserve the shape.

A really worn edge may need a completely new ground bevel before re-honing: see pages 185 -187 for more details. But for everyday sharpening – ie, re-honing – you simply hold the tool at the required angle to the stone or abrasive sheet and work it to and fro, bevel-down, until you feel a slight burr of metal on the back of the blade. Then turn it over, lay it absolutely flat, and move it to take off the burr.

There are just two main points to remember. Firstly, keep the tool properly aligned throughout. If you let it rock in either direction, its edge will become rounded and virtually useless. However, you do need practice to achieve the necessary control; the trick is to move from the shoulder, not the wrist.

What's more, if you apply uneven pressure the edge will be out of square. A honing guide, of course, removes these problems, and also ensures the correct angle.

Secondly, do work over the entire surface of a stone, rather than merely grinding away at a central strip. Otherwise the stone's surface will eventually become slightly concave (in severe cases, actually rutted) and thus useless for producing accurate edges in the future.

The chisel or plane iron should now be razor-sharp and ready for use as soon as you've wiped off any lubricant. But you can check by sighting along the edge. If it's really keen, it will be invisible. Roughnesses will show up as bright spots.

On smoothing-and jack-plane irons, an extra refinement is sometimes added. The former can have the corners of the cutting edge rounded off so they won't dig into the timber, while the latter can have the edge slightly rounded across its whole width to help speed up the work.

Planes

Every so often it's also well worth taking your plane apart and giving it a thorough clean – very lightly oiling the moving parts. The only snag is that you're then faced with re-assembling it correctly and, what's worse, re-setting it. (The anatomy of a plane is illustrated on page 16).

The first step is to secure the frog – the wedge-shaped component that holds the blade at an angle on all except block planes. Tighten its two screws only partially, then re-fit the adjustment screw at the rear and use that to position the frog for the required size of mouth (the mouth is the opening in the sole). This size depends on the timber you're working, a narrow mouth being used with difficult grain. When you've got the setting right, check that the frog is square in position, then tighten up the securing screws.

Next, screw the cap iron to the cutting iron. The curved end of the cap iron should fit snugly against the cutter's flat back, up to 1.5mm from the end depending on whether you're doing fine or coarse work, and parallel to the cutting edge.

To secure the cutter assembly, add the lever cap screw and lever cap. Just how firmly the lever cap grips depends on how far you've driven in the screw. While a firm fixing is essential, don't tighten the screw so far that you need real force to move the locking cam. The lever cap may well crack.

Always store a plane with the iron fully retracted. In fact, the edge is so vulnerable that you shouldn't even lay the tool sole-down on the bench while working.

Router bits

Tungsten-carbide and tungsten-carbide-tipped router bits are best passed to experts for sharpening (the same applies to masonry bits). An ordinary high-speed-steel router bit, however, can be tackled at home.

You'll need a stone, because the technique is simply to rub the inside (ie, the flat face) of each cutting edge in turn on the top of the stone, while the centre of the bit overhangs the stone's edge.

As with drill bits, the important thing is never to interfere with the outside faces of the cutting edges, or you'll change the bit's diameter and hamper its clearance of waste.

Files and rasps

Apart from ensuring that files and rasps are secure in their handles, your main task is to keep them clean. Remove any waste material trapped between the teeth, using either a wire brush or a file card (page 21).

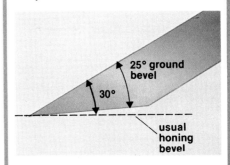
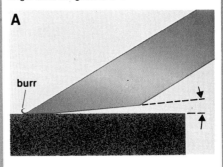
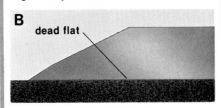

BLADE ANGLES

An ordinary plane iron (A) is ground to 25°, honed to about 30° and mounted at 45°. Most block-plane irons are mounted bevel-upwards at 20° (B). Some are set at only 12°, but sharpened more steeply (C).

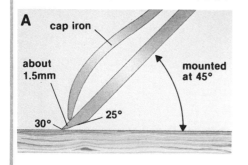

A
cap iron
about 1.5mm
mounted at 45°
30° 25°

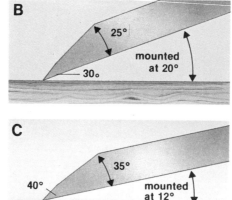

B
25°
30°
mounted at 20°

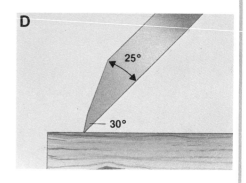

D
25°
30°

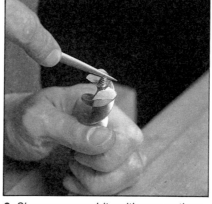

C
35°
40°
mounted at 12°

All wood chisels (D) are ground to 25°. In most cases, like plane irons, they're honed to about 30°. A few models come factory-honed as well as ground.

HAND SHARPENING: DRILL BITS

1 To sharpen twist bits correctly by hand, you need a guide like this. You clamp the bit in position twice – once for each side of the tip.

2 Sharpen auger bits with a smooth or dead smooth needle file. Lightly hone the insides of the spurs – never the outsides, or you'll upset the cut.

3 Renew the bevels on the cutting edges by filing through the 'throat' of the bit. Here too, you must never work from the other side of the edge.

4 For a spade bit, a fine-grade 'knife-edge' slipstone is as good as a file. Preserve the same bevel on the cutting edges, and keep them identical.

5 Gently renew the bevel on each side of the tip as well. But don't hone the bit's outside (parallel) edges, or you'll alter its cutting diameter.

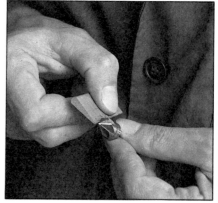

6 If necessary, sharpen a countersink by touching up the inside of each cutting edge with a file or slipstone. Again, leave both outside faces alone.

SHARPENING TOOLS BY MACHINE

For sharpening cutting tools properly and quickly, without the bother of sending them away, powered equipment is best. But it doesn't have to be expensive or complex: here are the choices that are available to you.

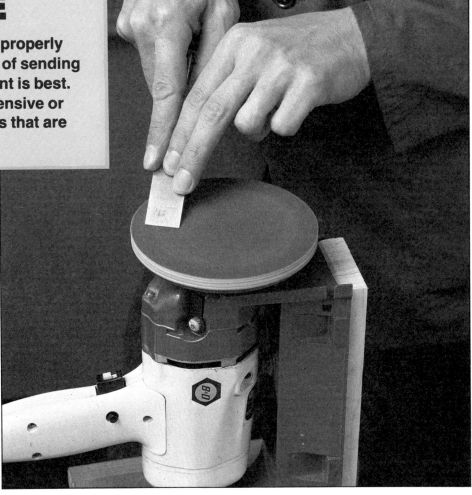

Sooner or later, the cutting edges of your chisels and plane irons will reach the stage where simply re-honing them (as detailed on pages 180 -184) is no longer enough. Repeated honing will have created unevenness, and accidental impact may have chipped them. That's the time for them to be re-ground to their original bevel, generally 25°.

You can, of course, get a shop to do this. But in fact the job is well within the capabilities of any do-it-yourselfer who has a power drill.

The machine used in many trade workshops is a bench (or high-speed) grinder. Home versions of this are available, both as power drill attachments and as integral tools (see overleaf). The latter are usually double-ended, consisting of an electric motor with a spindle sticking out of either side; that way you can fit two different wheels, and use one for final honing.

Wheels come in various types and grades of artificial abrasive. Aluminium oxide is the best for all-round use on woodworking tools; its white form is harder, and is used for high-speed-steel as opposed to carbon-steel tools. 60 grit is about right for initial grinding. Tungsten carbide edges need a green (silicon carbide) wheel, and on the whole are best left to professionals.

Never use a grinding wheel except in a purpose-built grinder or grinding attachment, where it will be properly guarded. There's always the risk of its disintegrating.

With use, all wheels develop a hard glazed surface, which impairs their cutting. They may also wear unevenly. A wheel dresser – either a block of diamond abrasive, or a hand tool with small diamond-tipped serrated wheels – is needed periodically to set things right.

Using a bench grinder

It's important, of course, to keep the tool you're grinding at the correct angle to the wheel (working against the wheel's edge, not its face). A tool rest, supplied or improvised, is pretty well essential for this. You should also keep the tool square or you'll get an angled cutting edge.

And, since the wheel revolves very fast, you must be careful not to overheat and thus weaken the steel. The risk is highest with fine wheels. To avoid it, remove the tool from the wheel every couple of seconds to cool (this is better than dipping it in water, which hardens it and thus makes it more brittle). If it turns blue, you've failed, and you'll have to grind away the discoloured part.

The basic rules are to apply only light pressure, not trying to grind away too much steel in one go, and to pass the tool's edge fairly rapidly from side to side against the wheel. In fact, sharpening by machine takes just as steady and careful a touch as sharpening by hand – more, if anything, because it's easier to harm the edge if you slip or approach at the wrong angle.

Lastly, **always** wear goggles. Grinding makes sparks (ie, tiny fragments of red-hot metal) and it may dislodge abrasive particles. Don't risk your eyes.

Other machines

The snags associated with the bench grinder's speed do count against it. A better though generally more expensive alternative is the traditional grindstone or whetstone (see photograph again), which can be made of natural sandstone instead of man-made abrasive. This revolves very much more slowly, and is usually lubricated with water (if the stone lies flat like a gramophone record, lubricant drips from a container above it; if it's mounted upright like a grinding wheel, its lower half is immersed). These factors make it safer to use, and it poses no threat of overheating your tools' edges.

Like bench grinders, grindstones are available as integral tools, or as attachments for power drills. Moreover, you can get integral tools which combine both machines.

Because of their wheels' curvatures, bench grinders and upright grindstones leave a slightly hollow bevel on your tools, rather than a flat one. However, this doesn't often matter in practice.

A third, though again usually quite expensive, method uses a small fixed belt sander (or 'linisher') in which the belt faces upwards or outwards. Purpose-built models are called 'belt grinders'. They too may be combined with bench grinders; refer to pages 46 -47 for an example.

SHARPENING MACHINES

1 *The grindstone or whetstone is a traditional way of sharpening; its slow speed means you won't overheat the steel. This version is powered by a drill, and its natural stone wheel revolves in water.*

2 *This self-powered machine combines a grindstone and a high-speed grinder. Use the latter, with its artificial wheel, for initial grinding, and the former for honing.*

3 *High-speed grinders also come as drill attachments. Both types include tool rests, like the grindstones shown, and also transparent guards for protection against sparks.*

4 *The standard high-speed bench grinder is double-ended, so you can fit both a coarse wheel and a fine one to cope with final honing.*

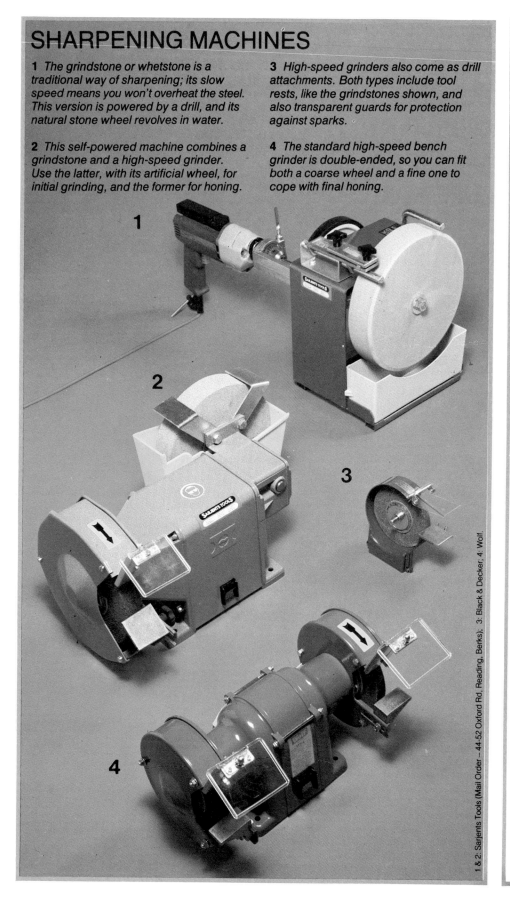

1 & 2: Sarjents Tools (Mail Order – 44-52 Oxford Rd, Reading, Berks); 3: Black & Decker; 4: Wolf.

READY REFERENCE

GRINDING WHEELS SAFETY RULES

These vital safety rules must be followed when you're using a bench (high-speed) grinder. The other powered sharpening tools – grindstones (whetstones) and abrasive discs – are safer, although some solid discs are meant for use with a guard such as that on a circular saw or angle grinder.

Before you start:
● handle grinding wheels carefully and don't drop them
● don't let them get wet or even damp
● before fitting a wheel, make sure it's undamaged. Examine it carefully; then suspend it vertically and tap it lightly with a non-metallic object. If it makes a dull sound instead of a clear ringing, it's cracked. On no account use a faulty wheel – throw it away immediately
● it's best to fit washers of blotting paper under the metal washers which clamp the wheel in place, to ensure even pressure. Before switching on, see that the wheel fits well onto the spindle and is tightly secured there – but without over-tightening
● any tool rest should be clamped firmly, and as close to the wheel as possible. Don't adjust it while the wheel is turning
● a wheel should come marked with its maximum safe speed. Never run it faster than that, or it may break up

When using a wheel:
● after starting a wheel, stand clear while letting it reach and run at full speed for at least a minute. If it's going to break up, this is when it's most likely to do so
● always wear goggles to protect your eyes from sparks. The machine itself should have a transparent guard over the area where the tool meets the wheel; in our step-by-step photographs, this has been removed to show the operations more clearly
● grinding wheels should revolve towards you ('into' the tool's edge) – whereas grindstones, abrasive discs and rubberised abrasive wheels should revolve away from you, so the tool can't suddenly dig in and jerk. When you're working on the face of a grindstone, disc or rubberised wheel, that means holding the tool to the right of the spindle, if the rotation is anti-clockwise.
● only use the edge of a grinding wheel – never its face
● it's best not to re-grind bolsters and cold chisels, since the tips are specially tempered. But you can certainly use a grinding wheel to remove any metal which has 'mushroomed' over the head.

SHARPENING BY MACHINE

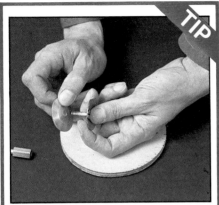

1 To make a sharpening disc, cut a 12mm (½in) plywood circle, drill it, fit an arbor (page 40) and glue on some heavy-duty abrasive sheet.

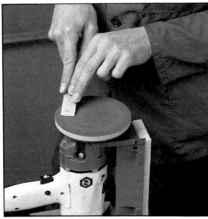

2 Fit the disc into a drill which has been clamped upright. Hold tools so it rotates away from them, and move blades from side to side as you work.

3 Twist bits are best sharpened with the drill horizontal. Practise to get the correct angle. Rotate the bit smoothly, sharpening each side in turn.

4 Bench grinders demand care. Clamp the blade in the tool rest if possible (at the correct angle) and always pass it lightly and evenly across the wheel.

5 A grinding wheel sometimes needs 'dressing' to level and re-texture it. A wheel dresser, such as a diamond block, is held against it as it turns.

6 The belt grinder is an especially good sharpening machine. As with the others, you fit coarse and fine abrasives for grinding and honing respectively.

Simpler methods

Even if you're unwilling to go to the expense of setting up such professional facilities (as may well be the case, unless you're grinding tools constantly) there are cheap and simple alternatives.

In the absence of any power tools at all, you can only grind edges on a coarse stone (usually the coarse side of a combination stone), or on an 80-100 grit artificial abrasive sheet glued to a stiff board.

But this does take a lot of time and labour. Perhaps the best option of all for the home worker is to improvise with a power drill – mounting it firmly in a vice or drill stand, and fitting a suitable abrasive disc. Consisting of 80 or 100 grit aluminium oxide or silicon carbide, this can be a solid disc made for an angle grinder or circular saw (page 143). Alternatively, the grit may be backed with paper, or with fibre (for toughness) or cloth, and glued to a disc of plywood. Like the bench grinder and belt grinder, this set-up is also capable of final honing; use a finer grit instead.

There will be no risk of over-heating. The only snag, present with wide blades, is that the disc turns faster near its centre. In all cases, use the slowest speed available.

A fairly new sharpening material is a compound of rubber and silicon carbide grit. This comes in the form of wheels – for mounting in a drill or bench grinder – and also sticks, which are used like slipstones. It's vital always to work so that the wheel rotates away from the edge being sharpened (the opposite procedure to that for an ordinary grinding wheel); otherwise, because of its slightly resilient surface, the wheel may snatch the tool from your hands.

A rubberised wheel will sharpen on either its edge or its face.

Sharpening twist bits

A grinding wheel or abrasive disc provides the fastest and cheapest means of sharpening twist drill bits (others are suggested on pages 180-184). However, you'll have to develop a certain amount of manual skill to get it right every time. It may be a good idea to practise on an old bit.

The important features are the angles of the cutting edges at the tip of the bit, and their curvature. Both of these features should be equal on either side, and the pointed straight edge between the cutting edges should be kept fairly narrow.

On the whole, good results are easier to achieve on a sideways-facing abrasive disc, 100 or 120 grit, than on a grinding wheel. Either way, the trick is to hold the bit at the correct angle (against the tool rest, if you're using a grinding wheel) and to rotate it smoothly as the wheel or disc turns – working first on one side of the tip, then on the other.

188

TOOL STORAGE

Careful storage of your tools will protect them from accidental damage and ensure that they are always to hand when needed. There are many storage methods you can use, ranging from purpose-made products to home-built systems.

No matter how small your tool kit may be, there are lots of very sound, practical reasons why the tools should be stored away properly when not in use. Careful storage prevents damage and so keeps them in good condition. It also makes the workshop a safe place by keeping sharp edges well out of your way. But perhaps the best reason of all for providing a well thought-out storage system is that never again will you suffer the frustration of discovering that the very tool you need has vanished without a trace; you'll have everything to hand when and where you need it.

The type and amount of storage you need will depend on the number and kind of tools you own. Here is a run-down of some of the options open to you.

Shelving
Although shelving is a fairly obvious form of storage – and there are many variations in both fixed and adjustable types suitable for garage or workshop use – there are a few important points to consider for workshop use.

Make sure the shelves are made from a durable, easily-cleaned material so that they will stand up to the sort of rough treatment workshop furniture tends to receive. If the material has a certain amount of chemical resistance, so much the better – spillages will be much easier to clean up.

Wall-mounted adjustable shelving should be strong enough to carry whatever you want to store, and so strong wall fixings are essential. In timber sheds, make your fixings into frame members only; in concrete buildings, bolt timber battens to the walls and make your fixings into those.

Although the things you'll be putting on the shelves may be no heavier than ordinary domestic bits and pieces (such as books, television sets, etc), they will be taken off and put back more frequently, often without much care, which can place quite a strain on the system. If there is any doubt, you may be better off going for a

free-standing, heavy-duty adjustable shelving system made from perforated steel racking.

Finally, if you are storing planes on a shelf, keep the blades clear of the surface by laying them on their sides or by resting their soles on a wooden batten fixed along the front edge of the shelf.

Cupboards
Cupboards, like shelving, are an obvious form of storage. However, make sure any you use are adequately ventilated – drill a few holes in the sides if necessary –

otherwise condensation may form on the metal parts of tools, leading to rust.

If any cupboard is at low level, and there are inquisitive children about, make sure it is fitted with a lock. This is particularly important if you are using it to store poisonous chemicals, although sharp tools alone are sufficiently dangerous to justify this precaution.

Beware of purpose-made tool cupboards that are claimed to double as portable tool chests. These are tempting, especially as they are often sold complete with a set of tools, but many are too unwieldy or just too heavy to be carried with ease.

Pegboard
Relatively lightweight, awkwardly-shaped items such as saws, marking tools, small hammers and so on can be wall-mounted with the aid of pegboard – hardboard perforated with a regular grid of round holes. Cut the pegboard to size and glue 50x25mm (2x1in) battens to the back so that they are flush with the edges of the sheet. To fix the board to the wall simply drive screws through the battens into wall plugs.

The cheapest way of fixing the tools to the board is merely to rest them on dowels inserted in the holes. However, this isn't a very strong fixing and you would do better to acquire a collection of spring clips made for the purpose; they are available from good hardware stores.

As an alternative, a ready-made pegboard storage system is available as a complete package. It comprises boards, board supports and a set of clips.

Battening
As a slightly less versatile alternative to pegboard, a wall-mounted rack can be made from timber battening. Simply screw 50x25mm (2x1in) battens vertically to the wall, setting them 300 to 450mm (12 to 18in) apart. Then glue and pin 38x12.5mm (1½x½in) horizontal battens to the vertical battens, spacing them at 50mm (2in) intervals. Many tools can be slotted through the battens, or hung from them on metal hooks made from stout wire – from coathangers, for example.

A simple wooden rack is ideal for storing chisels and similar tools. Fixed to a wall or to the side of the

STORAGE SYSTEMS FOR SMALL ITEMS

The simple glass jar (bottom) is a cheap, effective container for nails, screws and other bits and pieces.

Small items, in small quantities,

can be kept in a compact stack of clear-topped boxes (right); for a larger number, a cabinet with plastic drawers (centre) is better. A

plastic bin system (top) is suitable for more bulky items, including small tools. Carry tools to the job in an inexpensive bag (far left).

workbench, it will keep them safe, yet leave them readily to hand. All you need is a batten, or a strip of plywood, about 32mm (1¼in) wide and 6mm (¼in) thick, plus a few 32mm (1¼in) square 12mm (½in) thick timber blocks for spacers.

Glue one spacer to each end of the batten and then glue on the intermediate spacers at approximately 230mm (9in) centres.

For bench fixing, simply secure the assembly in place with screws through the spacer blocks. For wall fixing, screw a 25mm (1in) thick timber batten to the wall and then screw the rack to this. The batten provides enough clearance for the tool handles.

Hooks and brackets

Cup hooks screwed to the underside of a shelf provide a simple means of holding tools. Use loops of string to attach the tools to the hooks.

Alternatively glue lengths of dowel into holes drilled in a timber batten and fix the batten to the wall with screws and wall plugs. Hang the tools directly on these pegs. This method is particularly suitable for holding garden tools, so much so that ready-made versions are available, either separately or as part of a garden tool set.

Finally, for really awkward items such as ladders, garden hoses and so on, look out for purpose-made brackets and storage fittings. Where ladders and steps are to be stored in an outhouse, though, be sure to padlock them to the wall, otherwise a burglar may use them to break into your home.

Screw and nail storage

For screws, nails, wall plugs and similar small items, a collection of small boxes is fine, and old tobacco tins have long been the handyman's favourite for this purpose. However, these are becoming increasingly hard to find, even for smokers, and a number of manufactured alternatives are available to take their place.

For very small bits and pieces look for cabinets containing a set of clear plastic drawers. These are excellent in so far as you can see what each drawer holds. Don't put too much store in the unit's portability; many have carrying handles, but the drawers tend to slide out at the least provocation and can spill their contents all over the floor. It would be better to take advantage of the pre-drilled holes in most versions and screw the cabinet to the wall.

Larger items can be contained in a system that makes use of moulded plastic bins which can either be stood on a shelf or hung on special wall bars or a wall panel.

Another cheap receptacle for storing screws, etc, is the humble

CARRYING TOOLS

Quite often, you will need to carry a selection to tools to a job away from your workshop.

The metal cantilever tool box (top) is a popular way of providing both storage and portability, but it is more suited to mechanics' tools. Below it is a handy wooden tool box which can be bought with a selection of tools and may be a convenient way to start your tool kit. The plastic box (bottom) is tough and will carry large, heavy tools, but is not particularly suitable for long-term storage.

Steel racking will provide a strong and durable shelving system for heavy items.

screw-top glass jar. A space-saving trick is to fix the lid to the underside of a shelf with two screws and then screw the jar into the lid.

Drill stands

Most sets of twist bits come complete with a wallet or case for storage, but there is a more convenient way to store drill bits.

Take a fairly substantial block of wood – say, 75x25mm (3x1in) in section – and use each drill to bore its own mounting hole, taking care not to drill right through the block.

Arrange the holes so that they are in order of size and label each clearly so you know the size of bit it contains.

An advantage of this kind of drill storage is that you can use it as a gauge. If, for example, you need to bore a hole to receive a bolt of unknown size, you simply try the bolt in the various drill holes until you find the one that provides the best fit; then use that drill to make the hole. In this case, it would be better to make the stand out of hardwood to reduce wear and tear.

Tool chests and boxes

For a relatively small, everyday sort of tool kit, an ordinary tool chest will provide adequate storage; its main virtue is that it is portable. However, such a chest has limitations; few are capable of accepting long items such as panel saws, which means these must be carried separately – though you can glue the saw's cardboard sleeve to the chest to overcome this problem. More importantly, though very large chests are available, there comes a point where the advantage of

INDEX

Abrasives
    for curves, 77, 78
    for metalwork, 159
    for sharpening tools, 181, 187
    types of, 30-1
Adhesive, 49, 54, 80, 81
Adjustable square, 130
Allen key, 15, 37, 156
Aluminium oxide abrasive, 30, 181
Angle brackets, 36, 57
Angle brushes, 144
Angle drive, 39
Angle grinder, 141, 143
Angle irons, 53
Annealing, 165
Annular nails, 32-3
Asbestos gloves, 150-151
Auger, 24, 25
Auger bits, 25-6

Ball-pein hammer, 12, 158
Band saws, 43, 44, 78
Barefaced housing joint, 62, 63, 65, 121, 123
Batten staging, 178
Battening, 188-9
Beam cramps, 27
Belt sanders, 30, 45-6, 47, 185
Bench disc sanders, 46
Bench grinder, 47, 160, 185, 186, 187
Bench hook, 50, 51, 130, 131, 132
Bench rebate plane, 18, 19
Bevel-edged chisels, 23, 63, 69
Block joints, 36
Block plane, 17, 59, 183
Blowlamp, 150, 151, 152-3, 159
Blowtorch, 152-3, 159
Bolts, 154, 155, 156, 170
Box spanner, 156
Braces
    bits for, 15, 25-6
    types of, 24, 25, 149
Brackets, 189
Bradawl, 24, 25, 147
Breast drill, 24
Brick bolster, 141, 142
Brick hammer, 13, 141, 142
Builder's steps, 174, 175
Bullnose rebate plane, 18, 19
Bullnose shoulder rebate plane, 18, 19
Butcher's hook, 178
Butt joints
    adhesives for, 49
    in chipboard, 52
    marking out, 49
    sawing, 50, 51
    strengthening methods for, 50-3

Cabinet connecting screw, 37
Cabinet rasp, 20, 21
Cabinet scraper, 18, 19
Cabinet screwdrivers, 14
Cabinets, 189
Cable stripper, 147

Callipers, 106, 108, 110, 111
Cam clamps, 27
Cam joint, 37
Carpenter's mallet, 12
Carpenter's pencil, 8-9
Carpenter's rule, 8
Centre bits, 26
Centre punch, 160, 163, 165
Chasing saws, 141
Chipboard connector screw, 37
Chipboard plug, 37, 52
Chipboard screws, 34, 64, 65
Chisels
    cold 141, 142, 148, 160, 181
    wood
        blade angle, 22, 184
        choosing, 22
        safety, 22
        sharpening, 22, 181, 182, 183, 184
        types of, 23, 148
        mentioned, 55, 56, 63, 73, 74, 75, 78, 190
        woodturning, 104-5, 106, 110, 111
Circular saws
    anatomy, 42, 94-6
    attachment for power drill, 40, 42, 43-4, 94, 95
    basic cutting technique, 44, 96-7
    bench, 44, 98
    blades, 42, 44, 98, fitting, 42, 96
    care of, 180, 181
    choosing, 94
    cross cut fence, 99, 101, 102
    cut-off discs with, 160
    for masonry work, 141
    joints cut with, 62, 63, 64, 97-8, 101, 103
    laminates cut with, 98
    mitre fence, 44, 101
    rip fence/cutting, 44, 96, 97-8, 100-1
    safety, 94, 99, 101
    saw table with, 43, 44, 98, 99-103
    size and power, 42, 94
    using a batten, 97, 99, 101, 102, 103
clamps see cramps
Claw hammer, 12, 148
Clout nails, 33
Club hammer, 12, 13, 141, 142, 148
Clutch head screws, 34
Coach (or carriage) bolt, 154, 155, 156
Coach screws, 34
Combination ladder/steps, 174, 175
Combination plane, 18, 19, 183
Combination screwdriver, 15
Combination spanner, 156
Combination square, 8
Compass (or circular) plane, 18, 19

Compression coupling, 151
Concrete point chisel, 141
Continuity tester, 149
Coping saw, 10, 11, 78, 181
Core drill bits, 141
Corner halving joint, 54-6
Corner plates, 36
Countersink bit (for brace), 26
Countersink drill bits, 86, 88, 184
Cramp heads, 27, 28, 83
Cramps
    types of, 27-8, 83
    using, 80-3
Crescent spanners, 156
Cross halving joint, 55, 56
Cross-cut cold chisel, 141
Cross-cut fence, 99, 101, 102
Cross-cut saw, 10, 11, 77, 181
Cross-pein hammer, 12
Crow's-foot spanner, 150-151
Crutch screwdriver, 14
Cupboards, 188
Curves
    compound, 76, 78, 79
    concave, 78, 79
    convex, 77, 79
    cutting in plan, 76
    making a cut out, 76, 77, 78
    marking out, 76
    planes used for, 18, 78
    working in section, 78, 79
Cut clasp nails, 32, 33
Cut floor brads, 32
Cut tacks, 33
Cut-off discs, 160
Cut-off saw, 141
Cutting gauge, 8, 9, 73
Cutting wheel, 40
Cutting-in brushes, 144

Deep-throat cramps, 27, 28
Depth gauge, 60, 61, 87
Depth stop, 68, 87
Diamond-point cold chisel, 141
Dome nuts, 155
Dooking iron, 141
Dot punch, 160
Dovetail joints
    anatomy of, 71
    cutting tails and pins, 73-5
    drilling, 90-1, 93
    housing, 62, 73, 123
    marking out tails, 71-3
    putting together, 75
    router used for, 121, 122, 123, 125-6
    types of, 73
Dovetail nailing, 50-1
Dovetail saw, 11, 73, 74
Dowel drill bit, 25, 85-6, 88, 181
Dowelling jig, 60, 61, 87, 88
Dowels
    buying, 59
    chamfering ends, 59
    cutting, 60
    fixing and finishing, 60-1

    marking and cutting holes for, 60, 61
    pellets, 59, 61
    problems, 61
    size of, 58, 59
    types of joints made with, 58-60
Drill and counterbore bit, 86, 88
Drill and countersink bit, 25, 86, 87
Drill guide, 39
Drill sharpener attachment, 41
Drilling
    hand, 24-5
    power see Power drills
Drum sander attachment, 41
Duplex rebate plane, 18, 19

Edge cramps, 27, 28, 83
Electric hammer, 141
Electric percussion drills, 141
Electrical jobs, tools for, 147-9
Electrician's bolster chisel, 148
Electrician's brace, 25
Electrician's pliers, 147
Electrician's screwdrivers, 14, 147
Electronic speed reducers, 40
End mill, 86, 88
Engineer's pliers, 158
Engineer's screwdrivers, 14
Engineer's try-square, 8, 160
Epoxy resin, 151
Expansive bits, 26
Extension ladders, 174, 175, 176

File brush, 159
Files
    care of, 21, 183
    sharpening with, 181
    types of, 20-1
    used in metalwork, 159, 165, 167
    mentioned, 77, 78, 150, 151
Firmer chisels, 23
Fixed spanners, 160
Fixed-jaw cramps, 27, 28
Flat files, 20, 159, 165
Flat paint brushes, 144, 145
Flat-cut cold chisel, 141
Flexible drive, 39-40
Floorboard saw, 148, 149
Flux, 151, 152, 159, 162, 171, 172
Fore plane, 16-17
Fret cramps, 27, 28
Fret saw, 11, 78

G-cramps, 27, 28, 80, 82, 83
Garnet paper, 31, 77
Gimlet, 24, 25
Glass (spear point) drill bit, 87, 88
Glasspaper, 30-1, 50, 51, 77, 111
Glue guns, 47
Gluing, 80, 81 see also Adhesives
Goose neck scraper, 18-19
Gouges, 22, 23, 78, 105, 106, 109, 110, 111, 112
Grinding machines/attachments, 41, 47, 160, 185-7

Grindstones, 47, 185, 186
Groove punch, 168, 169
Grooving planes, 18, 19
Guide dowel, 37

Hacksaw, 148, 150, 151, 158-9, 165, 166 181
Half-round cold chisel, 141
Half-round files, 21, 159, 165
Halving joints
    circular saw used for, 101, 103
    corner, 54-6
    cross, 55
    dowels used in, 59
    router used for, 124
    strength of, 54
    tee, 55
    tools for, 55
    where to use, 55
Hammer adaptor, 40, 85
Hammers
    care of, 180, 181
    for electrical jobs, 148
    for masonry, 141
    hints on using, 13
    types of, 12-13
    see also under type of hammer
Hand countersink, 24, 25
Hand drills
    bits for, 24-5, 26
    types of, 24
Hand files, 21
Hand router (router plane), 18, 19, 63
Handsaws
    care of, 181
    for electrical work, 148
    for masonry work, 141
    types of, 10-11
    using, 10, 50, 51
    see also under type of saw
Hanger bolt, 37
Hardboard pins, 33
Hedge trimmer attachment, 41
Hole saw, 86, 88, 163, 164
Hooks, 189
Hot air stripper, 152
Housing joints
    circular saw used for, 62, 63, 64, 97, 98
    making, 62, 63, 64, 65
    router used for, 62, 63, 118, 121, 123
    tools for, 63
    types of, 62, 63
Hydraulic breakers, 141

Impact drivers, 15
Instrument screwdrivers, 14

Jack plane, 16, 183
Jet cramp, 27
Jeweller's files/rifflers, 21
Jig saws
    attachments for power drills, 40, 43-4
    blades, 43, 44, 160
    care of, 180
    features of, 42-3
    using, 44, 76, 77
Jointer (trying) plane, 17
Jointing blocks, 53

Jointing compound, 150, 151
Jointing jig, 57
Joints, 49-75 see also under type of joint
Joist brace, 25, 149
Jumping bit, 141, 143
Junior hacksaw, 148, 151, 159

KD (knock-down fittings), 36-7
Keyhole saw see Padsaw
Knife
    handyman's, 148
    marking, 8, 9, 49
Knife and scissor sharpener, 41

Ladder
    accessories, 177-8
    carrying, 176, 178
    extending, 176
    positioning, 176, 178
    safety, 176, 178
    securing, 176, 178
    types of, 174-5
Ladder brackets, 176, 177
Ladder platform, 177
Ladder stay, 176, 177
Laminates, 44, 98, 120, 121-2
Lathe
    attachment for power drill, 41, 107
    choosing, 107
    how it works, 107
    parts of, 108
    safety, 108
    using, 108-112
Lean-to steps, 174, 175
Levelling feet, 177
Lockable wrench, 150, 151
Locking nuts, 155
London pattern screwdriver, 14
Long-nosed pliers, 147, 160
Lost head nails, 32, 33

Machine bolts, 154-5, 156
Machine screws, 154, 155, 156
Mains testers, 14, 149
Mallets, 12, 160, 165, 167
Marking, tools for, 8-9
Marking gauge, 8, 9, 54, 55, 60, 67, 73
Masonry drill bits, 25, 86, 88, 141, 143, 148
Masonry nails, 32
Masonry saw, 141, 143
Masonry tools
    breaking tools, 141, 142
    cutting and shaping, 141, 142
    drilling, 141, 143
    electric hammers, 141
    hydraulic breaker, 141
    saws, 141, 143
Mason's bolster, 141
Mason's chisel, 141, 142
Measuring, tools for, 8-9
Metalwork
    bending metal over a former, 165, 167
    correcting hole centres, 165
    cutting metal, 165, 166
    grooves, 165
    drilling holes in metal, 163-5
    filing, 165, 167

making a box seam, 170
making seam joints, 168, 169
marking out, 163
riveting, 168, 169, 170, 171
safety, 163
soldering, 168, 171, 172 see also soldering irons
tools for, 158-62
Mill files, 21
Mini block joint, 36
Mini-hacksaws, 159
Mirror screws, 34
Mitre blocks, 57, 132
Mitre box, 57, 132
Mitre cramps, 27, 28, 57, 80
Mitre fence, 44, 101
Mitre joints
    aids, 57, 132
    circular saw used for, 97, 98, 101
    dowels in, 59, 61
    making, 56-7
Mitre shooting board, 131, 132
Mitre templates, 132
Modesty block, 36
Monkey wrench, 156
Mortise and tenon joints
    assembling, 67, 70
    marking and cutting the mortise, 67, 69, 93
    marking and cutting the tenon, 66, 67, 68, 101, 103
    router used for, 126, 127, 128
    types of, 66
Mortise chisels, 23, 66, 67, 69
Mortise gauge, 9, 66-7, 68
Moulding pins, 33
Multiple ring spanners, 156

Nails, types of, 32-3
Needle files, 21
Needle rasps, 20, 21
Neon tester, 14, 149
Nuts, 37, 155, 168, 170

Offset screwdrivers, 15, 147
Offset spanners, 156
Oil stone, 22, 106, 181
Open-ended spanner, 156
Orbital sanders, 30, 41, 46
Oval wire nails, 32, 33
Overlap, 50-1

PTFE tape, 150, 151
Padsaw, 11, 148
Paint brushes
    choosing, 144-5
    cleaning, 146
    storing, 146
    types of, 144
    using, 145
Paint mixer attachment, 41
Paint pads, 144, 146
Paint rollers
    choosing sleeves, 145-6
    cleaning, 146
    storing sleeves, 146
    types of, 145
    using, 145
Paint sprays, 146
Panel butting connectors, 37
Panel pins, 33

Panel saw, 11, 77, 181
Paring chisels, 23
Parting tool, 104, 105, 106, 110
Pegboard storage, 188, 190
Percussion drill bit, 86
Phillips screws/screwdrivers, 15, 34
Pickaxe, 141, 142
Pillar files, 21
Pin hammer, 12, 148
Pipe benders, 150, 151
Pipe cutters, 150, 151, 156
Plane irons
    angle of blade, 17, 184
    description, 16
    sharpening, 181, 182, 183, 185
Planes
    bench
        parts of, 16
        types of, 16-17
        using, 17
    care of, 181, 183
    power, 45, 46
    specialist, 18-19
    storing, 188
    mentioned, 59, 61, 78
    see also Plane irons
Plane board, 130
Plasterboard nails, 33
Plastic bins, 189
Platform steps, 174, 175
Pliers, 147, 158, 160
Plough plane, 18, 19, 183
Plug cutter, 86, 88
Plugging chisel, 141, 142
Plumb bob, 149
Plumbing jobs, tools for, 150-1
Power drill
    attachments, 39-41
    bits, 85-7, 88, 141, 148, 181, 184
    choosing, 85, 148
    drill stand used with, 86, 87-8
    drilling techniques
        basic, 87
        precision, 87-8
        wall plugs, 88
    routers compared with, 89
    shaping cutters for, 89-93
    using a dowelling jig with, 87
Power routers see Routers, power
Power tools see under name of tool
Pozidriv screws/screwdriver, 15, 34
Pressurised paint systems, 146
Prick punch, 160
Proprietary cutters, 165
Pump attachment, 41
Push drills, 24, 25

Quick-release cramps, 27, 28, 83

Radiator brushes, 144
Rak cramps, 27, 28
Rasps, 20, 21, 77, 78, 183
Ratchet screwdriver, 14, 147
Rebating planes, 18, 19
Reduction gears, 40
Reinforcing blocks, 52
Rifflers, 20, 21
Ring spanners, 156

Rip fence/cutting, 44, 96, 97-8, 99, 100-1
Rip saw, 10, 11, 181
Riveting, 168, 169, 170, 171
Roof hook 178
Roof ladders, 174, 175
Round files, 21, 159
Round wire nails, 32, 33
Router, hand, 18, 19, 63
Router, power
    bits for, 89, 114, 115, 116-7, 119, 120, 122, 183
        self guiding, 119, 120, 121, 125, 128
    choosing, 45
    cutting, circles, 122
    edges, 119-21
    fixed-base, 45, 114
    freehand routing, 122
    joints made with, 62, 63, 121, 122-3, 124, 125-6, 127, 128
    lathe, 128
    overarm, 125, 126, 128
    parts of, 114, 115
    plunging, 45, 114-6, 123
    power drill compared with, 89
    problems, 116
    routing grooves, 117-8
    safety, 116, 123, 126
    setting up for a cut, 116
    table, 125, 126
    trimming laminates, 120, 121-2
    using a jig, 124, 127
    using a spindle, 126, 127
    using a template, 125, 128
Router drill bit, 86, 88

Safety feet, 177
Safety tie, 177
Sanding, 30-1
Sanding blocks, 30-1
Sanding machines see Belt sanders; Orbital sanders; Stripping and finishing attachments
Sash brushes, 144
Sash cramps, 27, 28, 64, 67, 80, 82, 83
Saw horse, making, 130, 133-4
Saw table, using a, 43, 44, 98, 99-103
Saws see Band saws; Circular saws; Handsaws; Jigsaws
Scaffold boards, 177-8
Scan fitting, 37
Scrapers, 18, 19, 105-6, 110, 112

Scratch stock, 19
Screw fittings (self assembly), 37
Screw-holding (self grip) screwdrivers, 15
Screwdrivers
    attachment for power drill, 41
    care of, 180, 181
    for electrical work, 14, 147
    types of, 14-15
Screws
    accessories, 34
    heads, 34
    hiding, 34
    materials and finishes, 34
    recessed, 15, 34
    sizes and gauges, 34, 35
    special purpose, 34
    threads, 34
    using, 35
    see also Machine screws; Self-tapping screws
Scribers, 160, 163
Seam joints, 168
Self assembly fittings, 36-7
Self-tapping screws, 154, 156, 168, 170
Series ladders, 174, 175
Set screws, 154, 156
Shaping cutters, 89-93
Shaping wood, 76-9
Sharpening
    hand, 22, 106, 181, 182, 183, 184
    machine see Grinding machines
Shelving, 188, 190
Shooting board, 130, 131, 132
    mitre, 131, 132
Shoulder rebate plane, 18, 19
Shrinkage plates, 36
Side cutters, 147
Side rebate plane, 18, 19
Silicon carbide paper, 30, 31, 159, 181
Simple joints, 49-53
Single section ladders, 174, 175
Skew, 104-5, 106, 110, 111
Skew nailing, 53
Sledge hammer, 12-13, 141, 142
Slide calipers, 160
Sliding bevel, 8, 9, 71, 72, 73
Smoothing plane, 16, 183
Socket screws, 154, 155, 156
Socket spanner, 156
Soft-faced hammer, 13, 165, 167
Soft-faced mallet, 160

Solder, 151, 152, 159, 162, 169, 171
Soldering, 168, 171, 172 see also Soldering irons
Soldering guns, 162
Soldering irons
    bits for, 162, 172
    choosing, 162
    description, 161-2, 172
    for electrical jobs, 149
    for metalwork, 159-60, 161-2, 171, 172
    stand for, 162
    using, 171 172
Spade drill bit, 85, 87, 88, 181, 184
Spanners, 148, 150, 151, 155, 156, 159, 160
Spin grip cramp, 27, 28
Spiral ratchet screwdrivers, 15
Spirit level, 149
Split ring spanners, 156
Spokeshave, 18, 19, 78, 181, 182
Sprigs, 33
Spring dividers, 160
Spring steel fasteners, 154
Square tipped chisels, 105
Staples, 33
Star drill, 141, 143
Steel rule, 160
Steel tapes, 8, 49
Steel wool, 150, 159
Stencil brushes, 144
Stepladders, see Ladders
Stones, sharpening, 22, 106, 181, 183, 187
Stopped housing joint, 62, 63, 64
Stopping compound, 32, 50
Storage of tools, 180, 188-90
Straight-edges, 8
Stripping and finishing attachments, 40-1
Stubby screwdrivers, 14
Supadriv screws, 15, 34
Surforms, 20, 21, 77, 78
Swingbrace see Braces

T-bar cramps, 27, 28
T-nut, 37
Table shrinkage plates, 36
Tapes, measuring, 8, 149, 150, 151
Template, guide, 125, 127, 128
Templates, 76, 78, 125, 128, 132
Tenon see Mortise and tenon joints
Tenon saw, 10, 11, 63, 67, 148, 181

Tension file, 159
Thread sealers, 150
Three-square (triangular) files, 21
Timber connectors, 51, 57
Tinsnips, 165, 166
Tool bags and rolls, 190
Tool chests and boxes, 189
Tool tray, 177
Tools general information on care and maintenance of, 180-4
    sharpening, 181, 182, 183, 185-7
    storage, 180, 188-90
Torch, 148, 150
Trestles, 174, 175
Try-squares, 8, 9, 49, 60, 160, 163
Trying (jointer) plane, 17
Turn screw bit, 26
Twist drill bits, 24-5, 26, 85, 86, 88, 148, 159, 181, 184, 187
Twisted shank roofing nails, 33

Universal drill bit, 86

Veneer pins, 33
Vernier calipers, 160
Vices, 27, 28, 135, 137, 139

Wall brushes, 144
Wall plugs, 88, 151
Washers, 155, 170
Water stone, 106, 181
Web cramps, 27, 28
Wheel dresser, 185, 187
Wheelbrace see Hand drills
Whetstone, 47, 185, 186
Wing compasses, 160
Wing nut, 155
Wire brush, 160
Wire strippers, 147
Wood files, 20
Wood rasp, 20
Woodturning
    cutting tools, 104-6, 110
    face-plate turning, 107, 112
    lathe, 41, 107-8
    spindle-turning, 107, 109-111
    timber for, 107-8
Woodwork aids, making, 130-4
Workbench
    design features, 135-7
    making, 137, 138
    materials for, 137
    vices, 27, 28, 135, 137, 139
Workmate, 29
Wrenches, 148, 150, 151, 159